Paris, Capital of the Black Atlantic

A *MODERN FICTION STUDIES* BOOK
John N. Duvall, Series Editor

PARIS, Capital of the Black Atlantic

Literature, Modernity, and Diaspora

Edited by Jeremy Braddock and Jonathan P. Eburne

The Johns Hopkins University Press
Baltimore

© 2013 The Johns Hopkins University Press
All rights reserved. Published 2013
Printed in the United States of America on acid-free paper
9 8 7 6 5 4 3 2 1

The Johns Hopkins University Press
2715 North Charles Street
Baltimore, Maryland 21218-4363
www.press.jhu.edu

ISBN 13: 978-1-4214-0779-1
ISBN 10: 1-4214-0779-5

Library of Congress Control Number: 2012935068

A catalog record for this book is available from the British Library.

Chapters 1, 2, 4, 5, 6, 9, 10, 11, 12, 13, and the Afterword were originally published in *Modern Fiction Studies,* issue 51.4 (2005).

Special discounts are available for bulk purchases of this book. For more information, please contact Special Sales at 410-516-6936 or specialsales@press.jhu.edu.

The Johns Hopkins University Press uses environmentally friendly book materials, including recycled text paper that is composed of at least 30 percent post-consumer waste, whenever possible.

Contents

Acknowledgments   vii

Introduction   1
Jeremy Braddock and Jonathan P. Eburne

Afro-Modernism

CHAPTER 1   Cultural Artifacts and the Narrative of History: W. E. B. Du Bois and the Exhibiting of Culture at the 1900 Paris Exposition Universelle   17
Rebecka Rutledge Fisher

CHAPTER 2   "The Only Real White Democracy" and the Language of Liberation: The Great War, France, and African American Culture in the 1920s   52
Mark Whalan

CHAPTER 3   "No One, I Am Sure, Is Ever Homesick in Paris": Jessie Fauset's French Imaginary   78
Claire Oberon Garcia

CHAPTER 4   Writing Home: Comparative Black Modernism and Form in Jean Toomer and Aimé Césaire   101
Jennifer M. Wilks

CHAPTER 5   Embodied Fictions, Melancholy Migrations: Josephine Baker's Cinematic Celebrity   124
Terri Francis

Postwar Paris and the Politics of Literature

CHAPTER 6   Assuming the Position: Fugitivity and Futurity in the Work of Chester Himes   149
Kevin Bell

Contents

CHAPTER 7 "One Is Mysteriously Shipwrecked Forever, in the Great New World": James Baldwin from New York to Paris 175
Douglas Field

CHAPTER 8 Making Culture Capital: *Présence Africaine* and Diasporic Modernity in Post–World War II Paris 200
Cedric Tolliver

CHAPTER 9 Richard Wright's "Island of Hallucination" and the Gibson Affair 223
Richard Gibson

CHAPTER 10 Entering the Politics of the Outside: Richard Wright's Critique of Marxism and Existentialism 248
Jeffrey Atteberry

From Négritude to Migritude

CHAPTER 11 René, Louis, and Léopold: Senghorian Négritude as a Black Humanism 275
Michel Fabre (translated by Randall Cherry and Jonathan P. Eburne)

CHAPTER 12 *Nos Ancêtres, les Diallobés*: Cheikh Hamidou Kane's *Ambiguous Adventure* and the Paradoxes of Islamic Négritude 290
Marc Caplan

CHAPTER 13 Redefining Paris: Transmodernity and Francophone African Migritude Fiction 312
Pius Adesanmi

CHAPTER 14 Interurban Paris: Alain Mabanckou's Invisible Cities 330
Dawn Fulton

Afterword: Europhilia, Francophilia, Negrophilia in the Making of Modernism 350
T. Denean Sharpley-Whiting

List of Contributors 353
Index 357

Acknowledgments

We thank John N. Duvall and Nancy Peterson for their aid and advice throughout the process of editing the special issue of *Modern Fiction Studies* where this project began. And we are happy to express our gratitude to Suzanne Flinchbaugh, who guided the book through production at the Johns Hopkins University Press and enthusiastically supported its expansion. We also thank the anonymous reader of the manuscript for advice and encouragement.

We would also like to thank Randall Burkett, the staff at Emory University's Special Collections, and the Center for Humanistic Inquiry at Emory for their resources and assistance in making use of Emory's archival holdings in African American literature. Thanks also to Randall Cherry, Brent Edwards, T. Denean Sharpley-Whiting, Siobhan Somerville, and the late Michel Fabre for their generosity throughout the development of this topic.

Paris, Capital of the Black Atlantic

Introduction

Jeremy Braddock and Jonathan P. Eburne

Ten of the fourteen essays in this volume were first published as a special issue of the journal *Modern Fiction Studies*. Bearing the title "Paris, Modern Fiction, and the Black Atlantic," the special issue appeared in December 2005. As the issue was going to press, a wave of riots broke out in the Parisian suburb of Clichy-sous-Bois, a largely Arab and African working-class neighborhood. Sparked by the death of two teenage boys, Zyed Benna and Bouna Traoré, who were electrocuted after climbing into a power substation as they allegedly hid from police, the riots broke out on the night of October 27, 2005. Two days earlier, then Interior Minister Nicolas Sarkozy had incited rage with his public statement that crime-ridden suburban neighborhoods were full of "scum" and should be "cleaned with a power hose."[1] Two nights later, on October 27, the streets of such neighborhoods were instead bathed in fire. Rioters overturned and set fire to parked cars, while marches and demonstrations spread through the northeastern suburbs of Paris. With Sarkozy pledging "zero tolerance," the unrest spread throughout urban France during the month of November; the government declared a state of emergency, establishing curfews and forbidding public gatherings.

Fueled by the prevalent anti-Muslim sentiment of post–9/11 Europe, the "crise des banlieues" of late 2005 was cited as a breakdown not only of French public order but of its assimilationist national ideology. In 1998 the multiracial French national football team had won the World Cup to chants of "Beur! Blanc! Noir!" (Berber, White, Black), but in 2005 the suburban riots and their political aftershocks seemed a foreclosure on the myth of an egalitarian France. One writer for the socialist newspaper *Libération,* for instance, referred to the burning cars of Clichy-sous-Bois as fires that symbolized the failure of "the French style of integration," which was burning at the stake (bûcher).[2] Was the event to be the harbinger of new forms of insurrection or even new revolutionary movements? So claimed an anonymous 2007 pamphlet, *The Coming Insurrection,* which cited other recent protests in Mexico and Greece as further evidence of pan-European unrest (such events have since found their refrain in the U.K. riots of 2011). Or did the French suburban crisis have more to do with a rightward shift in French immigration politics, as well as an increasingly disenfranchised population of urban immigrants from France's former colonies, long since priced out of the urban villages of the central Paris *arrondissements?* Such unrest—as alive in 2013 as it was during the winter when "Paris, Modern Fiction, and the Black Atlantic" first appeared—seemed at odds with the issue's more celebratory vision of Paris as a site for intellectual ferment. Yet even the most fortuitous of the intellectual exchanges examined in the pages of this volume are often marked with the intensity of such explosive outbursts of collective violence, deep civic unrest, and contentious political upheaval throughout the long twentieth century.

A strong measure of how far the *crise des banlieues* resonated throughout the Francophone world came in December 2005, when the great Martinican poet Aimé Césaire, along with other public and political figures, refused to meet with Nicolas Sarkozy on a planned state visit to the French Overseas Departments of Martinique and Guadeloupe. Césaire's refusal responded not only to Sarkozy's role in the suburban riots but especially to his efforts to introduce a law that would require French schools to teach the "positive role" of colonization. Césaire's gesture of refusal was formalized, in turn, in a manifesto written by the Caribbean novelists Edouard Glissant and Patrick Chamoiseau in September 2007. Entitled *When the Walls Fall Down: An Outlaw National Identity?* (Quand les murs tombent: L'identité nationale hors-la-loi?), the tract calls for a collective refusal of the "walls" of immigration policy, nationalism, and essentialist notions of identity alike, which increasingly threaten to disrupt the very possibility of human relations.

This series of events confirms the continued, though transformed, importance of Paris as a site of diasporic convergence. Through the lens of the French capital we can witness simultaneously the persistent forging of relations—whether artistic, literary, intellectual, political, amorous, or polemical—as well as the conditions that threaten such relations. It is to this end that the essays collected here study the travels to and within Paris—whether literal or imaginative—by black writers of American, Caribbean, African, or European descent, with the collective aim of examining the historical formation and transformation of Black Paris throughout the twentieth century and into the twenty-first.

Understanding diasporic modernism means recognizing the conceptual range and scope of transnational black cultures that have emerged since the Middle Passage, as well as the forms of geographic mobility that have made such internationalism possible. As a subject and location of black literary interest, Paris has long been seen as one of the key sites at which this conceptual and geographic activity comes into focus. At the same time, Paris continues to be understood as the city with the phantasmagoric appeal whose allegorical dimension informs Walter Benjamin's writings about the political subtext of modernity. Indeed, some scholarly books appearing in the past decade have attested to Paris's role as the "Capital of Modernity" (Harvey) and, more ambitiously still, as the "Capital of the World" (Higonnet). It is in a similar Benjaminian spirit that the essays in this volume prompt us to consider Paris as the capital of the Black Atlantic.

We mean this in two senses. First, the essays collected here explore the city of Paris as a historically charged site for the transcontinental and transatlantic circulation of ideas, texts, and objects. As significant for its imaginary topography as for its actual landscape, the Paris inhabited by black writers throughout the twentieth century refers as much to the product of such international traffic as it does to the real conditions of Parisian life itself.[3]

Historians have documented the extent to which revolutionary French ideas about "liberty, equality, and fraternity" have been by turns offered and withdrawn, suppressed and defended, throughout the nation's long history of colonial intervention in Africa and the Caribbean. From the Haitian revolution to the war for Algerian independence, the role of Paris as the metropolitan seat of colonial power has been necessarily complemented, and contested, by the forms of agitation and dissent that have circulated through it. If the city serves as a "capital" of such political and intellectual ferment, it is because Paris obtains the form of *Kapital*—that is, acts both as a sign and a commodifiable product of black intellectual commerce—as much as it resembles a geopolitical capital or *Hauptstadt* for such commerce.[4] As a publishing center, for example—Pascale Casanova upholds Paris as the capital of "The World Republic of Letters"—the city has offered the tools and means for circulating ideas, while also acting, we propose, as a metonym for this circulation itself.

This does not mean, however, that Paris's status should be understood as purely mythical or allegorical. Just as Paul Gilroy stresses in *The Black Atlantic* that transnational black culture (as a "counterculture of modernity") is not just a set of "tropes and genres" but a "philosophical discourse" that simultaneously involves "ethics and aesthetics, culture and politics" (Gilroy 38–39), so too does Paris's status as a symbolic artifact trafficked among black intellectuals demand that we pay attention to the historical specificity of the ideas, texts, and forms of subjectivity that circulated under the aegis of "Black Paris." Indeed, attending to such specificity at discrete points throughout the long twentieth century reveals the ways in which the symbolic capital of Paris has been transformed, illuminating its evolving relationship to the very notion of a "Black Atlantic."[5] The value of Paris as a "special space for black transnational interaction, exchange, and dialogue" (Edwards 5) is remarkable to the extent that such transnational interactions have been, in turn, instrumental to the broader intellectual, literary, and political projects that fought against the domination of capitals, empires, and colonial forms of subjectivity.

The second sense in which we invoke Paris as capital of the Black Atlantic is in the Benjaminian sense of a "wish image" of the diasporic imagination. In place of the romanticized image of Parisian cafés and book stalls as the cosmopolitan meeting place of great literary minds, the essays collected here reveal Black Paris to be the product of a dialectical relationship between actual and virtual conditions of intellectual life, through which black writers of international origin made a "resolute effort to distance [themselves] from all that is antiquated" (Benjamin 4). Most immediately, this meant a separation from the "antiquated" conditions of colonialism, segregation, and racial violence from which Paris could be construed, however problematically, as a refuge. Paris was, and perhaps remains, very much a colonial city, as Jennifer Boittin and others have contended—a city in which, Boittin writes, "the specter of 'empire' guided the self-identification of its residents as well as their social and political interactions" (Boittin xiv). Yet even such dystopian conditions further dramatize the urgency—the exigency—of sustaining an intellectual life, to the point of refiguring Paris (as well, more recently, as its immediate suburbs) as a metonym for this very demand. As T. Denean Sharpley-Whiting has noted, numerous black intellectuals, such as the Dahomean (Béninese) writer Kojo Tovalou-Houenou and the Martiniquan novelist René Maran, "resuscitated the myth of France as tolerant and enlightened with respect to race" (Sharpley-Whiting 32). It is crucial to emphasize that they did so both as a deliberate fiction and also as an implicit critique of the glaring divergence between Parisian "tolerance" and France's far more violent overseas colonial policies in the Antilles and Africa. And for many African American writers, the idea of Paris as a refuge from racial violence and discrimination in the United States also corresponded, as Tyler Stovall and Michel Fabre have documented, to both real and imagined experiences of Parisian life, with France's assimilationist colonial policy providing a stark, if also ambivalent, contrast to the United States's politics of segregation. Not only are such paradoxes constitutive of the very notion of Black Paris itself as "the elision of black French culture in all its forms" (Edwards 6), but the divisions and differences between and among African, Antillean, and African American constructions of Parisian experience were likewise constitutive of the dialectical interplay between real and possible versions of black modernity that the wish-image of "Black Paris" articulated.

The "wish image" of Black Paris refers just as strongly to the role it has played in historical and literary-critical assessments of black internationalism: Paris has offered scholars, too, a means for recognizing the poetics of relation among a seemingly discontinuous body of black writers, artists, and intellectuals whose work converges through Parisian channels. In doing so, it has also brought into contact the fields of scholarly specialization that study such convergences: literary study in English, French, and Comparative Literature; African American and Africana Studies, as well as History, Sociology, and Philosophy.

Even so, the cultural and literary history of Black Paris refuses to adhere to a singular narrative, nor does it manifest a singular ideology of black internationalism. The numerous scholarly studies of Black Paris—including works by Lilyan Kesteloot, Michel Fabre, Tyler Stovall, Benetta Jules-Rosette, T. Denean Sharpley-Whiting, Brent Hayes Edwards, Christopher Miller, F. Abiole Irele, James Campbell, Alec Hargreaves, Odile Cazenave, and others—already attest to the multiple genealogies of black literary and intellectual life in, and concerning, Paris. The essays in this volume are concerned precisely with this historical as well as conceptual dynamism. The notion of Paris as a "capital" and the concept of the "Black Atlantic" as a circuit of transnational exchange haunted by the slave trade are themselves heuristic. We seek not to proselytize an ideology of "Parisianism" or cosmopolitan belonging, but instead to investigate the forms of intellectual and cultural work that have been made possible by the dimensions of the Parisian capital, while also appropriating and transforming them: from the expansion (and politicization) of literary careers to the formation of experimental journals and the organization and attendance of pan-African conferences.

For not only did Black Paris's historical conditions of hybridity and international exchange yield multiple conceptions of diasporic modernism and black internationalism, they also produced differential and often conflicting theories of anticolonial and postcolonial practice. Some of the black literary movements formed in Paris championed, both aesthetically and ideologically, the conditions of hybridity of their international origins: the pan-Africanism of W. E. B. Du Bois, for instance, and the cosmopolitanism of the Harlem Renaissance, as well as the Négritude movement. But not all the intellectual products of Black Paris reflected the cultural hybridity at work socially and environmentally. Indeed, as Robin D. G. Kelley has argued in the context of African American communists of the 1920s and 1930s, ethnic nationalism—what might seem to be the antithesis of cultural hybridity—could in fact be coextensive with the universalist revolutionary program of an international movement such as communism (see Kelley 37; see also Robinson). Analogously, the anti-universalist nationalism advocated by Frantz Fanon in *The Wretched of the Earth,* his landmark critique of Négritude, was itself a political platform forged by means of—and in response to—the same international commerce with French, African, and Antillean thought that Négritude celebrated.

In the years since the *MFS* special issue, the fields of black European studies, diasporic modernism, and Black Paris studies, in particular, have continued to grow. Dominic Thomas's groundbreaking study of immigrant literature in the era of migritude, for instance, has emphasized "the bilateralism and transversal nature of African and French relations . . . acknowledg[ing] the centrality of Paris, but also broaden[ing] and decenter[ing] the symbolic territory to provincial sites" (9–10). Scholars have devoted increasing attention to diasporic relations that do not rely solely on European mediation, figuring, for instance, a "Black Atlantic" that privileges direct Afro-Caribbean circuits of continuity and exchange. Other studies orient their examinations of Africa and its diaspora toward oceanic bodies other than the Atlantic: the Indian Ocean, the Southern Hemisphere, and the Mediterranean and Red Seas. Such expansions of the fields of black internationalism according to an exploded world map testify as much to the richness of this growing field of inquiry as to the urgency and heatedness of its political demands. Even as new global routes of affiliation and intellectual commerce come into focus, the symbolic and political importance of Paris has hardly waned, as indicated by the 2005 uprisings, as well as by Sarkozy's prominent position in response to the events of the 2011 Arab Spring. Whether Paris retains its character as a site of actual or virtual exchange among black intellectuals, its example remains a powerful case study in the past, present, and future of transnational thought and practice.

The essays in this volume are grouped into three sections. Part I, entitled "Afro-Modernism," is concerned with the conceptions of history forged by black writers in the early decades of the century. In each of this section's five essays, Paris serves as the place of encounter between conflicting notions of modernity—that is, between celebrations of and challenges to the Hegelian progress of the European West, as well as to racialized assumptions about African American and diasporic primitivism and countermodernity. Emerging from these encounters are developing conceptions of black modernism that no longer situate people of African descent outside or beyond the scope of modern historiography, sociology, or consciousness. As Rebecka Rutledge Fisher's essay argues, the exhibition of photographs, books, and data presented by W. E. B. Du Bois at the 1900 Exposition Universelle in Paris represented both a literal and a figurative intervention of African Americans into the narratives of European sociology and historiography. The 1900 Paris Exposition became the world stage upon which Du Bois used European and American sociological methods not only to call such narratives into question but also to construct and popularize the autonomous and self-generated epistemological development of African American culture.

In these first five essays, Paris serves, too, as the fictional and metaphorical sign of this historical intervention. As Mark Whalan demonstrates, numerous Harlem Renaissance writers presented the ability to speak French both as a sign of cosmopolitan sophistication and also, more significantly, as a marker or even repository of geographic, social, and historical mobility. Claire Garcia's study of Jessie Fauset's Paris-themed writing reveals a dialectical critique of the phenomenon Whalan identifies. In Fauset's fiction, competency in the French language is implicated within a wider series of pedagogical structures that are profoundly inflected by regimes of racialized power, thus challenging the myth of an emancipatory France. At the same time, however, Fauset's critical writing reveals—as does that of her contemporaries Paulette and Jane Nardal—the historical agency of diasporic women writers working in Paris.

Such mobility demanded a necessary confrontation between local and "foreign" or internationalist values. For Jennifer M. Wilks, Paris serves as a shared, if virtual, point of intersection for the tensions and problems of comparative black modernism articulated in the work of Jean Toomer and Aimé Césaire. Transatlantic in scope, the works of both writers share a conception of black modernism as a set of encounters through which one becomes aware of the spectral presence of the local, the past, and the native land within the subjective experience of the contemporary metropole. Many white U.S. and European audiences celebrated this haunting as a form of racial primitivism—as demonstrated by the "vogue" of Harlem and the "tumulte noir" of Josephine Baker in Paris. Wilks argues, however, that Toomer and Césaire established a historical circuit of conflict and connection between the United States and Paris, and between the Caribbean and Paris, in order to demand that the transatlantic experience of black modernity exist as a form of subjectivity to be struggled with and shared, rather than imposed as a form of exoticism.

Terri Francis's study of Josephine Baker argues similarly that Baker's public persona (itself celebrated precisely as an embodiment of exotic blackness) represents a complicated performance of what Francis refers to as the "embodied fictions" of blackness, transatlantic mobility, and colonial assimilation that proliferated in interwar Paris. Like the jazz-era Paris she both eulogized and stood for, Josephine Baker's celebrity was invested with multiple and often conflicting perspectives: French and American forms of racial primitivism and ethnic entertainment, as well as quintessentially modernist notions of bodily and political freedom.

Part II, "Postwar Paris and the Politics of Literature," focuses on African American writers whose post–Second World War careers or exiles in Paris were marked not merely by their distance from the United States but also by their engagements with competing ideas about the responsibilities of black intellectuals, whether communist, pan-Africanist, or existentialist. The stakes of writing fiction demanded both a philosophical and a personal negotiation of the divergent ideological positions occupied by blackness in the postwar era marked by massive decolonization, Algerian conflict, and the Cold War. As Kevin Bell argues, Chester Himes's relocation to Paris in the 1950s represented less his own abstraction from U.S. racial politics than his eradication of a subject position circumscribed, Bell writes, by "the American literary rules of 'professional' blackness." For Himes, the work of thinking—whether political or otherwise—was no longer the provenance of writers as individual subjects but was the product of writing itself, something that happens to thinkers from without.

In a different key, Douglas Field approaches the transformative effect of Paris on the writing of James Baldwin. Baldwin's Paris years, and his transformation from reviewer to essayist, were marked by a pronounced ambivalence toward the paradigm of diasporic identification and exchange that motivated other of his fellow African American expatriates and exiles such as Himes and Richard Wright. Baldwin's essays instead emphasize the particularity of African American political subjectivity. Yet even so, Field suggests that Baldwin's novel *Giovanni's Room* (a novel, famously, with no black characters) can be read as evincing Baldwin's attraction to the ways in which a concept of black internationalism could undermine hegemonic formations of French and American national identity. And in a later essay, *No Name in the Street,* Baldwin rethinks his earlier particularist position in the context of anticolonial struggles in Viet Nam and Algeria.

A notable black diasporic institution that goes unnamed in Baldwin's essays of the 1950s is the seminal journal *Présence af-*

ricaine, which had been founded by the Senegalese intellectual Alioune Diop in 1947. Given its enormous importance, its absence in Baldwin's essays conspicuously underscores Baldwin's own uncertainty about black transnationalism. Cedric Tolliver's essay confirms the place of *Présence africaine* at the center of postwar Paris black culture and traces the journal's ideological evolution by means of its strategic relationship to the concept of *culture.* In its early, postwar phase the editors' principal aim was to assert and insist upon an African presence at the heart of European modernity. As the journal grew and in the context of the Cold War's turn toward the Third World, culture increasingly became figured as a resource for political action and, indeed, as a form of politics itself, affirming the political role of artists and intellectuals in anticolonial struggle.

Whereas Kevin Bell cites an argument among Himes, Richard Wright, and James Baldwin at a famous Left Bank café as a critical moment in the development of Himes's antihumanist notions of political writing, Richard Gibson's autobiographical essay on the politics of 1950s Black Paris centers on a series of clashes, physical as well as ideological and literary, that came to bear his name as the Gibson Affair. Gibson uses Wright's unpublished *roman à clef, Island of Hallucination,* as a means of revealing how the expatriate African American community was impelled not only by American racial politics and the vicissitudes of the Cold War but also by divergent political strategies concerning the Algerian war and disagreement about the role of communism in anticolonial struggle. Informed by Anglophone pan-African thinkers like George Padmore, C. L. R. James, and the Ghanaian president Kwame Nkrumah, as well as by French thinkers, these pressures fueled the polemics among African American writers in postwar Paris.

In his essay on Richard Wright, Jeffrey Atteberry similarly characterizes the intellectual climate of postwar Paris as one of conflict and debate. Focusing on Wright's conceptual disputes with communism and existentialism, rather than on explicit polemics, Atteberry discusses the development of a political theory in Wright's novel *The Outsider,* which sought to account ontologically for the emergence of a new form of political subjectivity—what Atteberry calls the "politics of the outside." Whereas Bell argues that Wright's contemporary Himes found a similar "outside" to be a function of the vicissitudes of a written vernacular, Atteberry discusses how Wright's fiction seeks the philosophical bases for understanding, in its own right, the changing status of colonial and postcolonial spaces that had previously, if disingenuously, situated outside the scope of the West.

Part III, "From Négritude to Migritude," focuses on the conceptual stakes of literary movements that have taken black internationalism as their ideological basis, as well as their actual historical condition. Michel Fabre's essay documents René Maran's lifelong attention to Léopold Senghor's career, as well as to the Négritude movement of which Maran was dubbed a "precursor" but never an active adherent. Fabre's account of the sustained relationship between the Martiniquan novelist Maran and the future Senegalese president emphasizes both writers' insistence upon cultural hybridity—or *métissage*—as an at once aesthetic and ideological weapon against European colonialism. While privileging Senghor's fidelity to the less radical, reformist Francophone writers like Maran, Jane and Paulette Nardal, and Jean Price-Mars, Fabre nevertheless argues against the tendency to consider Senghor's version of Négritude to be, at best, a form of essentialism and, at worst, a form of racism. He demonstrates instead that Senghor's Négritude mobilized its rhetoric of the "black soul" as a strategic form of black humanism that strove to take advantage of the cross-cultural and transnational contacts that black internationalism made possible.

In Marc Caplan's essay, Cheikh Hamidou Kane's *L'Aventure ambiguë* is presented as a novel that stages the conflicts Hamidou Kane found integral to Négritude's internationalism. Pointing to a dramatized paradox between the aspirations of African nationalism and the cosmopolitan humanism learned in Paris, Kane's novel emphasizes the alienation of a Négritude intellectual, or "native intellectual" (in Fanon's phrase), from his own country. Although Fanon embraces hybridity, as a critique of the cosmopolitan native intellectual's paradoxical rejoinder of "the people" and creation of national works of art, Samba Diallo's "ambiguous adventure" to Paris actually begins at home by means of a colonial education that is fundamentally inimical to the tradition. In Caplan's reading, it is by means of this very dynamic that Kane delivers a thorough critique of Négritude as an ambivalent set of principles incapable of preventing modernity's subsumption of tradition (here signified by orality and Islam).

Pius Adesanmi's account of contemporary Francophone African fiction begins by considering how the Paris of Kane's generation figured as a site where the metropole could be subjected to the gaze of the African outsider; Adesanmi describes this reversal of the colonial encounter as a process of "transmodernity" that has worked to situate black subjectivities "beyond the epistemic claims of Euromodernity." In the tradition of Négritude, these novels describe outsiders who accept a position of non-belonging and inevitably stage an alienated return to Africa. The significant change for the last twenty years of African Francophone writing is a refusal of this return and of the position of transient outsider it implies. For contemporary Migritude writers like Calixthe Beyala and Sami Tchak, Paris is affirmed as home and, thus, in Adesanmi's phrase, "yesterday's passing outsiders now lay claim to an inclusiveness that constantly escapes them."

Dawn Fulton's study of the contemporary Congolese novelist Alain Mabanckou focuses on that author's interest in movement and traffic between Africa and Europe and between the Congolese city Pointe-Noire and Paris, in particular. Mabanckou's 1998 novel *Bleu-blanc-rouge* takes as its example the underground form of migratory trade known as *la sape,* in which young men travel to Paris to acquire designer clothing, which they bring back home to Kinshasa and Brazzaville. Manbanckou uses the phenomenon of the *sapeurs* to demonstrate the persistence of the myth of Paris, yet, as Fulton insists, the fact that *la sape* is an underground economy—and that its participants strive for anonymity while in Europe—raises the "crucial question of recognition and legitimacy in . . . conceptions of the French capital." This insight attains a metafictional dimension as well, with *la sape* ultimately forming a common concern with the structure of the Francophone publishing market; in this way, Mabanckou's writing provides a crucial and canny counterexample to Pascale Casanova's influential thesis on Paris as the capital of the "world republic of letters."

As each of the essays in this volume attests, the dialectical wish-image of Black Paris as a site of idealism and unrest alike is reflected perhaps most of all in the figure of the black intellectual. Indeed, the well-known formulation of Paris as "a city of the mind, a legendary place of refuge whose boundaries correspond only in part to those of earthly urbanity" (Stovall 300), can be understood to signify a city whose intellectualism has been a fundamental cultural product. Yet it would be a mistake to presume that such a product existed in the mind alone; rather, the forms of intellectualism privileged in twentieth-century Paris represented a set of material practices, as well as a spiritual activity and an ethical stance.

It is this Paris-oriented commitment to intellectualism that the narrator of Bernard Dadié's *Un Nègre à Paris (An African in Paris)* praises, albeit ambiguously, as the material practice representing all the liberatory activity promised by Parisian culture itself. In his mock-ethnographic, thick description of Parisian life through the eyes of an African visitor, Dadié writes of the "journalists" and intellectuals of Parisian history:

> One by one, they've managed to rescue our rights and freedoms from kings, emperors, and dictators, the same rights and freedoms we enjoy today that make life worth living. We love Paris because here, far more than back home, we can say what we think, even to the head of the war department. People here feel they're worth something, and they never forget that. The Paris of minstrels and their descendants is, however, a city built from blood and full of dreams yet to be realized (Dadié 82).

Dadie's paean to Paris as a space of liberation is, as his last line suggests, hortatory rather than celebratory; not only does the Parisian "city of the mind" still await realization, but, in more immediate terms, the commitment to truth manifested by its intellectuals renders France's actual colonial injustices all the more shameful. The promise of "say[ing] what we think" guarantees neither liberation nor a refuge from colonial relations. Indeed, "Intellectualism," though famously a term born from public involvement of writers and professors in the Dreyfus affair, has no fixed definition, instead designating a social category whose terms—political involvement, disinterested idealism, wielders of symbolic capital—have themselves been subject to debate (see Debray). But even if, or perhaps because, its boundaries were never defined, the participation of writers, artists, and thinkers in the political and moral life of Black Paris was practiced in ways that could not be absolutely policed.

Notes

1. "Timeline: French Riots," BBC News online (14 Nov. 2005), at http://news.bbc.co.uk/2/hi/europe/4413964.stm.
2. See Duhamel, "Le Bûcher de l'intégration à la française." See also Barrett. On the 2005 uprisings and their impact on the notion of a "Black Paris," see Constant and Keaton; also Begag, Hargreaves, and Tshimanga et al.
3. On the "imaginary" quality of Paris see, for example, Miller 55–89 and Stovall 300.
4. For an elaboration of such notions of finance capital in light of the slave trade's fundamental influence on the history of modernity, see Baucom.
5. See Kenneth Warren's critique of what he calls Gilroy's "experential essentialism," which in rendering its cultural objects as similar allows for an insufficiently historicized account of black transatlanticism (118–19).

Works Cited

Archer-Straw, Petrine. *Negrophilia: Avant-Garde Paris and Black Culture in the 1920s*. London: Thames and Hudson, 2000.
Barrett, Tristan. "Crise des banlieues: State, Media and the Imaginary in the National Press Coverage of the French Rioting of November 2005." *European Social and Political Research* 13 (2006–2007): 1–24.
Baucom, Ian. *Specters of the Atlantic: Finance Capital, Slavery, and the Philosophy of History*. Durham: Duke UP, 2005.
Begag, Aziz. *Ethnicity and Equality: France in the Balance*. Trans. Alec Hargreaves. Lincoln: Bison Books, 2007.
Benjamin, Walter. "Paris, Capital of the Nineteenth Century (Exposé of 1939)." *The Arcades Project*. Trans. Howard Eiland and Kevin McLaughlin. Cambridge: Harvard UP, 1999. 14–26.
Boittin, Jennifer. *Colonial Metropolis: The Urban Grounds of Anti-Imperialism and Feminism in Interwar France*. Lincoln: U of Nebraska P, 2010.
Campbell, James. *Exiled in Paris: Richard Wright, James Baldwin, Samuel Beckett and Others on the Left Bank*. New York: Scribner, 1995.
Constant, Fred. "Talking Race in Color-Blind France: Equality Denied, 'Blackness' Reclaimed." *Black Europe and the African Diaspora*. Ed. Darlene Clark Hine, Trica Danielle Keaton, and Stephen Small. Urbana: U Illinois P, 2009. 145–60.
Dadié, Bernard Binlin. *Un Nègre à Paris* (1959), trans. *An African in Paris*. Trans. Karen C. Hatch. Urbana: U of Illinois P, 1994.
Debray, Régis. *Le Pouvoir intellectuel en France* (1971), trans. *Teachers, Writers, Celebrities: The Intellectuals of Modern France*. Trans. David Macey. London: New Left Books/ Verso, 1981.
Duhamel, Alain. "Le bûcher de l'intégration à la française." *Libération*, 9 November 2005.
Edwards, Brent Hayes. *The Practice of Diaspora: Literature, Translation, and the Rise of Black Internationalism*. Cambridge: Harvard UP, 2003.
Fabre, Michel. *From Harlem to Paris: Black American Writers in Paris, 1840–1980*. Urbana: U of Illinois P, 1991.
Gilroy, Paul. *The Black Atlantic: Modernity and Double Consciousness*. Cambridge: Harvard UP, 1993.
Hargreaves, Alec. *Multi-Ethnic France: Immigration, Politics, Culture and Society*. London: Routledge, 2007.
Harvey, David. *Paris, Capital of Modernity*. London: Routledge, 2003.
Higonnet, Patrice. *Paris: Capital of the World*. Trans. Arthur Goldhammer. Cambridge: Harvard UP/Belknap, 2002.
Invisible Committee. *The Coming Insurrection*. Los Angeles: Semiotext(e), 2009.
Irele, F. Abiola. *The African Imagination: Literature in Africa and the Black Diaspora*. New York: Oxford UP, 2001.
Jules-Rosette, Benetta. *Black Paris: The African Writer's Landscape*. Bloomington: Indiana UP, 2000.

Keaton, Trica Danielle. "'Black (American) Paris' and the French Outer-Cities: The Race Question and Questioning Solidarity." *Black Europe and the African Diaspora*. 95–118.

Kelley, Robin D. G. "'Afric's Sons with Banner Red': African-American Communists and the Politics of Culture, 1919–1934." *Imagining Home: Class, Culture, and Nationalism in the African Diaspora*. Ed. Sidney J. Lemelle and Robin D. G. Kelley. London: Verso, 1994. 35–54.

Kesteloot, Lilyan. *Black Writers in French: A Literary History of Négritude*. Trans. Ellen Conroy Kennedy. Philadelphia: Temple University Press, 1974.

Miller, Christopher L. *Nationalists and Nomads: Essays on Francophone African Literature and Culture*. Chicago: U of Chicago P, 1998.

Robinson, Cedric J. *Black Marxism: The Making of the Black Radical Tradition*. 1983; Chapel Hill: U North Carolina P, 2000.

Roitman, Janet, ed. "Racial France." Spec. issue of *Public Culture* 23.1 (2011).

Sharpley-Whiting, T. Denean. *Negritude Women*. Minneapolis: U of Minnesota P, 2002.

Stovall, Tyler. *Paris Noir: African Americans in the City of Light*. Boston: Houghton Mifflin, 1996.

Thomas, Dominic. *Black France: Colonialism, Immigration, and Transnationalism*. Bloomington: Indiana UP, 2007.

Tshimanga, Charles, Didier Gondola, and Peter Bloom, eds. *Frenchness and the African Diaspora: Identity and Uprising in Contemporary France*. Bloomington: U of Indiana P, 2009.

Warren, Kenneth. "Taking the Measure of the Black Atlantic." *States of Emergency: The Object of American Studies*. Ed. Russ Castronovo and Susan Gillman. Chapel Hill: U of North Carolina P, 2009. 116–23.

AFRO-MODERNISM

CHAPTER 1

Cultural Artifacts and the Narrative of History
W. E. B. Du Bois and the Exhibiting of Culture at the 1900 Paris Exposition Universelle

Rebecka Rutledge Fisher

In much of his work from the last decade of the nineteenth century through the first half of the twentieth, W. E. B. Du Bois's major intellectual thrust was the narrating of American history in such a way that the African American was transformed in the popular imagination from historical victim to historical actor. At the same time, Du Bois was alive to the possibilities present in imagining the African American as not simply an American citizen but a citizen of the modern world. Paris proved to be an apt locale for such a cosmopolitan notion of global belonging. Home to the 1900 Exposition Universelle, Paris continued a tradition of large, cosmopolitan cities hosting international events that, additionally, gave expression to nationalist desires. London had done so in 1851 and 1862 when it hosted the exhibition; likewise, Chicago served American interests as the setting for the World's Columbian Exhibition of 1893.[1] Each fair underscored the ideologies of nationalism that inhabited the collective consciousness of the host countries.[2]

Viewing Paris as a cosmopolitan world capital is important to the work I propose in this chapter, an examination of Du Bois's gold-medal-winning exhibit of African American history and culture, which he mounted for the 1900 Paris Exposition Universelle. I discuss the sort of story Du Bois narrates through imagery and the exhibiting of artifacts (including more than 200 books written by black authors and collected by African American Assistant Librarian of Congress Daniel Payne) alongside data in the form of graphs and charts. In proposing to read imagery as narrative, I read the images Du Bois presents as certain attempts at African American self-determination in the face of what Frantz Fanon refers to, in *Peau noire, masques blancs,* as an "over-determination from without" via the larger social context (116). At the same time, my work underscores the instability of these images, Du Bois's role in mediating them for presentation on an international stage, and how these images articulate at once a metaphoric African American "presence" in the modern context as well as a metonymic African American "absence" in modern social discourses. Attention to Paris as the site of such making and unmaking of meaning serves to contextualize my discussion. For while the Paris fair provided, perhaps for the first time in the history of the world's fairs, a broad opportunity for African Americans to represent themselves at such an event,[3] it also reinforced, in ways that I shall discuss, a narrow nationalistic insistence upon the metaphysics of race and society that sought to but did not quite succeed at leaving them voiceless in the matrix of western discourses.

In this essay, I suggest that a consideration of the relationship of some aspects of the images in Du Bois's collection to the historical development of the discourse of sociology and its claims to propositional truth can teach us something about the dual nature of exhibiting cultural artifacts at venues such as the Paris Exposition and perhaps, at least partly, explain why Du Bois's collection, in particular, was capable of attracting the attention of a sociological world against whose values his work largely ran counter. Sociology is a realm rarely discussed in literary circles. Indeed, from Carl Van Vechten's introduction to the second edition of James Weldon Johnson's *The Autobiography of an Ex-Coloured Man* (1912; 1927) to Ralph Ellison's many essays on culture and literature, sociology has received harsh treatment for its tendency to place African Americans under a dissecting light. However, Du Bois's embrace of this discipline, an equivocal embrace at the time of the exposition, means that we, too, must examine it, if only to understand its function in relation to our subject. His gesturing toward ontology within the discourse of social science demands that we, as humanists, make an advance toward the genealogy of sociology, however hesitant and halting that advance might be.

Du Bois's sociological writings, those that appeared around the time of his participation in the exposition, are, when considered together and in a way that forecasts the reactions of Van Vechten and Ellison, particularly ambivalent in their stance toward the discipline of sociology. I see the nature of this ambivalence as something of an implicit internal opposition (internal to Du Bois's own poetics, that is), such that it gives shape to or motivates Du Bois's own sociological practice and methodology. This opposition exists in Du Bois's purposeful act of critiquing the particular elements that make up sociological theory and methodology. As we shall see later on, Du Bois's elementary critique, which we may speak of as an analytical fragmentation of the field, allows him to comment upon the discipline at large and his own work in particular, in such a way that these fragmentary sociological elements become intelligible units that carry meaning when placed in relation to one another. In other words, Du Bois's exhibit emerges as an example of his insistence on analyzing and revising sociological theory and practice. This he does to the extent that his holistic analysis of sociological discourse and its Comtean foundations (which he indirectly engages in his introduction to *The Philadelphia Negro* [1899] and directly undertakes in the 1904 essay "Sociology Hesitant"[4]) leads him to decompose (or deconstruct, de-sediment, as it were) the leading analytical and methodological ideas of the discipline. At the same time that Du Bois works to undo sociology as an intellectual object, he refashions it in such a way as to demonstrate sociology's vast potential, especially where the African American was concerned. Sociology becomes a mode of representation for Du Bois, and Du Bois, in deconstructing sociology and its objects of study, becomes a mediator whose intellectual activity mid-wifes the birth of some new thing: the cultural artifact of American blackness, the exportable image of the "New Negro," the cultural subject whose identity is transnational and pan-African.

I will begin with a contextualization of Du Bois's work at the fair, and within this framing I will discuss what I take to be the theme or thesis of the exhibit, and that is the ability Du Bois sees in the cultural artifact to do sociological and historical work. Thus, I discuss Du Bois's use of the image as a guiding idea or thetic principle. Further, I examine the intersection of the visual artifact with practices prevalent in nineteenth-century sociology. A review of the early roots of sociology, whose methods were highly dependent on observable fact, along with a discussion of the difficulties Du Bois experienced as a proponent of a discipline to which he unceasingly posed questions, reveals to us the problems inherent in the discipline at the turn of the century. The diffidence with which Du Bois embraced his chosen discipline of sociology was clearly articulated in his own writings on the subject. However, he seemed unwilling to allow for sociology's shortcomings in his exhibit on the American Negro. Instead, his few brief writings that deal with his participation in the fair yield no hint of his ambivalences toward the discipline. They convey, rather, a sense of Du Bois's revisionist faith in the abilities of sociology, employed not as theory alone but as a discourse with pragmatic, utilitarian possibilities, not only to proffer indicators of the Negro's social reality but to act as an intelligible bridge of continuity between the Negro's past and his or her present, at the very moment that it offered avenues leading to social reform and uplift.

Of moment also is sociology's role in the promotion of world's fairs themselves. Sociological thought was central to the organization of world exhibitions in the nineteenth and early twentieth centuries. In turn, the specularity at the core of sociological discourse, in addition to the sorts of structuralist perspectives and political ideologies at work in much sociological thought, all of which I discuss in this chapter are, in paradoxical ways, contended with by Du Bois in his display of cultural artifacts. Such imagery, fraught as it was with political and economic import, is employed by Du Bois in such a way that he historicizes without writing; he narrates without words. There is something, then, in the ineffable nature of Du Bois's highly visual sociological exhibit that, nonetheless, articulates his project quite clearly. His project is one that, on some level, employs the force of silence to drive these images into contemporary critical discourse, such that they are both given to and pose challenges before various perspectives of sociological thought. It is through a forced silence of sorts that the Negro takes the historical world stage at the 1900 Exposition. The differentiated language of Du Bois's silent images calls our attention to both the metaphorical presence of the Negro as well as his metonymic absence.

The tropes of metaphor and metonymy usefully designate two central, perhaps even simultaneous tendencies in Du Bois's work at this exhibit. The first is an effort to "identify" black people by way of various modes of sociological documentation in a way that I find to be metaphoric. That is, by presenting various sorts of imagery that constitute condensed data (processed after the collection of "observable facts" regarding the realities of black life in the United States), Du Bois actually presents a collection of signs that stand in for—serve as hypostases of—black subjectivity. Thus, these signs (which we might also think of as "citations" of black social reality) are useful metaphoric representations in the discourse on black history that Du Bois works to construct. The second tendency is manifested as an effort to demonstrate the diversity, the plurality of what he called the African American "type." This effort I read as metonymic: Du Bois's collection entails a multiplicity of detail that easily defies a single interpretation. They evoke a host of responses from those who view (or read, or seek to classify) Du Bois's presentation. Neither of the two tendencies, it seems, achieves primacy; they are always in competition in Du Bois's meaning-making process.

Both tendencies, as part of a semiological process, operate on the basis of fragmentation and differentiation in that each proceeds by way of the analogies I describe above. In metaphor and metonymy alike, words act in concert with conceptual or actual objects, and, by virtue of this interaction, produce a sort of independent meaning. If we allow, as semiology does, that not words alone but also other sorts of signs, such as bodies or images, participate in this process as well, we can begin to see the value of such an analysis in relation to Du Bois's exhibit. Du Bois's work, which puts forth its ideas through an interplay of source material, pretends toward immediacy by purporting to present to the international community representations of African Americans as gnostic creatures constituting themselves. The artifacts were, Du Bois contends, of the African American people's own making, thus providing proof of their noetic viability, their collective intellectual and social progress. And yet in generalizing the African American experience through symbols or artifacts, as Du Bois does, the interior relation of each sign he presents is brought into play, to the extent that each individual image functions as a signifier relating to its own signified. At the same time, each relates to other graphic representations in the display, interacting within a structure or system of meaning. Du Bois as exhibitor becomes not simply *homo pictor*, but also *homo significans;* the images he proffers function both syntagmatically and paradigmatically; they are alternately metaphorical and metonymic; their borders facilitate a fluid movement between presence and absence.

A fuller discussion of these visual signs as elements of a history of African American consciousness will follow in the latter portion of this chapter. Here we remark first Du Bois's general tendencies toward historiography, even in his role as sociologist. In the *Autobiography,* Du Bois describes the Exhibit on American Negroes as occupying a small alcove of about 20 square feet in a large exhibition space set aside for American displays.

A diagram of the display hall shows that the Negro exhibit was allocated space practically equal to, if not more than, that of other exhibits located there. All displays included in the U.S. exhibit hall in the Palace of Social Economy were required to conform to two

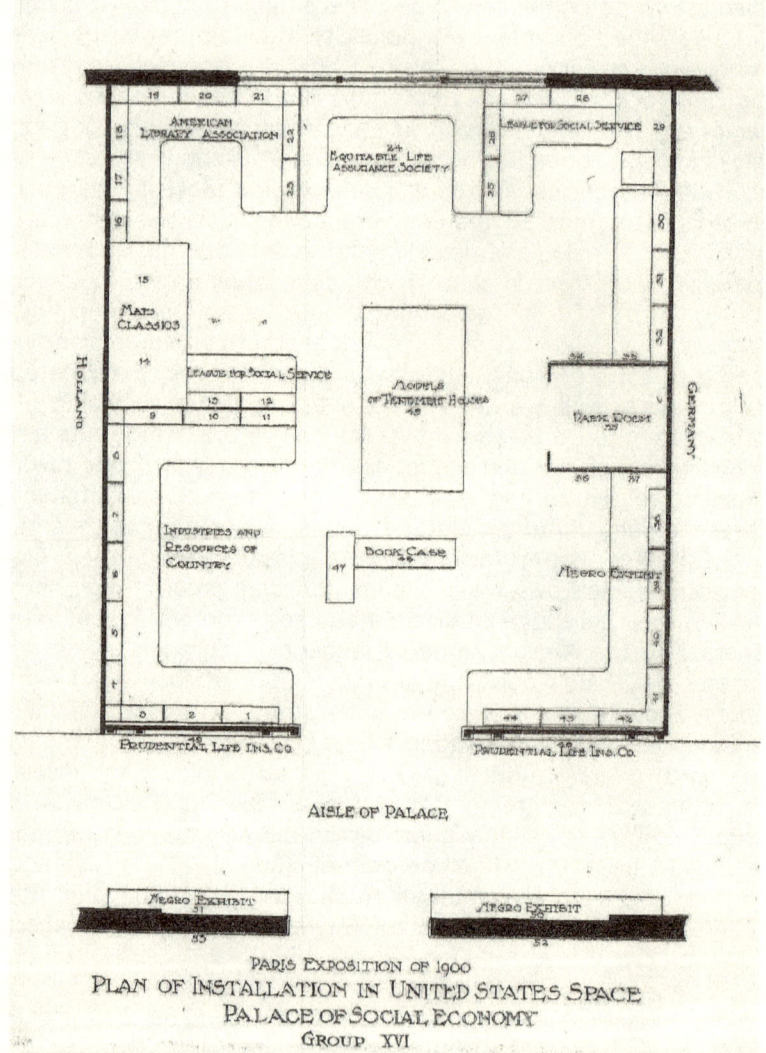

"American exhibit hall space at the Palace of Social Economy." Space allotted to Du Bois's work is labeled "Negro Exhibit" (lower right corner of room). *Report of the Commissioner-General for the United States to the International Universal Exposition, Paris, 1900. Vol. 2.*

stipulations: each had to function as "a spectacle for the entertainment as well as the instruction of visitors," and each had to present a "record of the state of each science or art and the progress accomplished" in that area (*Report of the Commissioner-General* 2: 390). Josiah Strong and William H. Tolman's League of Social Science exhibited in the American space, as did the Prudential Life Insurance Company and the American Library Association. In spite of this, the United States section of the Palais de l'Économie Sociale et des Congrès, an Italianate palace devoted to exhibits in social economy and the meeting of more than 150 congresses, was "small, and not, at first glance, particularly striking," Du Bois writes in his November 1900 essay, "The American Negro at Paris" (575).[5] Its models of tenement houses, its stereopticon room (a photographic darkroom), and its maps showing the general distribution of industries were overshadowed (and, it seems, easily so) by the Negro exhibit. The Negro exhibit stood out, Du Bois opined, because it was "more than most others in the building . . . sociological in the larger sense of the term." That is, it represented, in ways that the other exhibits in the American section did not, "an attempt to give, in as systematic and compact a form as possible, the history and present condition of a large group of human beings" ("American Negro" 576).

In "The American Negro at Paris," the only extensive writing Du Bois undertakes on his work at the exposition, he points out that the most striking, and thus most significant element of his exhibit lay in the various sorts of illustrations that worked together to provide visitors with a sociological understanding of the history, social condition, education, and literature of the American Negro (576). Underscoring the significance of what he calls the "usual paraphernalia for catching the eye," Du Bois felt assured that the exhibit effectively fulfilled the commissioner-general's requirements of "spectacle" and "instruction" via a display of "photographs, models . . . and pictures" (576). Further, the artifacts demonstrated the "state" and "progress" of the discipline of sociology by way of the structure Du Bois conceived for their presentation, "a carefully thought out plan" designed to argue convincingly that African Americans were constructing a particular epistemology of their own (576).

More than these things, which are specific to his work at the Paris fair, the Exhibit on American Negroes responded in important ways to the radical crisis in African American history and culture that Du Bois remarked in 1900. He was certain that what was needed in the long shadow cast by Frederick Douglass's death in 1895 was the establishment of a solid black intelligentsia and leadership. The leadership provided by Douglass—an ex-slave, a fierce abolition-

"A postcard bearing an image of Frederick Douglass's statue." Reproduced with kind permission of the Department of Rare Books and Special Collections, The University of Rochester Library.

"W.E.B. Du Bois in Paris, 1900." Reproduced with kind permission of the Department of Special Collections and Archives, W.E.B. Du Bois Library, University of Massachusetts, Amherst.

ist, a statesman, and a cosmopolitan traveler—had been taken up (unnaturally, Du Bois insists) by the southern educator Booker T. Washington. Washington's greatest rival for national prominence at the time of Douglass's death was the feminist anti-lynching crusader Ida B. Wells-Barnett. Yet, even as Du Bois dares to castigate Washington, first in 1901 in his review of *Up from Slavery* (Washington's autobiography) and again in 1903 with the publication of *The Souls of Black Folk,* Wells-Barnett garners little of Du Bois's attention. Her international tour in the early 1890s, when she took the podium at a number of venues across the United Kingdom, was undoubtedly a gutsy and admirable move in Du Bois's eyes. Du Bois had been a graduate student at the University of Berlin between 1892 and 1894, and Wells-Barnett's activism might have served as unacknowledged inspiration for the strong feminine protagonists of some of his works of fiction. However, in his non-fictional essay "Of Mr. Booker T. Washington and Others," an essay that is essentially

"The American Negro Exhibit, Paris 1900." *Report of the Commissioner-General for the United States to the International Universal Exposition, Paris, 1900.* Vol. 2.

a study and critique of black male leadership, Wells-Barnett figures not at all. The crisis in American Negro leadership could be resolved only by way of an infusion of informed masculine initiative, Du Bois seems to argue in a manner that appears strikingly unequivocal. Thus, as maker and recorder of history, Du Bois traces a hypothetical genealogy from Douglass—whose sculpted image occupied a prominent place in the exhibit—not to Washington or Wells-Barnett, but to himself.

Thus, while the statue of Douglass (see far left of exhibit photo) is obviously an image at play with other images that abounded in the exhibit, it is also an image at play with the self-image Du Bois worked to project. By displaying a miniature of Douglass's statue, which had been dedicated in Rochester, New York (with then-

Governor Theodore Roosevelt in attendance) in June of 1899 as the first public statue of an African American, Du Bois paid homage to a great black leader whose heritage and legacy he unabashedly claimed as his own. As Du Bois would be after him, Douglass had been drawn to the process of historiography. Douglass's *Narrative* was widely embraced as an archetypal document of free and intelligent black manhood and leadership. His published orations and circulated *cartes-de-visite* (calling cards Douglass had made at different times in his life and that carried different images of him) likewise became markers of history. To my mind, the photographs, graphs, charts, and myriad textual inscriptions displayed by Du Bois at the fair are, in essence, instantiations of sociological practice that are themselves deeply embedded within a field of linguistic practice. What is more, if images operate in the mode that Roland Barthes indicates—that is, if the various images Du Bois presents operate as a language, as a site of discourse that enters into a heteroglossic discursive context and, in so doing, effects an historical and cultural difference—then Du Bois's images exist as so many attempts at conveying sociological meaning that is, at once, ostensibly fixed in historical discourse and also shifting and desedimentary. That is to say, we may, as we shall in this chapter's final section, draw examples from Du Bois's exhibit that demonstrate his attempt—and success—at advancing Douglass's liberatory efforts on behalf of the Negro. We may view them as examples of Du Bois's work in altering the discourse and genealogy of the history of the Negro.

It is a curious paradox of Du Bois's oeuvre that his work at the fair, which has in recent years garnered increased academic attention,[6] should have been treated so sparely by him in his own writings. As I mention above, Du Bois's most complete word on the exhibit is found in "The American Negro at Paris," published in the *American Monthly Review of Reviews*. Otherwise, he seems to take notice of Paris only fleetingly, as his thoughts and writings move on to other notes. "To the Nations of the World," his address to the meeting of the first Pan-African Conference in July of 1900, speaks of the French Republic in passing but leaves Paris and the exposition, which Du Bois and Thomas J. Calloway (the special agent in charge of the exhibit) had quit only a few weeks before, without mention. His reference to the Paris expo in "The Immortal Child" (published in *Darkwater: Voices from within the Veil*, 1920), a memoir of the composer Samuel Coleridge-Taylor in which Du Bois writes briefly of "the beautiful World's Fair at Paris" (193), is no more informative. He touches on the fair again in his 1940 autobiography *Dusk of Dawn* (in the chapter entitled "Science and Empire") and in the opening pages of his revisionist book of history called *The World and Africa*

(1947), but it is not until *The Autobiography of W. E. B. Du Bois,* published posthumously in 1968, that he works to place the exposition experience into greater perspective, albeit in limited fashion. There, he acknowledges that his work in Paris had been "a significant occurrence which not until lately have I set in its proper place in my life" (220), yet he does little more than recount the story in brief yet again, relating it to the commendations he was sure would come as a result. Accolades did pour in, he writes, "not only for this particular exhibit but for the work of the Atlanta conferences in general" (221). Nonetheless, he lamented that he still found himself struggling for support to carry out future sociological studies.

Du Bois's short word on the exhibit is informative, and yet we wonder why it comes only in brief. His interactions with Thomas Junius Calloway and Booker T. Washington demonstrate its importance to him. Calloway, a steadfast supporter of Washington, was tapped for the position of special commissioner to the Paris Exposition on Washington's recommendation to national organizers of the United States exhibits. He had been Du Bois's classmate at Fisk, graduating from the university in 1889, the year after Du Bois finished his studies, and it was Calloway who recommended Du Bois to Washington as the scholar best suited to prepare an exhibit on the American Negro. In spite of Calloway's long collaboration with Washington, Du Bois in the *Autobiography* describes him as "a pal of mine" who "remained so for 40 years" (112). Calloway served as a clerk in the War Department in Washington, D.C., and briefly held tenure as the president of Alcorn A & M College in Mississippi in 1895. He was, for a time, a northern agent of Washington's Tuskegee Institute. In this role, he would oversee the transport to Paris of the now well-known collection of Hampton photographs that launched the career of Frances Benjamin Johnston, a white American documentary photographer with ties to some of America's leading families. African American photographers Thomas Askew and Harry Shepard also contributed to the print collection displayed in Paris, along with some other photographers whose names are now lost to history. The photos taken by Johnston comprise The Hampton Album, a collection of 159 plates taken between December 1899 and early 1900.[7] Those photos by Johnston that were included in the 1900 Paris exhibit were, according to the editors of *The Booker T. Washington Papers,* "designed to promote industrial education for blacks along the Hampton-Tuskegee model" (Harlan 177), a model of which Du Bois soon became a vociferous critic.[8]

It is not certain that it was Booker T. Washington's shadow-like involvement in the Exhibit on American Negroes that alone caused Du Bois to downplay his own participation. His early questioning of

"Agriculture. A class judging swine." *The Hampton Album: 44 Photographs by Frances B. Johnston from an Album of Hampton Institute.* New York: The Museum of Modern Art, 1966. Digital image © The Museum of Modern Art-Licensed by SCALA-Art Resource, NY.

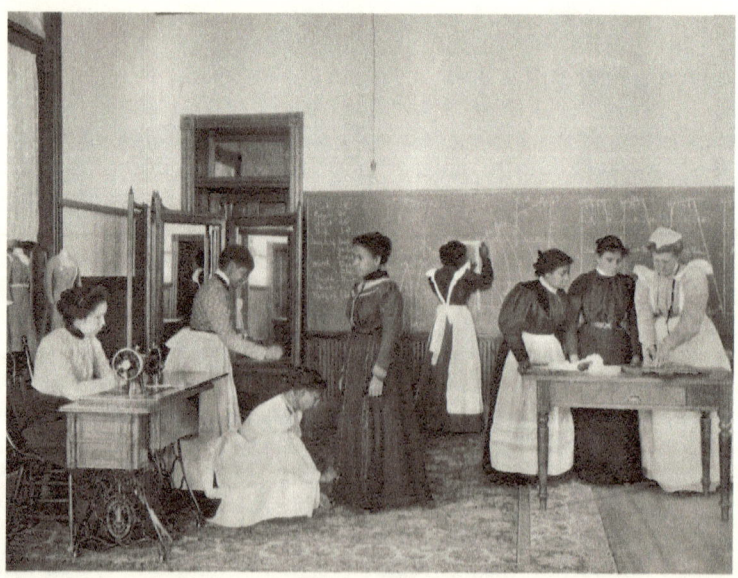

"A class in dress-making." *The Hampton Album: 44 Photographs by Frances B. Johnston from an Album of Hampton Institute.* New York: The Museum of Modern Art, 1966. Digital image © The Museum of Modern Art-Licensed by SCALA-Art Resource, NY.

Washington's educational method, which could be described as the educational corollary of the types of social control of the lower classes employed by industrialists such as Andrew Carnegie, has already been well documented.[9] Du Bois's questioning of Washington's way would not, of course, stop him from appealing to Washington for employment once he had graduated from Harvard in 1894. The two did not meet in person, and Du Bois would not emerge as an apparent threat to Washington's dominance, however, until March of 1899, when Du Bois, Paul Laurence Dunbar, and Washington took the stage in Boston's Hollis Street Theatre for a series of talks (*Biography of a Race* 229). Washington had been trying to get Du Bois to come to Tuskegee "to conduct sociological studies that will prove helpful to our people," and he wrote Du Bois in October of that year "to renew the proposition that you connect yourself permanently with this institution" (Washington 245). Du Bois would take a while to answer definitively, but skillfully queried Washington in February of 1900: "Would not my department be regarded by the public as a sort of superfluous addition not quite in consonance with the fundamental Tuskegee idea?" (Washington 443).

It is clear that Du Bois saw his own ideology as being inconsonant with that of Washington, and it is just as clear that he and Calloway held similar views on the work that could be accomplished by a successful exhibiting of African American history and culture at the fair. Calloway and Du Bois, as did all other African American leaders of that time who sought high levels of governmental and philanthropic funding, needed Washington's support in order to get money to carry out their work. To further ensure Washington's endorsement of his efforts to secure funds, Calloway wrote the Tuskegee principal in the fall of 1899, employing words that echoed much of Du Bois's own thought:

> Every one who knows about public opinion in Europe will tell you that the Europeans think us a mass of rapists, ready to attack every white woman exposed, and a drug in civilized society. This notion has come to them through the horrible libels that have gone abroad whenever a Negro is lynched, and by the constant reference to us by the press in discouraging remarks. The social and political economists of the Old World put down the erroneous accounts of such cases as that of Sam Hose as truth, and, not hearing the actual facts, reach conclusions which do us wrong. How shall we answer these slanders? Our newspapers they do not subscribe for, if we publish books they do not buy them, if we lecture, they do not attend.
> To the Paris Exposition, however, thousands upon thou-

sands of them will go and a well selected and prepared exhibit, representing the Negro's development in his churches, his schools, his homes, his farms, his stores, his professions and pursuits in general will attract attention as did the exhibits at [the] Atlanta and Nashville Expositions [sic], and do a great and lasting good in convincing thinking people of the possibilities of the Negro.

Not only will foreigners be impressed, but hundreds of white Americans will be far more convinced by what they see there than what they see, or can see, every day in this country, but fail to give us credit for. (Washington 226–27)

With Washington's positive response to this query, Calloway was able to raise some $15,000 to support the work of the exhibit, the excess of which went, according to the Commissioner-General's Report, into the bursary for support of other fair-related needs. Du Bois and his students at Atlanta University produced, in a very brief window of time, numerous hand-drafted color charts and graphs presenting their documented sociological research. Somehow, little of the $15,000 and little of Washington's articulated support reached Du Bois, for he tells in his *Autobiography* of the difficulties of finishing the "50 or more charts, in colors, with accuracy" when he had "little money, limited time and not too much encouragement" (221). However, Du Bois and Calloway felt certain that their work, presented in a land other than America and argued before an international conclave of some of the world's best thinkers, would afford them some leverage in their fight against American racism. Indeed, as Du Bois tells it, the "American press, white and colored, was full of recommendation and in the end, the exhibit received a Grand Prize, and I, as its author, a Gold Medal" (221).

It is, perhaps, the Sam Hose incident, mentioned by Calloway in his letter to Washington, along with Du Bois's late realization of the stealth power of Booker Washington that, in his writings, distracts Du Bois from discussing the Paris expo to any great length. Du Bois mentions Hose, an itinerate farmer who was arrested for murder little more than a year before Du Bois sailed for Paris, in a number of his major works, including *The Souls of Black Folk, Dusk of Dawn,* and the *Autobiography*. It was the lynching of Sam Hose that wrought a significant change in his professional outlook. Hose's murder in April 1899 by a mob of whites, who afterward fought over his remains for souvenirs, "cut across [the] plan which I had as a scientist" and caused him to "turn aside from my work." Hose's lynching was a "red ray," the consideration of which "broke in upon my work and eventually disrupted it: first, one could not be a calm, cool, and detached scientist while Negroes were lynched, murdered and starved; and secondly, there was no such definite demand for scientific work of the sort that I was doing, as I had confidently assumed would be easily forthcoming" (*Autobiography* 221–222). The shock that Hose's murder brought to Du Bois's consciousness was rendered more acute by his understanding, some years later, of the power Washington wielded behind the scenes. In the *Autobiography*, Du Bois draws a link between the rise of Booker Washington to power after Douglass's death in 1895 and the wave of disfranchisement laws that were passed between 1890 and 1910 in many states of the former southern confederacy (231). Hose's lynching had ridden the crest of this wave. Jim Crow legislation, which gave birth to a violent American caste system of color and race, eventually forced Du Bois from his sociological work at Atlanta University, he writes. It explains, Du Bois tells us, why he left Atlanta to take up a position as Director of Publications and Research for the National Association for the Advancement of Colored People, which he helped to found in 1910 (231–32).

So, it appears that the truncated description of the Exhibit on American Negroes that Du Bois provides in the *Autobiography* must be read in the context of these other forceful factors. In fact, by his action of inserting into the text what would appear as part of the *Autobiography* material that had not been explored in his previous memoir, *Dusk of Dawn*, Du Bois insists that we must interpret the exhibit as part of this furious context.[10] His work at the fair came at a pivotal moment in both his career and his self-conception as a sociologist, as a "seeker of truth" who slowly came to see "the ruins of some ideals about me" (228), working, "deliberately" as he puts it, in the South (232) before migrating, as did many other African Americans, toward a large city in the North. And as he traversed the Atlantic Ocean during June of 1900, he undertook a different sort of migration that would forecast the global importance of his move to the cosmopolitan city of New York—a temporary, transnational migration to a temporary, international space where he hoped his work would be perceived as an "honest straightforward exhibit of a small nation of people, picturing their life and development without apology or gloss" ("American Negro" 577).

Du Bois's exhibit, then, is both historical document and revisionist sociological practice. At the time he wrote *Dusk of Dawn*, and by the time he penned his *Autobiography*, Du Bois was well aware of the high regard in which many held his work. His exhibit was displayed again in 1901 at the Pan-American Exposition in Buffalo, New York, where President William McKinley met his untimely end at the hands of a self-proclaimed anarchist. By the time of the

Jamestown Tercentennial Exposition in 1907, Du Bois would condemn the Negro exhibit organized by Giles B. Jackson of Richmond, Virginia, as being a sort of "Jim Crow" endeavor, and he sent out a circular dated March 29, 1907, that made clear that he had no involvement whatever with the enterprise.[11]

What was important to Du Bois was that it be quite apparent that the artifacts that appeared as part of his own exhibit be deemed, collectively, an autonomous exercise of African American cultural expression. The Paris exhibit was, he insists, "above all made by themselves," that is, made by the Negro people alone (577). Such an insistence discloses Du Bois's tacit argument that the meaning conveyed through the various images there assembled bore the imprint of no one person's mediating hand, not even his own. They were, Du Bois seems to say, immediate presentations of black life and existence, put forward collectively and presenting the disparate collectivity of the African American people as a cohesive and unified nation, one that vied with other nations (the Spanish and the Russians appeal to Du Bois as points of comparison) for light and recognition on an international stage.

Of course, if my reading of Du Bois's position is just and correct, if his pretensions to immediacy are not simple pretensions but constitute something greater, viz., a critical commentary on the prevalent practices and methods of sociology, then we have some further ground to cover in our examination of his work. For if this is so, and I believe it is, Du Bois's practice works to support the critical stance he takes vis-à-vis the metaphysics of sociology. Du Bois's critique, especially as we find it in "Sociology Hesitant," tells the story in full, as we shall shortly see. In claiming immediacy, Du Bois returns to what he sees as the fundamental theoretical problem that sociology was called, in his opinion, to confront. That problem consisted in nineteenth-century sociology's insistence upon a transcendent "idea." Du Bois rejected such thought on the grounds that sociological theory was too far removed from sociological reality. The study of African American sociological reality could, Du Bois argues in "American Negro," do society a great amount of good, and it was to such study that he had devoted the bulk of his time since joining the faculty of Atlanta University in 1897.

Du Bois had approached this problem in his introduction to *The Philadelphia Negro* (1899) but would not pose it as a problem until the composing of "Sociology Hesitant," which was written in 1904 or 1905 but was never published during Du Bois's lifetime.[12] And yet in 1900, he sought, through the exhibit, to work out this problem, to solve it practically by attention to a sociological object as opposed to a sociological concept. He is not completely successful in avoiding the idealist schemata he worked to overturn. Yet he does succeed in identifying certain artifacts that manifested or demonstrated the effects of social structure among African Americans in particular, while recognizing that this specific structure operated within a larger American social structure that itself existed mainly on the basis of racial and class inequities.

We can, therefore, regard the cultural artifact, the image, as something of a guiding tenet, a thetic principle undergirding Du Bois's work at the Expo, a principle that enfolds his intellectual engagement with the discipline of sociology and his immersion in African American culture and historiography into a display of material culture. In his essay "The American Negro at Paris," Du Bois conveyed his sure sense that the Palais de l'Économie Sociale et des Congrès would have disappointed those visitors who came in search of displays that actually engaged the "'science of society,'" a sort of code phrase that indicated for Du Bois the problematic set of metaphysical positionings that plagued sociology.[13] This sentiment was attended by his equal certainty that those "who [had] followed historically the development, out of the old Political Economy, of a miscellaneous body of knowing chiefly concerned with the larger aspects of human benevolence" would have found "much of interest" in the "charts, statistics, models, and photographs" prominently displayed in the booths occupied by not only the exhibit on the American Negro but also such organizations as the "mutual-aid societies of France" and "the working-man's circles of Belgium" (575).

To get at the thesis of the exhibit, a kind of iconography that I take to reside in Du Bois's own conception of and preoccupation with race, history, and sociology, is to engage the rationalist notion of the "'science of society'" and the discipline of political economy to which Du Bois refers above. (It was through gains made in sociological discourse that early political economy, which had resulted from the rise of science during the Enlightenment, lost much of its force and focus as it gained currency in the new field of sociology, although it coincided well with the concomitant rise of capitalist thought.) The iconography that inhabits the thesis of the exhibit—the mounting of an exhibit that shows African Americans to be gnostic creatures deeply engaged in the development of their own cultural and historical epistemology—was itself at the heart of late nineteenth-century sociological methods. Named sociology by its founder, August Comte, in 1838, at the turn of the century the "science of society" was still quite a young discipline in American institutions of higher learning. Indeed, as is perhaps well known by now, Du Bois's 1899 book, *The Philadelphia Negro: A Social Study*, was a pioneering sociological work in the United States. However, sociology was a discipline toward which Du Bois openly expressed misgivings, even as he undertook a number of that discourse's most important investigations. (I am thinking here as well of the Atlanta University sociological studies; Du Bois had completed five of these studies by the time of the 1900 Paris fair.) For Du Bois, the questions surrounding sociological methods were far from insignificant. In the introduction to *The Philadelphia Negro,* he lays before the reader his concerns about the "credibility of the results," which, due to the tendency of even "the best methods of sociological research" lean toward such

> inaccuracies that the careful student discloses the results of individual research with diffidence; he knows that they are liable to error from the seemingly ineradicable faults of the statistical method, to even greater error from the methods of general *observation,* and, above all, he must ever tremble lest some personal bias, some moral conviction, or some unconscious trend of thought due to previous training, has to a degree distorted the *picture* in his view. (*Philadelphia Negro* 2–3; emphasis added)

Du Bois would return to an exposition of his halting concerns for the discipline, which he describes here in terms that underscore the metaphor of the visual (for example, "observation" and "picture"), in the recently rediscovered essay "Sociology Hesitant." The piece falls in line with other of Du Bois's writings that articulate his theoretical positioning vis-à-vis western sociological methodology and philosophy. In "Sociology Hesitant," he castigates the practitioners of sociology in general and the positivist sociologist Auguste Comte in particular for failing to shed the burden of metaphysics in their framing and application of sociological theory. This "[fixing of] scientific thought on the study of an abstraction"—society, that is—Comte had not meant to do, Du Bois concludes (38). "[R]ather he meant to call attention to the fact that amid the bewildering complexities of human life ran great highways of common likenesses and agreements in human thoughts and action, which world-long observation had already noted and pondered upon" (38). Nonetheless, the persistence of "society" as an abstraction that guided the efforts of scientists who called themselves sociologists (or, Du Bois seems to say, sociologists who called themselves scientists) spelled, for Du Bois, the terms of sociology's great failing.

Such shortsightedness on Comte's part was willfully assumed by England's great social scientist, Herbert Spencer. A contemporary of Charles Darwin, Spencer is credited with developing the notion of Social Darwinism.[14] He also published his very popular *Descrip-*

tive Sociology (1870–1890), a compilation of works by various social scientists. Though widely heralded by sociologists for its scope, Du Bois found the work to be severely "limited," to the degree that its findings were dangerously predicated upon "woefully imperfect" data that were in turn dependent upon "hearsay, rumor and tradition, vague speculations, travellor's [*sic*] tales, legends and imperfect documents, the memory of memories and historic error" ("Sociology Hesitant" 39).[15] It appears without question that Du Bois deemed Spencer's sociological method in particular to be of little value—either extrinsic or intrinsic. To Du Bois's mind, Spencerian sociologists failed miserably in their attempts to grant greater understanding to human deeds because their work examined not deeds but theories. More than this, they did not gather data in order that it be used to effect social progress; rather they collected information simply to theorize. In Du Bois's words, they gave a "description of those Thoughts, and Thoughts of Things, and Things that go to make human life an effort to trace in the deeds and actions of men great underlying principles of harmony and development" (39). Sociology's attempt to escape Hegelian metaphysics ultimately failed in Spencerian thought, specifically with the establishment of what Spencerians called the "sociological element."

Looking back on his participation in sociological discourse from a vista of forty years and commenting upon the work he produced in the closing years of the previous century, Du Bois would draw roughly the same conclusion regarding the shortcomings of the discipline he had once claimed as his own. He writes in *Dusk of Dawn:*

> Social thinkers were engaged in vague statements and were seeking to lay down the methods by which, in some not too distant future, social law analogous to physical law would be discovered. Herbert Spencer finished his ten volumes of Synthetic Philosophy in 1896. The biological analogy, the vast generalizations, were striking, but actual scientific accomplishment lagged. For me an opportunity seemed to present itself. I could not lull my mind to hypnosis by regarding a phrase like "consciousness of kind"[16] as a scientific law. But turning my gaze from fruitless word-twisting and facing the facts of my own social situation and racial world, I determined to put science into sociology through a study of the condition and problems of my own group.
>
> I was going to study the facts, any and all facts, concerning the American Negro and his plight, and by measurement and comparison and research, work up to any valid generalization which I could. I entered this primarily with the utilitarian ob-

ject of reform and uplift; but nevertheless, I wanted to do the work with scientific accuracy. Thus, in my own sociology, because of firm belief in a changing racial group, I easily grasped the idea of a changing developing society rather than a fixed social structure. (590–91)

Certainly, the state of social theory in the year 1900 and his own disagreement with the theory and methods of that discipline were not lost on Du Bois as significant historical markers of what he calls in *Dusk of Dawn* the "era of empire" and "industrial imperialism" (591). Indeed, sociology was often viewed as an instrument of industrial and imperial might. According to Sanford Elwitt, mid-nineteenth-century sociology in the United States (and sociological thought at the time closely adhered to the system set forth by Comte) "was best expressed in George Fitzhugh's *Sociology for the South* and Henry Hughes's *Treatise on Sociology*. Both argued for the value, the virtue and the logic of hierarchical social relations characteristic of slavery" (209). While following the systems laid down by Comte, Fitzhugh in particular decried the more egalitarian socialism espoused by the French social scientist Claude Saint-Simon, himself mentor to Comte. Instead, in books such as *Cannibals All! Or, Slaves without Masters* (1857), Fitzhugh readily embraced the economics of slavery as a social panacea. So, while Du Bois saw well the potential of sociological study, he also voiced his concerns for research among a field of scholars whose leading lights were, at times, biased toward the theoretical and away from the practical. Likewise, currents in the field from its early days in American practice had sanctioned the sort of racist pretensions evident in the work of Hughes and Fitzhugh.

There was, then, a question central to sociological discourse at the time Du Bois mounted his exhibit at Paris, and this question is demonstrated in the latter elements of the commentary we find in *Dusk of Dawn,* which echo much of the sentiment he expressed in "Sociology Hesitant." He states clearly that he developed his own stream of thought on the discipline and points us toward a consideration of his own methodology apart from that developing in his chosen field. Sociology, emerging as it did in the middle of the nineteenth century and crystallizing under the thoughts and pens of Comte and the autodidact Spencer, took a decided turn away from the sort of activist social reform Du Bois envisioned. Indeed, contrary to Du Bois's desire that the sociological method be used for the practical "object of reform and uplift," it was often employed in an effort to maintain what was broadly termed the "social peace." Such a thematic element of sociological discourse pertained not only to the traffic among enterprises but also to the intercourse among nations. "French social scientists," Sanford Elwitt writes, "elevated social economy to the 'science of social peace,' thereby offering it as a political weapon for the French ruling classes. The examples of the 1889 and 1900 Paris Exhibitions testify to the fact," he tells us: "the Social Economy exhibits in both cases were dominated by displays relating to the working class" (212). Sociology suffered from a rather overt collusion between science and capital.

In fact, William H. Tolman, a leader in American sociology who was a jurist at the Paris exposition[17] and who undoubtedly attended a number of the congresses held at the Palais de l'Économie Sociale, took "as his primary task the promotion of the 'interdependence between capital and labor and the sympathy which should exist between these two elements in the successful promotion of a business'" (Elwitt 210). Tolman, whom Elwitt describes as a social engineer, was also founder of the American Institute of Social Services. His "vocation," Elwitt writes, might be called "sociology in the classical sense of the term and following in the habit of industrial corporations to label their personnel offices departments of sociology" (210).

Industrialists in America and Europe alike underscored the importance of the international fairs not simply for their ability to promote global capital and to foster the so-called "social peace" but also for their role in national identity building. As Wolfram Kaiser puts the matter, the French, like their counterparts in the West, used the expositions to create "temporarily . . . not only a national, but a kind of global public space which [they] also tried to use to create a favourable national image abroad" (227). Other national entities, including the United States, essayed to accomplish much the same through leading industrialists who acted as *portes-parole* of the nation's nationalist and internationalist desires. In an 1894 article entitled "Value of the World's Fair to the American People," the steel magnate Andrew Carnegie, reflecting somewhat wistfully upon the grandeur of the World's Columbian Exhibition of 1893 (and using the ironically appropriate image of Shakespeare's Prospero—himself a fictional seventeenth-century imperialist—to convey the sense of magic the exhibition was thought to have exercised over its visitors), expressed his opinion that international exhibitions were of such value in bringing together Americans from disparate states that they should be held "[a]t least once every twenty years" (422). Such reunions would serve not only to "[draw] together . . . the people of the United States," itself "a work of great difficulty"; they would allow the diverse citizenry of the nation to meet "their fellow citizens" and to converge "in harmony upon one point at least,—

their intense Americanism" (422). Alfred Goshorn, who had been involved in the mounting of several industrial fairs in Cincinnati, Ohio, and who had drawn upon this experience in his post as director-general of the Centennial Exhibition held in Philadelphia in 1876, also lent his voice to this special issue of the *Engineering Magazine*. For him, the importance of the fairs was not simply their ability to solidify national sentiment and nationalist sensibilities. Rather, he concluded that the "[i]nternational exhibitions are among the most effective of national educators. They tend to raise each of the cö-operating nations to the level of the highest in artistic, industrial, and scientific advancement, and they stimulate that one [nation] to still more energetic efforts to preserve supremacy" (423). According to Goshorn, the world's fairs were themselves a sort of bloodless field of international striving upon which each nation contended for artistic, scientific, and technological advancement. While the theme of the 1900 Paris fair may have been "Le Bilan d'un Siècle" (loosely translated as "The Fruit of the Century," in terms of an assessment or evaluation of its achievements), its more readily apparent theme might be identified as "Progress." In Carnegie's estimation, the theme of the 1893 fair could well have been the same. The palaces of Chicago's great White City (aptly named for its white masculinist agenda) seemed to shout unabashedly, through their "unrivalled" beauty, the very slogan of progress. That an unnamed but "eminent Frenchman" openly concurred is proffered by Carnegie as so much proof of the same: "'these buildings at Chicago seem as if they must have been produced by us in Paris,'" the anonymous Frenchman effused, "'and those that we boasted of in Paris seem now as if they must have been designed and erected in Chicago'" (419).

Carnegie's need for foreign affirmation of American supremacy is less surprising when compared to France's equally fervent desire for international recognition from the community of nations. Wolfram Kaiser argues that the "exhibitions in Philadelphia in 1876 and Chicago in 1893 were at least partially politically motivated—one by the centenary of American independence, the other by the fourth centenary of the discovery of America by Columbus—but they were not nearly as important for the nation as a whole as those in Paris were for France" (228). The political import of the 1900 Paris expo "was mostly expressed through symbolic sign arrangements," Kaiser continues, "including art, architecture and colonial exhibits, which the French visitor was expected to easily comprehend" (230).

This dependence on spectacle for the conveyance of political messages was not exclusive to the 1900 fair, nor was it peculiarly French in nature. Carnegie, in his general review of the 1893 Columbian expo, opined that "the grandest thing about the exhibition was the scene from without": "I make bold to say that after every work of art, every ponderous engine, every invention, everything that proved the cunning brain and hand of man, has faded away, the general effect of the purely artistic triumph attained by the buildings and their environment will remain vividly defined in the memory and recorded there unmixed with baser matter" (418–19). Carnegie's emphasis upon the specularity of the fair, and his pointing up of the mental image (that which "will remain vividly defined in the memory and recorded there") echoes Du Bois's own judgment of the importance of the visual in his exhibit at the 1900 Exposition Universelle. When Du Bois underscores the significance of what he calls the "usual paraphernalia for catching the eye," which fulfilled the commissioner-general's demand that all exhibits not simply demonstrate the state of the field, but also "entertain" the exposition's visitors, he seems not far afield from the conclusions Walter Benjamin would later draw regarding the Paris fairs. The Paris Expositions grew out of industrial fairs that themselves were organized "to entertain the working-class." It was the Saint-Simonians, the early sociologists of France who practiced a brand of sociology that was, erroneously to the mind of Karl Marx, deemed somewhat socialist, who envisioned "the industrialization of the earth [and took] up the idea of world exhibitions," Benjamin tells us (7). The phantasmagoric fantasies of the world exhibitions "modernized" the universe, he argues (8).

The sociological method, put into place by Saint-Simon and Comte, modernist in its role in world exhibitions, structuralist in its very nature, provides the methodology that emerges from a certain sort of poetics that Du Bois both embraces and rebels against in specific ways through his work at the exposition. "Poetics" becomes a quite useful way of supplying a nomenclature that links the methods of social science to methods of representation—imagery, or what we might call, following Roland Barthes in "The Structuralist Activity" (1963), "simulacrum." Poetics, as we may use the term in recalling Du Bois's work, refers to a set of principles, implied or articulated, that are remarkable and observable in a work such as his exhibit. It is also used to refer broadly to the "theory" back of a specific field of work (for example, Comte's theory of sociology), and in Greek etymology, it has to do with artistic creativity. In other words, it has to do with the making or creation of some form or other. As it pertains to the structuralist activity, Barthes argues that structuralist thinkers and practitioners create something new by virtue of their work. It is not simply that they take unformed elements and give them form by virtue of pure, noetic activity. Instead, they may take objects that are fully formed, de-form or decompose them, and recompose them in such a way that they reappear as a new thing. The process of mediation at the center of this type of work cannot, it seems to me, be overstated, although Barthes and, as we have seen, Du Bois decline to underscore the importance of mediation. What each thinker emphasizes instead is the end-product of this structuralist manipulation, a simulacrum that is at once old and new. The structuralist activity, as Barthes describes it and as we see in the work of Du Bois, thus stands at the border between two objects and two tenses, past and present.

In Du Bois's exhibit, the prior object, presented to us as existing anterior to a process of mediation and decomposition, is representative of the past and elicited from a demonstrable history from which Du Bois calls the various images forth. For our purposes in examining this process, we shall be content with studying some of the photographic representations Du Bois displays and, in particular, we shall give attention to the anonymous subjects of these photos as individuals who are absent from the scene of the exhibit itself, but who are also, nonetheless, present in the new objects. In other words, and I argue this point somewhat vicariously, as the claim exists nowhere in Du Bois's own recounting of his work at Paris, we might speak in certain terms of the "New Negro" Du Bois obviously sought to re-present to the American public and to present to the international community. For this argument and its demonstration, I extrapolate on a number of bases from Du Bois's various historical, cultural, and sociological critiques, which I have set out above and will restate here.

I see three concomitant streams of thought at work in Du Bois's exhibit. First, Du Bois was intent upon challenging and revising the genealogy of western history in such a fashion that the "gifts of the Negro people," as he would refer to black peoples' contributions to world civilization in works such as *The Souls of Black Folk*, "The Star of Ethiopia" (1913), and *The Gift of Black Folk* (1924), would be seen as undeniably essential to the dialectic of history. Second, his engagement with black culture and his quarrel with what he came to see as Booker T. Washington's blatant conciliations to white racism in both the North and the South led him to vie contentiously for the intellectual leadership of black America, although he in no way saw himself as a charismatic leader. And third, his questioning of sociological theory led him to develop his own sociological method apart from the major theoretical currents of the day, such that he challenged Comte as well as Spencer (who had himself referred to Comtean positivism as pseudoscientific cosmogony, and yet had, in Du Bois's eyes, produced "sociological theory that was lagging in 'scientific accomplishment'" and was riddled with "fruitless word-twisting" [*Dusk of Dawn* 590]).

These three complex streams merge as Du Bois undertakes a definitive act of mediation, of calling forth and re-presenting a historical Negro (with all of the weight the word *historical* connotes and denotes) poised to take his/her place—albeit in absentia—at Paris at the dawn and premiere of the new century. Barthes would argue that the simulacrum produced by this sort of act is "intellect added to object" and might say in particular that this specific addition of intellect "has an anthropological value" (150). It would be equally correct to view the simulacra presented by Du Bois as work by one of America's greatest intellects imbued with sociological value, in the very manner that Du Bois himself intended. That is (recalling Du Bois's stated aims of the exhibit as articulated in "The American Negro at Paris"), the exhibit moved in simultaneous diachronic and synchronic time by presenting the history and progress of the Negro at the very moment that it spoke to the Negro's "present" condition. Further, it sought to present cultural artifacts that were, themselves, useful objects of study in that they shifted what Du Bois saw as sociology's usual interest in the construction of vast generalizations to the observation of particular, living individual elements of a large society. They focused the sociologist's attention upon the working contributions of singular people to a vast functioning social structure.

In discussing specific, isolated (yet interrelated) elements of Du Bois's exhibit, I return to the two tropes that frame my analysis of his use of the image, metaphor and metonymy. In my introduction, I pointed out that the visual signs Du Bois employs in his exhibit may be seen as metaphoric representations that act as hypostases of an African American social reality, necessarily absent and existing in an anterior state because the images were captured prior to their being shown. At the same time, I see certain images operating metonymically, in that they are given as representations of what Du Bois called the African American "type"; they are detailed examples of such types that are arranged in relation to other types in the exhibit. I would like to explore further what I take to be a semiological process at work in Du Bois's display, one that operates on the basis of fragmentation and via the contending forces of metaphor and metonymy. It is through such intellectual ferment that Du Bois's exhibit makes meaning that contextualizes the advent of the New Negro in the new century.

Let us begin with a general discussion of four photos included in Du Bois's photo albums entitled *Types of American Negroes,* now unbound and in the holdings of the Library of Congress's Prints and Photographs Division. The first three images were found in the first volume and were located close together. They are, clockwise, numbers 59, 60, and 51, respectively. The third volume held the final photo, labeled number 217.

The photos I have selected are of African American children. The first two are young girls who posed in the same studio for the same photographer (note the curtain in the right background); the second two, babies in what appear to be christening gowns. These images, similar in composition, lighting, and study, were, like many others shown in Paris, displayed without commentary and without identification of the subject or the photographer. I regard these four photographs as forming a certain class or paradigmatic unit (in the sense in which linguistics employs the term) within the larger paradigm of the entire photographic essay. My reference to the collection in linguistic and literary terms is quite purposeful, for it allows me to speak of the photos in question as a strictly limited collection of units from which we might draw one or two examples for commentary and analysis. In fact, we might relate our own process of drawing out these four to the process Du Bois undertook in choosing and arranging each of the five hundred photos for display. In so doing, we call forth those that we choose to endow with a certain meaning. And while we do so with words and commentary, Du Bois does so silently, or so it seems. In his collection as in our own small paradigmatic unit, the images themselves are left to do the work of producing some sort of meaning as they relate to one another. Paradoxically, this meaning is produced most readily in the similarities and differences observable between and among them, to the extent that these observable similarities and differences allow us to draw conclusions about the meaning or identity of one artifact vis-à-vis the meaning or identity of another artifact.

Without words and given arbitrary numbers (or so it seems), we communicate with the images of the bodies of these children, bodies that themselves illustrate (bring to life) other graphic representations found in the exhibit. These four photographs, although random, adumbrate some theory of the image as it is employed in Du Bois's exhibit and allow us to escape the heterogeneity of the rest. They form a relation of theme, pose, and, somewhat outstandingly, an attitude of innocence. Further, they relate in brief the importance Du Bois placed on reproduction among African Americans, that is, the importance of the longevity of the black race. They animate Du Bois's graphs and charts illustrating the birth rate among African Americans. Likewise, they speak to the percentage of racial amalgamation that had taken place in Georgia, another aspect Du

"African American girl, full-length portrait, seated on stool." W. E. B. Du Bois, *Types of American Negroes* (1900), v. 1, no. 59. The Daniel Murray Collection, Library of Congress, Washington, D.C.

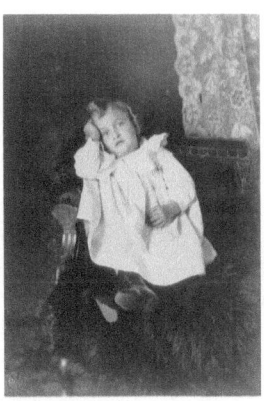

"African American girl, full-length portrait, seated in chair." W. E. B. Du Bois, *Types of American Negroes* (1900), v. 1, no. 60. The Daniel Murray Collection, Library of Congress, Washington, D.C.

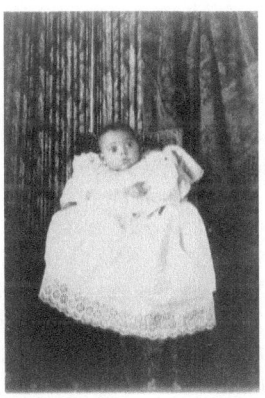

"African American baby, full-length portrait, wearing christening gown." W. E. B. Du Bois, *Types of American Negroes* (1900), v. 1, no. 51. The Daniel Murray Collection, Library of Congress, Washington, D.C.

"African American infant, seated in chair, facing front." W. E. B. Du Bois, *Types of American Negroes* (1900), v. 3, no. 217. The Daniel Murray Collection, Library of Congress, Washington, D.C.

Bois documented through graphs; the two young girls are very fair-skinned and, phenotypically, approximate the appearance of a white child. We may take this representation to act in support of Du Bois's own position on race, what he describes in *Dusk of Dawn* as his own "firm belief in a changing racial group" that varied in accordance with "a changing developing society" (591). Racial lines were not "fixed and fast" (628) but were instead a sort of construct that gained force "because the economic foundation of the modern world was based on the recognition and preservation of so-called racial distinctions" (629). To my mind, this paradigmatic group of photos demonstrates Du Bois's early understanding of the dynamics of race and social structure and not, as he says of the prevailing sociological thought of his day, that of a "fixed social structure" (591) that supported false ideas of racial essentialism.

This unit of photos, then, works within the larger collection in ways that appear deceptively simple but in reality are complex. We may take the collection at large as a reflection of a veritable world of black folk that, in its resemblance to the original, undoes what Thomas Calloway describes in his letter to Booker T. Washington as "the horrible libels that have gone abroad whenever a Negro is lynched." It exists as a representation of an immense and productive black community that Du Bois and his collaborator knew to be real and not merely something imagined or written about by whites. More than this, we should see it as an object that exists beyond Du Bois's own "impression" of that world and its culture but also as evidence of a sort of mimetic activity that Du Bois undertakes. We might think of the collection as analogical, that is, as a photographic and metaphoric reflection of black reality, black realism that points the way toward an intelligible black world without providing ways of grasping that world's limits. But the photos are much more. The collection derives from Du Bois's process of analyzing a multitudinous black world, documenting, that is, historicizing, it through his sociological work, and then choosing and arranging visual representations of that world, often metonymic in their singularity, such that he arranges out of these dissected fragments a new, multivalent aesthetic object. By virtue of his actions, he brings about new meanings of the object itself.

According to Du Bois, sociology and its practitioners were caught up in "metaphysical wanderings"; they were engaged in noting "the grouping of men, the changing of government, the agreement in thought, and then, instead of a minute study of men grouping, changing, and thinking, proposed to study the Group, the Change, and the Thought and call this new created Thing Society" ("Sociology Hesitant" 39). They ought instead, he opined, to recognize that they were confronted with a paradox that they had, at the turn of the century, not yet given sufficient consideration. The paradox was the juxtaposition of what he called "the Hypothesis of Law and the Assumption of Chance" (42). The object of sociology ought not simply to be the study of an abstraction called society, Du Bois argues, but instead should be the analysis of the actions and deeds of individuals within that society. At the same time, the astute sociologist should perceive that his or her work is not so much in conceiving stable, finite, and "true" meanings regarding the social entity; instead, the sociologist should see clearly the intersection of law and chance. The sociologist's challenge, the way out of the paradox, was the recognition of something "incalculable" at the very foundation of sociological study because the incalculable stood at the heart of human existence. The "'Ought,'" or that which remains undefinable, "is the greatest thing in human life," Du Bois writes (43).

Du Bois's work at the exhibit is exemplary of the revised sociological method he champions in "Sociology Hesitant." His work at Paris is not a battle against chance; it is not a sociological enterprise submitted to the constraints of sociological formalism. Rather, it presents a simulacrum of the black world that proceeds by way of metaphorical reality—the representation of black folk in a Parisian exhibit that stands in for the black folk themselves. Yet it is the very limits of these representations that Du Bois seeks. The limits are demonstrated in the numerous and precise charts and graphs in his display; they are shown, for example, in "the rhythm in birth and death rates and the distribution by sex" that Du Bois documents. But the limits are also exercised by the deeds of individuals within that society, those nameless faces of all ages that appear in his three volumes of photographs. Essentially for Du Bois, the limits are found in the specifics of culture, in "human customs" and "the operation of a woman's club" (44). Thus his insistence upon visual documentation through a display of culture at the exhibit is actually the wedding of African American history and American and European sociology. The cultural artifacts Du Bois mounts at Paris are intelligent and interrogating, articulate yet silent. They announce the arrival of the New Negro who speaks with a language that, Du Bois insists, will rise out of history.

Notes

Grateful acknowledgment is made to the Department of Rare Books and Special Collections, The University of Rochester Library, for permission to reprint the postcard bearing an image of Frederick Douglass's statue.

1. Andrew Carnegie notes that several individuals involved in organizing the 1893 fair had serious doubts as to whether Chicago, because of its Midwestern location, would serve the event well (417). New York was a strong contender, as many felt that the eastern city was more appropriate to an international gathering.

2. I use the term *collective consciousness* as it is defined by sociologist Émile Durkheim. It refers to a body of belief or sentiments common among members of a society.

3. African Americans had been allowed self-representation at the 1893 Chicago fair, but it was quite limited and came only after much agitation on the part of Ida B. Wells, Frederick Douglass, and others.

4. For some reason, Du Bois chose to keep "Sociology Hesitant" out of the field of professional interchange. Du Bois's biographer David Levering Lewis imagines that, had Du Bois published the essay at the time it was written, he would have "boldly challenged the giants of contemporary sociology and declared that the discipline's methodology was based on theoretical fallacies that ignored the ineradicable element of chance in human affairs" (*Biography of a Race* 202). Instead, Du Bois kept the essay among his personal papers. It was published only in 2002, in a special issue of the journal *boundary2*.

5. Du Bois's use of the preposition "at" in the title of his essay corresponds with the French "à": "Le nègre américain à Paris" would be the French translation of the title, which would translate back to the English as either "The American Negro *in* Paris" or "The American Negro *at* Paris." Thus we might imagine that Du Bois allows himself to be influenced by French grammatical patterns in the titling of his essay. But, as we see in Thomas Calloway's letter to Booker T. Washington, cited on page 29 of this chapter, the use of "at" in the context of speaking of the exhibits seems to be common usage. (Calloway writes of the exhibits "at Atlanta and Nashville" [226].) Nonetheless, it might be fruitful to imagine that the use of the preposition *at* reflects in some way Du Bois's sensitivity to place, to his feeling of being in Paris but certainly not of it. My thanks to Professor Jonathan Eburne for his underscoring of this point.

6. Shawn Michelle Smith's work on the exhibit is extensive and excellent but was published well after my ideas for this essay were conceived. Please see, for example, *Photography on the Color Line: W. E. B. Du Bois, Race, and Visual Culture,* where Smith focuses on Du Bois's photo albums, *Types of American Negroes,* and argues for seeing Du Bois as "an early visual theorist of race and racism" (2). See also essays by David Levering Lewis (for a historical contextualization); Deborah Willis (for a discussion of Du Bois and the cultural history of African American photogra-

phy); Eugene F. Provenzo, Jr. (for an electronic reconstruction of the exhibit); and Robert Rydell. Rydell sees Du Bois and Calloway alike as being firmly entrenched in Booker T. Washington's camp and argues that both sought to render Washington's ideology in iconic form through graphic representations of African Americans. Of course, I reject that stance in this chapter.

7. Prints for The Hampton Album were made from 159 glass plates; reproductions of 44 of these prints would be published as *The Hampton Album,* a photographic essay first exhibited at MOMA's Edward Steichen Photography Center in January 1966. Photographer Lincoln Kirstein, who wrote the foreword to *The Hampton Album,* describes Johnston as "a fascinating figure of American feminism in the decades from 1882–1952" (5).

8. Indeed, Albert Shaw, founding editor of the *American Monthly Review of Reviews,* the periodical in which Du Bois's "The American Negro at Paris" first appeared, published a number of Johnston's photographs in an April 1900 article he wrote entitled "'Learning by Doing' at Hampton." Shaw, who styled himself a reformer, praised the educational method he found documented in Johnston's photography, which captured what he called "the conception of . . . *integral education"* (418). By this, Shaw meant industrial and vocational education intended to mold young people and guide them into those professions that social leaders thought most appropriate. He was unequivocal in his opinion that Hampton gave an example of "the finest, soundest, and most effective educational methods in use in the United States," methods found largely, he opined, in "certain schools for negroes [sic] and Indians, and in others for young criminals in reformatory prisons" (419). Shaw, who has been described by his biographer, Lloyd J. Graybar, as a believer in white supremacy and a supporter of Jim Crow laws, likely imagined himself to paraphrase one of Hampton's most distinguished graduates, Booker T. Washington, when he wrote that the future of blacks in the American South lay in the "thorough and contented acceptance of agriculture by the colored race." "[F]arming must go on in the South," Shaw maintained, "and the negro [sic] race must continue to do the bulk of the farm work. The negro's best chance for the advancement of his personal fortunes now lies in the purchase and cultivation of a piece of land" (422). The educational methods of Hampton would, Shaw intimates, lead to a happy and peaceful South; on his visits to Hampton Institute he writes that he noted "the atmosphere of serenity and happiness that exists everywhere. I saw no evidence of pressure or anxiety or of that pitiable condition that results in schools where learning is merely based upon books and where the supreme test of knowledge is the successful passing of examinations" (425).

9. See, for instance, chapter 10 (238–64) of Lewis's *W. E. B. Du Bois: Biography of a Race, 1868–1919.*

10. A reading of page 602 of *Dusk of Dawn* alongside pages 220–21

of the *Autobiography* shows two new paragraphs on the exposition inserted into material that had appeared in *Dusk*. Thus, the *Autobiography* explores Du Bois's participation in the fair in ways that *Dusk of Dawn* does not.

11. The circular reads: "The statement sent out by the Jamestown Exposition management that I am preparing an exhibit for Jamestown or intend to is an impudent lie, and quite in keeping with this whole shameful and discredited enterprise" (*W. E. B. Du Bois Papers*, reel 1, frame 124.). A letter dated April 8, 1907, to the editor of the journal *Appeal to Reason* expands on Du Bois's criticism:

    > My dear Sir:—My reasons for opposing the Jamestown Exposition are twofold. In the first place, I do not like the treatment that they are going to accord Negroes. The Negroes are to be separate in practically all things and are to be treated as a separate caste and to that I am opposed. If the separation were voluntary on the part of the colored people that would be a different thing but for them to accept Jim-Crowism and then work to make the exposition a success is a thing in which I do not believe. Then too, I am opposed to the exposition because it represents so distinctly the military and naval spirit, the idea of force and war, the things of which we ought to be thoroughly ashamed in the twentieth century." (*W. E. B. Du Bois Papers*, reel 1, frame 126.)

12. "Sociology Hesitant" forms an odd element in Du Bois's oeuvre. His body of work includes few, if any, other pieces that engage, as "Sociology Hesitant" does, in addressing a topic without directly or even obliquely dealing with the question of race or the so-called "Negro Problem" that so preoccupied Du Bois, along with such figures as Booker T. Washington, Pauline Hopkins, Anna Julia Cooper, and Charles Waddell Chesnutt. "Sociology Hesitant" lacks, as no other major work by Du Bois does, any mention of race whatever. It maintains a distance from a rhetoric of social awareness based upon democratic reform; it fails to argue that sociological study, correctly conceived and applied as the study of groups and not abstractions, could be of great benefit in the advancement of the Negro people. Nonetheless, it advances a critique that Du Bois had raised in 1899 in *The Philadelphia Negro* and again in 1900 in "The American Negro at Paris."

13. The notion of a "science of society" was proposed by Auguste Comte, who (following the example set by Claude Saint-Simon) founded the discipline of positivism, described as a philosophy of science. Positivist sociology ostensibly rejected metaphysics and strove toward empiricism. According to Du Bois, however, Comtean sociology failed on this count, for although metaphysics was, for Comte, a stage of knowledge that must be overcome, Du Bois forcefully critiques Comte in "Sociology Hesitant," arguing that his ideas remained mired in metaphysical thought.

14. See Hofstadter, 31–51.

15. In spite of his criticisms of Spencer and his rejection of Spencer's methods, Du Bois nonetheless seems to have found elements of Spencer's early thought somewhat valuable, so much so that he places Spencer's *First Principles* (1862) in the library of his heroine in *The Quest of the Silver Fleece* (1911). *First Principles* addresses the question of the relationship between science and religion and argues that there is no real contest between the two. According to Spencer, the friction that surrounds the relationship between science and religion actually emerges from the tension between what was knowable (the realm of science) and what was unknowable (the domain of religion).

16. The phrase "consciousness of kind" has a relationship to the sociological concept of community, usually a "common sense" identity distantly related to nationalism. The sociology of community, which promotes the concept of consciousness of kind, has encountered much resistance in the field, largely because it is a highly imprecise term.

17. Tolman produced a number of works of social engineering, one of which, *Industrial Betterment,* was written expressly for the Paris fair. Its subject was classed as industrial sociology. It was simultaneously published in French as *Progès industriel.* His book *Social Engineering: A Record of Things Done by American Industrialists Employing Upwards of One and a Half Million People* was introduced by Andrew Carnegie for its American printing. For the French edition, published as *L'Oeuvre de l'ingénieur social,* Carnegie's introduction was translated and was accompanied by a preface from the French sociologist Émile Levasseur. Tolman and Du Bois's friend Jane Addams, founder of the famous Hull House in Chicago and an early luminary of the Chicago school of sociology (which would later produce, among others, the noted sociologist E. Franklin Frazier) who would contribute to Du Bois's Atlanta University studies, were among the judges of exhibits in Du Bois's class at the fair. Please see *Report of the Commissioner-General for the United States to the International Universal Exposition, Paris, 1900,* volume 2, page 379.

Works Cited

Barthes, Roland. "The Structuralist Activity." *The Structuralists: From Marx to Lévi-Strauss.* Garden City, NY: Doubleday, 1972.

Benjamin, Walter. *The Arcades Project.* Trans. Kevin McLaughlin and Howard Eiland. Cambridge: Harvard UP, 1999.

Calloway, Thomas J. Letter to Booker T. Washington. 4 October 1899. *The Booker T. Washington Papers.* Ed. Louis R. Harlan. Vol. 5. Urbana: U of Illinois P, 1976, 2000. 226.

Carnegie, Andrew. "Value of the World's Fair to the American People." *Engineering Magazine* 6.4 (1894): 417–22.

Du Bois, W. E. B. "The American Negro at Paris." *American Monthly Review of Reviews.* Nov. 1900: 575–77.

———. *The Autobiography of W.E.B. Du Bois: A Soliloquy on Viewing My Life from the Last Decade of Its First Century.* New York: International, 1968.

———. *Dusk of Dawn: An Essay toward an Autobiography of a Race Concept.* New York: Library of America, 1986.

———. *The Philadelphia Negro: A Social Study.* 1899. Philadelphia: U of Pennsylvania P, 1996.

———. "Sociology Hesitant." *boundary2* 27.3 (2002): 37–44.

———. "To the Nations of the World." 1900. *W. E. B. Du Bois: A Reader.* Ed. David Levering Lewis. New York: Henry Holt, 1995.

———. *Types of American Negroes, Georgia, USA.* 1900. 3 vols. Daniel Murray Collection, Prints and Photographs Division, Library of Congress.

Elwitt, Sanford. "Social Science, Social Reform and Sociology." *Past and Present* 12 (1988): 209–14.

Fanon, Frantz. *Black Skin, White Masks.* Trans. Charles Lam Markmann. New York: Grove, 1967. Trans. of *Peau noire, masques blancs.* 1952.

Goshorn, Alfred T. "Effects of the Centennial Exhibition." *Engineering Magazine* 6.4 (1894): 423.

Harlan, Louis R., ed. *The Booker T. Washington Papers.* Vol. 5. Urbana: U of Illinois P, 2000.

Hofstadter, Richard. *Social Darwinism in American Thought.* Boston: Beacon, 1955.

Kaiser, Wolfram. "Vive la France! Vive la République? The Cultural Construction of French Identity at the World Exhibitions in Paris, 1855–1900." *National Identities* 1.3 (1999): 227–244.

Kirstein, Lincoln. Foreword. *The Hampton Album: 44 Photographs by Frances B. Johnston from an Album of Hampton Institute.* Ed. Lincoln Kirstein. New York: The Museum of Modern Art, 1966. 5–11.

Lewis, David Levering. "A Small Nation of People: W. E. B. Du Bois and Black Americans at the Turn of the Twentieth Century." *A Small Nation of People: W. E. B. Du Bois and African American Portraits of Progress.* New York: Amistad, 2003. 24–49.

———. *W. E. B. Du Bois: Biography of a Race, 1868–1919.* New York: Holt, 1993.

Museum of Modern Art, New York. *The Hampton Album: 44 Photographs by Frances B. Johnston from an Album of Hampton Institute.* Ed. Lincoln Kirstein. New York: The Museum of Modern Art, 1966.

Papers of W. E. B. Du Bois, The. Microfilming Corporation of America (1980): reel 1, frames 124, 126.

Provenzo, Eugene F., Jr. "The Exhibit of American Negroes: Paris 1900 International Exhibit." *The African American Multimedia Collection.* CD-ROM Archive and Online Data Source (New York: Facts on File, 2004).

Report of the Comissioner-General for the United States to the International Universal Exposition, Paris, 1900. 6 Vols. Washington: Government Printing Office, 1901.

Rydell, Robert. "Gateway to the 'American Century': The American Representation at the Paris Universal Exposition of 1900." *Paris 1900: The 'American School' at the Universal Exposition.* New Brunswick: Rutgers UP, 1999. 119–144.

Shaw, Albert. "'Learning by Doing' at Hampton." *American Monthly Review of Reviews,* April 1900: 417–32.

———. "Paris and the Exposition of 1900." *American Monthly Review of Reviews,* June 1900: 679–88.

Smith, Shawn Michelle. *Photography on the Color Line: W. E. B. Du Bois, Race, and Visual Culture.* Durham: Duke UP, 2004.

Washington, Booker T. *The Booker T. Washington Papers.* Vol. 5. Champaign: U of Illinois P, 1976.

Willis, Deborah. "The Sociologist's Eye: W. E. B. Du Bois and the Paris Exposition." *A Small Nation of People: W. E. B. Du Bois and African American Portraits of Progress.* New York: Amistad, 2003. 51–78.

CHAPTER 2

"The Only Real White Democracy" and the Language of Liberation
The Great War, France, and African American Culture in the 1920s

Mark Whalan

> I found that many subjects were taboo from the white man's point of view. Among the topics they did not like to discuss with Negroes were the following: American white women; the Ku Klux Klan; France, and how Negro soldiers fared while there; French women; Jack Johnson; the entire northern part of the United States; the Civil War; Abraham Lincoln; U. S. Grant; General Sherman; Catholics; the Pope; Jews; the Republican Party; slavery; social equality; Communism; Socialism; the 13th and 14th Amendments to the constitution; or any topic calling for positive knowledge or manly self-assertion on the part of the Negro.
> —Richard Wright, "The Ethics of Living Jim Crow"

The Great War, France, and African American Culture (1920s)   53

Richard Wright's famous—and famously lengthy—list of taboos for interracial conversation in 1920s Tennessee exhibits much of his talent for grim humor on the subject of white southern racial prejudice. It is also a revealing litany of the totems and shibboleths around which African American struggles for social, material, and cultural inclusion were enacted in the first half of the twentieth century. Each item on Wright's list had historically been a site of contestation for the status of African American masculinity, a contest the white southerners at the Memphis optics company Wright was working for avoided by their prohibitive silence. France is the only country whose name is subject to this taboo, a prohibition due to African American participation in the Great War of 1914–18, which the United States joined in April 1917. The largest transatlantic movement of black men since the days of the Middle Passage (200,000 African Americans served in France during and after the Great War), was to a country without the social and sexual racial segregation of the United States, and it left a lasting legacy—in France, in the white South, and in African America. Wright's inclusion of France among the unmentionable aspects of "living Jim Crow" from the distance of 1938 is perhaps only the best known of several testaments to the fact that the figure of the African American soldier returning from the Great War retained a powerful range of political connections in the imaginations of both black and white Americans long after the immediate social consequences of demobilization.[1]

Despite this, critics have often been silent on the importance of France and French culture to the prolific outpouring of cultural experimentation known as the Harlem Renaissance. This is surprising as the Great War in France afforded African American men opportunities many had not experienced before. As Wright noted, participating in models of masculinity grounded in martial heroism and "manly self-assertion" was crucial, but so was the engagement with a range of global cultures far removed from their peacetime experiences. Such an engagement was often written about in fiction and memoirs dealing with African American participation in the Great War through the trope of the acquisition of the French language, a language that often came to represent democracy, liberty, and a cosmopolitan sophistication. Indeed, white writers committed to the racist paradigms of eugenics or minstrelsy would attempt to mollify the type of white fears that Wright referred to above by dramatizing episodes of inept, or incompetent, African American assimilations of French language and culture. African American servicemen acquiring French culture and language became an area of racial and political conflict, both in terms of representation and in the realities of servicemen returning home.[2] Such a conflict exemplified that the mobility in which African American members of the American Expeditionary Force (AEF) engaged was not exclusively spatial, as their participation in what Modris Eksteins described as the single most important event in establishing the "life in the fast lane" mentality of modern consciousness represented an inclusion in the temporal configurations of modernity (xiv). It was a chance to escape the historical-political system that proclaimed the temporal "belatedness" of peoples of African descent, to assert that the temporal lag so often used to justify their exclusion from the privileges of modernity was a chimera.

While it is true that the transatlantic and diasporic traffic in culture and language were sites of change, agency, and emancipatory politics for what came to be known as America's *soldats noirs*, I do not wish to suggest that the Great War was a uniformly positive experience for those African American servicemen who participated in it. The harshness of work in the Services of Supply labor battalions in which most African American soldiers were posted, the widespread racism within the army and the government (which continually curtailed opportunities and privileges for promotion, leave, and training for African American soldiers), the rough justice many of those soldiers received at the hands of white MPs and a disproportionately southern, white officer cadre, and the often hostile reaction from whites on their return to southern communities—not less than the casualties of front line combat—were all very real. Nonetheless, what Alain Locke described as the "brilliant opportunity" for the American Negro to implement "cultural democracy and the concept of cultural pluralism" that the cosmopolitan possibilities of service in France in the Great War provided existed in constant tension and often struggle with these hardships and oppressions, just as it frequently sat uneasily with French colonialism and primitivism (qtd. in Butcher 294). Rather, it was an opportunity that was often recognized, explored, and celebrated, and how this was so is the subject of what follows.

There is often a tendency to see the significance of the Great War to the Harlem Renaissance in nationalistic terms, to view its major effects on African American cultural experience as the impetus it gave to the Great Migration from rural South to urban North and its configuration of an aggressive new militancy in postwar black literature and politics.[3] Yet such a focus on the Harlem Renaissance as a movement rooted in the indigenous cultural products of American regionalism, with the heavy emphasis on folk art that this often involves, has served to elide the sheer frequency and significance

The Great War, France, and African American Culture (1920s)   55

of the figure of the returning African American soldier in New Negro literature. Current or former African American soldiers are major characters in numerous Harlem Renaissance novels.[4] Moreover, many white writers of the time—Howard Odum, I. A. R. Wylie, John Dos Passos, e. e. cummings, George Mack, Ransom Rideout, and others—represented black soldiers in fiction, autobiographical fiction, film, and drama. This cultural response—and the journalism, popular science, photography, and popular history that accompanied it—was, of course, of various opinion over the legacy of the war to the African American community. Many saw it as another broken promise on the part of white America, as wartime service did not correlate to the peacetime political gains many had hoped for. Conversely, in the case of white America, cultural responses to African American military service were often nervous about the implications of mass black martial masculinity. Yet many of the more optimistic examples of this wide range of material configured African American participation in the Great War in ways that proposed it as a basis for greater civic entitlement, for the radical revision of black male subjectivities, for reimaginations of the African American body and the African American mind, and as a chance to engage with a form of cosmopolitanism that would indeed serve as a "brilliant opportunity" for political and social advancement.[5] In the past ten years critics have begun to take more interest in the international and transnational paradigms of African American and black cultural production in the 1920s and 1930s, yet few have focused on the representation of African American soldiers in that production and how those figures engage with what Brent Hayes Edwards has recently called the "practice of diaspora."[6] The use of France as a rhetorical figure for a truly egalitarian and democratic politics was important in many of these representations, as was the acquisition of French as a gateway to new and progressive subjectivities.

In his account of inspecting African American troops in Europe following the armistice, W. E. B. Du Bois remarked that "there is not a black soldier but who is glad he went,—glad to fight for France, the only real white Democracy; glad to have a new, clear vision of the real, inner spirit of American prejudice" ("An Essay" 922). Similarly, in his welcome address to returning African American soldiers in Washington in April 1919, the Reverend F. J. Grimké told the troops that in France they had had "the opportunity of coming into contact with another than the American type of white man; and through that contact you have learned what it is to be treated as a man, regardless of the color of your skin or race identity. Unfortunately you had to go away from home to receive a man's treatment, to breathe the pure, bracing air of liberty, equality, fraternity" (242). In the writing by African American leaders and activists in the immediate aftermath of the war, this trope of a truly democratic and unprejudiced France is often mentioned as a powerful example of the possibility of interracial democratic equality and served as a political spur to the Civil Rights struggle in the United States. Such enthusiastic celebrations of the "colorblindness" of France were not new and, as Tyler Stovall has discussed, grew from a tradition of similar reports from nineteenth-century visitors such as Ira Aldridge, Bishop Daniel Payne, Booker T. Washington, and Frederick Douglass (3). In the writing of Du Bois, Grimké, and others following the war, however, such an example of democracy, brought back as the direct experience of servicemen who had fought or worked in France, was often configured not just as a political but also as a cultural experience, something—to paraphrase Grimké—*en l'air*.

This move was, to a degree, strategic. Figures like Du Bois were well aware of the economic exploitation of African colonies within France's extensive empire, and indeed in essays written before U.S. entry into the conflict he had seen competition for colonial spheres of influence and African natural resources as one of the main reasons the war began in the first place.[7] Moreover, in his extensive travels in Europe before the war he must have been aware that most French people were far from free of demeaning preconceptions about black people; Stovall suggests that "for the average French man and woman, blacks meant Africa, where sensuous dark-skinned natives danced in the jungle or labored under the benevolent tutelage of the French Empire" (16). France had conscripted 620,000 soldiers from its colonies to fight the war, often under deeply unpopular and brutal circumstances, and its treatment of colonial labor troops was often as harsh as the treatment black American labor troops received at the hands of white American officers. Yet for Du Bois—facing a government locked into the patterns of reaction, red-baiting and curtailing civil liberties, and seeking to galvanize a *Crisis* readership disquieted by his accommodationist editorial "Close Ranks" of June 1918—lauding French democracy as a tactical move seemed necessary to address these problems and thereby maintain the pressure for reform in the United States.[8] However, this tactic would not have had the longstanding resonance that it did had it not enjoyed such a widespread appeal and if so many returning soldiers had not written about the revelatory experience of living without a color line during their time in France. In addition to well-established figures like Grimké and Du Bois, new radical black socialist and black nationalist publications such as *The Messenger* and *The Crusader* praised French standards of democracy and hailed them as a territory on which they could pivot demands for greater civil rights in the United States.[9] In the African American imaginary, France became both a romantic location of liberation and a set of codes for articulating political demands at home. In this willful blindness, this phenomenon gestures both to what Gilroy has called "the tension between . . . local, parochial, and more cosmopolitan commitments" and to the way that political models with the severest of limitations for black self-determination could be appropriated and through a kind of radical romanticism become a set of cultural reference points for bolstering black political struggle in the United States (289).

It is this that lies behind Grimké's discussion of the relevance of returning servicemen having experienced the "bracing air of liberty, equality, fraternity" (242). In configuring this experience as cultural—and therefore learnable—Grimké tacitly challenges the primacy of personal experience in the memory of army service and combat, the widespread epistemological configuration of warfare which suggests that "not only did their experiences authorize soldiers to speak, they denied that right to those that had not shared them" (Sherman 16). Often, the vehicle through which this wartime experience of color-blind France could be transmitted, learned, and become part of African American political sensibility was figured as language. Through drawing on the Romantic ethnolinguistics of cultural nationalists like Herder, writers such as Du Bois suggested that the medium of a foreign language could reconfigure black soldiers' personal experience of greater racial tolerance in a predominantly white country, turning it from something distinctly individualized and in a sense nontransferable into a cultural experience. Rather than seeing French as a colonial language, and in finding "in the conversion of an enslaving medium into an insurgent weapon" a use of what Wole Soyinka has called the "linguistic blade" to carve "new concepts into the flesh of white supremacy"—a tactics of linguistic appropriation that a later generation of anticolonial black intellectuals would advocate—African American writers often chose to take the French political rhetoric of liberty, egalitarianism, and fraternity at face value (88). Accordingly, acquisition of the French language— the medium and the structuring grammar and vocabulary of that culture—often comes to represent a powerful vehicle of democracy in its own right in much of this writing. One example is an often overlooked African American account of the war, Addie Hunton's *Two Colored Women with the American Expeditionary Forces* (1920).

Hunton had worked in France from June 1918 until late 1919 as an assistant for the YMCA and later wrote a fascinating memoir of her service looking after African American soldiers.[10] It recounted both the bravery and decency of these soldiers in France and also the difficult and aggravating working conditions faced by African American workers in the voluntary support organizations that accompanied the American Expeditionary Forces to Europe. Indeed, so often were they hampered by military disregard for African American soldiers' welfare that until spring 1919 there were only three African American women YMCA workers for the 150,000 African American men stationed in France. Hunton's memoir is unsparing in its criticism of the military authorities and many of the white elements in the YMCA organization, whose often rigid policies of segregation and callousness meant that "the service of the colored welfare workers was more or less clouded at all times with that biting and stinging thing which is ever shadowing us in our own country" (27). Yet Hunton saw the war as highly significant in the development of American racial politics and African American subjectivity, as "there was being developed in France a racial consciousness and racial strength that could not have been gained in half a century of normal living in America. Over the canteen in France we learned to know that our young manhood was the natural and rightful guardian of our struggling race" (197).

Like many others, she remarked on the relative absence of racism in France and the warm welcome extended by the French to the African American servicemen stationed there; as she said, "the relationship between the colored soldiers, the colored welfare workers, and the French people was most cordial and friendly and grew in sympathy and understanding, as their association brought about a closer acquaintance" (230). In these circumstances, learning French became a mode of "racial strength"; it represented a cultural expression of (and conduit toward developing) the political "sympathy" she believed existed between the French and the African American servicemen, their shared commitment to humanistic and democratic principles. Hunton saw this affinity as existing at very deep levels of the culture and consciousness of both groups and believed it was most manifest through the ability of African American soldiers to learn French quickly. She noted that "the understanding ear of the colored man seemed attuned to the French language, and he learned more quickly, it seemed, how to converse with this romantic people. The French people are affectionate and demonstrative, which corresponds to the deep emotional spirit which seems the heritage of the colored American" (249). This was not intended to extol the supposed African American talent for "universal mimicry" that was such a common assumption and which Zora Neale Hurston would see as significant to the "Characteristics of Negro Expression" (Hurston 1019). Instead, it betokened an affinity born of a feeling of "delight" at being in a "sister democracy" which "furnished to some of us the first full breath of freedom that had ever come into our limited experience" (230).

Such a repetition of Grimké's notion of democracy and racial equality existing in the "air," an image that suggests its nature as an enveloping and naturalized milieu, indicates again the cultural configurations of democratic politics that Hunton hoped could be learned and transported (242). Accordingly, she intimates that, if African Americans were adept at picking up the French language, it is because French democracy and the absence of racial discrimination in France is part of a national spirit that is implicit in that language. As such, in a Barthesian process of mythologization, Frenchness becomes naturalized as democratic and egalitarian, with all of the historical and specific complexities of French involvement with those concepts being cast aside (especially, for an African American context, the complexities of French colonial rule). Such a step implies that the adequate practice of democracy relies on more than democratic electoral and legislative procedures being in place. Instead, the guarantee of a fully democratic practice relies both on these procedures being in place and on a consensus on democratic ideals within a nation akin to a democratic *consciousness* or style. As Ken Hirschkop suggests, "one cannot underestimate the importance of legally sanctioned democratic procedures; but where these have an impact, it is because they coexist with a democratic consciousness which supports them" (34).

This democratic consciousness, which underpins adequate democracy and prevents the kind of hypocrisy that saw the fourteenth and fifteenth amendments regularly ignored in the United States, is a fundamentally cultural phenomenon; it was clear that authors such as Hunton and Du Bois saw this culture as embedded in the French language. In a *Crisis* editorial of April 1919, Du Bois himself would urge all African Americans to learn French and Spanish, remarking that it was essential for any pan-African movement but also because "the only white civilization in the world to which color-hatred is not only unknown, but absolutely *unintelligible* is the so-called Latin, of which France and Spain are the leading nations" ("French and Spanish" 269; emphasis added). Du Bois suggests that racial prejudice does not translate into French, that its grammar and vocabulary refuse the accommodation of discrimination, and that its conceptual range allows only for a *Weltanschauung* of universal justice free from a racialized vocabulary and practice found in languages of Germanic origin. Such a comment built on his remarks in the earlier essay "The Conservation of Races," in which he described a temperament in what he called the "Romance nations" which had a deeply unique "spiritual, psychical" character (86, 87). In the later editorial he clearly hitches a "democratic consciousness" into this "spiritual, psychical" character, a character both embedded and reproduced in romance languages. In an echo of Herder—a thinker who had often informed Du Bois's theories—and supporting recent developments in linguistic theory by anthropologists such as Edward Sapir, Du Bois therefore unfolds a concrete link between national-racial character, political history, and language, a linkage that stresses that racial egalitarianism can be lexicographically encoded and learned. As Sapir noted, "Would we be so ready to die for 'liberty,' to struggle for 'ideals,' if the words themselves were not ringing within us? And the word, as we know, is not only a key; it may also be a fetter" (17). For Du Bois, the Romance languages were both free from the "fetter" of "color-prejudice" and replete with the "key" of democratic consciousness.[11]

The seeming self-contradiction of a committed pan-African such as Du Bois espousing French as a language of democracy was only exacerbated by the fact that this article appeared in the same number of *The Crisis* as his report from the Pan-African Congress in Paris in 1919, a report that also praised French democracy and repeated (without demur) the words of Blaise Diagne, the black representative for Senegal in the Chamber of Deputies, in support of French colonial rule.[12] Yet this report also included a list of proposals that the Congress resolved to be given to the postwar Peace Conference of the Allied governments then in session, and it included resolutions against the economic exploitation of colonial labor, in support of native land ownership, and asserting the right of colonial subjects to education in both native and European languages. As David Levering Lewis notes of these resolutions, "while their immediate and practical consequences would be negligible, a powerful idea to bind up the wounds of the world had been launched in Paris" (*W. E. B. Du Bois* 578). Du Bois's seeming enthusiasm for France's colonial *mission civilisatrice* and rapturous endorsement of the French language must be placed in balance with these commitments to anticolonialism and native cultural self-determination. For Du Bois French was valuable both as a conceptual vehicle for democracy and as a medium for communicating across the diaspora for the purposes of contesting white global hegemony—ideas that at best had an uneasy relation to each other. Accordingly, he can of course be faulted here for Eurocentrism, placing national struggles for black civil rights over internationalist commitments in his tactical use of French, or favoring a political system grounded in the benevolent leadership of cultured elites. Yet to do so misses much of the complexity of his engagement with French language and culture at this moment and ignores the fact that diasporic communication is commonly marked precisely by such complexity and misrecognition. As Brent Hayes Edwards has recently reminded us, the cultures of black internationalism are typified as much by "new and unforeseen alliances and interventions on a global stage" as by "unavoidable misapprehensions and misreadings, persistent blindness and solipsisms, self-defeating and abortive collaborations, a failure to translate even a basic grammar of blackness" (5).

If Du Bois's grand vision for the political possibilities of French saw its primary importance both as a somehow racially neutral language and as a medium for pan-global exchange among peoples of color, other writers who dealt with the trope of soldiers learning French were much more interested in the concrete examples of advantage such fluency could provide. Indeed, in certain stories a local, tactical use of French becomes something so localized that it becomes a tool for personal advantage uncoupled from a progressive drive for racial uplift, indeed from any kind of collective politics. As exemplified in Rudolph Fisher's short story "City of Refuge," French in the vocabulary of the returning African American soldier becomes a marker and a medium of cosmopolitanism and urbanity that is used not just to exploitative purpose but to the exploitation of another black resident of Harlem. Yet the hitching of the acquisition of French to notions of African American modernity—a move that becomes a forceful challenge to the "racial politics of temporality" that Gilroy has discussed as so important in the racial configurations of modernity—make Fisher's text an interesting one to examine (Gilroy 334). Although all of these authors seek to configure French as a medium for eliminating the racist chronologies of black temporal lag, the shift in focus Fisher introduces—from French as *langue* to French as *parole*—also becomes an implicit critique of generalizations about the meaning of French as made by figures like Du Bois and Hunton. Specifically, the critique lies in the reminder that language only generates meaning through the concrete utterances wherein it appears. A particular use of French might endorse a democratic and egalitarian politics—but then again, it might not.

Fisher's story, which appeared in the *Atlantic Monthly* in 1925, centers on the greenhorn migrant King Solomon Gillis, recently arrived in Harlem from South Carolina. The opening sections describe his awe-stricken reaction to the sensory barrage of urban Harlem; he is both excited and bewildered by the subway, the crowds, and the dense traffic. Yet it is the sight of a "colored policeman" that totally dumbfounds him. As Maria Balshaw notes, this reflects his surprise that urban space can be African American; indeed, "he cannot get over the sight of a thoroughly developed, socially progressive urban race capital" (15).[13] The visceral shock that Gillis experiences at being faced with this "Bang Clash" modernity is indicative of the contemporary perception that African Americans occupied a different temporal schema to the epoch of modernity, a modernity often conflated with Anglo-Saxonism (qtd. in De Jongh iii).[14]

The racialization of temporalities was a common feature of primitivism in the 1920s, and what Felipe Smith calls segregated "racial time spaces" were often exercised to position black people as exterior to modernity (37). Indeed, such a temporal schema has a history of being "invoked by white supremacism as a principle of exclusion and social discipline" (Gilroy 334). Yet such exclusions do not work solely on a racial basis in Fisher's story; Gillis had learned about Harlem from the Uggams, a family he had known in South Carolina, who were "always talking about" Harlem because one of their own had been drafted to serve in France and stayed in New York on his return (1176). In contrast to Gillis, the drafted Uggam—Mouse by name—is located firmly in the fast lane of modernity, and this is often linked to his experience of wartime service in France.

Gillis is soon befriended by Mouse, who sees in Gillis exactly the gullible fall guy he had been seeking to do the dirty work of his drug-dealing business. Mouse's ability to carry off his plan is based in his three-point geographic mobility, in his experiences in South Carolina, New York, and France, and this is communicated through the range of what linguists would term his language repertoire. For example, in defending Gillis against an irate West Indian shop assistant, Mouse remarks "this here's my friend, an' I'll be john browned if there's a monkey-chaser can gyp him in Harlem if I know it, see? Bes' thing for you to do is catch air, toot sweet" (1180). This performance—mixing black Harlem speech with the Anglicization of the French *tout de suite*—helps persuade Gillis to take up Uggam's seemingly aboveboard offer of a job. Soon afterward, Uggam persuades Gillis that the pills he wants him to sell are legitimate because "in France he had learned about some valuable French medicine" as yet unavailable in the United States (1181).

In contrast to the idea of the returning soldier as a militant "soldier of democracy" (to use Du Bois's phrase) replete with a cultural equipment capable of fighting for a more egalitarian American racial politics, then, Fisher sees martial service as serving Uggam well in the quasi-Darwinian struggle occurring within the newly African American urban space of Harlem (Du Bois, "Returning Soldiers" 171). This street-sharp brand of cosmopolitanism decisively shifts Mouse from his Carolina origins into the temporal schema of modernity, and this shift is one which he reflects upon directly. Earlier in the story, he dismisses Gillis as a "baby jess in from the land o'cotton and so dumb he thinks ante bellum's an old woman" (1178). Mouse links Gillis's status as a "baby" to his lack of awareness of the division between the pre- and postwar eras; both testify not just to his lack of intelligence but to his inability to understand the complexities of an urban space that is relentlessly coded as emblematic of modernity. Although "antebellum" is probably a reference to the Civil War, there is a conflation here, collapsing the vast difference in the situation of African Americans before and after the Civil War with a similar difference in the situation of African Americans before and after the Great War. Awareness of these two wars as watersheds in African American identity and temporalities of subjectivity is crucial, Mouse suggests: in positioning Gillis as ignorant of these, and therefore "antebellum," he jokingly identifies him as a hapless ingénue in the urban space of black modernity. Awareness and experience of the war thus conferred a cosmopolitanism and what Balshaw calls an "urbanity" on certain African Americans in Harlem. Urbanity in Balshaw's account is a complex and often contradictory social ideal, but for Fisher and for Mouse the expression of the concept that applies is where "the pursuit of urbanity [functions] as a mode of self-projection," a projection which allows for the successful negotiation of urban space (36).[15]

In the urban space of Harlem, Mouse's use of French works as one such mode of self-projection. Recalling Henry Louis Gates's discussion of signifying—in which meaning derives "not [from] what is played or said [but rather from an] on-the-streets exercise in the use of troping, in which the play is the thing—not what is said, but how" (69–70)—Mouse's French becomes a style with a set of associations far beyond the concrete referent of the sentence.[16] His use of the French phrase codes him as a soldier, as worldly, experienced, and dangerous, but it also codes him as having an affiliation with a specifically French type of urbanity and ability in "self-projection." That this is embedded within an African American tradition of signifying illustrates that the French language added a significant range of possibilities to this rhetorical tradition of self-affirmation, a new lexicon and range of options in the "on-the-streets exercise" of verbal mastery. This incorporation of French also potentially presented useful strategies for negotiating "attempts at domination," particularly the domination of a white culture not attuned to the complexity and dexterity of the resources of Black English—a negotiation which Gates found central to the practice of signifying (77).

However, in Fisher's example, Mouse's use of French serves a much more intraracial agenda. His signification verbally outwits the shopkeeper but simultaneously employs a much more subtle tactic with Gillis—namely an example of the "indirect intent" which Gates sees as one of the signal features of signifying (85). Through his performance the direct intent is that Mouse triumphantly vanquishes the shopkeeper, but also more insidiously he gains Gillis's trust, which he goes on to abuse to his own advantage. Gillis's fate of arrest is therefore the upshot of Mouse's verbal mastery, reflecting Fisher's awareness of the polyvalence of linguistic strategies, their ability to be used in a huge array of different and even contradictory ways and to a vast range of purposes. Such an opinion is a more pragmatic approach to the uses and potential advantages of French than is offered by Du Bois and Hunton. French is still coded as a tool in "self-projection" and proof of a passage that is both transatlantic and about passing into the temporalities of modernity, but Mouse's self-projection in this story is at the expense of Gillis's liberty.[17] That this is so implicitly casts Du Bois and Hunton's view of French as both overly utopian and hopelessly generalized; while French is still seen as a potent resource in the African American lexicon and is of decided personal benefit to Mouse, it carries within it no inherent commitment to democracy, racial solidarity, or freedom.

The converse of the trope of the possibilities inherent in African American soldiers learning French was the failure of that process. For both black and white American authors, the inability of African American soldiers to learn French tended to indicate the inevitability of the status quo of American racial politics—an inability that was consequently represented as either frustrating or reassuring, depending on the racial politics of the writer. The African American writer Gwendolyn Bennett's short story "Wedding Day" is one such example, wherein the inability to learn French becomes a marker for the protagonist's inability to shrug off a racialized inferiority complex that is represented as inextricable from Anglophone culture.

Bennett's story follows the fortunes of the expatriate African American musician Paul Watson, loosely based on the famous airman, drummer, and nightclub owner Eugene Jacques Bullard (Stovall 3-4, 36). Watson's inability to learn French demonstrates how the sexualization of American racial inequality has been deeply stamped into his identity and determines the pattern of his sexual life. Paul is an expatriate living and playing music in Montmartre; he has a furious temper when faced with white American racism and is eventually imprisoned for shooting two white sailors who call him "nigger." He is freed to fight for the French in the Great War, in the aerial division, and becomes a hero. Following the war he resumes his old life, which—to the bewilderment of his friends and acquaintances—is a celibate one. He tells a friend that French women are "all white" and that "I ain't got nothing for no white meat to do. If a woman eva called me nigger I'd have to kill her" (366). Yet he falls for a white American prostitute in Paris, Mary, and plans to marry her; the talk of the bars is that "that's the way with them spades. They beat up all the white men they can lay their hands on but as soon as a gang of golden hair with blue eyes rubs up close to them they forget all they ever said 'bout hatin' white folks" (367). On his wedding day he finds out that his fiancée, Mary, can't go through with marrying a black man and thinks this over while riding in a "subway" coach:

> A bit out of breath he stood inside the train and looking down at what he had in his hand he saw it was a tiny pink ticket. A first class ticket in a second class coach. The idea set him to laughing. Everyone in the car turned and eyed him, but that did not bother him. Wonder what stop he'd get off—funny how these French said descend when they meant get off—funny he couldn't pick up French—been here so long. First class ticket in a second class coach!—that was one on him. Wedding day today, and that damn letter from Mary. (369)

This passage couples Paul's feelings of cultural awkwardness—despite having lived in France for many years he still feels like an alien—with (it is suggested) a very American sense of racial abjection. Inadvertently, Paul enters the second-class coach, despite holding a first-class ticket—a situation enforced on African Americans traveling by rail in several southern states at the time and one that discouraged many people, especially middle-class black women, from traveling at all. The ignominy of having imposed an episode of Jim Crow on himself parallels his inability to escape the straitjacket of a history of the racialized psychosexuality of America, where hatred of whiteness among African Americans was often represented as coexisting with powerful sexual desire for the white body.[18] That Paul's sexuality exists within these contours illustrates his inability to escape the closed circuit of hate and impersonal desire of interracial sexuality which exists in the "psychological-economic" system of racism; indeed, his violent swings from vitriolic aggression to abased devotion signify the stranglehold that America's Manichean racial politics has on him (Fanon 35). Yet Paul's inability to become "un-American" is represented by his failure to learn the French language, which becomes the synecdoche of his failure to embrace a more democratic, racially egalitarian frame of mind. The story ends with Paul literally going nowhere on the tellingly misnamed "subway" (or, more properly, Metro) and with his complete alienation: from his adopted homeland, from an American system he despises but cannot escape, and from himself.

If Bennett's story was a cautionary tale about the persistence of racialized psychology and the problems this might cause for dreams of a more egalitarian society, other writers dealing with African Americans failing to learn French had different motives. Indeed, Bennett's subtle tale about the persistence of racialized ideology, dramatized through Paul's inability both to unlearn his own culture and to learn another, was crudely paralleled in how the trope of African American soldiers unable to learn French was treated in the racist writing of white apologists for segregation. In 1928 the white minstrel author Charles E. Mack published *Two Black Crows in the A.E.F.*, a spin-off of his popular blackface vaudeville act with George Moran. Known as the "Two Black Crows," the pair were famous stage entertainers before embarking on a radio career, and *Two Black Crows in the A.E.F.* was also made into a film in 1930 entitled *Anybody's War*. Mack's novel represents African Americans, particularly its two Tennessee protagonists, Amos and Willie, as exactly the type of "happy-go-lucky, singing, shuffling, banjo picking . . . more or less pathetic figure[s]" that James Weldon Johnson had railed against at the beginning of the decade (Preface xl). They spend most of their time avoiding work, thieving corn, or gambling, and they speak in comedy-dialect that doubtless formed the backbone of Mack and Moran's stage act; they are prone to drunkenness and superstition, and when they are drafted, they are physically incapable of being drilled. They are cowardly and self-interested, and the only exception to this is their filial attachment to certain white, male authority figures such as Steve Reinhart or Major Crawford Robinson. Shiftless, unreliable, and childish, they are the exact opposite of the type of black masculinity Du Bois hailed as the "soldiers of democracy" returning from France.

A racial politics of temporality was at play in "The City of Refuge" in the story's representation of African American participation in the space-time of modernity, evident in Mouse's ability to learn French, and a similar politics is at play in *Two Black Crows in the A.E.F.*—but with opposite intent. We are told early on that Amos, "like the rest of his race, never wasted time worrying about the future," and much of the comedy of the book rests on the unchanging nature of its protagonists, despite their first experiences of sea travel, a different country, a different language, military life, and combat (27). One way in which this perpetual sameness generates humor is in Amos and Willie's encounters, often ending in incomprehension, with different languages. French proves perplexing to them; at one point they ask a Frenchman for directions to the levee of the river, hoping to find a catfish joint. The Frenchman provides his reply, which prompts Amos to exclaim "sound like, 'Jenny say pa'. . . . De words was good American but way he put 'em together was just foolishness. Don't help us find no levee" (228). Later, after getting lost, they end up in a trench with a regiment of Senegalese soldiers—a moment ripe with the unvoiced white apprehension of exactly what would happen if these armed, trained, and exploited men from across the black diaspora could communicate. Shortly afterward, though, Willie and Amos are captured by the Germans and interrogated in French. This is conducted by a professor in linguistics and an expert on African languages. He begins by asking them "Parley voo Frawn-say?"—which Willie translates as "Polly jump over de fence today" (284). The pair are interrogated in Senegalese, a "Gold Coast dialect," "Zulu, Congo, Somali, Moroccan, and fifteen other African dialects" before the professor calls in a Major Lohman (at great inconvenience, as he is a five-hour journey away) because he is a specialist in "Tanganyika" (285). He realizes that they are American and had been talking English to each other all along—a realization humiliating in the extreme for the professor, as he had spent five years at Harvard. The punch line comes when Lohman informs the professor that "they are American Negroes and they speak English. But it is not the kind of English used at Harvard" (286).

The racial politics of Amos and Willie's encounters with French culture and the French language is deeply conservative: in being unable to learn or understand French, they illustrate their occupation of a static temporality wherein dynamism or change is impossible and which relegates them as exterior to the progressive space-time of an Anglo-Saxon modernity. This is similar to what James Snead calls a "metaphysical stasis" in representations of black people, which typifies "the black . . . as eternal, unchanging, unchangeable" and which serves to "justify blacks' continuing economic disadvantage" (3). Moreover, this confirmation of the "naturalness" of the racial status quo in Tennessee is reinforced by the explicit renunciation of any affinity between French democracy and what Hunton called the "emotional spirit which seems the heritage of the colored American"; if the language is strange and becomes gibberish in translation for Amos and Willie, then so, by implication, do French racial politics (249). Finally, their English is not of the variety that Bakhtin called the "unitary language," namely the dialect variety of a language invested with prestige and authority and which often represents a literary and national standard. Instead, their dialect is so far from that standard that a speaker of that standard finds their language incomprehensible. They become both parochial and immutable, a literal embodiment of "local color," and statements of the inevitability and naturalness of the prewar rural economy in the southern states.

In *Two Black Crows in the A.E.F*, therefore, the alien and unlearnable nature of French language and culture for the two black protagonists becomes confirmatory and reassuring for the racial status quo, rather than providing a progressive politics of cosmopolitanism as envisaged by writers like Hunton—and the comedy (such as it is) of *Two Black Crows in the A.E.F.* frequently rests precisely on this reassurance. If, in "Wedding Day," the reason for the African American soldier's inability to learn French is the persistence of American racial ideology, in Mack's story it is racial essence— but the solidity of the American racial status quo is affirmed either despondently or triumphantly in both. In making such an affirmation, both authors gesture toward the extremely politicized terrain of language acquisition and the significance that France had in the postwar imagination of a racially emancipatory politics.

Both the imaginative appeal of France as a space of democracy and black freedom and misgivings about that appeal continued to be present in the African American press well into the 1920s. *The Crisis* published accounts in the early 1920s about France's colonial failings, remarking on the practices of forced labor in the French Congo, unrepresentative elections in Guadeloupe, and the colonial promotion of the opium industry in Indochina.[19] Alain Locke was taken to task by the Martiniquean writer Renè Maran for praising France's treatment of its colonial troops in their exchange of open letters in *Opportunity* in 1924 (261-63).[20] Similarly, Du Bois had been far from a consistent champion of French involvement in the war or of French culture. As well as his observations in 1915 about the "African Roots" of the Great War, the battle for colonial territory that had undergirded the European hostilities, in 1916 he had remarked that the war exhibited the bankruptcy of Enlightenment thinking, the "cruelty of the civilization of the West" ("Battle" 88). Yet the vocal presence of black delegates in the French chamber of deputies, the warm reception of black troops by the French population during and after the war, and the lavish praise and decorations given to black American units deployed with the French army during the conflict led to many African American leaders overlooking the details of how colonial rule actually worked. Instead, they chose to emphasize these wartime events to their African American audience, an embrace of a French rhetoric of equality and democracy that provided useful leverage for their struggles at home—effecting a situation where, at its crudest, "transnational black solidarity [was] traded in for a certain kind of national currency, an anti-racism in one country" (Edwards 6). Limited as it was, the "national currency" of a particularly French-inflected vocabulary of democratic Enlightenment thinking appealed as a political strategy to African American leaders during a time when other political strategies began to seem more difficult and risky.

This was evident as early as September 1917, when Du Bois remarked on the American "Black Bastille of Prejudice," a "monstrous superstructure" that had swallowed up the "democracy of a nation" and that cried out for destruction in the manner of 1789, to be replaced by "that liberty, fraternity and equality which is in verity the pride of France" ("Black Bastille" 217). Du Bois's revolutionary choice of metaphor, in the year of the two revolutions in Russia, gives a good indication of some of the reasons that France became such an important cultural resource for the spokespeople of American black civil rights both during the war and in its immediate aftermath. France provided an alternative emancipatory political model to Soviet Russia at a time that the American mainstream parties were in the midst of the first-ever American "red scare," a scare that resulted in overbearing scrutiny on African American leaders for any signs of communist affiliation. Indeed, *The Chicago Defender* and *The Crisis* were nearly suspended from the mails in 1919; the editors of *The Messenger*, A. Philip Randolph and Chandler Owen, were arrested on charges of sedition in the same year.[21] In establishing France's seeming ability to combine democratic procedure with democratic consciousness, the embrace of French culture by African American intellectuals proposed a return to the ideals of an earlier revolutionary moment, a moment much less threatening than a Bolshevik vision of proletarian revolt. Such a proposal took the less confrontational strategy of striking at American hypocrisy over its democratic constitution, rather than representing a frontal assault on its economic principles.

However, this tactic should not be seen solely as a parochial move to co-opt French democratic rhetoric for a national civil rights program, one which necessitated the cool overlooking of French colonial policy and the refusal of transnational black solidarity. As Du Bois demonstrated in 1919, he hoped the use of such a tactic would better situate African Americans in the vanguard of a pan-African movement—a movement whose goals were to effect greater self-determination of colonized peoples, including self-determination in the sphere of culture. Moreover, whatever the limitations or ironies of this position, the embrace of France as "the only real white democracy" demonstrated a faith in the politics of culture that George Hutchinson found typical of much of the Harlem Renaissance—a movement marked by the belief that "aesthetic experience could be a powerful impetus to the destruction of social convention, the awakening of new types of consciousness, and the creation of new forms of solidarity across traditional boundaries" (13).

The writings of Du Bois, Hunton, and Fisher are full of new solidarities across traditional boundaries. Fisher's writing exemplifies how the incorporation of French lexical items into African American English increased its already considerable resources for play, creativity, self-affirmation, and resistance to authority—even if he was circumspect about the rather utopian claims for French culture being promulgated by some of his contemporaries. Du Bois and Hunton were more eager to believe that the French language was the repository of the "democratic consciousness" that America so urgently needed to fulfill the racially democratic legislation of the fourteenth and fifteenth amendments—a belief that can also be tacitly seen in the distinctly nervous rejection of that language in the comedy of Mack. Moreover, the African American use of French emphasized their place within the landscape of urban modernity and accentuated a brash confidence, urbanity, worldliness, and quick-wittedness long associated with urban culture. These features were to appear in much of the distinctive (and often self-congratulatory) Harlem style that was to emerge in the 1920s.

As Jessie Fauset said in a *Crisis* essay entitled "Nostalgia"—which again eulogized the experience of France for African American soldiers—the "great principles" of America always seemed "just beyond, always beyond," rooted in a "dream country . . . founded on that document which most realizes and sets forth the primal and unchanging needs of man—the Constitution of the United States" (157). Yet both for rhetorical purpose and in the lived experience of many black soldiers France seemed like this "dream country," and this easily became configured as a story linking travel with emancipation in a way that had long been important as an inspiring principle in African American culture. Osceolo E. McKaine, a black officer with the 367th, alluded to this fairly directly when he conflated traveling to France with a narrative of Christian salvation; in February 1919 he remarked that "The Black Crusaders landed in France with the same emotions Elijah must have had when he landed in heaven." Moreover, this journey was "from the terra firma where they had played and toiled, which they hated and loved, to a strange semi-mythical region, where a grand reception and a cordial welcome, where a square deal and an absolute equality awaited them" (3). It was this tangible location for emancipatory idealism, as well as the embedding of this idealism in the resources of a culture that could be brought back to the United States, that was one of the main reasons the Great War was so exciting for African American writers. France's role was indeed "semi-mythical," both real and imagined; it emerged as a trope through a type of romantic radicalism that despite its blind spots over colonialism held a real power in U.S. postwar struggles for black rights. Conversely, these were also the reasons it proved so threatening to segregationist white authors. Experiences (and representations) of France also informed the Harlem Renaissance in more thoroughgoing ways than have been previously acknowledged, of which language acquisition was just one; they provided a significant counterweight to the currents of cultural nationalism and Afrocentrism in the movement that have taken up so much critical attention. Service in France undoubtedly involved racism, disappointment, injury, and death for many. Yet it also provided the experiences of linguistic expansion, defamiliarization, technological modernity, and mobility that would typify much of the African American writing of the decade, and much of this served to unsettle the naturalized foundations of the racial status quo in the United States. Perhaps the last word in this regard should go to Addie Hunton:

> The many ports of France were particularly the home of the colored soldiers, so that landing at Bordeaux it did not seem strange to be greeted first of all by our own men. But it did seem passing strange that we should see them guarding German prisoners! Somehow we felt that colored soldiers found it rather refreshing—even enjoyable for a change—having come from a country where it seemed everybody's business to guard them. (17)

The "passing strange" experience of colorblind France—however myopic, strategic, or romanticized—would continue to be a touchstone for the writers of the Harlem Renaissance. Whether unsettling the ethics of living Jim Crow, making white people guarded, or seeming like the promised land, France indeed proved a rich store of the refreshing and enjoyable in the African American imagination.

Notes

1. This influence was brutally realized in the spate of lynchings of ex-servicemen in uniform in the aftermath of the war. For summaries

of the African American role in the Great War, see Arthur E. Barbeau and Florette Henri; also Bernard C. Nalty, especially chapters 7–9; W. E. B. Du Bois's "An Essay toward a History of the Black Man in the Great War"; Robert H. Zieger, particularly chapter 5; David M. Kennedy; Jack D. Foner; Gerald Astor; and Tyler Stovall, chapter 1.

2. Examples of how these conflicts were played out in representation will be discussed later in the essay. For a detailed assessment of how black Americans' experiences in France fuelled often brutal clashes between black and white Americans over civil rights in Texas, see Steven A. Reich.

3. This is obviously a highly abbreviated charge, but books dealing with the impact of the Great War on the Harlem Renaissance that broadly (if not absolutely) follow this pattern include David Levering Lewis's *When Harlem Was in Vogue,* George Hutchinson, Ann Douglas, and Houston Baker.

4. Some examples include Claude McKay's *Home to Harlem* and *Banjo* (1928 and 1929), Walter White's *Fire in the Flint* (1924), Langston Hughes's *Not without Laughter* (1930), and Jessie Fauset's *There Is Confusion* (1924). The war plays a significant role in Zora Neale Hurston's *Jonah's Gourd Vine* (1934) and in Dorothy West's *The Living Is Easy* (1948). African American protagonists fought in the war in stories such as Rudolph Fisher's "City of Refuge," "High Yaller" (both 1925), and "Fire by Night" (1927), in "Wedding Day" (1926) by Gwendolyn Bennett, and in poetry by Georgia Douglas Johnson (a section entitled "Martial" dealing with the Great War is included in her 1922 collection *Bronze*), Jean Toomer ("Seventh Street," in *Cane* [1923]), Sterling Brown ("Sam Smiley" [1932]), Langston Hughes ("The Colored Soldier" [1931], "Poem to a Dead Soldier" [1925], and "America" [1925]), and James Weldon Johnson ("St. Peter Relates an Incident of the Resurrection Day" [1930]). The war is also featured in one-act plays such as Mary Burrill's "Aftermath" (1919), Alice Dunbar-Nelson's "Mine Eyes Have Seen" (1918), and Joseph Seamon Cotter Jr.'s "On the Fields of France" (1920).

5. Such a range of ways in which African American participation in the Great War affected the Harlem Renaissance lies outside the scope of this essay but will be addressed in the monograph I have in preparation (*Soldiers of Democracy: The Great War and the Culture of the New Negro,* appearing with the University Press of Florida). The account of how the Great War affected the discursive configuration of African American bodies and intelligence is closely connected to the mass physical and IQ testing of recruits to the army, which governed much discussion of African American intelligence and bodily characteristics for the next decade. For more information see Gould, 222–63, and Daniel J. Kevles.

6. Important recent work in this field includes Brent Hayes Edwards, Tyler Stovall, Michel Fabre, William J. Maxwell, Sieglinde Lemke,

and Michelle A. Stephens. Key points of transatlantic exchange addressed by several of these writers are international socialism, popular culture and entertainment, relations between the African American and the black Francophone press, and also the imperialistic black nationalism of Marcus Garvey's Universal Negro Improvement Association.

7. See Du Bois's 1915 essay "The African Roots of War."

8. For details of the way the wartime Espionage and Sedition acts curtailed what African American periodicals were able to publish, as well as the huge increase in the size and power of the American intelligence services which resulted from the war, see Theodore Kornweibel, especially chapters 3 to 5. Du Bois's "Close Ranks" editorial was one of the most controversial of his long career; it urged African Americans to "forget our special grievances" in order to "close ranks with our fellow white citizens" for the duration of the war (170). This caused a storm of protest within the African American press and the NAACP, which only intensified when it transpired that Du Bois had recently been offered a commission in the Military Intelligence Bureau. For a full discussion of this incident, see Mark Ellis and also David Levering Lewis's *W.E.B. Du Bois: Biography of a Race, 1868-1919*, 552-57.

9. See, for example, William N. Colson's "Propaganda and the Negro Soldier," "An Analysis of Negro Patriotism," and his "The Social Experience of the Negro Soldier Abroad." See also Lieut. Osceolo E. McKaine; Steven A. Reich, 265-267; and Cyril V. Briggs.

10. Michel Fabre provides a brief account of Hunton's memoir and her experiences with the YMCA in France. See pages 55-58.

11. For a discussion of Herder's importance for Du Bois, see Helbling, 19-41. Sapir's theory, while disavowing the concrete links between language, nation, and culture that Herder's cultural nationalism was famous for, nonetheless saw language as the fundamental conceptual medium for political systems. See Sapir, 16-17.

12. Du Bois's most authoritative biographer, David Levering Lewis, accounts for Du Bois's praise of France and benign attitude to its colonial rule in 1919 by suggesting this was "a measure of the eccentric Eurocentrism and radicalism-from-above that still resided in the marrow of the author of the *Souls of Black Folk*. Perhaps European imperialism was ultimately reprehensible to Du Bois less for its inequities than because, at its Anglo-Saxon worst, it was founded on skin color" (566-67). For Lewis's detailed account of the 1919 Pan-African Congress, see 564-78.

13. Important for this section is Maria Balshaw's reading of Fisher's oeuvre.

14. The phrase is Amiri Baraka's. For more on how racialized temporalities functioned in the United States at this time, see Felipe Smith (37).

15. For a fuller explanation of the multiple and complex meanings of "urbanity" at this time, particularly in the work of Robert Park, see Balshaw 18.
16. Gates discusses Mezz Mezrow's definiton of signifying in particular in this section of his account.
17. Such use of French in "on-the-streets" exercises of troping and self-projection can also be seen in Iceberg Slim, in which verbal dexterity is a key distinguishing factor between those who are successful on the Chicago streets and those who are not. As proof of this, Slim includes a glossary of Chicago Black English of the 1920s and 1930s; it includes the term "boo koos," an Anglicization of *beaucoup,* which Slim lists as meaning "plenty" (273).
18. This dynamic of racialized psychosexuality forms a key point of Fanon's. It also formed an important part of the black power movement: see Eldridge Cleaver, particularly section IV, "White Woman, Black Man." This dynamic was also described in the Harlem Renaissance; see James Weldon Johnson's poem "The White Witch." Fanon and Cleaver's accounts have been criticized for their privileging of male sexuality in their texts, and Cleaver's in particular for its misogyny; see Gwen Bergner. As Cornel West has noted of the contemporary period, in observations which apply with even more force in the early twentieth century, the mythologizing of black sexuality in America has led to a situation where "much of black self-hatred and self contempt has to do with the refusal of many black Americans to love their own black bodies" (85). Such a situation is implicated in the assumption of a "machismo identity" by many young black men, as a form of "self-identification and resistance in a hostile culture" that "usually results in a direct confrontation with the order-imposing authorities of the status quo, that is, the police or criminal justice system"—much as Paul seeks confrontation with white southerners (85, 90–91). Yet such a system also means that instead "of black women being the most sought after 'objects of sexual pleasure'—as in the case of black men—white women tend to occupy this 'upgraded,' that is, degraded [situation], primarily because white beauty plays a weightier role in sexual desirability for women in racist patriarchal America" (90).
19. See the anonymous "The Reverse of the Medal" (227–28).
20. Edwards discusses this exchange; see 104–18. See also Locke 6–9.
21. See Theodore Kornweibel, especially chapters 3 to 5.

Works Cited

Astor, Gerald. *The Right to Fight: A History of African Americans in the Military.* Novato, CA: Presido, 1998.

Baker, Houston A. *Modernism and the Harlem Renaissance.* Chicago: U of Chicago P, 1987.
Balshaw, Maria. *Looking for Harlem: Urban Aesthetics in African-American Literature.* London: Pluto, 2000.
Baraka, Amiri. "The Return of the Native." Rpt. Ed. In *Vicious Modernism: Black Harlem and the Literary Imagination.* James De Jongh. Cambridge: Cambridge UP, 1990. iii.
Barbeau, Arthur E., and Florette Henri. *The Unknown Soldiers: African-American Troops in World War I.* New York: Da Capo, 1996.
Barthes, Roland. *Mythologies.* Trans. Annette Lavers. St. Albans: Paladin, 1973.
Bennett, Gwendolyn. "Wedding Day." *The Portable Harlem Renaissance Reader.* Ed. David Levering Lewis. London: Penguin, 1994. 363–69.
Bergner, Gwen. "Who Is That Masked Woman? Or, the Role of Gender in Fanon's *Black Skin, White Masks,*" *PMLA* 110 (1995): 75–78.
Briggs, Cyril V. "Fighting Savage Hun and Treacherous Cracker." 1919. Hill. 257–60.
Butcher, Margaret Just. *The Negro in American Culture: Based on Materials Left by Alain Locke.* New York: Knopf, 1956.
Cleaver, Eldridge. *Soul on Ice.* New York: Dell, 1970.
Colson, William N. "An Analysis of Negro Patriotism." *The Messenger* (August 1919): 23–25.
———. "Propaganda and the Negro Soldier." *The Messenger* (July 1919): 24–25.
———. "The Social Experience of the Negro Soldier Abroad." *The Messenger* (October 1919): 26–27.
De Jongh, James. *Vicious Modernism: Black Harlem and the Literary Imagination.* New York: Cambridge UP, 1990.
Douglas, Ann. *Terrible Honesty.* London: Papermac, 1995.
Du Bois, W. E. B. "The African Roots of War." 1915. *W. E. B. Du Bois Speaks.* Ed. Eric D. Foner. New York: Pathfinder, 1991. 244–57.
———. "The Battle of Europe." *The Crisis* 12 (1916). *W. E. B. Du Bois: An A.B.C. of Color.* New York: International, 1969. 86–88.
———. "Black Bastille." *The Crisis* 14 (1917): 217.
———. "Close Ranks." *The Crisis* 16 (July 1918): 111. Rpt. *The Selected Writings of W.E.B. Du Bois,* ed. Walter Wilson. NY: New American Library, 1970. 170.
———. "The Conservation of Races." 1897. *Race.* Ed. Robert Bernasconi. Oxford: Blackwell, 2001. 84–91.
———. "An Essay toward a History of the Black Man in the Great War." *W. E. B. Du Bois: Writings.* Ed. Nathan Huggins. Cambridge: Cambridge UP, 1986. 879–922.
———. "French and Spanish." *The Crisis* 17 (1919): 269.
———. "Returning Soldiers." *The Crisis* 18, May 1919. Rpt. *The Selected Writings of W.E.B. Du Bois,* ed. Walter Wilson. NY: New American Library, 1970. 170–72.
Edwards, Brent Hayes. *The Practice of Diaspora: Literature, Translation, and the Rise of Black Internationalism.* Cambridge: Harvard UP, 2003.

Eksteins, Modris. Preface. *Rites of Spring: The Great War and the Birth of the Modern Age.* London: Papermac, 2000. xiii–xvi.
Ellis, Mark. "'Closing Ranks' and 'Seeking Honors': W. E. B. Du Bois in World War I." *Journal of American History* 79 (1992): 96–124.
Fabre, Michel. *From Harlem to Paris: Black American Writers in France, 1840–1980.* Chicago: U of Illinois P, 1991.
Fanon, Frantz. *Black Skin, White Masks.* Trans. Charles Lam Markmann. London: Pluto Press, 1986.
Fauset, Jessie. "Nostalgia." *The Crisis* 22 (August 1921): 154–58.
Fisher, Rudolph. "City of Refuge." 1925. Gates and McKay 1175–87.
Foner, Jack D. *Blacks and the Military in American History.* New York: Praeger, 1974.
Gates, Henry Louis, Jr. *The Signifying Monkey: A Theory of African-American Literary Criticism.* Oxford: Oxford UP, 1988.
Gates, Henry Louis, Jr., and Nellie Y. McKay, eds. *The Norton Anthology of African American Literature.* New York: Norton, 1997.
Gilroy, Paul. *Against Race: Imagining Political Culture beyond the Color Line.* Cambridge: Harvard UP, 2000.
Gould, Stephen Jay. *The Mismeasure of Man.* Rev. Ed. London: Penguin, 1997.
Grimké, F. J. "Address of Welcome to the Men Who Have Returned from the Battlefront." *A Documentary History of the Negro People in the United States.* Ed. Herbert Aptheker. Vol. 3. New York: Citadel, 1973. 241–43.
Helbling, Mark. The *Harlem Renaissance: The One and the Many.* Westport: The Greenwood Press, 1999.
Hill, Robert A., ed. *The Crusader. A Facsimile of the Periodical.* New York: Garland, 1987.
Hirschkop, Ken. *Mikhail Bakhtin: An Aesthetic for Democracy.* New York: Oxford UP, 2000.
Hunton, Addie, and Kathryn M. Johnson. *Two Colored Women with the American Expeditionary Forces.* 1920. New York: G. K. Hall, 1997.
Hurston, Zora Neale. "Characteristics of Negro Expression." 1934. Gates and McKay 1019–32.
Hutchinson, George. *The Harlem Renaissance in Black and White.* Cambridge: Harvard UP, 1995.
Johnson, James Weldon. Preface. *The Book of American Negro Poetry.* Ed. James Weldon Johnson. New York: Harcourt, Brace, 1922. vii–xlviii.
———. "The White Witch." *Saint Peter Relates an Incident: Selected Poems by James Weldon Johnson.* London: Penguin, 1993. 34–36.
Kennedy, David M. *Over Here: The First World War and American Society.* Oxford: Oxford UP, 2004.
Kevles, Daniel. "Testing the Army's Intelligence: Psychologists and the Military in World War I." *Journal of American History* 55 (1968): 565–81.
Kornweibel, Theodore, Jr. *"Seeing Red": Federal Campaigns against Black Militancy, 1919–1925.* Bloomington: Indiana UP, 1998.
Lemke, Sieglinde. *Primitivist Modernism: Black Culture and the Origins of Transatlantic Modernism.* Oxford: Oxford UP, 1998.

Lewis, David Levering. *W. E. B. Du Bois: Biography of a Race, 1868–1919.* New York: Holt, 1993.
———. *When Harlem Was in Vogue.* New York: Oxford UP, 1981.
Locke, Alain. "The Black Watch on the Rhine." *Opportunity* 1 (1924): 6–9.
Locke, Alain, and René Maran. "French Colonial Policy: Open Letters." *Opportunity* 2 (1924): 261–63.
Mack, Charles E. *Two Black Crows in the A.E.F.* Indianapolis: Bobbs, 1928.
Maxwell, William J. *New Negro, Old Left: African-American Writing and Communism between the Wars.* New York: Columbia UP, 1999.
McKaine, Lieut. Osceolo E. "With the Buffaloes in France." 1919. Hill 185–86.
Nalty, Bernard C. *Strength for the Fight: A History of Black Americans in the Military.* London: Macmillan, 1986.
Reich, Steven A. "Soldiers of Democracy: Black Texans and the Fight for Citizenship, 1917–1921." *The Journal of American History* 82 (1996): 1478–1504.
"The Reverse of the Medal." Anonymous. *The Crisis* 23 (1922): 227–28.
"Rewarding the Battlers for Democracy." Anonymous. 1919. Hill 265–67.
Sapir, Edward. *Language: An Introduction to the Study of Speech.* New York: Harcourt, Brace, 1921.
Sherman, Daniel J. *The Construction of Memory in Interwar France.* Chicago: U of Chicago P, 1999.
Slim, Iceberg. *Pimp: The Story of My Life.* 1967. London: Payback, 1996.
Smith, Felipe. *American Body Politics: Race, Gender and Black Literary Renaissance.* Athens: U of Georgia P, 1998.
Snead, James. *White Screens, Black Images: Hollywood from the Dark Side.* London: Routledge, 1994.
Soyinka, Wole. "Language as Boundary." *Art, Dialogue and Outrage: Essays on Literature and Culture.* London: Methuen, 1993. 82–94.
Stephens, Michelle A. "Black Transnationalism and the Politics of National Identity: West Indian Intellectuals in Harlem in the Age of War and Revolution." *American Quarterly* 50 (1998): 592–608.
Stovall, Tyler. *Paris Noir: African Americans in the City of Light.* Boston: Houghton, 1996.
West, Cornel. "Black Sexuality: The Taboo Subject." *Race Matters.* Boston: Beacon, 1993. 81–91.
Wright, Richard. "The Ethics of Living Jim Crow." *Uncle Tom's Children.* 1938. New York: Harper, 1993. 1–15.
Zieger, Robert H. *America's Great War: World War I and the American Experience.* Lanham: Rowman, 2000.

CHAPTER 3

"No One, I Am Sure, Is Ever Homesick in Paris"
Jessie Fauset's French Imaginary

Claire Oberon Garcia

Paris in 1925 witnessed several events that have become iconic moments in conventional histories of modernism: Josephine Baker arrived in Paris with the Revue Nègre; Ernest Hemingway and F. Scott Fitzgerald met for the first time in the Ritz Hotel bar; the International Exhibition of Arts Décoratifs showed the world what modern looked like; and Picasso painted his *Three Graces*. Mentioned less often in narratives of modernism is the encounter between Anna Julia Cooper and Jane Nardal that took place on March 23, 1925, in the Salle du Doctorat at the Sorbonne. Cooper, 65, was an American public high-school teacher who had been born in slavery. The black-gowned woman stood alone before the elevated seats of three male "jurors" to defend her dissertation (Keller 5). Her thesis, *L'Attitude de la France à l'égard d'esclavage pendant la Révolution*, though written in a carefully dispassionate, academic style, went against the grain of French historical scholarship in that it placed the issue of slavery at the center of an analysis of the French revolution. Her work suggested that the conditions for European modernity were created through relationships of power between Europeans and people of color.[1] Working out of a lifelong commitment to bringing "the feminine flavor" to scholarly inquiry (Cooper, *The Third Step*, 3–4 quoted in Keller), Cooper's dissertation reminded historians that "enslaved blacks in Sainte-Domingue are a flesh-and-blood *living* negation of [France's] noble principles" (May 114), and that narratives of revolution in Europe could not be disentangled from issues of slavery and domination.

The presence of this middle-aged black woman in such a venerable public arena was itself a living challenge to contemporary constructions of race and gender in France, in that it instantiated a black woman's determination to inscribe her own historical agency. As an education reformer and political activist, Cooper spent her long career resisting and re-writing limiting narratives imposed upon women and people of color. Cooper's new interpretation of the French Revolution, which involved remapping the power relationship between the metropole and its colonies and foregrounding African-descended people as agents of French history, rather than merely its subjects, prefigured the questions and concerns of a younger generation of black women who crossed the Atlantic to study in Paris during the interwar years. As an effect of the increased interest in African American culture and education during the 1920s, dozens of New Negro women from the United States had their studies in France underwritten by sororities or foundations. They joined the first generation of women from the Antilles who, as their sisters had customarily done, sailed to the hexagon to achieve university degrees in preparation for professional careers. As Jenny Alpha writes in her autobiography, *Paris Créole Blues*, "Mes parents voulaient que je quitte la Martinique, pour continuer mes etudes. . . . [M]es parents voulaient que j'aille à la université pour devenir professeur, ou à la rigueur que je travaille à la douane ou à la poste comme eux" (My parents wanted me to leave Martinique to continue my studies. . . . My parents wished that I might go to university to become a teacher, or if need be, to work in the customs or post office, as they did) (51).

Watching Cooper from the gallery was a young Martiniquaise who was also studying at the University of Paris, Jane Nardal. Nardal, who later described herself as someone who had been, until that moment, "une bonne négresse française," wrote of the transformative power of this scene two years later in a letter to Alain Locke, as she was asking Locke's permission to translate his anthology, *The New Negro*. "Pourtant," she wrote, "ma curiosité, mon intéret, déja sollicité par d'autres faits nègres, commencaient à s'éveiller" (Nevertheless my curiosity, my interest, already drawn out by other negro accomplishments, began to awaken).[2] For Nardal, the moment was a catalyst for her own discovery of and dedication to a transnational "ésprit de race" founded upon common origins in Africa that she later explored in her own writing and political activism. Nardal believed that her generation of scholars would use their European educations to study the spirit and history of their race, with a new critical energy.

Jane's sister, Paulette Nardal, also identified a key political development in black women's new presence and experiences in Paris, emphasizing in particular the sense of dislocation, marginality, and struggle that characterized the lives of the first handful of female students who went to the city to study during the interwar years. In narrating her history of "l'éveil de conscience de race" (the awakening of black consciousness) among Antillean intellectuals, Paulette describes the initial small "stirrings," unarticulated transgressive questions, and upstart periodicals that provided the groundwork for the eventual bold critiques and demands of the black liberation movements of the twentieth century. Nardal writes:

> [P]arallel to the isolated efforts above mentioned, the aspirations which were to be crystallized around "The Review of the Black World" asserted themselves among a group of Antillean women students in Paris. The coloured women living alone in the metropolis, until the Colonial Exhibition, have certainly been less favoured than coloured men who are content with a certain easy success. Long before the latter, they have felt the need of a racial solidarity which would not be merely material. They were thus aroused to race consciousness. The feeling of uprooting which they experienced . . . was the starting point of their evolution. (350)

Paulette Nardal locates the catalyst for racial consciousness in the sense of uprooting and dislocation more dramatically experienced by young Antillean women. Together with her sister's memory of the spectacle of the older American Anna Julia Cooper, truant from her respectable job in her nation's capital, this insight highlights the often overlooked but significant "présence feminine" in modernist transatlantic black discourses. This black female presence was fraught and paradoxical by its very nature, as the Nardal sisters' fellow student, Roberte Horth, would depict in her 1932 essay, "Histoire sans importance" (A thing of no importance), recounting how a bookish Martiniquaise's dream of the intellectual delights and transcendent "truths" of a Parisian university education clashes with the social and emotional alienation that characterized a black woman student's daily life in the metropole.

Written in January 1925—and published in the NAACP's journal *The Crisis* the same month that Cooper defended her dissertation—

Jessie Fauset's essay "The Enigma of the Sorbonne" likewise demands that readers confront the presence of black women in modernist Paris through their intrusion into the halls of academe, and posits that presence as a sign of modernity itself. Fauset, who was fluent in French, was at that time studying for a certificate from the Sorbonne. Her article begins as a summary of the history of one of the greatest universities in the world for the middle-brow African American reader, but Fauset closes the essay with a description of her vision of "[t]wo absolutely black girls. . . . Their hair, stiff, black and fuzzy frames. . . . their voices clear . . . and staccato; their movements free and unrestrained" striding beneath the indifferent and tolerant gazes of the statues of Louis Pasteur and Victor Hugo (219). In Fauset's view, the Haitian girls whom she inscribes in the Place de la Sorbonne are not the passive beneficiaries of French republican tolerance; they are active agents whose very presence testifies to a historical intervention: "In this atmosphere so completely are they themselves that tolerance is a quality which they recognize only when they are exercising it toward others" (219). The young women's distinctively black female bodies, and the intellectual work that they are engaged in, disrupt and reorient the historical narrative of the elite institution, much as the Haitian revolution disrupted and challenged French national narratives. However, Fauset is careful to emphasize the students' self-possession; *bien dans leurs peaux*, they are the ones who "recognize" and "exercise" tolerance. Fauset herself, as the black female tourist recounting the history of the Sorbonne for the readers of *The Crisis*, assumes in turn the power to observe the girls, and place them in the historical narrative of the esteemed university.

Jane Nardal's account of the impact of witnessing Cooper's thesis defense at the Sorbonne signals and symbolizes the opening of a new chapter in black women's history in the West. Against all odds, Jane and Paulette Nardal, Jessie Fauset, and other black women modernists such as Gwendolyn Bennett, Suzanne Césaire, and Augusta Savage inscribed themselves and their peers in narratives of western history, modernism, and the struggles for liberation across the black diaspora. In "talking back," as Cooper did, to the institutional narratives that sought to define, control, and restrict black women, these young modernists also inscribed gender into projects of racial, cultural, and political liberation. They all spent significant time in Paris when that city was the major contact point for intellectuals, artists, and writers from around the world. The city's multiple identities as the global artistic and intellectual capital, imperial metropole, sexual and racial free zone, and haven for refugees from dozens of countries made it a generative imaginary site in these women's fiction and non-fiction writing. For the Antillean women, a degree from a French university was the necessary authentication of French professional and social identity. For the African American women, study in Paris was both an opportunity to become acquainted with the most significant aspects of European culture as well as to be present as witnesses and actors on the artistic and intellectual frontiers of the future.

Although not all of the women knew each other, and between them held a variety of political commitments and aesthetic perspectives that changed and evolved over the course of their lives, read collectively, their work reveals interesting new dimensions of interwar black modernism. Emerging from cross-cultural, transnational, and multi-lingual environments, their texts make clear that gender consciousness is part of the warp and woof of race consciousness. Many of their texts share particular characteristics and questions. They remap the relationships among the United States, European metropoles, and their African and Caribbean colonies, placing women's perspectives and points of view at the center of their discussions. In their critiques of colonialism and other manifestations of white supremacy, they foreground issues of gender as socially and politically constructed. They portray women—including themselves—as agents and interpreters of history and culture, problematizing issues of dislocation and translation to explore and critique representations of black women's identities in the modern world.

In an era characterized by unprecedented disruptions and transgressions, the presence of black women in areas of life and discourse where they had been either invisible or objects of (mis) representation was yet another consequence of dramatic economic, political, and social shifts in the aftermath of the First World War. In this essay, I will examine Jessie Fauset's comprehension of the contributions of black women writers to the new "self-understanding" of black people confronting modernity, contributions often overlooked or undervalued by scholarship on the history and literature of the New Negro and Négritude movements. In her fiction and in her essays, Fauset elaborates what I will call a "French Imaginary," a mode of appropriating and transforming the received image of Paris as a romanticized city of refuge for black intellectuals. Fauset's French Imaginary issues forth from a specifically gendered perspective that testifies to the intellectual agency of black women's presence to historical events, at home and abroad. Against the backdrop of critiques and debates about the changing understandings of gender, as well as the meaning and function of racial identity, in anticolonial movements, women who were the descendants of slaves in the New World were uniquely positioned to critique and create new concepts of racial and gender agency. Their gendered experiences of dislocation and isolation informed their efforts to articulate what united people of African descent throughout the black diaspora beyond the "common condition" Alain Locke identified as having been forged by slavery and the ideology of white supremacy (7).

As Edouard Glissant has argued, the experience of an uprooted and transplanted people "severed from their original nature," and marked by profound cultural and material distress and loss, nevertheless offers "the opportunity to assert a considerable set of possibilities. For instance, the possibility of dealing with 'values' no longer in absolute terms but as active agents of synthesis. The abandonment of pure original values allows an unprecedented potential for contact" (Glissant 16). Glissant's "for instance" is borne out in the exemplary cases of the black women who ventured across the Atlantic to Paris in the early decades of the twentieth century to continue their formal education or enhance their artistic aspirations. These women engaged self-consciously with issues of translation and representation, as well as with their own historical and institutional positioning, in ways that sought at once to abandon the "absolute terms" of racial and gender identification and to usher in new forms of solidarity. As I will argue next, this thesis obtains a striking articulation in examples from Fauset's fiction, where a female character refuses the "benefits" of the cultural capital that apparently accompany a relationship with French language and culture.

"The value of a translation lies in its adequacy"

In her short fiction no less than in her novels, Fauset explores the ways in which linguistic exchange records and reshapes historical understanding and experience alike. While knowledge of French language and culture was often a sign of sophistication in the non-Francophone Americas, for Fauset among other black women modernist writers the status of France and Frenchness opened up often perplexing questions about the connections between language, culture, and experience. To the extent that language structures perception—including self-perception—black Francophone writers struggled with the problem of how to come to Lockeian "self-understanding" through the language of the colonizer. In addition, black women writers during this period also challenged the linguistic misrepresentations of black womanhood. In Roberte Horth's "Histoire sans importance/A Thing of No Importance" (1932), which appeared in Paulette Nardal's *La Revue du Monde Noir*, a young Martiniquaise laments the disconnection between the academic ideals of her French education and social and emotional experiences of being a black woman in France:

> Her mind, strong like a man's, by turns influenced by Western literature and disciplined by different methods of thinking, had taken on the best of a clear and precise logic. They moulded her reason, her heart, and her ways. She entered a great university whose sole concern was to lead minds into the path of progress, regardless of class or race . . .
>
> But what of the world and its pleasures? . . . One might excuse a narrow-minded people . . . for considering her only as a fetish, but that the best of them while opening wide the doors of their spiritual treasure should guard closely that of their hearts . . . that passed understanding. In this country, she will never be a woman like the others . . . because she will never be able to blot out, for the others, the absurdity of her soul fashioned by Occidental culture but concealed by an objectionable skin. (Horth 119–20)

The substance of Horth's politically explicit critique of the determinative presence of colonial ideology within French culture and institutional life is both anticipated and addressed in Fauset's own, much earlier, sketches of pedagogical structures. These, tellingly, often employed French language and culture as complex signifiers of colonial ideology.

Fauset specifically linked problems of representation and translation, institutional knowledge and self-knowledge, in two early short stories, "Emmy" (1912) and "There Was One Time: A Story of Spring" (1917). Both stories foreground the role of educational institutions in the construction of generating "knowledge" of black womanhood. Issues of translation in "Emmy" raise questions about how black women read and resist society's often vicious representations of both their gender and their racial affiliations. In "There Was One Time," pointless French lessons serve to unite two young African American lovers not only to each other but to a diasporic consciousness that unites oppressed African Americans to colonized people around the globe. In the opening of the story, an exasperated French teacher in a segregated school launches "for the fiftieth time . . . into an explanation of the translation of idioms" that make no sense in the black American children's world (524); the story's title emphasizes the point that conventional marriage plots are irrelevant for African American women by mistranslating the traditional opening of French fairy tales. "There Was One Time" and "Emmy" both use the protagonists' associations with French as a means of articulating and resisting racial and gender constraints and of allowing the heroines to imagine a more satisfying counter-narrative.

"Emmy" appeared in *The Crisis* in two installments in December 1912 and January 1913. The story opens with a schoolgirl, Emilie Carrel, being asked to identify her racial affiliation from a choice of five visual representations. To her teacher's relief Emmy chooses the "correct" image, the "Hottentot, chosen with careful nicety to represent the entire Negro race" (51). But the reasoning that Emmy uses to make the choice is definitely counter-cultural and, in a country governed by white supremacy, appears to be subversive and irrational, though the narrator pointedly insists that Emmy is "always severely logical" (53). To Emmy, the Hottentot "had on the whole a better appearance" (51).[3] Emmy arrives at the socially-sanctioned conclusion, but does so with counter-cultural reasoning: dominant American aesthetic and social standards would never allow that the paradigmatic African is never more beautiful than the paradigmatic European. When a white friend expresses sympathy after Emmy publicly affirms her black identity, Emmy retorts, "We're just the same, only you're white and I'm brown"; her response is similar when her biracial friend wishes that he "were a good sure-enough brown like you": "But what difference does it make?" (52).[4] Although as Emmy grows up and learns "what color means" to other people, she manages to graduate from high school "mak[ing] them see she was perfectly satisfied with being colored" (56). The opening sequence is the first of several in which Emmy is confronted with a representation of "blackness" and required to position herself in relation to the inferiority that that representation suggests.

Emmy's non-compliance with the racial norms of her central Pennsylvania village is not understood by its citizens to be the product of Emmy's autonomous reasoning, but is instead attributed to what is called Emmy's "foreignness." Her mother "used to live in France" (53), has a French maid, and makes a good living by translating: "Seems so funny for a colored woman to speak and write a foreign language," asserts one of Emmy's teachers. "I like colored people to look and act like what they are" (53). The teacher's words assume a correspondence between white representations and expectations of blackness and the conditions of their existence. Emmy and her mother's association with French language and culture is a cause for suspicion, not privilege, in their community. Their "Frenchness" is bound up in the history of slavery and the social and legal constraints against miscegenation: Emmy's grandmother was a slave and her mother's father was a slave master.

In one instance, Emmy's knowledge of French is a form of capital that might allow her to buy off some of the stigma of blackness—a classmate offers to allow Emmy to join her club if she helps her with her French verbs, asserting to Emmy that "'colored folks can't expect to have what we have, or if they do they must pay extra for it'" (82). But Emmy's racial pride prevents her from acquiescing to the rules of that particular game. Emmy's teacher, Miss Wenzel, had earlier made a misguided attempt to help Emmy learn her place in American society, by presenting her with a stone engraved with a series of mottos from a Robert Louis Stevenson poem titled "A Task"—among them, "To renounce when that shall be necessary and not embittered" (82). However, Emmy's instinctive racial pride and self-satisfaction cause her to misunderstand her teacher's condescension and she interprets the poem's message to suit her own life and perspective on her dilemma. According to the white supremacist mores of American society, Emmy not only misreads the poem but also misreads her place in the world. In rejecting her classmate's racist invitation to exchange her French skills for a discount on the social cost of her blackness, Emmy declares that she finally understands a line in the poem, emphasizing (by taking out of its original context) these lines: "To keep a few friends, but these without capitulation" (82).

By contrast, her friend Archie, whose olive skin has also caused his neighbors to imagine him as a "foreigner," is all too eager to accept others' representations of him. Archie decides to pass for white when he allows his imagination to be sparked by a "quixotic" young white man's construction of a racial narrative. The white man, interested in Archie's "history," spins a fanciful tale of Archie's present and future life:

> "By George! How exciting your life must be—now white and now black—standing between ambition and honor, what? Not that I don't think you're doing the right thing—it's nobody's confounded business anyway. Look here, when you get through, look me up, I may be able to put you wise to something. Here's my card. And say, mum's the word, and when you've made your pile you can wake some fine morning and find yourself famous simply by telling what you are. All rot, this beastly prejudice, I say." (84)

Archie unquestioningly accepts the white man's blithe narrative as his own. Later, in Philadelphia, Archie is unmasked as a "Negro" when his employer confronts the melodramatic scene of Archie "mooning" over Emmy's photograph. To the white male spectator, Archie's performance of a young white gentleman in love becomes a performance of sexual perversion when the object of his romantic yearning is a black woman, and then becomes a major disruption of the order of things—both in his office and in the larger social world—when Archie reveals himself as a black man.

Significantly, the moral crisis in the story surrounds Emmy's reaction to (or reading of) her mother's cautionary tale about the perils of misreading a situation based upon the lexicon of racial and sexual exploitation, violence, silence, and pride. Based on her own experience of love and marriage, Mrs. Carrél relates how her husband, coming home unexpectedly, found her in the arms of a white man. He accused his wife of infidelity, and struck her "—you mustn't blame him, child. Remember it was the same spirit showing in both of us, in different ways. I was doing all I could to provoke him by keeping silence and he merely retaliated in his way. The blow wouldn't have harmed a little bird" (141). Insulted by his accusations, Mrs. Carrél banned him from her house and her life rather than explain that the white man was her father, her own "mother's guardian, protector, everything, but not her husband." The Carréls' reconciliation is aborted by a shipwreck that kills Emmy's father en route back to his wife; "his body was so badly mangled, they wouldn't even let [her] see him" (141).

The irony of the chapter from family history lies in the fact that Mrs. Carrél's father, on his fateful visit to her, "had come after all these years to make some reparation. It was through him that I first began translating for the publishers. You know yourself how my work has grown" (141). Her translation work serves as both a means of independence and liberation as well as the death knell of her marriage. Emmy, however, characteristically misreads this didactic tale, along with its nineteenth-century prescription of womanly sacrifice ("If you really loved Archie . . . you'd let him marry you and lock you off, away from all the world, just so long as you were with him"). Rejecting the literary trope of the secret black female sexual playmate (as popularized in Charles Chesnutt's *The House behind the Cedars*, William Wells Brown's *Clotel*, and others), Emmy finds that her mother's prescription only increases her "gloom" and bitterness about the poisonous role of "color" in black women's relationships. While her mother ascribes Emmy's romantic dilemma to Emmy's "pride" and "talk of color," Emmy has a different interpretation of both her mother's romantic tragedy and her own:

> "It wouldn't have happened at all if we hadn't been colored," she told herself moodily. "If grandmother hadn't been colored she wouldn't have been a slave, and if she hadn't been a slave—That's what it is, color—color—it's wrecked mother's life and now it's wrecking mine." (141)

Emmy goes as far as to wish, for a moment, that she were white, before she "checked herself angrily" (141). Yet although she rejects her mother's advice of self-suppression and self-silencing and refuses to crawl back to Archie, Emmy does resolve to adopt the nineteenth-century woman's mask of "cheerfulness," but the cheerfulness is performed before her mother, not her lover. Fortunately for her, and crucial to the ideology of race pride that the story affirms, Emmy does not have to resort to a self-annihilating compromise.

Archie nevertheless returns to her, full of apologies, and asks her to marry him and join him in the Philippines, where Emmy's mother's connections have assured him a job, as it seems impossible for him as a black man to pursue his career in the United States. Yet unlike the racial outsiders in nineteenth-century novels such as George Eliot's *Daniel Deronda* and Helen Hunt Jackson's *Ramona*, the couple need not leave their native country to live a fulfilling life: a Christmas Eve change of heart on the part of Archie's white employer ensures that he can pursue his career and their class-appropriate marriage there in Pennsylvania. Despite the story's coincidences and conventional language, the story is radical in its insistence on Emmy's emphatic rejection of archaic racial and gender identities and life-narratives prescribed for black women, as well as in its rejection of the notion that African Americans must expatriate themselves to find professional and personal freedom. At this same time, it thus also challenges the notion of France and the French language as an emancipatory place and object of experience and knowledge.

The other early story we are examining here, "'There Was One Time!' A Story of Spring" (1917), also ends with a black couple eschewing an easier career in another country—this time, France itself—and resolving "to live that wonderful fairy tale" in New York (15). The protagonist of "'There Was One Time!' A Story of Spring," Anna Fetters, is a "typical American girl done over in brown" who graduates with "the quota of useless French . . . vocabulary which the average pupil brings out of the average High School" (273). Because of intractable discrimination in the job market of her small Pennsylvania town, she finds herself obliged to "teach foreign languages—always her special detestation" (272). Trained in a business school and excelling in mechanical drawing, Anna bitterly "realize[s] the handicap of color" when she discovers that no business will hire her, and that the only opportunities open to a black woman are teaching or domestic service. Deeply angry, frustrated, and resentful, she has already, before the story's opening, spent two years working as a waitress and her mother, who takes solace in the delusions of religion, worked as a maid while Anna attended night school for teacher training. She is finally hired to teach at a "colored school," "[b]ut Fate, with a last malevolence, saw to it that she was appointed to teach History and French." At the opening of the story, the French language, rather than being a marker of education and class status, is for Anna a symbol of discrimination, humiliation, and "the merciless indifference of life" (272).

The French fairy tale romance that Anna tries to get her students to understand is far removed from her life and from theirs, and when a brief bolt for temporary freedom is cut short by a white tramp's attempted sexual assault upon her, Anna ruefully concludes, "[t]his is what could happen to you if you are a colored girl playing at being a French shepherdess" (275). A Prince Charming does rescue her, but irony permeates her lived version of the fairy tale of the shepherdess and the prince. As part of a series of "anti-fairy-tale" turns of the plot, the potential prince rescues Anna, but then disappears for several weeks. While many critics have identified the fairy-tale plot structure in Fauset's novels, this story, which features a prince whose spring fever is an actual illness ("I get it every spring, darn it!" [277]) rather than amorous, suggests that Euro-American fairy tale tropes are inappropriate for "two young colored people" (275) in America.[5] Her nameless savior's bout with malarial fever contracted in colonized Guiana makes him a weak and apparently fearful defender of his damsel's virtue. In fact, when Anna (whose French language skills are rudimentary, despite the fact that she is a French teacher) returns several weeks later to her laborious translation of the fairy tale, she speculates that it will end with the prince giving the shepherdess a job, rather than making her queen: "Perhaps, she thought fancifully that Thursday evening—the shepherdess meets the prince again and he gives her a position as court-artist" (11). When Anna does finish the story, her translation is woefully inadequate; the narrator describes it as a "mutilation" (12) rather than translation of the story.

Anna's Prince Charming also has connections to the French language, but that language for him is a sign of his migratory life in the colonized black diaspora. The nameless stranger is a foreigner yet American—born in New Jersey, he spent his childhood in British Guiana, then ran away and lived a vagabond life in England and France before making a kind of reverse migration "home to Harlem." A critic of the white imperial "cold-bloodedness which enables a civilized people to maim and kill in the Congo and on the Putumayo, or to lynch in Georgia" (276), his politics of racial uplift is informed by his transnational experiences and diasporic perspective.

Translation and mistranslation, reading and misreading, are tropes that course their way through the story, from the students' insistence on mistranslating the conventional opening lines of French fairy tales to Mrs. Fetter's habitual misuse of Biblical phrases and her propensity to turn common phrases "upside down" (12). It is the effort of translation and deferral of comprehension that unites the lovers at the end of the story—Anna's thick-headed pupil in French class miraculously starts turning in apt translations, thanks to his uncle's help. His uncle, pointedly bearing the name "Winter" in "A Tale of Spring," had misinterpreted his nephew's interest in his uncle's German books, not realizing that Tommy was one of Anna's pupils until several weeks after meeting her. Although Anna and Richard plan a future together involving a return to the freedom of Europe, where Richard would "build bridges and [Anna could] draw the plans" (14), they must wait until after the war, in the meantime "liv[ing] that wonderful fairy tale" in Harlem.

"France, Sweet France": Fauset's Black Parisian Imaginary

Fauset herself, of course, was unlike these protagonists in the sense that she made several visits to Paris throughout the 1910s and 1920s, experiences she represented in several innovative nonfiction pieces she wrote for *The Crisis*. Paris has always shown a multiplicity of faces to the black people who migrated, were transported, or aspired to sojourn there. Before the twentieth century, there had been a black presence in France, but the interwar years saw an increase in the number and spheres of activity of black people, especially in Paris. The participation of thousands of soldiers from the United States, West Africa, and the Antilles in the war "to keep the world safe for democracy" and French popular and avant-garde interest in black forms of cultural expression marked a new and modern chapter in the history of black people in France. African American veterans returned to the United States with renewed determination to fight for their citizen rights at home after experiencing a taste of social and educational freedoms in France. For the first time, a small but active number of women from the Antillean families of the *gens de couleur* joined the sons of the elite who came to France to study at the universities before returning to take their places among the professional though not ruling classes on the islands. Although it was assumed that the women would also return home to take their pre-determined places in Antillean society, this first generation of female university graduates, as Paulette Nardal often noted, saw themselves and their place in society differently after their sojourns in Paris.[6]

As a major nodal point in the African diaspora, Paris has long served as a laboratory for exploring the alchemies of national, racial, and cultural identities and testing the practical, modern applications of Enlightenment values and claims. By the interwar period, however, the Parisian myth had become overdetermined for black artists and intellectuals; its tropological status was both firmly established and yet freshly tempting for black writers examining their racial and cultural identities with new eyes. Fauset was one of the New Negro writers who most frequently drew on her own experiences in France to explore the tensions between common conditions and common consciousness in the black diaspora. Although many critics have painted her as a genteel Francophile, Fauset's French writing—what I will call her French imaginary—is nuanced, complex, and far from romanticized, and in this way can be seen as an extension of the short fiction we have already considered. Though she never fully expatriated herself, Fauset visited France at least four times—first in 1914, as France entered the Great War, the second time in 1921 as a delegate to the Second Pan-African Congress, the third time in 1924–25, to study French at the Sorbonne and the Alliance Française, and then in 1934. With the exception of the first trip, each of these sojourns involved extensive journeys to other European countries, and during her last two trips, Fauset traveled to Algeria and Morocco. In Fauset's French writings, France figures as a politically and aesthetically charged space that functions as more than simply an idealized society of liberty and mobility, and the overdetermined tropes associated with France and Frenchness figure strategically as challenges to dominant constructions of race, gender, power, and citizenship.

In a letter to NAACP luminaries Mr. and Mrs. Arthur Spingarn in 1925, Fauset complains that the French were "a little too coldly rationalistic and entirely too chauvinistic."[7] While acknowledging that being in France "is just heaven. Particularly for one of us," Fauset also recognizes that France is far from a paradise: "I should hate to be genuinely poor and have to live in Paris or anywhere else in France for that matter."[8] She appreciates, however, the transformative power of Paris, enjoying the delicious irony of dancing at a *bal nègre* with an acquaintance who "had never danced a step" before he came to Paris, but now danced exquisitely: "Well, I was outdone, a colored man from America who had learned to jazz over here!" In an interview with Pierre Loving in the *Paris Tribune*, Fauset declares:

> I like Paris because I find something here, something of integrity, which I seem to have strangely lost in my own country. It is the simplest of all to say that I like to live among people and surroundings where I am not always conscious of "thou shalt not." I am colored and wish to be known as colored, but sometimes I have felt that my growth as a writer has been hampered in my own country. And so—but only temporarily—

I have fled from it. I adore my own people and I like to be among them, despite the race issue in America.

The "integrity" Fauset attributes to her first visit to Paris derives neither from Frenchness itself—as some sort of autochthonous characteristic—nor from expatriate liberation. Rather, it emerges through the tensions and displacements such affective relations foster within her everyday experience.

Fauset's first published depiction of her experiences in France, which appeared in *The Crisis* in 1915, provides an early example of her use of the Parisian imaginary and lays the groundwork for her later, more mature writing. The essay, "Tracing Shadows," is ostensibly a description of the France she saw in the summer of 1914 at the outbreak of the Great War, as well as a meditation on the French national character. Yet the central preoccupation of the essay—as the title indicates—concerns problems of interpretation and creativity. As in many of her early articles and stories, the piece starts with the presentation of a truism: in this case, the notion that "Coming events cast their shadows before." The essay then situates its author on a train ride from Calais to Paris, during which a fellow passenger remarks on the "terrible news" of the murder of the Archduke and Archduchess of Austria. Fauset thus inscribes herself as both a witness to and interpreter of history. In so doing she makes several bold claims for a black woman's authority and agency, not only in recording history but also in asserting the value of her own imaginative writing as the medium that both dramatizes and displaces this history. The "France" of this essay is primarily a fanciful construction—an arena of creative innocence which, in Fauset's writing, speaks more to the narrator's imagination than anything else. The essay, despite its ominous topic, is an almost playful testimony to Fauset's story-making faculties, her own declaration to the world that she is a writer "upon whom nothing is lost." Indeed, the essay's opening lines position the narrator as an imaginative observer: "Few things, it seems to me, offer so much ground for speculation as the psychology of the proverb. I like to pause and consider the series of striking incidents and co-incidences which have finally moved some man to utter the remark which afterwards becomes the trite aphorism of all the ages" (247). Paris becomes the site of pleasure against which world events can be both measured and suspended: "I wonder," Fauset's speaker intercedes, "if great joy ever bursts on one with the same unexpectedness as does disaster" (248).

The narrator does not mention her racial identity at all in this text. Although this was her first trip to Paris, Fauset departs from the narrative conventions established by nineteenth- and early twentieth-century African American visitors to Europe. Writers such as Frederick Douglass, Mary Church Terrell, James Weldon Johnson and others describe their experiences of being "de-raced" in the course of European travel; these "de-racing" scenes often take place mid-Atlantic on board a ship. They then use their experiences abroad to generate comparisons, almost always to the detriment of the United States, between their treatment in France and in America. Fauset's narrative de-races itself far more definitively. The author does not need a doorman, a waiter, or a white American shipboard table companion to authorize the claim that "color does not matter" here; there is no one moment, either mid-Atlantic or in a café, that brings home to the protagonist that Jim Crow is behind her on the receding western horizon. The narrator of Fauset's essay talks to other "ladies" and they talk to her; men treat her and her traveling companion with respect and sometimes gallantry; they check into hotels, change money, and picnic in the park without any mention of color. All we know about the text's narrator is that she is a traveler, a writer, and a student of an unnamed discipline, writing under the byline of "Jessie Fauset." The narrator turns herself and her small group of fellow travelers into almost generic figures of tourists, referring to them only as "The Musician," "Our Lady of Leisure," "The Artist," and "The Other Student" (Fauset herself, presumably, is "The Student"), although several people they encounter in their Parisian adventures are given names, fanciful or true. In France, identities other than racial ones can come to the fore, and one is free not to be "raced" in any situation.

Throughout "Tracing Shadows," Fauset reminds the reader of the consciousness constructing the narrative, repeatedly using the authorial "I" and drawing attention to the work involved in recalling, selecting, and organizing apparently random incidents, as well as interpreting and recognizing connections between them. The speaker is frequently the subject of verbs such as "supposing," "imagining," knowing," "believing," "hoping," and "fancying," and thus actively engages her senses as she sees, hears, tastes, and touches the city of Paris. The brief essay maintains attention on three discrete moments simultaneously: the summer of 1914, the time of writing the following year, and the intervening months of reflection and connecting the "shadows" to the events that eventually unfolded between the summer and the process of writing. The simultaneity of these moments on the page underscores the narrator's role in creating the meaning of the connections she is "tracing," establishing the relations among incidents and their recollection, just as former slave writers used a constant juxtaposition of their slave existence and current free status as a writer as a trope in their narratives.[9]

"In that time, I think, my brain must have become a camera," Fauset writes of her weeks in France (249). Her authority derives not, however, from her invisible recording of French characters, events, and feelings, but from her subtle framing of the essay itself: though an essay about the onset of war, it centers on specifically female perspectives and forms of authority, starting with her own. Indeed, Fauset's claim for her own authority echoes that of the female American slave writers of the previous century, as it is her own personal experience rather than social status or institutional affiliation that gives her authority to speak: "I am grown-up now. I have lived in two or three large cities. I have seen and known many people. I have seen and felt sorrow and grief and pain" (240). Later, in their hotel, it is another woman, the proprietor's wife, "her eyes red with weeping now, I suppose," who takes up the thread of the story begun by the woman on the train. While her husband performs as a hotel proprietor would on any ordinary day, his wife wonders aloud about what the future might hold in light of the terrible news.

The final scene, which Fauset describes as "the most important because [the] most indicative incident of all," centers on the sorrow of a restaurant proprietor's wife over her husband's departure for the front. Her perseverance with her domestic chores epitomizes French stoicism in the face of disaster. Playing with the domestic and martial connotations of the verb "to shell," the narrator explains:

> Well that was France, that is France. Because of her delicate sensibilities, when her tragic hour came, she wept careless that all the world could see and know, but falter, shrink, hesitate—never! Were peas to be shelled there were her women choking back sobs, and working with eyes too blinded by tears to see. Were guns to be shouldered. (251)

Underscoring the juxtaposition of the time of experiencing and the time of writing, Fauset's "Tracing Shadows" entrusts its historiography of the domestic impact of the oncoming war to a temporal displacement that is characteristic of proverbs. Fauset's figuration of the French Marianne is not the familiar dramatically heroic, bellicose beauty mounting the barricades, but the wife of a petty bourgeois, whose husband had called the possibility of France going to war "absurd" only a week before. From its depictions of the "polyglot woman" on the boat train who provides Fauset with her first social interaction on Continental soil to the tears of a common Frenchwoman, this early travel sketch prefigures Fauset's preoccupation with imaginative agency and the forms of authority and solidarity that a female-identified cosmopolitanism could offer a black woman artist.

Despite the sentimental idealization of France that closes "Tracing Shadows," this early article prefigures themes and commitments that would mark Fauset's later work: the placement of women and their experiences at the center of her writing, a self-conscious exploration of her own agency and authority as a writer, a fascination with France as an arena where issues of national, racial, and gender identities are contested, and an interest in what the experiences of travel, with its attendant dislocations and disruptions, can reveal.

"The voyage, the danger, the foreign language and new customs went to her head like wine."

As is perhaps more familiar to readers, France serves as a significant setting in three of Fauset's four novels, *There Is Confusion* (1924), *Plum Bun* (1928), and *Comedy, American Style* (1933). Here, too, one finds Fauset's protagonists challenging the received image of France. In *Plum Bun*, although Paris "at first charmed and wooed her" (374), the protagonist, Angela, sees the city primarily as a temporary refuge and a place to get necessary work done. When not single-mindedly engrossed in her work, she experiences "periods of utter loneliness and boredom" (376). Although her lover joins her unexpectedly in the city renowned for romance, Fauset emphasizes that the Parisian setting does not contribute to the romantic aspect of the reunion.

Maggie, one of the protagonists of *There Is Confusion*, finds a sense of direction and purpose as a nurse to the African American soldiers in France:

> It was the thing for her. . . . Maggie was taken out of herself completely. The voyage, the danger, the foreign language and new customs went to her head like wine. . . . A new sense of values came to Maggie. (258–59)

Though it is the service to the brave young mistreated soldiers and the drama of war that inspire her, French culture, language, and "foreignness" allow her to be open to completely new experiences and perspectives.

Fauset's last and bitterest novel uses its French setting most vigorously and critically. Teresa Cary, driven by her mother to desire the social and financial security of whiteness, marries a Frenchman after her engagement with a black man is poisoned and broken by her suggestion that he try to escape some of the painful inconveniences of blackness to appease her mother. Teresa discovers that she can gain some financial independence and help her family by tutoring American undergraduates in French. Although Teresa delights in "the precious fillip too that came from speaking a foreign language for the first time in the land of its origin, and finding it succeed," it is significant that "Paris . . . offended her" (168):

> Teresa did not like it. She could see that it was a great, a beautiful city but staying as they did on the Avenue de l'Opéra, near the Rue de la Paix, she found it too full of the remembered noise and traffic of New York, too cosmopolitan, not enough French and far, far, too hot. . . . And over everything and everywhere Americans, loud-voiced, determined, pushing. . . . (166)

However, the appealing smaller and slower city of Toulouse, where she has come to improve her French in an effort to start her own French school in the United States, becomes a prison after her marriage to a domineering, miserly French professor. Teresa, another of Fauset's disillusioned French teacher characters, has fatally misread her husband and the possibilities of a stable, free life in France distant from the vexations of the American color line.[10] Her entrepreneurial desire, developed out of her attraction to the French language, becomes a mere pipe-dream when she chooses what she assumes will be an easier life that will both free her from as well as appease her mother. She betrays her younger brother, who commits suicide when she fails to offer him a home with her as an alternative to his loveless home with his mother, and "settle[s] down to an existence that [is] colorless, bleak, and futile" (183). Her mother, Olivia, is condemned to a lonely and disconnected life in a shabby Parisian hotel, though she continues to lie to herself and the American divorcée with whom she tries unsuccessfully to kindle a friendship:

> "I'm like you, Mrs. Reynolds, I love the life and the freedom of Paris. It is so broadening to live here. Think of the people one meets," said Olivia, oblivious to the fact that she had met no one in Paris, not a soul, except this woman from Connecticut who had a part interest in the world's smallest hairdressing establishment. (324)

Olivia's Paris is as small and constrained as a prison cell, consisting of a predictable route she shares with the other dislocated and untethered American woman:

> They walked down teeming *rue Sèvres*, entered the *pâtisserie*, then passed the delicatessens with the horrid little stuffed

larks, reassembled in the window with their miserable feathers and their toothpick legs. They turned the corner past the cobbler, in his five-by-six-foot shop, working slowly, painfully under the light of a kerosene lamp. At the far end of *la rue Romain* they entered the courtyard of Olivia's pension. (322)

Despite the crowded streets and air of what Fauset called in *Plum Bun* "the intent application of the business of living. So noticeable in the French" (322), Olivia's Parisian existence is much like that of the "horrid" larks and their facsimile of living.

Fauset's three essays on her own year-long residency in Paris while she studied French at the Sorbonne in 1925 reveal the various and sophisticated ways that she deployed the idea of "Frenchness" in her explorations of questions of identity, dislocation, and ideologies of race, gender, and class. As in her fiction, Fauset suggests that translation always involves representation, and vice versa. The processes of translation and representation are particularly hazardous for black women, who at the time of her writing were not in control of discourses of race and gender, and had few forums in which they could exercise and affirm their own perceptions of themselves in a racialized patriarchy. Taken as a piece, Fauset's French writing exposes and explores the fissures as well as the possibilities of a transnational feminist racial consciousness, a "French imaginary" that has the courage to engage the ambiguities and complications of gender, class, and assumptions about national identity on the part of both beholder and beheld. Fauset's multilayered identity as both implied and explicit narrator in these works questions the ontological status of the categories of nation, race, and gender that are fundamental to any black diasporic political project. Emmy's question "What's the difference?" (later repeatedly echoed by *Plum Bun*'s protagonist Angela) haunts these early narratives with the possibility of the response that finally, there might only be "difference." If this is the case, the political and cultural project, which depends upon cross-cultural and transnational articulation, is doomed to failure. These stories' depiction of misplaced and disappointed idealism, vignettes of misreading as well as being misread, and deft evocation and undermining of stereotypes remind us of the difficulties of being a black cosmopolitan feminist in the New Negro and Négritude era. In Fauset's texts, the black woman's creative subjectivity dramatizes the problems of modernist ideas of the self as a fragmented, fluid consciousness negotiating a world whose only coherence is that imposed upon it by the imagination. The New Negro and later the Négritude writers discovered the difficulties inherent in delegitimizing essentialist ideas of race left over from nineteenth-century pseudo-science while trying to identify qualities of "Négritude" which could transcend national, social, and linguistic identities upon which modern black people could build a global agenda for political liberation and black culture building. France, far from being an idealized space of social and artistic liberation for educated black women, represents the challenges of constructing a black feminism in the modern world.

Notes

The author gratefully acknowledges permission to quote from the Alain Locke Papers and from the Arthur B. Spingarn Papers, Moorland-Spingarn Research Center, Howard University.

1. Vivian May, in her biography of Anna Julia Cooper, argues that "Cooper rejects the notion that colonialism and slavery entail a simple one-sided relationship or unidirectional power dynamic. That is, by focusing on the political life of Saint-Domingue as well as the transatlantic circuits of communication and ideas, Cooper stretches the bounds of what constitutes the French nation . . . and alters the parameters of who should be considered among history's central agents (i.e., gens de couleur, free blacks, and slaves, and not just the principal 'French' characters of this history)" (111). Citing the work of David Pellow, Charles Lemert, and Esme Bahn, May contends that Cooper's move was a risky one, given the Eurocentric, white supremacist bias of the French academy, as epitomized by her chief doctoral examiner, Célestin Bouglé, who believed in "an evolutionary hierarchy of world civilizations" (73).

2. Jane Nardal, letter to Alain Locke, Alain Locke Papers, Box 164 Folder 74.

3. It is difficult not to also read into this vignette an allusion to the so-called "Hottentot Venus," Sarah Baartman, who was put on display in circuses and studied as a racial specimen by eminent scientists, among them Georges Cuvier and other members of the Académie Française who were particularly fascinated by her genitalia.

4. This question is also a major ground note of *Plum Bun*, as the protagonist Angela realizes that racial identity is in the eye of the beholder, and not inherent in any physical or internal characteristics.

5. On Fauset's fairy-tale plots, see for example Deborah E. McDowell's introduction to *Plum Bun*.

6. See, for example, her "Éveil de conscience de race/Awakening of Race Consciousness."

7. Arthur B. Spingarn Papers, Box 3.
8. Jessie Fauset, letter to Harold Jackman, 21 December 1924, James Weldon Johnson Memorial Collection, Beinecke Rare Book and Manuscript Library, Yale University.
9. The most famous example of this trope probably appears in Frederick Douglass's *Narrative* of 1845, as he meditates on how the pen with which he is writing his words would fit into the gash he received from his whipping as a slave.
10. Fauset herself was a reluctant and resentful French teacher, and resorted to teaching only when she was unable to find writing or editorial work to support herself.

Works Cited

Alpha, Jenny. *Paris Créole Blues*. Paris: Editions du Toucan, 2011.
Boittin, Jennifer. *Colonial Metropolis: The Urban Grounds of Anti-Imperialism and Feminism in Interwar Paris*. Lincoln: U of Nebraska P, 2010.
Du Bois, W. E. B. "An Essay toward the History of the Black Man in the Great War." *Writings*. Ed. Nathan Huggins. Cambridge: Cambridge UP, 1986. 879-922.
Edwards, Brent Hayes. *The Practice of Diaspora: Literature, Translation, and the Rise of Black Internationalism*. Cambridge: Harvard UP, 2003.
Fauset, Jessie. *Comedy, American Style*. New Brunswick: Rutgers UP, 2009.
———. "Dark Algiers the White." *The Crisis* 29 (Apr.-May 1925): 16-22.
———. "Emmy." *The Crisis* 5 (Dec. 1912, Jan. 1913): 79-87, 134-42.
———. "The Enigma of the Sorbonne." *The Crisis* 29 (Mar. 1925): 216-19.
———. *Plum Bun: A Novel without a Moral*. Boston: Northeastern UP, 2003.
———. *There Is Confusion*. Boston: Northeastern UP, 1989.
———. "'There Was One Time!': A Story of Spring." *The Crisis* 13 (Apr. 1917, May 1917): 14, 11-15.
———. "Tracing Shadows." *The Crisis* 10 (Sep. 1915): 247-51.
Ford, Hugh, ed. *The Left Bank Revisited: Selections from the Paris Tribune 1917-1934*. University Park: Pennsylvania State UP, 1973.
Glissant, Edouard. *Caribbean Discourse: Selected Essays*. Trans. Michael Dash. Charlottesville: U Virginia P, 1992.
Horth, Roberte. "Un Histoire sans importance/A thing of no importance." *La Revue du Monde Noir/The Review of the Black World*. (1931-32): 48-50. Rpt. Paris: Jean-Michel Place, 1992. 118-20.
Hughes, Langston. *The Big Sea: An Autobiography*. New York: Hill and Wang, 1940.
Johnson, James Weldon. *Along This Way*. New York: Viking Press, 1973.

Locke, Alain, ed. *The New Negro*. New York: Athenaeum, 1968.
May, Vivian M. *Anna Julia Cooper, Visionary Black Feminist: A Critical Introduction*. New York: Routledge, 2007.
Nardal, Jane. "L'internationalisme noir." *Dépêche Africaine* (Feb. 15, 1928): 5.
Nardal, Paulette. "Eveil de la conscience de race/Awakening of Race Consciousness." *La Revue du Monde Noir* (1932): 25–34. Rpt. Paris: Jean-Michel Place, 1992. 343–52.
Walker, Corey D. B. "'Of the Coming of John [and Jane]': African American Intellectuals in Europe, 1888–1938." *Amerikastudien/American Studies* 47.1 (2002): 7–22.

CHAPTER 4

Writing Home
Comparative Black Modernism and Form in Jean Toomer and Aimé Césaire

Jennifer M. Wilks

If I could feel that I came to the South to face it. If I, the dream (not what is weak and afraid in me) could become the face of the South. How my lips would sing for it, my songs being the lips of its soul.
—Jean Toomer, *Cane*

"Embrassez-moi sans crainte . . . Et si je ne sais que parler, c'est pour vous que je parlerai." . . . "Ma bouche sera la bouche des malheurs qui n'ont point de bouche, ma voix, la liberté de celles qui s'affaissent au cachot du désespoir."

"Embrace me without fear . . . And if all I can do is speak, it is for you I shall speak." . . . "My mouth shall be the mouth of those calamities that have no mouth, my voice the freedom of those who break down in the solitary confinement of despair."
—Aimé Césaire, *Cahier d'un retour au pays natal*

While there is no evidence of an actual encounter between the enigmatic American author Jean Toomer and Martinican poet-statesman Aimé Césaire, the many points of convergence between their works illustrate the ways in which interwar African diasporic intellectual communities developed in print as well as in person. The role of Paris in this multilayered development is key in that the French capital not only hosted those diasporic encounters that did take place, such as that between African American Langston Hughes and Martinican René Maran,[1] but also, as the center of the *vogue nègre* (Negro vogue) and a diverse expatriate community, opened up that which Brent Edwards calls "transnational circuits of expressive culture" (18). Thus, although Toomer traveled to Paris in the mid- to late 1920s and Césaire lived there between 1931 and 1939,[2] what interests me more than literal historical gaps are virtual literary connections. The Harlem Renaissance was shaped in large part by francophiles Jessie Redmon Fauset and Alain Locke, who followed the emergence of black "expressive culture" on both sides of the Atlantic, and African American literature reached Francophone audiences through translations in the *Anthologie de la nouvelle poésie américaine* (1928) and pre-Négritude periodicals such as *Légitime défense* (1932) and *La Revue du monde noir* (1931–1932), the latter a bilingual publication coedited by anglophile Paulette Nardal. Indeed, the strong impression left by Harlem Renaissance depictions of African Americans as independent, proud, and culturally distinct subjects prompted Aimé Césaire to observe, "Ils ont été les premiers à dire: 'Le Noir est beau'" (They were the first to say, "Black is beautiful") (qtd. in Fabre, "Du mouvement" 149; my translation).

Césaire's statement is brought to life by the striking resonance between the two epigraphs—one, the tortured musings of Toomer's Ralph Kabnis, the other, the tentative overture of Césaire's unnamed persona. Both bespeak the manner in which the tension between community and creation informs African diasporic modernisms differently than their French and Anglo American counterparts. In an essay on early French readings of *Cane,* Michel Fabre contends that most critics of the 1920s overlooked the "interplay of the folk tradition of communal wisdom and the voice of the solitary modernist" in Toomer's groundbreaking text ("Reception" 204). This critical oversight casts the folk and the modern, the communal and the individual, as competing rather than complementary elements of modernism, yet it is precisely in such pairings that I locate the black modernist aesthetics of Toomer and Césaire.[3] While *Cane* exudes the "'folk spirit'" that Toomer encountered during his two-month stay in Sparta, Georgia (McKay 32), Césaire's *Cahier,* partially composed during his eight-year sojourn in Europe, renounces "poetic expression for its own sake" in order to present a persona who "sees himself as both poet and leader, the spokesman for a people not yet aware of their uniqueness" (Arnold 146). Toomer and Césaire not only write to the U.S. South and to the Caribbean, then, seeking to restore the link between an exiled modernist subject and his respective ancestral or geographic home, but also write of both locales, transforming them from noncoeval, premodern backdrops into stages for defining modernist encounters. Through these literary migrations, themselves mirrors of the writers' physical relocations, Toomer and Césaire recast the modernist journey from the familiar to the foreign, reduce the gap between the individual and the collective, and revise their native lands as complicated sites that are as concrete as they are metaphorical (Arnold 147). What results are texts that challenge not only the role of place in constructing modernist identities but also the notions of modernity on which such constructions are based.

Modernity/Modernism

If from an Old World perspective modernity might signal the march of progress and the attendant emergence of new economic, national, and cultural identities (a prime example of this march being Christopher Columbus's 1492 voyage), the New World reality is that such models often do not accommodate African American and Caribbean perspectives. On the contrary, the designation of 1492 as inaugural modern moment posits modernity as that which happens to, rather than that which is effected by, indigenous American populations and the enslaved and indentured transplants who succeeded them: "if Columbus's 'discovery' of the Americas and his initial encounter with the peoples of the New World have paradigmatic value in the European episteme because they usher in a brave new world, a world of modernity and modernist forms, . . . these events also trigger a contrary effect on the people who are 'discovered' and conquered" (Gikandi 1). Paul Gilroy extends the critique of Eurocentric narratives of modernity by faulting them for discounting slavery, which is either deemed the "special property [of blacks] rather than a part of the ethical and intellectual heritage of the West as a whole" or declared "a premodern residue that disappears once it is revealed to be fundamentally incompatible with enlightened rationality and capitalist industrial production" (49). As a result, to question modernity, to move beyond the limited options of ahistorical concern and premodern residue, is to interrogate not only historical timelines but also the soundness of the historical enterprise as a whole. It is, in brief, to assert the role of formerly silenced voices and bodies in the formation of the brave New World.

Given the degree to which notions of progress always already inform concepts of modernity, one may ask whether these newly asserted New World voices can indeed exorcise the specter of Columbus. Edouard Glissant, deeming History "un fantasme fortement opératoire de l'Occident, contemporain précisément du temps où il était seul à 'faire' l'histoire du monde (a highly functional fantasy of the West, originating at precisely the time when it alone "made" the history of the world; 227, 64), notes the persistence with which totalizing historical narratives trade the disruptive complications of the conquest for cohesive stories of European expansion.[4] Yet rather than posit a Caribbean-centered seamlessness, Glissant embraces complication as constitutive of and even necessary for American literary production:

> Il leur faut tout assumer tout d'un coup, le combat, le militantisme, l'enracinement, la lucidité, la méfiance envers soi, l'absolu d'amour, la forme du paysage, le nu des villes, les dépassements et les entêtements. C'est ce que j'appelle notre irruption dans la modernité. (330)
> They [national literatures] must include all at once struggle, aggressiveness, belonging, lucidity, distrust of self, absolute love, contours of the landscape, emptiness of the cities, victories, and confrontations. That is what I call our irruption into modernity. (100)[5]

Marked by renegotiation and reinvention as much as dissociation, the Glissantian rendering of modernity recasts African American and Caribbean subjects' relationship to the chain of events set in motion by Columbus. What was a static self-other dichotomy in Old World paradigms becomes a "dynamic state" in Glissant's New World model, and it is in this cultural and theoretical fluidity that alternative modernities emerge (Richardson 30).

The construct of modernity is not to be dispensed with, then, but reconsidered through Caribbean and African American lenses. Accordingly, J. Michael Dash dates Caribbean modernity from the 1804 Haitian Revolution "because it was in Haiti that Caribbean thought first emerged as a contestation of the reductive mystification of colonialism" (42). Neither African nor European yet both, Haiti asserted its independence by asserting itself as a "new composite culture" (45). As befits the political context of the late-nineteenth-century United States, where the emergence of an independent African America was not imminent, Houston A. Baker Jr. traces the advent of African American modernity to the rise of a national leader: Booker T. Washington. Baker designates Washington's 1895 "Atlanta Exposition Address" the inaugural moment of African American *modernism,* but his choice echoes Dash's identification of Caribbean *modernity* with the assertion of black agency through radical social change. Baker maintains that, when read in the larger context of *Up from Slavery* (Washington's autobiography and the volume in which the speech was reprinted), the Atlanta address represents a seismic shift in African American political discourse. If minstrelsy was a "device . . . designed to remind white consciousness that black men and women are *mis-speakers* bereft of humanity," Baker writes, Washington's discourse was a device that appropriated that tradition in order to "[set] forth strategies of address . . . designed for Afro-American empowerment" (21, 31). This revision of Washington's career encourages a provocative comparison between his appropriation of minstrelsy to champion African American agency and Toussaint L'Ouverture's use of Enlightenment principles to foster Haitian independence. Despite the apparent gulf between Washington the accommodationist and L'Ouverture the revolutionary, both examples demonstrate that which Gilroy considers a key element of black modernity: the reciprocity of culture and politics (38).

As a means of recognizing the prominence of plurality and ambivalence in life in African America and the Caribbean, I posit all of the aforementioned defining moments—Columbus's New World "encounter," the Haitian Revolution, and Washington's "Atlanta Exposition Address"—as points along a continuum of black modernity rather than competing historical coordinates. The unexpected echoes between Washington's rhetoric and L'Ouverture's philosophy suggest the collective, multivoiced accounts that Glissant invests with the power to revise History: "'Là où se joignent les histoires des peuples, hier réputés sans histoire, finit l'Histoire.' (Avec un grand H.)" (History [with a capital *H*] ends where the histories of those people once reputed to be without history come together; 227, 64). If, in the settlement of the Caribbean, otherness emerged as a category to distinguish between conquered and conqueror, enslaved and free, in the declaration of Haitian independence it became that which separated Haitian from foreigner, Caribbean from European.[6] In advocating for African Americans, Washington, however problematic his approach, used his rhetorical skills to relocate blackness from the minstrel show to the national stage. When reconsidered individually and collectively, these stories provide a hemispheric framework within which to read African American and Caribbean modernities as well as foreshadow the struggles to come for the black modernist writers whose negotiations of artistry and mastery would echo their historic predecessors' interrogations of humanity and citizenship.

Much like the early colonial period in the Americas, the early twentieth century ushered in its own brave new world, one "of science, war, technology, and imperialism" (Baker 4). When imperialist expansion increasingly forced the West to confront its colonial and/or domestic others, European and Anglo American writers seeking to process the altered social landscapes produced by this confrontation developed "a fresh and unprecedented aesthetic response . . ., generally by way of formal, structural, and linguistic innovation" (Jameson 50). As members of groups whose cultural and political emergence contributed to the perceived upheaval, however, African American and Francophone Caribbean writers had a much different relationship with language, literature, and form. Often their work was "faulted for its 'failure' to produce *vital, original, effective,* or 'modern' art" (xiii, emphasis in original), as Baker notes was the case for many Harlem Renaissance authors, or, when deemed innovative, was attributed to natural impulse. Jean-Paul Sartre's 1948 essay *Orphée Noir* (*Black Orpheus*) offers a classic example of this conflation of modernist criticism with primitivist stereotypes. After a careful comparison of the respective politics of surrealist and Négritude poets, Sartre attributes the latter group's linguistic experimentation to atavism more than art:

> C'est le rythme, en effet, qui cimente ces multiples aspects de l'âme noire, c'est lui qui communique sa légèreté nietzschéenne à ces lourdes intuitions dionysiaques, c'est le rythme—tam-tam, jazz, bondissement de ces poèmes—qui figure la temporalité de l'*existence* nègre. (xxxv)
> In effect, rhythm cements the multiple aspects of the black soul, communicates its Nietzschian lightness with heavy Dionysian intuitions; rhythm—tam-tam, jazz, the "bounding" of these poems—represents the temporality of Negro *existence.* (43)

More striking than Sartre's essentialism alone is the resemblance between his presentation of Négritude poets and Eurocentric History's placement of New World subjects vis-à-vis modernity. That is, the refusal or inability to read Francophone writers—and their African American counterparts, if one returns to Baker's critique of cursory dismissals of Harlem Renaissance literature—as modernists or, for that matter, creative agents posits modernism as that which can draw from nonstandard, noncanonical sources (as in T. S. Eliot's use of dialect in *Sweeney Agonistes* [1926] and André Breton's celebration of the Caribbean in *Martinique charmeuse de serpents* [1948]) but not originate in them or in the cultural groups with which they are associated.[7]

But as I insisted earlier on retaining the term "modernity," so I will insist here on using the word "modernism." Much of the African American and Francophone Caribbean literature of the early twentieth century is not insufficiently modernist but distinctly so. Although assumptions such as Sartre's complicated the "linguistic rebellion" characteristic of modernism for writers of color, in the U.S. context "modern writers of both races [African and Anglo American] were attempting in dramatically different ways to free" language from "the political and cultural forces that were constricting" it (North 11). Similarly, the depersonalization augured by early-twentieth-century science, technology, and mass culture and targeted by canonical modernism recurs as a theme in the work of black writers such as Aimé Césaire, René Maran, Jean Toomer, and Nella Larsen.[8] What complicates modernism for these and other black artists is not an inability to access certain creative tools but the difficulties posed by the intersection of said tools with the political undercurrents of the various modernist discourses. Where black modernist embraces of nonstandard language entailed negotiating the fine line between cultural celebration and self-exoticization, any decision by African American and Caribbean writers to reject mass society for personal autonomy likewise risked being overdetermined by the competing politics of racial uplift and racial or colonial assimilation. Such tensions confirm the Glissantian characterization of modernity as a multifaceted "irruption" rather than a neat, linear process and, as demonstrated by Jean Toomer's prose-poetry cycle *Cane* and Aimé Césaire's epic prose-poem *Cahier d'un retour au pays natal (Notebook of a Return to My Native Land)*, shape the very dynamics of comparative black modernism.

Jean Toomer's Song to the South

The artistic, cultural, and political contradictions of black modernism are perhaps nowhere more evident than at the intersection of Jean Toomer, the man, and *Cane*, the manuscript. Born to a fair-skinned but black-identifying family in Washington, D.C., in 1894, Toomer claimed to belong to the "American" race (McKay 21).[9] Although he considered his choice a conscious effort to acknowledge all of the "seven bloodlines" which constituted his heritage (McKay 57), Toomer's stance nonetheless corresponds to Langston Hughes's description of "the racial mountain" facing African American artists as "this urge within the race toward whiteness, the desire to . . . be as little Negro and as much American as possible" (1267). With his repeated refusals to identify as "Negro," Toomer seemed at best to elect the role of the solitary modernist independent of any community, racial or otherwise, and at worst to exhibit what Hughes diagnoses as a "desire to run away spiritually from [the] race" (1267). Yet even as Toomer rejected racial labels, he viewed himself and his art as a means of rescuing African American culture, especially its rural variants, from the early-twentieth-century threats of primitivism, propaganda, and industrialization. In his first published writings, Toomer sought to depict African American life as it was, not as it was imagined or spun by the Anglo and African American intelligentsia, and to record an experience he sensed was "'walking in to die on the modern desert'" (McKay 32). His ultimate goal was not to separate African American from American culture but to ensure the recognition of the former's place within the latter.

If *Cane*, the brilliant collection of fiction and poetry that resulted, realized Toomer's artistic goal, it also frustrated his personal quest to dissociate himself from a single racial identity. Toomer faced the challenge articulated by Houston Baker in his critique of the underestimation of Harlem Renaissance literature: friends, publishers, and critics alike associated Toomer's literary accomplishment with his African American heritage.[10] How, then, should one read *Cane*, with its two sections inspired by Toomer's brief tenure teaching at a black school in rural Georgia joined by a middle section about African American urban life in the nation's capital and points north? Is the text, which evokes the South as an ancestral home, a Toomerian "return to the native land" where internal migrations speak to racial exile and return as much as if not more than geographic and cultural ones? How does *Cane*, in spite—or perhaps because—of its author's self-identification, exemplify the African diasporic modern(ist) concerns of renegotiation, reinvention, and fluidity? In brief, should it be a surprise that a seminal black modernist text, written in a dynamic, internationalist context in which publications met where people could not and intellectual communities coalesced, however conditionally, across linguistic and cultural differences, was written by an author who refused to be called "black"?

In his 1923 essay "The South in Literature," Toomer presents the region not as a racial native land, but as a national one: "The South has a peasantry, rooted in its soil, such as neither the North nor West possesses. Therefore, it has a basic adjustment to its physical environment (in sharp contrast to the restless maladjustment of the Northern pioneer) the expression of which the general cultural body stands in sore need of" (11).

Bringing the rootedness of one region to the maladjustment of the other, *Cane*, as did its author, refuses rupture and instead yields an aesthetic fusion of South and North, African American and American. The inaccessible rural beauty "Karintha" finds an urban counterpart in "Avey," the woman visionary from "Fern" foreshadows the unwanted prophet of "Box Seat," and the pine needles and sawmill smoke that envelop Karintha rustle and smolder again in "Carma," "Song of the Son," and "Georgia Dusk" before setting the mood for the fevered reveries of "Kabnis," *Cane's* final section. With these abundant symbiotic relationships, embodied in the text's shifts between prose/poetry, poetry/song, fiction/drama, Toomer produces literary correspondence and inscription out of racial ambivalence and exile.

Despite his text's mutability, Toomer presents both South and North as spaces fraught with the burdens of New World modernity. Unlike Alain Locke's New Negro, who rose out of the ashes of the southern-affiliated Old Negro and gravitated toward urban centers such as Harlem, the black modernist subject of "Kabnis" emerges through a journey that reverses the migration heralded by Locke and shares none of its triumphant, optimistic spirit. The drama opens with northern transplant Ralph Kabnis contemplating his relocation to Sempter, a small southern town: "If I could feel that I came to the South to face it. If I, the dream (not what is weak and afraid in me) could become the face of the South. How my lips would sing for it, my songs being the lips of its soul" (81). This individual song to the South remains unrealized, however, because the character's dream-self cannot accommodate his human weakness, here graphically rendered separate by parentheses. Gikandi argues that Caribbean modernism is characterized in part by "the negotiation of a historically engendered split between the self and its world, between this self and the language it uses" (20); what Toomer illustrates in the American context of "Kabnis," I would argue, is what happens when such negotiations fail. When confronted by menacing night winds, Kabnis, rather than articulating his fear and isolation, responds primarily with unconvincing variations on a theme of stoicism and self-reliance. As the piece progresses, he seems only to unravel further, losing his livelihood and will as he struggles to comprehend his surroundings. The closing image of the character is one of a man defeated, a spirit drained: "And then, seeing Carrie's eyes upon him, he swings the pail carelessly and with eyes downcast and swollen, trudges upstairs to the work-shop. Carrie's gaze follows him till he is gone" (116). It would seem that the once aspiring poet has become a voiceless, alienated soul.

Reading the conclusion through Fabre's juxtaposition of "communal wisdom" and "solitary modernis[m]," however, suggests another prospect, that of Kabnis's particular failure as a collective point of departure. For Toomer counters his positioning of Kabnis as individual protagonist—through the drama's title, its attention to Kabnis's interior life, and, despite Halsey's assurance that Kabnis "aint like most northern niggers" (86), the schoolteacher's outsider status—with the introduction of the character's double and foil: the mysterious old man who resides in Halsey's basement. In other words, the text itself negotiates the split that haunts Kabnis. The blind, near mute Father, later christened Father John, seems the antithesis of the South's would-be troubadour, but Toomer bridges the distance between the two men through the speech of an intermediary:

> Lewis: Father John it is from now on . . .
> Slave boy whom some Christian mistress taught to read the Bible. Black man who saw Jesus in the ricefields, and began preaching to his people. Moses- and Christ-words used for songs. Dead blind father of a muted folk who feel their way upward to a life that crushes or absorbs them. (Speak, Father!) Suppose your eyes could see, old man. (The years hold hands. O Sing!) Suppose your lips . . . (105)

Lewis's facetious elegy to the elderly, dark-skinned former slave recalls the younger, fair-skinned intellectual's quest to speak for and serenade others. Just as effectively, though, the prevalence of religious imagery also forecloses any idealistic collapse of elder and youth, leader and community, by recalling the "mingled fear, contempt, and pity" that organized religion produces in Kabnis (89). Toomer proposes instead that these voices be joined antiphonally, as indicated when Carrie scolds a feverish Kabnis for taunting Father: "Brother Ralph, is that your best Amen?" (116). Kabnis's subsequent walk upstairs is sorrowful, then, because he squanders the opportunity to join his words to those of Father John. Kabnis longs to sing for the South, but the text suggests that in order to produce what Houston Baker calls the defining component of black modernism—"poetic mastery discovered as a function of deformative folk sound" (93)—the character must first learn to join his voice to those of the people and natural forces around him.

Kabnis's inability to transform personal vision into collective song echoes an expressive bind that torments figures throughout *Cane*. Also a transplanted northerner, the narrator of "Fern" continually alludes to but ultimately does not articulate the "something [he] would do for" the title character (16). His stunning opening description of her eyes suggests that the unnamed accomplishment might involve a poetic tribute: "Face flowed into her eyes. Flowed in soft cream foam and plaintive ripples, in such a way that wherever your glance may momentarily have rested, it immediately thereafter wavered in the direction of her eyes" (14). Yet just as Kabnis's dream escapes him when confronted with life in Sempter, so the narrator's lyric sensuality proves elusive when he finds himself alone with Fern; an evening walk together leaves Fern enthralled and the narrator mystified. Suggesting the manner in which the sketch's gender politics mirror the cultural politics of black modernism, McKay traces the impossibility of the narrator's promise to his "inability to see [Fern] as a person rather than only as a woman" and contends that, "[a]s a metaphor for the relationship between the poet and the folk culture, the narrative points to the problems that those like Jean Toomer, removed in time and place from it, face in accurately trying to record and interpret it" (111). Like Kabnis, the narrator fails to grasp the importance of seeing those he wishes to represent as partners in the project of modernist expression rather than simply as beings in need of representation. Shortly after the aborted walk with Fern, her suitor returns North, apparently defeated.

With the conflicted urbanites in *Cane's* middle section, Toomer alters the dynamic between poet and folk by reconfiguring the landscape in which the two encounter each other. In "Box Seat," Dan is a poor southern migrant adrift in the social sea of Washington, D.C.'s African American community. If geography has distanced Dan from the night wind that preoccupies Kabnis, it does not release him from the strain that the wind symbolizes, that of reconciling one's interior self with the external world. As a result, when Dan manages to sing early in the story, the sounds he produces are neither beautiful nor harmonious but "shrill," painful, and discordant with his surroundings (56). If fully realized, Toomer suggests, Dan's song would be one of liberation, a means of freeing himself and his beloved Muriel from the self-censorship and internalized racism of bourgeois propriety. Indeed, Muriel reasons to herself that she cannot love Dan because, although he is able to save her, he refuses to do so: ". . . the town wont let me love you, Dan. Dont you know? You could make it let me if you would. Why wont you? Youre selfish. I'm not strong enough to buck it. Youre too selfish to buck it, for me. I wish you'd go. You irritate me. Dan, please go" (58–59). It is as if Muriel wishes to be rescued from the very "proper," propagandistic blackness that Toomer desired to counter. What Muriel does not confess is that she is unwilling to accept the ostracism that Dan's intervention, whether in the private sphere of her parlor or in the public one of the Lincoln Theater, would entail. Dan may be a liberator—from his childhood anointing "in a canefield" to his adult resurrection below Muriel's box seat ("A new-world Christ is coming up. Dan comes up"), the story abounds with messianic imagery—but he is a liberator without a people (56, 62). When Dan interrupts the theatrical performance with the outburst "JESUS WAS A LEPER!" he momentarily joins his social awkwardness to the grotesque difference of the dwarf onstage and to the repressive conformity of the audience (66). That Muriel succumbs to the audience's "steel fingers" signals a definitive refusal of the deliverance Dan offers; the story concludes with Toomer's latter-day prophet choosing a solitary peace over collective, conflict-ridden interaction.

The notion of modernism as a "quest for union [and] wholeness" that Dan embraces but his audience rejects seems to have a more likely champion in the suave, mysterious poet-philosopher of the Chicago-set "Bona and Paul" (Sollors 28). Visually different (that is, nonwhite) but racially indeterminate, Paul embodies the plurality that is central to Toomer's aesthetic vision. Indeed, the character's unspecified identity propels the story's narrative. Bona, his white southern classmate, struggles with her simultaneous attraction to Paul and revulsion at his possible blackness, and Art, his irritated roommate, repeatedly asks why Paul refuses to leave his racial closet. Satisfying neither, Paul draws from a dazzling palette to create human and social descriptions that are as much atmospheric as they are visual. In Paul's sight, Art is "a purple fluid, carbon-charged, that effervesces beside him," and Bona's words "are pink petals that fall upon velvet cloth" (73, 74). Yet in a world that demands the same fixed racial moorings sought by Bona and Art, these vivid portraits are unintelligible and unsatisfactory. By story's end, Paul, like Dan before him, experiences an epiphany that promises to transform his abstract philosophy into an articulate vision of modernist multiplicity:

> "I came back to tell you, brother, that white faces are petals of roses. That dark faces are petals of dusk. That I am going out and gather petals. That I am going out and know her whom I brought here with me to these Gardens which are purple like a bed of roses would be at dusk."
>
> Paul and the black man shook hands.
>
> When he reached the spot where they had been standing, Bona was gone. (78)

Using a series of organic symbols ("petals," "roses," "dusk," "[g]ardens"), Toomer connects Paul's dark face with Bona's white one, thus obviating the need for racial distinctions; however, Bona's disappearance leaves the black doorman the lone recipient of Paul's conciliatory message. The unity suggested by the coordinating conjunction of the story's title is destabilized, and the characters' lives on the last page seem as dissonant as the sentences Bona uses to describe Paul on the first: "He is a harvest moon. He is an autumn leaf. He is a nigger" (70).[11] As much as Paul attempts to free his speech from the limits of literalism, his counterpart and the society she represents ultimately champion the efficacy of clear, if also racist and reductive, expression.

The cycle of choral and poetic discord that intimates failure and alienation at the narrative level culminates metatextually in an artistic unity much like that found in Bona's inspired, offensive description. Like the characters' aborted romance, the semantic relationship between "Bona" and "Paul" recalls Glissant's rendering of modernity: "tout d'un coup, le combat, le militantisme, l'enracinement, la lucidité, la méfiance envers soi, l'absolu d'amour" (all at once struggle, aggressiveness, belonging, lucidity, distrust of self, absolute love; 330, 100). Indeed, Bona and Paul's first narrative interaction is a physical, sexually charged encounter on a basketball court. Thus, *Cane* represents that which Kabnis and his counterparts cannot achieve: the transformation of the disjunction between lyrical dreams and social realities from creative obstacle into artistic tool. Perhaps the most eloquent realization of this feat is "Portrait in Georgia," a brief poem from the work's opening section:

> Hair—braided chestnut,
> coiled like a lyncher's rope,
> Eyes—fagots,
> Lips—old scars, or the first red blisters,
> Breath—the last sweet scent cane,
> And her slim body, white as the ash
> of black flesh after flame. (27)

In this physical inventory doubling as the anatomy of a lynching, the benign, almost banal features on the left become, in the move from one side of the dash to the other, ominous signs of racial and sexual oppression, and the woman's white(ned) body becomes a means of expressing the inexpressible: the torture of African American bodies. Although one suspects that Kabnis cannot accommodate verses such as these in his song to the South, Toomer suggests that any composition meant to be collectively as well as personally gratifying must seek to connect, not sever, the beauty of pine needles and the brutality of lynch mobs. In making such connections, *Cane* embraces the spectral past that Gikandi associates with Caribbean modernism and extends it into an African American context.[12] For Toomer as for his character Dan, "Life bends joy and pain, beauty and ugliness, in such a way that no one may isolate them. No one should want to. Perfect joy, or perfect pain, with no contrasting element to define them, would mean a monotony of consciousness, would mean death" (59). With these words and with *Cane* as a whole, Toomer both writes the South and rights the modernist scripts depicting African American culture as a timeless, uncomplicated well of either artistic inspiration or social progress.

Aimé Césaire's Black Modernist Epistle

If Jean Toomer's writing reflects a quest "for a spiritual fusion analogous to the fact of racial intermingling," Aimé Césaire's work represents a search for an artistic fusion analogous to his reality of cultural intermingling (Turner xvi). A native son of Martinique, where he was born in 1913, and an intellectual child of France, in whose schools he was educated, Césaire writes from the perspective of one for whom home could seemingly be any number of places: the Fort-de-France of his youth, the Paris of his university days, or the "Africa of [his] heart" (Arnold 33). His "Caribbean imagination sustained by the tug of both Europe and Africa" was also inspired by the cultural production of North America (Gikandi 10). Although Césaire wrote a thesis "on the theme of the South in black American literature" during the 1937–38 academic year (Arnold 10), his 1941 essay "Introduction à la poésie nègre américaine" brought his first published appreciation of Toomer's work.[13] Along with translations of James Weldon Johnson's "The Creation" (La Création du Monde) and Claude McKay's "America" (A l'Amérique), Toomer's "Harvest Song" (Chant de la Moisson) follows Césaire's meditation on the role of the African American poet and his work.[14] Césaire praises the former for becoming "engagé dans la même aventure que ses héros les moins recommandables" (engaged in the same adventure as his least reputable hero; 38), and it is because of this engagement, he contends, that African American poetry has escaped the primitivist fascination with "[un] paradis nègre" ([a] black paradise) that is little more than "la poétique évasion d'un peuple meurtri" (the poetic avoidance of a wounded people; 40).[15] No such evasion can be found in "Harvest Song," perhaps one of *Cane's* starkest pieces with its depiction of a field laborer's hunger and thirst, nor can it be found in the work with which Césaire began his own poetic engagement: the epic *Cahier d'un retour au pays natal* (*Notebook of a Return to the Native Land*).

Though grand in scope and bold in its conclusion, the *Cahier* offers neither unifying narrative nor unified experience in following its persona's journeys between geographic, cultural, and imaginative sites. Like *Cane,* the *Cahier* unfolds through a tripartite structure in which sections echo their predecessors and foreshadow their successors. An opening movement of prose-poetry depicts the native land, a second departs from prose as the persona ponders the departures that have punctuated his life, and a final movement blends the two forms as the persona marshals the sum of his experiences to articulate—and celebrate—his Négritude. As the persona's consciousness evolves, so, too, does his ability to identify with as well as illustrate his "native land." Where *Cane* is Toomer's restoration of African American life to U.S. culture, the *Cahier* is perhaps, to borrow from Houston Baker, one of Martinique's "first *national* book[s], offering not only a description of streams of tendency in [the island's] collective lives but also an actual construction within its pages of the sounds, songs, images, and signs of [an island]" (85).

Before Césaire's persona arrives at any conclusive reunion or identification, he must first confront the alienation that has characterized his relationship with the Caribbean. This confrontation involves not only an explicit descriptive mode, a writing about, but also an implicit responsive mode, or writing to, through which Césaire counters reductive depictions of his island. Where Toomer's modernist project entails a careful re-presentation of the southern United States, Césaire's includes exploding exoticist notions of the Caribbean as a paradisiacal, timeless "elsewhere":

> Au bout du petit matin bourgeonnant d'anses frêles, les Antilles qui ont faim, les Antilles grêlées de petite vérole, les Antilles dynamitées d'alcool, échouées dans la boue de cette baie, dans la poussière de cette ville sinistrement échouées. (34)
> At the end of the wee hours burgeoning with frail coves, the hungry Antilles, the Antilles pitted with smallpox, the Antilles dynamited by alcohol, stranded in the mud of this bay, in the dust of this town sinisterly stranded. (35)

These opening stanzas demystify the Caribbean as they reclaim the archipelago from the impossibility of postcard perfection. As Mireille Rosello comments, "the [poem's] 'land' is not the idealized homeland towards which nostalgia turns" (180). Nor is it the lush creative source that André Breton would later present in his 1943 essay "Martinique charmeuse de serpents: Un Grand poète noir" (A Great Black Poet: Aimé Césaire): "C'est là et sous les auspices de cette fleur [du balisier] que la mission assignée de nos jours à l'homme de rompre violemment avec les modes de penser et de sentir qui l'ont mené à ne plus pouvoir supporter son existence m'est apparue" (It was there, and under the auspices of this [canna] flower, that the mission assigned in our day to man to break violently with the ways of thinking and feeling that have led him to the point of no longer being able to tolerate his existence, truly appeared to me; 121, 193).[16] Unlike Breton, the Césairean persona sees only inertia and stagnation in the island's geographic and cultural isolation. As his sunrise meditation continues, the persona wonders how a town could be filled with a people "si étrangement bavarde et muette" (strangely chattering and mute), "[une] foule qui ne sait pas faire foule cette foule, on s'en rend compte, si parfaitement seule sous ce soleil" (a throng which does not know how to throng, this throng, clearly so perfectly alone under this sun; 34, 35). This stranded, disjointed people cannot coalesce in order to articulate the pain and despair of its reality, much less to foment surrealist revolt.

The persona does not share the aphasia of his compatriots; nonetheless, it is only in breaking with the stagnant environment of the poem's first section that Césaire's modernist subject can move from merely describing the island's predicament to engaging it. Thus, the single-word verse "Partir" (To go away; 42, 43) opens the *Cahier's* second movement and liberates a first-person voice heretofore asserted solely through possessive pronouns. As the persona's newly excavated "je" emerges, so, too, does his sense of purpose vis-à-vis his land. Indeed, the persona imagines his return home before his departure is even well under way:

> Je viendrais à ce pays mien et je lui dirais: "Embrassez-moi sans crainte. . . . Et si je ne sais que parler, c'est pour vous que je parlerai."
> Et je lui dirais encore:
> "Ma bouche sera la bouche des malheurs qui n'ont point de bouche, ma voix, la liberté de celles qui s'affaissent au cachot du désespoir." (44)
> I would go to this land of mine and I would say to it: "Embrace me without fear. . . . And if all I can do is speak, it is for you I shall speak."
> And again I would say:
> "My mouth shall be the mouth of those calamities that have no mouth, my voice the freedom of those who break down in the solitary confinement of despair." (45)

Césaire situates this address amid the persona's growing appreciation of global oppression and regional history. While the "je serais un homme-juif" (I would be a jew-man; 42, 43) litany evokes the former, references to Toussaint L'Ouverture and the transatlantic slave trade invoke the latter. The result is a proliferation of expression and imagery that constitute, as Arnold notes, "surrealist practice" (147) but not the surrealism of "ciel bleu et cocotiers" (blue sky and coconut trees; Bernabé 15, 77) evoked by Breton. Rather, it is a surrealism which confronts the "*absurdité immédiate*" (*immediate absurdity*) of being trapped between the visual splendor of the

Caribbean landscape and the horrors of its slave, colonial past.[17] No longer troubled by this discursive contradiction, Césaire's persona embraces its illogic, in which "2 et 2 font 5" (2 and 2 are 5; 50, 51), and claims his formerly denigrated African roots.

This empowerment swells until the persona arrives in Paris, where the specter he must face is not Columbus, but himself. In the poem's most well-known episode of this new-Old World haunting, Césaire stages what Frantz Fanon would later call the psychopathology of the black man. The persona's version of southern U.S. night winds is a Parisian streetcar where he joins in the ridicule of a fellow black passenger. Like the behavior of the Fanonian subject, the persona's identification with whites is simultaneously compulsive and counterintuitive: "Le Noir cesse de se comporter en individu *actionnel*. Le but de son action sera Autrui (sous la forme du Blanc), car Autrui seul peut le valoriser" (The black man stops behaving as an *actional* person. The goal of his behavior will be the Other [in the guise of the white man], for the Other alone can give him worth; Fanon 125, 154). Césaire further complicates the scene with an indication that, even if courage had trumped cowardice, the persona's voice might very well have been drowned out by the clamor of the Jazz Age:

> Ou bien tout simplement comme on nous aime!
> Obscènes gaiement, très doudous de jazz sur leur excès d'ennui.
> Je sais le tracking, le Lindy-hop et les claquettes.
> Pour les bonnes bouches la sourdine de nos plaintes enrobées de oua-oua.
> Attendez. . . . Tout est dans l'ordre. Mon bon ange broute de néon. J'avale des baguettes. Ma dignité se vautre dans les dégobillements. (58)
> Or else quite simply as they like to think of us!
> Cheerfully obscene, completely nuts about jazz to cover their extreme boredom.
> I can boogie-woogie, do the Lindy-hop and tap-dance. And for a special treat the muting of our cries muffled with wah-wah. Wait . . . Everything is as it should be. My good angel grazes the neon. I swallow batons. My dignity wallows in puke. (59)

Instead of heralding a new era in race relations, the soundtrack of modernist exoticism celebrates a primitivist adoration that creates a "strategic zone of intense feeling" through which European audiences can lose themselves (Dash 34). As the trumpets sound, the persona finds that he has escaped the inertia of the colony only to be objectified in the metropole.

The *Cahier* eventually answers this discursive predicament with the creation of a new discourse. Through the articulation of *négritude* as a word and as an identity, Césaire subverts linguistic and social conventions; the root of the neologism is *nègre*, a derogatory term that Martinicans of Césaire's generation associated with Africans rather than themselves.[18] The move not only provides Césaire with artistic freedom but also emboldens and enriches the persona. His confidence grows as Césaire layers interior monologues upon mythic chants, personal anecdotes upon surrealist poems-within-the-poem, and bold exclamations upon more tranquil narrative rhythms. As Dan's outburst disturbs the spectacle of propriety in "Box Seat," so his Caribbean analogue challenges his listeners-readers with the cry "ASSEZ DE CE SCANDALE!" (ENOUGH OF THIS OUTRAGE!; 56, 57). Where Dan's speech ends prematurely, the persona's continues, allowing him to regain his composure long enough to voice what might very well be the first surrealist lullaby: "Calme et berce ô ma parole l'enfant qui ne sait pas que la carte du printemps est toujours à refaire / les herbes balanceront pour le bétail vaisseau doux de l'espoir" (Calm and lull oh my voice the child who does not know that the map of spring is always to be drawn again / the tall grass will sway gently ship hope for the cattle; 66, 67). Between the earlier exclamation and this later verse, the persona calls attention to and offers comfort for the calamities (malheurs) he once pledged to express.

As in Toomer, the Césairean narrative does not end with the modernist subject's emergence as lone spokesperson. The *Cahier*, through a series of reversals and returns, reveals the goal of the persona's journey to be union, not solitude. The excretory impulses of the second movement, punctuated by images of "les dégobillements" (puke) and "vomissure" (vomit; 60, 61), give way to unconditional acceptance: "j'accepte, j'accepte tout cela" (I accept, I accept it all; 76, 77). This incorporation allows the persona to fill the epistemological void that Glissant calls "nonhistory" with the thorny complexity of black modernism/modernity. Thus, although the isolated Caribbean of the first movement is replaced by an empowering, mythological Africa in the second, the native land that the persona ultimately claims in the third movement is the scarred, "deformed" (difformes) islands of the Caribbean (74, 75). The most pivotal acceptance comes in the persona's movement from representing and soothing his people to recognizing the force of collective action:

> je te livre l'intourist du circuit triangulaire
> dévore vent

je te livre mes paroles abruptes
dévore et enroule-toi
en t'enroulant embrasse-moi d'un plus vaste frisson
embrasse-moi jusqu'au nous furieux
embrasse, embrasse NOUS (82)
to you the nontourist of the triangular circuit
devour wind
to you I surrender my abrupt words
devour and encoil yourself
and self-encoiling embrace me with a more ample shudder
embrace me unto furious us
embrace, embrace US (83)

Surrendering his poetic gifts as a gesture of solidarity, the persona accomplishes the black modernist hat trick that eludes Toomer's characters; he is no longer writing/speaking to his community, but writing/speaking with them. His experience of blackness as an empowering, grounded identity does not simply involve the community: his Négritude depends upon it. The *Cahier* concludes with a triumphant resurrection—"monte/monte/monte" (rise/rise/rise; 84, 85)—rather than an uncertain retreat because, unlike Kabnis, the persona has understood his place and that of his words vis-à-vis collective expression. The community to which he belongs may be a "bitter brotherhood" (fraternité âpre; 84, 85), but it is a brotherhood nonetheless.

Jean Toomer and Aimé Césaire's investment in marshalling their poetic mastery to reclaim the U.S. South and the Caribbean, respectively, is evident. Yet just as Toomer's racial identity defied categorization and Césaire's cultural heritage spans three continents, so the significance of their work reaches far beyond their two homes. *Cane* and *Cahier d'un retour au pays natal* restore shattered diasporic pasts as they express and embrace culturally rich, regionally specific realities. In their respective explorations of modern black subjects seeking to negotiate and reimagine the worlds around them, these prose-poetry hybrids expose both the inadequacy of facile social and artistic categories and the potential of revised, expanded conceptions of modernism and modernity. Uncomplicated articulations of "hemispheric identit[ies]" can undoubtedly elide the cultural, linguistic, and social differences which exist across the Americas (Dash 60), but nuanced, comparative engagements of such identities can, in turn, reveal the internationalist underpinnings of a regional text, the diasporic richness of a national book. For Toomer and Césaire the paths from Washington to Paris and from Fort-de-France to Paris may not have crossed, but the stunning literary conversation between their works bespeaks the many ways in which individuals and ideas traveled the circuits of transatlantic black modernism.

Notes

1. See Lewis 86, Fabre 70. One of the means through which African American and Francophone intellectuals met was the salon held by Jane and Paulette Nardal, Martinican sisters living in Paris, and their cousin Louis-Thomas Achille at the Nardal home on Rue Clamart. For more on the writings of the Nardals, prominent intellectuals in their own right, see Edwards, *The Practice of Diaspora* 119–86 and Sharpley-Whiting 38–79. See also Fabre, *From Harlem to Paris*.

2. See Michel Fabre, "The Reception of *Cane* in France," *Jean Toomer and the Harlem Renaissance* 202–3; McKay 194–95; and Arnold 8–12. Toomer's French travels were prompted by his growing interest in the work of the mystic George Gurdjieff, whose Institute for the Harmonious Development of Man was housed at the Chateau du Prieuré in Fontainebleau. Césaire went to Paris to prepare for the entrance exams to, and later to complete his postsecondary studies at, the Ecole Normale Supérieure.

3. Here and throughout the essay I use "black" to indicate a sociocultural community defined but not rigidly bound by race. This distinction is especially important given Toomer's racial ambivalence/ ambiguity, which I discuss in greater detail later in the essay.

4. See Gikandi, *Writing in Limbo* 2, and Glissant, *Le discours antillais* 223, 61.

5. It is important to note that Glissant uses the modifier "American" in a broad regional sense rather than to refer exclusively to the United States.

6. Article 14 of the 1805 Haitian Constitution reads, "All acception [*sic*] of colour among the children of one and the same family, of whom the chief magistrate is the father, being necessarily to cease, the Haytians shall hence forward be known only by the generic appellation of Blacks."

7. See North 10 and Dash 38. Note that *Martinique charmeuse des serpents* is the title of both a 1941 Breton essay and his subsequent illustrated volume, which includes the former. See Breton, *Martinique charmeuse des serpents*.

8. See Aimé Césaire, "Poésie et connaissance," translated as "Poetry and Knowledge." See also René Maran's 1921 novel *Batouala*, Toomer's *Cane*, and Nella Larsen's 1928 novel *Quicksand* and 1929 novel *Passing*.

9. For more on Toomer's complicated, illustrious family background, see McKay 13–33 and Werner Sollors 18–37.
10. For a detailed discussion of Toomer's dissatisfaction with the racialized praise offered by friends and colleagues, see McKay 179–83.
11. Sollors 27.
12. See Gikandi, *Writing in Limbo* 1.
13. See also Fabre 207. According to Arnold, the thesis, written for Césaire's Diplôme d'Etudes Supérieures, is no longer extant; however, Fabre notes that the thesis examined the work of poet Sterling Brown.
14. The Toomer translation came from the 1929 *Anthologie de la nouvelle poésie américaine*, edited by Eugène Jolas and published by Editions Kra.
15. Translations mine.
16. Richardson notes that Breton wrote the essay in New York in 1943, hence, my reference above to that date rather than the essay's 1944 publication date. Breton visited Martinique—and met Aimé and Suzanne Césaire—in April 1941 on his way from France to the United States.
17. Breton, *Manifeste du surréalisme* (*Manifesto of Surrealism* 34–35, 24). For an explicit theorization of Caribbean surrealism, see Suzanne Césaire's essay "1943: Le Surréalisme et nous" (1943: Surrealism and Us).
18. See Arnold 36. For a history of the valences and appropriations of *nègre* in early-twentieth-century Francophone literature, see Edwards 25–38.

Works Cited

Arnold, A. James. *Modernism and Negritude: The Poetry and Poetics of Aimé Césaire*. Cambridge, MA: Harvard UP, 1981.
Baker, Houston A., Jr. *Modernism and the Harlem Renaissance*. Chicago: U of Chicago P, 1987.
Bernabé, Jean, Patrick Chamoiseau, and Raphaël Confiant. *Éloge de la créolité/In Praise of Creoleness*. 1989. Édition bilingue. Trans. M. B. Taleb-Khyar. Paris: Gallimard, 1993.
Breton, André. "A Great Black Poet: Aimé Césaire." Trans. Krzysztof Fijalkowski and Michael Richardson. In *Refusal of the Shadow: Surrealism and the Caribbean*. Ed. Michael Richardson. New York: Verso, 1996. 191–98.
———. *Manifeste du surréalisme*. 1924. *Manifestes du surréalisme*. Paris: Gallimard, 1969. 13–60.

———. *Manifesto of Surrealism*. In *Manifestoes of Surrealism*. Trans. Richard Seaver and Helen R. Lane. Ann Arbor: U of Michigan P, 1969. 1–47.

———. "Martinique charmeuse de serpents: Un Grand poète noir." *Tropiques* 11 (1944): 119–26.

Césaire, Aimé. *Cahier d'un retour au pays natal*. In *Aimé Césaire: The Collected Poetry*. Trans. and ed. Clayton Eshleman and Annette Smith. Berkeley: U of California P, 1983. 32–85.

———. "Introduction à la poésie nègre américaine." *Tropiques* 2 (1941): 37–50.

———. "Poésie et connaissance," *Tropiques* 12 (1945): 157–70.

———. "Poetry and Knowledge." Trans. A. James Arnold. *Lyric and Dramatic Poetry, 1946–82*. Charlottesville: CARAF Books/UP of Virginia, 1990. xlii–lvi.

Césaire, Suzanne. "1943: Le Surréalisme et nous." *Tropiques* 8–9 (1943): 14–18.

———. "1943: Surrealism and Us." Trans. Krzysztof Fijalkowski and Michael Richardson. *Refusal of the Shadow: Surrealism and the Caribbean*. Ed. Michael Richardson. New York: Verso, 1996. 123–26.

Dash, J. Michael. *The Other America: Caribbean Literature in a New World Context*. Charlottesville: UP of Virginia, 1998.

Edwards, Brent Hayes. *The Practice of Diaspora: Literature, Translation, and the Rise of Black Internationalism*. Cambridge, MA: Harvard UP, 2003.

Fabre, Geneviève and Michel Feith, eds. *Jean Toomer and the Harlem Renaissance*. New Brunswick: Rutgers UP, 2001.

Fabre, Michel. "Du mouvement nouveau noir à la négritude césairienne." *Soleil éclaté: Mélanges offerts à Aimé Césaire à l'occasion de son soixante-dixième anniversaire par une équipe internationale d'artistes et de chercheurs*. Ed. Jacqueline Leiner. Tubingen: Gunter Narr Verlag, 1984. 149–59.

———. *From Harlem to Paris: Black American Writers in France, 1840–1980*. Urbana: U of Illinois P, 1991.

———."The Reception of *Cane* in France." *Jean Toomer and the Harlem Renaissance*. Ed. Geneviève Fabre and Michel Feith. New Brunswick: Rutgers UP, 2001. 202–14

Fanon, Frantz. *Black Skin, White Masks*. Trans. Charles Lam Markmann. New York: Grove, 1967.

———. *Peau noire, masques blancs*. Paris: Seuil, 1952.

Gikandi, Simon. *Writing in Limbo: Modernism and Caribbean Literature*. Ithaca: Cornell UP, 1992.

Gilroy, Paul. *The Black Atlantic: Modernity and Double Consciousness*. Cambridge, MA: Harvard UP, 1993.

Glissant, Édouard. *Caribbean Discourse: Selected Essays*. Trans. and introd. J. Michael Dash. Charlottesville: CARAF Books / UP of Virginia, 1989.

———. *Le discours antillais*. 1981. Paris: Gallimard, 1997.

"Haiti: 1805 Constitution." *Bob Corbett's Haiti Page*. Ed. Bob Corbet. 8 March 2005, at www.webster.edu/~corbetre/haiti/history/earlyhaiti/1805-const.htm.

Hughes, Langston. "The Negro Artist and the Racial Mountain." 1926. *The Norton Anthology of African American Literature.* Ed. Henry Louis Gates Jr., Nellie Y. McKay, et al. New York: Norton, 1997. 1267–71.
Jameson, Fredric. "Modernism and Imperialism." *Nationalism, Colonialism, and Culture.* Ed. Terry Eagleton, Fredric Jameson, and Edward W. Said. Minneapolis: Field Day Company / U of Minnesota P, 1990. 43–66.
Larsen, Nella. *Quicksand* and *Passing.* Ed. Deborah E. McDowell. New Brunswick: Rutgers UP, 1986.
Lewis, David Levering. *When Harlem Was in Vogue.* 1981. New York: Penguin, 1997.
Locke, Alain. "The New Negro." *The New Negro.* Ed. Alain Locke. 1925. New York: Touchstone, 1997. 3–25.
Maran, René. *Batouala.* 1921. Trans. Barbara Beck and Alexandre Nboukou. London: Heinemann, 1973.
———. *Batouala: vértiable roman nègre.* Paris: Albin Michel, 1921.
McKay, Nellie Y. *Jean Toomer, Artist: A Study of His Literary Life and Work, 1894–1936.* Chapel Hill: U of North Carolina P, 1984.
North, Michael. *The Dialect of Modernism: Race, Language, and Twentieth-Century Literature.* New York: Oxford UP, 1994.
Richardson, Michael. Introduction. *Refusal of the Shadow: Surrealism and the Caribbean.* Ed. Michael Richardson. New York: Verso, 1996.
Rosello, Mireille. "'One More Sea to Cross': Exile and Intertextuality in Aimé Césaire's *Cahier d'un retour au pays natal.*" Trans. Robert Postawsko. *Post/Colonial Conditions: Exiles, Migrations, and Nomadisms,* vol. 2. Ed. Françoise Lionnet and Ronnie Scharfman. Spec. issue of *Yale French Studies* 83 (1993): 176–95.
Sartre, Jean-Paul. *Black Orpheus.* Trans. John MacCombie. *The Massachusetts Review* 5 (1964): 13–52.
———. *Orphée Noir.* Preface. *Anthologie de la nouvelle poésie nègre et malgache de langue française.* Ed. Léopold Sédar Senghor. Paris: PUF, 1948. ix–xliv.
Sharpley-Whiting, T. Denean. *Negritude Women.* Minneapolis: U of Minnesota P, 2003.
Sollors, Werner. "Jean Toomer's *Cane*: Modernism and Race in Interwar America." *Jean Toomer and the Harlem Renaissance.* Ed. Geneviève Fabre and Michel Feith. New Brunswick: Rutgers UP, 2001. 18–37.
Toomer, Jean. *Cane.* 1923. New York: Liveright, 1993.
———. "The South in Literature." In *Jean Toomer: Selected Essays and Literary Criticism.* Ed. Robert B. Jones. Knoxville: U of Tennessee P, 1996. 11–16.
Turner, Darwin T. Introduction. *Cane.* 1923. New York: Liveright, 1993. ix–xxv.
Washington, Booker T. "The Atlanta Exposition Address." 1895. *Up from Slavery: An Autobiography.* New York: Random, 1999. 142–54.

CHAPTER 5

Embodied Fictions, Melancholy Migrations
Josephine Baker's Cinematic Celebrity

Terri Francis

One night not long after the arrival of Anne's letter with its curious news, Helga went with Olsen and some other young folk to the great Circus, a vaudeville house, in search of amusement on a rare off night. After sitting through several numbers they reluctantly arrived at the conclusion that the whole entertainment was dull, unutterably dull, and apparently without alleviation, and not to be borne. They were reaching for their wraps when out upon the stage pranced two black men, American Negroes undoubtedly, for as they danced and cavorted, they sang in the English of America an old ragtime song that Helga remembered hearing as a child, "Everybody Gives Good Advice." At its conclusion the audience applauded with delight. Only Helga Crane was silent, motionless.
—Nella Larsen, *Quicksand*

What is Helga Crane thinking as she sits silent and motionless amid the enthusiastic audience? What is the relationship between the transnational migrations that take her, a biracial black American woman, between New York and Copenhagen and the alienation she experiences when she hears music from home at the Circus?

In Nella Larsen's *Quicksand* (1928), Copenhagen is initially a site that permits Helga's imagination to run free. There she explores the city and meets new people in her family's circle of artist friends. Dissatisfied with New York, Helga had set sail for Denmark's capital. Larsen describes Helga's feelings during the trip, "even the two rough days found her on deck, reveling like a released bird in her returned feelings of happiness and freedom, that blessed sense of belonging to herself alone and not to a race" (64). At first, Copenhagen seems to be a utopian space for "a new life" and "the realization of a dream that she had dreamed persistently ever since she was old enough to remember such vague things." Larsen describes the European capital as "where she belonged" and as Helga's "proper setting," where she felt "consoled for the spiritual wounds of the past." In Copenhagen, "she took to luxury as the proverbial duck to water. And she took to admiration and attention even more eagerly" (67). Helga's transatlantic journey takes her across national and class lines and she enjoys both public admiration of her racial difference and a newfound ability to afford her rare tastes.

But the European capital soon makes Helga restless, becoming yet another source of confinement. The scene at the Circus crystallizes Helga's internal conflicts without entirely explaining why the performance was so disturbing. When the dancers prance on stage, Helga seems to feel exposed somehow. Is an aspect of her character suddenly public and visible? Why does the public performance elicit such a personal reaction? Helga seems to experience an identity crisis, experiencing a sense of invisibility and crushing vulnerability. Perhaps in that instant she sees a distillation of how she appears in the eyes of her uncle's Danish family and her suitor Olsen. The fact that Helga recognizes the song is a crucial detail. Her recognition creates tension that makes Helga's silence at the end of the performance more than a simple rejection of the performance; she feels implicated in its aesthetics. In many ways, the novel builds to this moment. Rather than experiencing freedom from racism or The Race—the promise of racelessness, individuality, cosmopolitanism, affluence, whiteness—Helga finds herself entangled in the conundrum of black female existence—the condition of continually competing with myths about oneself as they manifest in the stated and unstated perceptions of others and in one's own mind. The fact that Olsen has been painting Helga's portrait, and that this has been not entirely to her satisfaction, underscores the novel's engagement with issues of black women's representation and creativity. Is Helga a work of art or entertainment? Are those dancers art—folk culture—or are they commodities of entertainment, stereotypes?

The tension that transfixes Helga at the Circus emerges from her conflicted response to the cultural history represented by the ragtime song and the cavorting or clowning of the performance, which offends her. It appears that Helga believes, to some degree, the manufactured distortions of blackness and cannot see the performers on stage outside of negative connotations placed on their performance style. As Larsen writes:

> The cavorting Negroes on the stage showed something in her that she had kept hidden. She felt ashamed, betrayed, as if these pale pink and white people among whom she lived had suddenly been invited to look upon something in her which she had hidden away and wanted to forget. And she was shocked at the avidity at which Olsen beside her drank it in. . . . They had divined its presence. (82–83)

Here Larsen touches on the racist concept of civilization as a veneer that hides a "primitive" black essential self. Helga seems to be in just such a predicament except that as a self-aware protagonist she struggles with both what she does feel and what she would like to feel. All of this occurs in the context of Helga's growing ambivalence in her feelings about Olsen. She imagines parallels between herself and the performers. If they clown and play to the enjoyment of the audience, as texts they register the audience's desires and pleasures on a variety of levels. In a flash, Helga may begin to see the narrative that she has entered and the role she has unwittingly played, as she faces the suspicions she tried to dismiss in the early days of her time in Copenhagen.

Frozen by the trauma of the way that this scene opened her eyes to the limitations of her self-representation, Helga "returned again and again to the Circus, always alone, gazing intently and solemnly at the gesticulating black figures, an ironical and silently speculative spectator" (83). She inhabits a continual nightmare in which her "jungle" essence is revealed to herself and, she fears, to others around her. Having run from one brand of blackness in the United States, Helga finds that it is an apparently inescapable visual paradigm that is only more intense in all-white environments like this fictional version of Copenhagen.

For Larsen, the Danish capital bears a significance that extends beyond its physical borders. Copenhagen, for instance, has biographical significance to Larsen, who was the daughter of a Danish mother and a West Indian father, who died when she was young (McDowell x).[1] More significantly, however, Copenhagen represents the idea of a home that can be a refuge from racism for all African Americans. As New York or Chicago is often used to reference black modernity in a variety of urban settings, so too is Copenhagen a synecdoche for European sites of black American travels. Copenhagen, like Paris, serves as a utopian possibility To Helga, the city represents freedom: "she gave herself up to daydreams of a happy future in Copenhagen, where there were no Negroes, no problems, no prejudice . . ." (55). Helga believes that isolation and leaving America will free her from the limitations and bonds of community—of blackness itself. In fact, her sense of blackness is intensified. She interprets her Danish relatives' curiosity about her hair and skin as admiration and casts singularity and public acclaim as freedom. But Larsen's critique of exoticism shows its social and personal dimensions through rendering Helga's interior thoughts as mostly unheard resistant responses to the family's objectifications of her. In *Quicksand,* Larsen complicates the already entangled relationship between exoticism and gender by emphasizing Helga's youth. Her social role as a young, unmarried woman of color makes her especially vulnerable to the wishes of her older, white family members. This intersection of social identities forms the basis for her experience. Because of the ways the novel articulates the entire early twentieth-century period of African American cultural movements through the multifaceted Helga Crane, this once neglected Harlem Renaissance gem lays the groundwork for a cultural history of Josephine Baker that accounts for her Parisian success within the context of race, gender, and performance.

Published three years after Josephine Baker's 1925 Paris debut, *Quicksand* offers a framework for reading the dancer's theatrical and cinematic celebrity. As Cheryl Wall suggests in her analysis of the novel, *Quicksand's* Black Atlantic trajectory has clear parallels with Baker's migrations as an international performer. Indeed, the novel explores how the dynamics of Baker's fame operated on the streets-turned-stages of Helga's everyday life. Wall's analysis addresses the idea of black women in art and as art in an international context where meanings shift with locations. *Quicksand's* plot takes Helga from Naxos, a black college in the American South, to urban dwellings in the North; to Europe and back to New York; and, finally, to the South once again. Analogously, Baker's travels took her from the Midwest to the routes followed by the black segregated Theater Owners Booking Association, through the North, and eventually to Paris and other European capitals. The richest association between the fictional character and the historical celebrity, however, is their shared position as key figures in the history of black female visibility.

Viewed through the lens of Larsen's text, Baker represents much more than the feathered mannequin she appeared to be in photographs and films. Despite attention to Baker wherever blackness, film, jazz-age France, and primitivism are discussed, she remains an under-analyzed cultural figure in her own right. Her biography, too, often serves as a site for celebrating the phenomenon of black American success in Paris, obscuring the complexity of her stage and screen roles and the command she held over them. When she is not being celebrated, Baker's victimhood is emphasized to the extent that her films, billed as musical comedies, explicitly use her blackness to exploit the dynamics of assimilation and migration toward their own ideological ends. Indeed, her status as caricature is often cited, which tends to foreclose a more complex consideration of, for example, how she indexes the parallels of black modernity and primitivism. I wish to illustrate instead how the figure of Baker embodies what Hazel Carby called "the crises of representation" that shaped early twentieth-century black popular culture and represents the limitations on forming a coherent public or private, collective or individual identity (169).

In what follows, I integrate the foregoing literary reading of *Quicksand* with a cultural history of Baker's dancing in order to make legible the bodily grammar of Baker's films and personas; put another way, I examine Baker as a performer of embodied fictions of race, transatlantic migration, and assimilation. Both in spite and because of the difficulty of separating Baker's persona from her personhood, especially since she and her representatives often used elements of her private life in creating her public image, I refer explicitly to "Josephine Baker" as the persona(s) she projected in her films and performances. The characters that Baker plays in films and on stage, in other words, all functioned as part of her overall celebrity persona. The fact that Baker was a celebrity means that her life, body, and words, once made public, circulated as consumable signs in an orbit beyond her ultimate control but that was nonetheless generated by her. The roles Baker performed on stage, in films, and in her general celebrity, which set off a storm of criticism and adoration in mid-twenties Paris, thus open up new ways to think about the issues of race and representation that marked the Harlem Renaissance and the phenomenon of European primitivism alike.

In her films, Baker typically plays the role of an anonymous girl who is introduced to the theater and carried away from her everyday life by her "natural" entertainment qualities. Meanwhile, Baker's characters enable the white male characters around her to have a break from their routines. Similar to the dynamic Larsen narrates in *Quicksand,* films like *Siren of the Tropics* (1927), *Les Hallucinations d'un Pompier* (circa 1927), *Zou Zou* (1934), *Princesse Tam Tam* (1935), as well as Baker's concert films, each establish visual tropes that make spectacular both blackness and womanhood. These tropes work in tension with their black female characters' sense of self and concept of beauty, with Baker's blackness functioning as a naturalizing sign for her abilities. Like the character of Helga in *Quicksand,* the figure of Baker represents the ways in which black womanhood functions as spectacle in the public sphere, almost to the exclusion of a private, anonymous everyday space for black women. The plots of Baker's films feature protagonists who long for love but get stardom instead of domestic bliss. Larsen's study of the ways that Helga is made exotic on both sides of the Atlantic thus illuminates the contradictory ways she was received as both exemplary of black womanhood and a spectacularly curious example of humanity.

Like Larsen's fictional Copenhagen, the real Paris is often imagined as a racial haven. Baker's success as a singer and dancer is often cited in celebratory narratives of the city. Michel Fabre has described the desire of African Americans at home to share in the international achievement of the expatriates as "lieux de memoire," or sites of recognition (122). Indeed, the phenomenon of black success in Paris permitted stateside readers to recognize themselves as contributors of culture, which vindicated accusations of inferiority and offered grounds for denaturalizing American racism. Fabre put it this way:

> What made Baker's success exceptional was, on the one hand the magnitude of its economic rewards (of which blacks had traditionally been deprived); and, on the other hand, the legitimization of her dancing as a highbrow aesthetic contribution (not only entertainment) in Europe—very much the way that jazz was considered there. Also, isn't it significant that in spite of the way black American women were seen by white Americans, this girl from St. Louis was viewed as one of the most attractive women on earth? (128)

While Baker's success is remarkable in itself, its exceptionality is an insufficient explanation. Baker's embodiment of carefree success must be understood in terms of a complex colonialist context and of her own complicity with it. From this perspective, I argue that her popularity depended on the way Baker performed her own fame and "freedom." Aesthetically, the figure of Baker galvanized the transformation of nineteenth-century ethnological inquiry and the exotic human display that was part of colonial fairs into mass entertainment. Her performances did facilitate artistic epiphanies for many prominent figures and groups, even if they saw Baker through a haze of misperceptions. Baker blurred lines between high and low and was a reference point many artists used to create high art out of "primitive" works. However, when Baker made moves to perform what she thought was artistic and legitimate, critics in the entertainment press were hardly united in their desire to see her work develop—they wanted the bananas. This resistance shows that Baker's success was specific to one role and that her audiences policed its boundaries. The very exceptionality on which Baker and many of her peers depended in many ways was a severely limited and unsustainable cultural experience for African Americans.

The internationalism that many in the black vanguard practiced in the 1920s formed part of the basis for the black renaissance that Alain Locke and others formulated. This cosmopolitan, modern figure also played a role in French concepts of its national self. The persona of the modern American African performed by Baker likely appealed to Parisian audiences because it could give the impression of being distanced politically, morally, artistically, and sexually from American racism, as well as from the taint of colonial guilt, Old World musical traditions, and conservative social mores. In my view, this combination of French colonial guilt and fascination toward black (American) people was managed by white Parisian consumption of the spectacle of the free black, which both black American performer-products and white audience-consumers invented. To a large extent, black Americans and white Parisians conspired to submerge actual racist practices and experiences under the desire for what they hoped would feel like freedom and behind the image and rhetoric of "race-less-ness." They created the myth of the free black in Paris, which was crucial, both to the imagination of a modern African America and to the invention of a progressive Paris. Americans writing about their Parisian sojourns rarely see their fate as linked to that of North Africans and French blacks, yet many writers treated diaspora in their writings.[2]

France's relationship to Africa and the conflict between its rhetorical humanism and active colonialism drove the phenomenon of black American success in Paris. African American performers like Baker uniquely permitted the combination of (fantastical) references to ancient Africa and to modern black America—bypassing actual, contemporary Africa. This capacity for a number of readings made Baker and black American jazz compelling to Parisians throughout the twentieth century, but particularly in the 1920s and 1930s, the height of colonial wealth and expansion. It's true that the waves of immigration that have resulted in the cosmopolitan Paris of today are largely a postwar phenomenon, but France has always had its own *nègres* in a variety of forms and across a number of public and private spheres.

When Baker made her 1925 debut in *La Revue Nègre,* she was incorporated into (even as she updated) longstanding narratives about black women, empire, and sexuality in the popular French imagination. Although she sought to command some authority in her self-production, she was "simultaneously locked into a derogatory and objectified essence of black femaleness," as T. Denean Sharpley-Whiting has argued (107). Crucial for Baker was the way in which a dual reading of her as either cute or savage would result in the elision of her artistic potential. Sharpley-Whiting's formulation of a phenomenon she has named the "black Venus narrative" in French literature (7), art, and performance explains how Baker's imported body, like nineteenth-century imaginary bodies, represented "the colonized black female body, that is, a body trapped in an image of itself, whose primitivity, exemplified in a childlike comedic posture, sexual deviancy, degradation, and colonization, is intimately linked with sexual difference" (10). The contradictions and doublings of Baker's career foreground the interpenetration of fantasy and racism, which crystallizes in her performances. Baker's complicated performances provide an occasion to point out that one of the ways racial discourse works is to make some bodies more available than others to a certain type of display.

Baker's diasporic performance takes its cues from the forms of ethnological entertainment that made a spectacle of the black Venus narrative[3]—that is, from human displays that translated a study of an ethnic group into a format fit for public amusement. Saartjee Baartman, the Khoi-Koi woman who, around the year 1816, was taken from South Africa to appear in fairs and other kinds of display in Paris and London, is one of the most famous examples of such ethnological entertainment. Existing scholarship on early cinema establishes the cinema's affinities with early popular entertainments such as natural history museums, and Fatima Tobing Rony and Alison Griffiths have shown that ethnological spectacles were protocinematic, not just theatrical. The formal and politico-cultural echoes between Baartman's live performances and the cinematic Baker are a striking example of this continuity, even as generational and historical differences are at play.

Older than cinema, ethnological entertainment is also a mass amusement form, whose influence can be seen in Baker's film roles. *Les zoos humains*, or freak shows, were popular in both France and the United States during the nineteenth century. "From 1877 to 1912, around 30 'ethnological exhibitions' . . . were produced at the *Jardin zoologique d'acclimatation* with unwavering success" (Blanchard, Bancel, and Lemaire 65). This park became one of the main sites of the French human zoos. However, Paris's famous music halls, particularly the Folies Bergère, where Baker would perform, were often settings for these race shows. African Americans were neither absent from nor immune to ethnologically inflected, colonization-inspired entertainment.

Sometimes produced apart from colonial fairs, the small-scale living dioramas of what was supposed to read as daily life in an African village still merited press coverage. For example, in a June 1895 issue of *L'Illustration,* a popular French weekly newspaper, I discovered an article on a new diorama in the public park known as Champs de Mars. I quote an excerpt here: "After the Ashantis, the Dahomeans . . . and other savages that have been exhibited for several years in the Jardin d'Acclimation or other areas, here at the Champs-de-Mars, an exhibition of nègres from central and western Africa. The organizers have bound themselves to reconstruct with precision a Sudanese village . . ." (my translation). This simulation of a Sudanese village required 350 uprooted men, women, and children, who had been transported to Paris from Africa. The article does not report on the compensation the people might have been promised or provided. For religious and architectural "precision," organizers built a mud mosque in the center of the village and maintained fidelity to the village's planning by building mud-clay houses and arranging them around the mosque. They even went to the trouble of constructing a 2000-meter artificial lake to replicate what was meant to represent the Sudanese landscape. However, the lake also served as a curious kind of wishing well in which visitors would toss coins and village-diorama children would dive after them, while other village-diorama natives glided by in canoes, dug out from whole tree trunks. This clash of spectacle, (normally invisible) daily life, and petty commerce raises the questions: What is the purpose of this display, isolated from a colonial fair? What exactly is the source or the original of this simulation? Is a particular Sudanese village represented? The title *"village nègre"* suggests that the reproduction was a composite of any and all perceptions of African villages. What does it mean for colonialist exhibition in general and for Baker's roles that specificity is erased in the name of greater "precision" and authenticity?[4] This human zoo exemplifies the way that engaging racial fictions of whiteness, blackness, Africanity, and Frenchness became a significant pastime on the Paris cultural scene.

"Un Village nègre au Champs de Mars" was a living diorama in which a culture's supposed daily life was exhibited for the entertainment of visitors playing the role of lay anthropologists. *L'Illustration* reported that there was a French *brasserie* at one corner of the scene and that visitors invited villagers to sit with them and talk. The organizers' attention to detail shows their concern with authenticity; however, it is clear that the diorama's realism is in direct proportion to its fakery. It had to fabricate its re-creation of village life. Consequently the diorama deepened the juxtaposition of the Sudanese village and the French capital, making the contrasts more striking and enhancing the frisson of the participation-spectacle. Ultimately, the *village nègre* plays with the idea of Africans coming to Paris as immigrants and colonial subjects. By making spectacular everyday aspects of their culture, the exhibit distanced the participants and those they represented from participating in French daily life. Unnaturalized in this way, their role was to perform themselves. Fundamentally, the exhibit epitomizes a scene of containment through exposure. In other words, despite the mobility that is implied by the travel involved in creating the exhibit, they were hardly free to move about the country. From the descriptions of the exhibition, it seems to me that the venue in which the Africans are displayed symbolizes and functions as the tool of their confinement. Their exposure as Other to French society nearly limits, or at least circumscribes, any capacity they might have had to lead private lives while in captivity.

The *village nègre* event is a key example of the overall ethnological entertainment backdrop from which Baker emerged because of its strategy of display. Blending displacement and display, the *village nègre* exhibit's very name demonstrates its discursive collapsing of a wide variety of African ethnicities into one composite black representative, despite the claims of specificity that *L'Illustration* reported. This idea of "black" as a general term versus particular ethnicities became a code that developed through other *villages nègres* and manifested itself in Baker's performances.

Baker was a transatlantic or, more specifically, a black diaspora phenomenon. This translated to her celebrity in the ways that she would portray characters of various ethnicities (drawn from the French empire) while grounding her repertoire in American dance. Baker was an American performer but, given the routes of her international career, she is best understood through an international approach to black performance; regardless of her origins in the United States, Baker's dancing and eventually her screen performances took shape in a colonialist context. Baker's position as a black American actress playing roles of colonial women in French films crystallizes only when viewed in terms of the racial performances that preceded it and the way in which by the mid-to-late 1920s and the 1930s audiences were able to enjoy Baker as a unique creature who was both a screen for the projection of colonialist fantasy and the bearer of black American modernist aesthetics. The colonialist European performance context in which Baker emerged was marked by ethnological entertainment, which formed a defining component of her aesthetic lineage.

In the age of Primitivism and the Harlem Renaissance, Baker's illusions were read in the context of quasi-scientific reproductions of African cultures. The live performers in ethnological spectacles are both objects of entertainment and objects of science because what they do—the dance, for example—is either presented as or perceived as evidence and their bodies are taken as in-the-flesh examples of the entire racial type. When Baker debuted as a live performer in 1925, she was the latest in a long line of black entertainers who were featured in Paris. Her performances played to fantasies about African female sexuality, enticing audiences to forget that she was American and reinventing her as *noire*—a fictional ethnicity elastic enough to encompass a variety of perceptions of Africans variously located in the diaspora. The Jazz Empress was in this way singular in her capacity to embody the current ideologies of race, women, and the body in interwar Paris. Baker was bodily conscious of her black American performance heritage and expressed a black Atlantic sensibility through bringing together her own repertoire of black moves and new dances from the eclectic and exoticist dance scene in Paris.

Across her fifty-year career, but especially during the interwar years, Baker was seen both as a member of French society and as an Other within it. This unstable position was reflected in the fact that Baker was often identified with her banana skirt, which served as a comic symbol of Baker's sense of movement and her overall blend of sex appeal and comedy. The *couronne des hanches* (hip crown) was her costume for the *danse des bananes.* Fleshing out the primitive persona that she established with her shocking 1925 debut in *La Revue Nègre,* the banana dance was a main number in the 1926 Folies Bergère production, *La Folie du Jour,* under the direction of Paul Derval. In fact, *Folie* was Baker's first show at the Montmartre music hall and she broke her contract with *La Revue Nègre* while on tour in order to take this starring role (Baker and Chase 56). The troupe of *danse des bananes* includes Baker as Fatou, several black men playing natives, and a white man in the part of a white explorer, and they are organized along the expected lines of colonialist power relations. The natives carry the explorer's packages and dock his canoe for him. Then, he appears to lounge while Fatou dances. In an attempt to represent an imaginary African landscape, the set simulates a tropical environment complete with a river (implied when the natives pull in the explorer's canoe) and an enormous tree whose branch extends over the stage. Potted plants and a tent on the stage add the finishing touches of fabricated, ethnological realism.

French directors Joé Francis and Alex Nalpas filmed scenes from *La Folie du Jour* in the spring of 1926, and under the titles *La Revue des revues* or *La Folie du Jour* they distributed the film among *Folie's* cast and management. The performance film may have had a wider audience for promotional purposes, since it was released officially in December 1927 shortly before Baker left Paris to embark on a twenty-five-country world tour. The banana dance also appears in another compilation film of Baker's music hall performances, *Joséphine Baker: Star of the Folies Bergère and Casino de Paris*. This short film was apparently made in the early 1930s after Baker's world tour and after she had begun performing at the Casino de Paris music hall. Its opening titles are in English and they recount semiaccurately Baker's rise to Parisian stardom from humble origins in "cotton fields." The inaccurate portions still work effectively for Baker's persona. Baker did not rise out of any cotton fields but her people did and this narrative is one way that her American identity remains active in the colonial persona she performs in Paris. The English titles suggest international distribution or specifically American distribution, but perhaps most importantly they figure Baker as an African American everywoman.

In *La Folie du Jour,* we see Baker dancing in front of an immobile camera that is positioned at the stage level. It is basically an extended tableau shot of the stage with a few cuts to medium long shots of Baker dancing and close-ups of her facial expression. Baker first appears in the frame crouched and wiggling her fingers. With thumbs hooked behind her ears, she makes a comic gesture toward the film's onstage surrogate audience, the lounging explorer. Then she appears to twirl down the length of the tree branch and a cut to a medium close-up shows her landing on a floor for a brief pose that makes her arms appear to blend into the foliage behind her. Cut back to Baker dancing in front of the explorer and pause. This footage gives access to Baker's early dance and serves as evidence of what it meant to film a stage performance in France in the twenties. In this case, we see a theatrical style with frontal framing, static camera, few cuts, and no variation in camera angle.

Baker's dance merits careful attention so that we can understand how it is translated cinematically. Two of Baker's most significant moves in the *danse des bananes* speak to what we could call a Black Atlantic or African diaspora movement sensibility. First, after her entrance and an initial shimmy, Baker appears to fling herself to the floor and in the next shot she has risen to face the white man with her arms extended overhead. She holds the pose for an extra beat and then twirls her hands slowly, shakes her head, smiles, and circles her hips quickly, while moving her stomach slowly. The bananas on Baker's costume shimmy in yet another sphere of rhythm as they independently knock against each other and against her legs. The drummers move around her creating a sense of musical flow from the drums to Baker's dancing and back again. Characteristic of African dance, polyrhythmic and polycentric movements feature prominently in Baker's dance practice.

In Baker's second key move, she bends the upper body forward at an angle with the arms hanging diagonally toward the ground, and the knees bent. This posture raises and isolates her buttocks and Baker pivots in a circle while shaking her hips very fast, the impression of speed enhanced by the shaking bananas. Baker does what appears to be a traditional African move in which the dancer shifts the lower body from left to right, with exaggerated hips, and throws the arms out to the opposite side. In the *danse des bananes* as in *danse sauvage* and other routines, Baker combines a series of postures and movements, going through them plotlessly and quickly, with only brief dance poses. However, the circling rump and the rocking tummy/shimmy recur in this dance like a bodily chorus. Thus, whereas the visual drama of the music hall relies on frequent costume changes, Baker made her body into a music hall by changing her movements and relying on juxtapositions. Earlier dance films tend to focus on a dancer or group of dancers doing a specific dance, such as the cakewalk or belly dance. In a Primitivist context, Baker's seemingly spontaneous dancing was (mis) interpreted as an expression of freedom of the body and the black essence. In a sense, her dancing came to represent the glamour and energy of Paris.

Details of her movements and costume reveal the ways in which Baker's dance combined American and African elements. The bananas make a tropical reference that could be either to the Caribbean or Africa. Baker's bright white brassiere is more of an American element than an African one. Covering her breasts was probably in response to Americans who were part of the imagined international audience for the film because Baker regularly performed topless in her music-hall shows.

The topic of hair bears a great deal of meaning for black female representation. Baker's hair is shiny and straightened. By straightening her hair, Baker represented the modern Black woman. In Baker's era, choosing to process one's hair helped to signify a break with "country" and older ways, because it involved being serviced by another person, engaging a chemical process, and reconstructing the self in order to play a public role, usually within white society. What was at stake in hairstyle was Baker's public identity as a modernized American woman, which was layered over the Africanist dancing she performed.

Baker's dance combines vague gestures toward Africa with her personal signature moves such as crossing the knees and eyes simultaneously. These moves and other improvisations add a playful and nonthreatening tone to Baker's dance. *Danse des bananes* is based in a colonialist imaginary but includes elements of an Americanized African-ness under an ethnographic gaze. As in the live performance of her *danse sauvage* in *La Revue Nègre*, Baker danced topless at the *Folies*, but she does not have a partner in this routine. The African male drummers who play and dance around the African American performer add to the spectacle of racial performance, and a lounging white explorer provides a conventional masculine presence for sexual tension as well as a colonialist audience surrogate. Baker's banana ballet shows strong influences from African dance traditions and includes black American movements as well as her signature eye crossing. The costume itself was meant to humorously concretize Baker's exotic colonial persona, and it took on a life of its own during and after *Folie's* run. Baker writes, "For this show, someone had the idea of having me wear only and for always a belt of bananas. Oh! How this idea has turned ridiculous! How many drawings and caricatures it has inspired! Only the devil, apparently, could have invented something like that" (Baker and Chase 137; my translation).[5] Indeed, the costume's designer is uncertain, as Jean-Claude Baker put it: the paternity is attributed to different people, particularly Jean Cocteau or Poiret, who did design evening gowns especially for *La Vénus Noire* (137).

In a sense Baker became the banana belt, a commodification of natural talent or raw material; she was a product of the Empire. In the banana dance, she's meant to be a fantastical creature, a bunch of bananas animated as a beautiful dancing girl, transformed by colonialist fantasy. Baker represented colonial commerce and abundance of raw materials. Like the bananas, Baker had become a transnational commodity. She was an advertisement come to life. Among Baker's most popular songs of the 1930s was the double-entendre ditty, *"voulez-vous de la canne à sucre?"* (Would you like some sugarcane?). As this material suggests, Baker's persona was associated with the products of colonialism. In this regard, Baker's signification is continuous with advertisements for rum, tobacco, or other colonial products that used images of black females to represent the product's faraway origins and its ability to arouse curiosity as pleasure.

Imperial and sexual politics within France are inscribed both in Baker's performance and in its reception. While her brand of novelty dancing was often called savage and animalistic early in her career, Baker's onstage sexuality was viewed as playful and nonthreatening in the thirties. Unlike her predecessors in freak shows, Baker was not seen as a monstrous freak. She performed a form of feminine sexuality that, when combined with her ethnic notions, or those projected onto her, made people laugh. Yet Baker seems to have been ambivalent about being a comic as well as about her famous banana costume.[6] Baker and the bananas became so closely associated that she had great difficulty separating herself from that 1920s performance when she sought to develop her singing and acting in pursuit of a more sophisticated persona in the 1930s. In her postwar onstage or made-for-television performances, however, Baker displayed a sense of humor about her early days. For example, during a performance recorded at Olympia music hall, she struggles to sit on the edge of the stage, but she laughs it off with a quip about her complications and how much easier everything was *"quand j'avais mes bananes"* (when I used to have my bananas) (*The Josephine Baker Show*). Such moments provide an occasion to look at two Josephines simultaneously: the mature chanteuse of ballads and novelty songs and the younger woman who performed as a belt of dancing bananas.

Looking back, the anonymous men, women, and children who portrayed village life at colonial fairs in the United States and in Europe are less easily assimilated into the fantasy of Paris as a refuge, when compared with the often celebrated history of early twentieth-century soldiers and jazz musicians who preceded Baker in Paris. These "actors," I suggest, are Baker's precursors because their spectacularity created a context for Baker's innovative creations and the audience's capacity to interpret them, though their conclusion was often that Baker was illegible. Baker's performances replaced the single-emphasis and illustrative function of early ethnic representations with the glib way in which she would layer African and American elements, confusing any distinction between those that were authentic and those that she choreographed. Through her dancing (and eventually its adaptation to musical comedy films) Baker created an entirely fictional, elastic ethnicity. Taking account of the invented nature of Baker's elastic ethnicity and its history problematizes the much romanticized relationship between the French and black people, particularly Americans.

In order to appreciate the heterogeneity of Baker's fictional ethnicity, it is important to consider the racialized images from

United States culture on which she drew. Alongside the live ethnographic displays of the nineteenth century, early African American dance films, in particular, figure into Baker's aesthetic lineage. The visual and kinetic aspects of the cakewalk phenomenon, to name perhaps the most salient example, were captured on film. These films last from twenty or thirty seconds to several minutes and isolate the dance from the revue from which it was likely extracted. The framing was relatively expanded for that purpose but not to the extent of revealing a context such as a stage or other background. These are single-subject films and might have been part of a longer program of dance or spectacle films. Early black dance films provided exposure for performers, while today they serve as texts that show key elements of particular dances. These films can be employed to speak to issues of race and representation precisely because they are performance pieces isolated from a larger narrative. As film, the performances become signs, at once more superficial and denser in their meanings and associations.

The dancing in cakewalk films appears to have been performed exclusively for the camera even when it is paired with acting sequences in a longer work. For example, in *Uncle Tom's Cabin* (1903), a sequence called "Tom and Eva in the Garden" breaks the narrative in order to feature a performance. In the dance, four couples cakewalk on a stage with a painted backdrop. In a tight shot, stylishly dressed women carry umbrellas and high step in circles. One of the women raises the hem of her dress with one hand, in a slightly flirtatious gesture. In a 30-second Biograph film, *Ballyhoo Cake* (1903), several couples perform the dance outdoors; however, there is minimal description of the space they occupy and the camera frames the bodies tightly. This method holds for films of non-American exotica such as *Fatima's dance du ventre* (1896). It shows Fatima, a woman in an Orientalist costume, moving her arms up and down, with some shoulder movement, but she concentrates her most dramatic series of moves on the belly. The Fatima of this earlier film may be the same performer who was later acclaimed as "the greatest Oriental dancer" and featured in the film *Fatima's Coochee-Coochee Dance* (by late July 1896). An April 1896 article in the *New York Clipper* described Fatima as "an oriental dancer who has become particularly well-known in this city and vicinity, also danced in the second scene of Marguerite, and apparently found much favor with the audience. Many of the objectionable features of her performance were omitted, but, nevertheless, her motions throughout the dance strongly suggested the 'couchee-couchee'" (qtd. in Musser 220). This excerpt implies that Fatima's film performance was edited as a means of censoring the overly sexualized aspects of her dancing. The unique possibilities of film material permitted spontaneous and repeated viewing that could be edited, as desired. Though these short films have a realist or documentary function, they nonetheless participated in the formation of racial and gendered fictions. The example of Fatima further illustrates this point.

A May 1896 advertisement also in the *New York Clipper* announced that Fatima had just closed "six weeks of successful engagement at Hammerstein's Olympia, N.Y. City" (qtd. in Musser 221). Fatima was "the lady whose graceful interpretations of the poetry of motion has made this dance (the *danse du ventre*) so popular of recent years" (qtd. Musser 220). Thus the film producer James White of Raff & Gammon sought to capitalize on the audience's desire to see her again or for the first time in the peep-hole kinetoscope (qtd. in Musser 220–21).[7] Novelties of motion, viewing, and the illicit, the couchee-couchee dance and the kinetoscope function symbiotically. Further, many black dance films can be best described as triple novelty. They showed "black" skin, motion (of image and figure), and the projection and enlargement of an image—or the miniaturizing of an image in the kinetoscope.[8] This was a crucial moment when African American identity was cast as an aesthetic construction by the medium of film. This cinematic blackness circulated with a variety of ethnic dances and exotic performances.

Through these early films, the spectator saw live performance brought closer to them as a recorded image. The screen showed a dancer or dancers directing their performance to the camera. The actors' gazes and bodies are directed toward the camera rather than toward the scene within the shot. Without a before and after, the performance appears unmotivated, which makes the absence of a narrative as much of a problem as a solution. Fatima's act and early black dancing such as the cakewalk foregrounded the special capacities of motion picture film while "documenting" and naturalizing the idea of blacks as entertainers. Images of black dancing made stars not just of the individuals on the screen but of all black people. It characterized them through the body and defined them in terms of their physicality. The material of film and the image of the black dancer create a double astonishment by combining the attraction of the body and the spectacle of film. Significantly, the films featured the dancing of particular cultural groups, and the isolation of the dancer and dance from their contexts tends to make them a sign of their culture. As such, they are quite different from the living dioramas and cultural replicas of African American or African cultures I described above, but they are linked discursively through the primary goal of exhibiting an Other.

As I have sought to show by bringing together black performances from the United States and France, as well as from theater, musical hall, and cinema, live ethnological spectacles could and did take many forms. One reason for this variety is that the European audience member had one way of looking at foreign peoples: as objects. And this ethnographic gaze was adaptable to several commercially viable performance venues, which served as enlargers or projectors, using light and visual language to transport an image of the live figure from the "real" to the realm of myth. In many ways, much writing about Baker presumes a white male spectator who provided a uniformly positive reception of Baker. If it was not entirely positive, it certainly brought Baker the kind of attention that helped to make her a star. However, black intellectuals, including the African American press, watched and reflected upon Baker's performances. Larsen's novel *Quicksand* is one of these responses.

Quicksand indexes the problematics of transatlantic black popular culture, formed in the cross-currents of European Primitivism and the Harlem Renaissance, both encountered and embodied by Josephine Baker. Larsen's novel stands apart from other Harlem Renaissance depictions of travels within and outside the United States, as one of the few sustained critical reflections on the visibility of black women performers like Baker, as well as on the resulting romanticization of their European context. Of course, numerous fictional and nonfictional works of the Harlem Renaissance share *Quicksand's* themes of mobility, utopian longings for home, and concern with the theatricality of identities. James Weldon Johnson's *The Autobiography of an Ex-Coloured Man* (1912 and 1927), Claude McKay's *Banjo* (1929) and his autobiography *A Long Way from Home* (1937), Jessie Fauset's *Plum Bun* (1929), Langston Hughes's memoir *The Big Sea* (1940), and Zora Neale Hurston's *Their Eyes Were Watching God* are some particularly illustrative examples of this interest in mobility. Using the conventions of passing narratives in some cases, these texts express the Harlem Renaissance's concern with migration, cultural hybridity, and representations of the body; this tendency is further reinforced when they evoke the atmosphere of the cabaret, circus, or dance, since such theaters of fantasy tended to generate a carnival atmosphere where symbolic borders of public roles are crossed. These spaces typically encourage patrons to experience and exploit social masks for their own pleasure; they allow greater play with and performance of identity than the home or workplace. Migration here is tied to identity formation and deformation.

Like Baker's art, however, Larsen's novel does not so much participate in this deformative play as embody the era's more pressing crisis of representation. As Carby explains, Nella Larsen creates a self-aware protagonist who explores "contradictions of her racial, sexual, and class position by being both inside and outside these perspectives" (169). Moreover, it is precisely Helga's alienation—a socially constructed, historically informed state of mind, rather than a "purely individual transformation"—that enables Larsen to treat issues of representation, the visibility of black bodies in a public sphere, within a framework that includes but is not limited to the circulation of negative black stereotypes (169). As I have discussed above, this circulation took a variety of historical forms that are each absorbed by the multi-disciplinary nature of the cinema: the European tradition of ethnological entertainment, the exoticist tastes in dance in 1920s Paris, and the tendency to idealize black beauty.[9]

Like Nella Larsen's Copenhagen, Paris was in no way an uncomplicated freedom zone for African American visitors. Americans traveling to European cities found themselves in a hall of mirrors, in which they negotiated their self-perceptions and ideas about America and about blacks in the diaspora with those that were projected onto them. The idealism of texts such as historian Tyler Stovall's *Paris Noir: African Americans in the City of Light,* which emphasizes the phenomenon of black success in Paris, seems to obscure the city's more complicated ethnic tensions. The framework of Helga's hopes about Copenhagen enables us to see how the city of light uniquely provided black Americans the cultural space to perform Blackness with pleasure; they finally felt free to embrace the very romance with blackness that many American and French whites have always enjoyed. But there was a cultural pay-off for the French as well. Investing its identity in Paris and the freedom of black expatriates to some extent, France attempted to resolve (for itself) the longstanding tension between its liberating principles and its colonizing activities, by seeing itself through the eyes of the black American refugees it harbored. Expressions of blackness became synonymous with expressions of freedom. What black American community there was in Paris was formed out of this shared expression. Thus, black Americans' expatriation to Paris is significant not only because they achieved success that they might not have found in the United States, but also because their work and lives constituted a new black identity. The phenomenon of black American success in Paris is not entirely the result of good will; it emerges from a mutually beneficial relationship between the French and black Americans rather than simply being one group's escape from racism.

Josephine Baker's Cinematic Celebrity   143

Notes

1. For more a more complete account of Nella Larsen's mytho-biography, see Thadious Davis.

2. Of special note are two biographies: Claude McKay and Langston Hughes. For a more comprehensive view of internationalist writing during this period, see Brent Edwards.

3. The term "ethnological entertainment" is an adaptation of Bernth Lindfors's usage in the title to his book. Fatima Tobing Rony uses a related term in her work, as well.

4. See Ivan Karp and Steven D. Lavine. Essays in this collection discuss the construction of ethnic identity through the objects of museum displays. They explain the ways in which iconic materials, representing the Other, serve as a prosthetic link to displaying culture's past. For an examination of black American images in colonial fairs, see Shawn Michelle Smith, 159–86.

5. In Jean-Claude Baker's and Chris Chase's biography of Josephine Baker, her speech is rendered in French, as the book is in the French language. It is not clear what language Baker said these words in originally. I have translated his quotation. The French is as follows: "Pour cette revue, on avait eu l'idée de me faire porter, en tout et pour tout, un ceinture de bananes. Oh! Comme cette idée a été tournée en ridicule! Combien de dessins et de caricatures elle a inspirées! Seul le diable, apparemment, aurait pu inventer une chose pareille."

6. Baker certainly engaged traditions of black humor, but her ambivalence toward being a comic registers her vulnerability in a world where blacks were more often the targets of humor. See Mel Watkins, 200–265.

7. Nonextant dance films provide an insight into the problematic roles that Blacks played at cinema's origins. *The Pickaninny Dance—From the Passing Show/The Pickaninnies* (Edison, 6 October 1894), an Edison film of Lucy Daly's "Pickaninnies," a troupe of black male dancers, appears to be the earliest moving picture images of African Americans (Musser 133). Edison's kinetoscope films of the 1890s featured popular black dancers performing their stage acts. For example, black vaudevillian James Grundy appeared in *James Grundy, [no. 1]/Buck and Wing Dance, James Grundy, [no. 2]/Cake Walk,* (both Edison, January 1895), and *Grundy and Frint* (Musser 174–75). Black music hall performer Elsie Jones was featured in *Elsie Jones [no. 1]* and *Elsie Jones [no. 2]* [both Edison, 26 November 1894] (Musser 157–58). *Dancing Darkey Boy* (October 1897) "shows a small colored boy, about ten years old, amusing the stable hands with a characteristic negro dance," according to the catalog description (Musser 327). Edison's images of African Americans were not limited to dance films, but with few exceptions, the films tended to mobilize plantation-era stereotypes, which showed the ex-slaves in comedic narratives

centered on eating watermelons or stealing chickens. However, images such as *Colored Troops Disembarking/24th U.S. Infantry* provide clues to a counternarrative (Musser 426). *The Pickannies* can be viewed online: www.indiana.edu/~bfca/clips.html. While early African American images must be understood in terms of a hostile social environment that emerged alongside mass cultural forms such as cinema, the fact of a black figure dancing, isolated from narrative, presents an ambiguous potential for a racist statement. The question becomes what is the status of dance, particularly black physicality relative to other content in moving images.

8. Early film materials raise questions of audience and reception that are not easily resolved. For example, it is difficult to know exactly which films were projected for an audience of spectators and which were seen in individual kinetoscopes. Knowing the difference would determine in large part how I would interpret an image. In terms of race and aesthetics, it is also difficult to reach conclusions on the formal qualities of the film in order to determine how lighting, skin tone, and other racial markers were handled because deterioration of the film heightens contrast.

9. What Carby calls an "intertextual coherence" among black women's writing in literary, autobiographical, poetic, and nonfictional forms opens up fresh routes to understanding personal, historical experiences in a wider social context (160).

Works Cited

Baker, Jean-Claude, and Chris Chase. *Josephine: The Hungry Heart.* New York: Random, 1993.

Ballyhoo Cakewalk. Biograph, 1903. *Ernie Smith Jazz Film Collection, 1894–1979,* Ben Publos, Franklin A. Robinson Jr., and Wendy Shay. National Museum of American History, 2001.

Blanchard, Pascal, Nicolas Bancel, and Sandrine Lemaire. "Les Zoos Humains: le passage d'un 'racisme scientifique' ver un 'racisme populaire et colonial' en Occident." *Zoos humains: de la vénus hottentote aux reality shows.* Ed. Bancel, Blanchard, Lemaire Gilles Boetsch, and Eric Deroo. Paris: Editions La Découverte & Syros, 2002. 63–71.

Bonini, Emanuel, and Eric Lange. "Filmography." *La Veritable Josephine.* Paris: Pygmalion, 2000.

Carby, Hazel. *Reconstructing Womanhood: The Emergence of the Afro-American Woman Novelist.* New York: Oxford UP, 1987.

Dance du Ventre. American Mutoscope and Biograph Company, Edison Manufacturing, 1894. *Ernie Smith Jazz Collection, 1894–1979.*

Davis, Thadious. *Nella Larsen, Novelist of the Harlem Renaissance: A Woman's Life Revealed.* Baton Rouge: Louisiana State UP, 1994.

Edwards, Brent. *The Practice of Diaspora: Literature, Translation, and the Rise of Black Internationalism.* Cambridge, MA: Harvard UP, 2003.

Ernie Smith Jazz Film Collection, 1894–1979, Ben Publos, Franklin A. Robinson Jr., and Wendy Shay. National Museum of American History, 2001.
Fabre, Michel. "International Beacons of African-American Memory: Alexandre Dumas père, Henry O. Tanner, and Josephine Baker as Examples of Recognition." *History and Memory in African-American Culture.* Ed. Geneviève Fabre and Robert O'Meally. New York: Oxford UP, 1994.
Griffiths, Alison. *Wondrous Difference: Cinema, Anthropology, and Turn-of-the-Century Visual Culture.* New York: Columbia UP, 2002.
Hallucinations d'un Pompier / Le Pompier des Folies-Bergères. Unknown credits. Circa 1927 (Lobster Films).
Hughes, Langston. *The Big Sea.* 1940. New York: Hill, 1993.
The Josephine Baker Show. Dir. Jacques Rutman. Radiodiffusion Télévision Française. 1964.
Karp, Ivan, and Steven D. Lavine, eds. *Exhibiting Cultures: The Poetics and Politics of Museum Display.* Washington: Smithsonian Institution, 1991.
Larsen, Nella. *Quicksand.* Ed. Deborah E. McDowell. New Brunswick: Rutgers UP, 1986.
Lindfors, Bernth. *Africans on Stage: Studies in Ethnological Show Business.* Bloomington, IN: Indiana UP, 1999.
McDowell, Deborah E. Introduction. *Quicksand.* By Nella Larsen. Ed. Deborah E. McDowell. New Brunswick: Rutgers UP, 1986. xi–xxxv.
McKay, Claude. *McKay: A Long Way from Home.* London: Pluto, 1937.
Musser, Charles. *Edison Motion Pictures, 1890–1900: An Annotated Filmography.* Gemona: Le Giornate del Cinema Muto; Washington, D.C.: Smithsonian Institute, 1997.
The Pickannies. "Early African American Images." Black Film Center / Archive. University of Indiana. Bloomington, IN. 27 September 2005. www.indiana.edu/~bfca/clips.html.
Princesse Tam-Tam. Edmond T. Gréville. Arys Production, 1935.
Sharpley-Whiting, T. Denean. *Black Venus: Sexualized Savages, Primal Fears, and Primitive Narratives in French.* Durham, NC: Duke UP, 1999.
Siren of the Tropics. Mario Nalpas and Henri Etievant. Production unknown. 1927.
Smith, Shawn Michelle. "Photographing the 'American Negro': Nation, Race and Photography at the Paris Exposition of 1900." *American Archives: Gender, Race, and Class in Visual Culture.* Princeton, NJ: Princeton UP, 1999.
Stovall, Tyler. *Paris Noir: African Americans in the City of Light.* New York: Houghton Mifflin, 1996.
Tobing Rony, Fatima. *The Third Eye: Race, Cinema and Ethnographic Spectacle.* Durham, NC: Duke UP, 1996.
"Tom and Eva in the Garden." *Uncle Tom's Cabin.* Edwin S. Porter, 1903. *Origins of Cinema, Vol. 1, 1989–1905.* Nostalgia Family Video, 1996.
"Un village nègre au Champ de Mars." *L'Illustration,* 15 June 1895, 508. Bibliotheque Nationale, Paris.

Wall, Cheryl. "Nella Larsen, Passing for What?" *Women of the Harlem Renaissance*. Bloomington: Indiana UP, 1995. 85–138.

Watkins, Mel. "The New Negro: Harlem and Hollywood . . . exotics, imposters and other misshapen identities." *On the Real Side: Laughing, Lying, and Signifying—The Underground Tradition of African-American Humor That Transformed American Culture, from Slavery to Richard Pryor*. New York: Simon, 1994. 200–265.

Zou-Zou. Marc Allégret. Les Films H. Roussillon Production, 1934.

POSTWAR PARIS AND THE
POLITICS OF LITERATURE

CHAPTER 6

Assuming the Position
Fugitivity and Futurity in the
Work of Chester Himes

Kevin Bell

> But there exist other values that fit only my forms.
> —Frantz Fanon, *Black Skin, White Masks*

In the disappeared third side of a Parisian triangle he draws between Richard Wright, James Baldwin, and Chester Himes, drinking and fighting, advancing and recoiling, all on the terrace of Les Deux Magots on a spring evening in 1953, *New Yorker* writer Hilton Als, describing the scene nearly fifty years later in a profile on Himes, detects the betrayal of an unspoken ideological mandate presumably governing the field of black American literature after the Second World War.

The alcohol consumed by the three writers that evening loosens the boundaries of a hazardous zone of dense interpersonal tension, already laced by an ancient intertwining of fiction's force and ideology's racialist insistence. The primary fabric of this tension is a ruptural, sarcastic word-play that, without drink, might have remained soberly submerged, repressed within a public sphere essentially tone-deaf to the agonistic gestures of an inchoate, expatriate black literature, defined from its very beginnings by the paradoxical task of making poetic sense of the multiply dislocated conditions of its own expression. What results that evening is a conversation between Wright and Baldwin that is as sharp in its mutually contemptuous edges as it is pointedly free in its accusatorial range.

The freedom of the dialogue's violence, however, is silently enframed and brutally circumscribed throughout by the American literary rules of professionalized "blackness." The rigors of such rules—policed as they are within the self-reproductive regimes of the publishing arm of the American culture industry—are amplified even as they are reconfigured by this interplay among artists who are rivals and, in the shared-ness of the ground each seeks, also brothers, writers who will never form an ideological or creative unit, yet who will ever be viewed within a certain unitary fusion.

The scene at Les Deux Magots in 1953 is originally recorded by Himes himself in the first volume of his memoir *The Quality of Hurt* (1972). By Himes's account, its very arrangement is born in an antagonistic swirl of egoism, betrayal, voyeurism, and perhaps, not-so-surprisingly, fraternity:

> Later, as we were preparing to leave for the party, the telephone rang. When Dick returned from answering it, he wore that look of malicious satisfaction which his close friends knew so well. He asked if I knew James Baldwin. I said no, but I had heard a great deal about him . . . I had read a review of *Lonely Crusade* that Baldwin had published in the Socialist Party's newspaper, the *New Leader,* but I had never met him.
>
> Dick said that he had been instrumental in getting Baldwin an award for eighteen hundred dollars and a renewal for nine hundred from Harper & Brothers to enable him to write his first novel. . . . He said Baldwin had "repaid his generosity" by "attacking him" in a number of published articles. . . . "Now Baldwin has the nerve to call me to borrow five thousand francs (ten dollars)," he said gleefully.
>
> He had made an appointment to meet him at the Deux Magots, and insisted that I go with him. I remember thinking at the time that he sounded as though he wanted a witness . . .
>
> Then we hurried to the Deux Magots and found Baldwin waiting for us at a table on the terrace across from the Eglise Saint-Germain. I was somewhat surprised to find Baldwin a small, intense young man of great excitability. Dick sat down in lordly fashion and started right off needling Baldwin, who defended himself with such intensity that he stammered, his body trembled and his face quivered. I sat and looked from one to the other, Dick playing the fat cat and forcing Baldwin into the role of the quivering mouse. It wasn't particularly funny, but then Dick wasn't a funny man. I never found it easy to laugh with Dick; it was far easier to laugh at him on occasion.

Dick accused Baldwin of showing his gratitude for all he had done for him by his scurrilous attacks. Baldwin defended himself by saying that Dick had written his story and hadn't left him, or any other black writer, anything to write about. I confess at this point they lost me. (199–200)

Somewhere within the sudden relocation of a conflict from the sphere of the personal and its competing narcissisms to the more abstracted planes of the political and the aesthetic, Chester Himes becomes unmoored from the contest's stakes. Where he becomes "lost" is on the idea of a somehow "proper" program by which to write or *re*-present the linguistic, aural, and textu(r)al fluidity of an immanent blackness that, in Himes's own work, is *always* antecedent to the local act of closure and exclusion that is racialization. Much of the cited passage gestures toward that realm of strangeness—that fevered, often ecstatic and megalomaniac blindness to the limits of one's own position in space; that blackness, which is prior to and always outside social orders of propriety, designation, and tradition. It is a plateau of nonidentity and ongoing incomprehensibility that, for Himes, designates the actual point of writing's commencement.

Stage directions toward this zone of private abandon gone public abound in Himes's account: the silent self-satisfaction with which Himes notes Wright's curiously "malicious" pleasure at Baldwin's embarrassing need for money; the more conspicuous editorial silence about what Himes thought of Baldwin's review of Himes's second novel; the wicked suggestiveness of the thought that Wright may have wanted and even needed "a witness" before his dealings with the suddenly suspect Baldwin; the studied attunement to Wright's supposedly defunct humor; the sharply critical opposition of Wright's "lordly" "fat cat" to Baldwin's effeminized, nearly infantilized "stammering," "trembling," "quivering mouse." Each of these characterizations transmits an enmity born of intimacy that disrupts the scene's reportage even as it reconstitutes it, and by way of caricature in the last instance, points toward the textures of the tragicomic absurd that Wright and Baldwin tend to abjure in their own work. But at the same time, these are the vertiginous textures of self-abyss and self-contradiction within which the writing of Chester Himes finds itself very much "at home."[1]

In his reconstruction of the conversation, Als notes with a momentary prescience that is nearly fatally compromised by a characteristic glibness, that Himes's quiet dis-identification that evening is at least partially a function of his aesthetic comportment, a salient feature of the singular philosophical freedom that enables his indifference to the personal and political rewards over which Wright and Baldwin now carp. As Als writes:

> He was not a skilled literary politician nor was he as adept as Baldwin or Wright at self-promotion. He had never been hungry enough or insecure enough to learn the game. So, on that Paris evening, he failed to recognize that his compatriots weren't discussing the finer points of *literature*—that, unlike the former college boy sharing their table, Wright and Baldwin were gladiators by necessity, fighting, at Les Deux and in parlors around the Faubourg Saint-Germain, to establish whose spear was long enough to pierce their largely white audience's consciousness, and anoint its wielder head literary Negro. (93)

As we observe, the vanishing side of this would-be triangle is more cutting in the totality of its self-effacing, its disappearance more playfully and indeed, drunkenly, free in its withdrawal than is the hyper-defensive aggression of either of the anxiously narcissistic combatants. Which is only to say that, in the absence of anything for which to compete against either Wright or Baldwin this particular evening, Himes dissolves into the unheard contouring of another articulation—into the soundless articulation of an altogether different mode of critical presence, belonging to a completely other set of critical imperatives. He abandons, or more precisely, is abandoned by what he imagines as a literary zone of social realist pathos, now demanding and regulating the aesthetic re-presentation of a black masculinity whose continual estrangement from any hope of self-possession would allegorize the entirety of twentieth-century black thought and experience in the United States.

In his disengagement from the performative protocols of such conventionality, Himes opens a silent investigation into the deeper implications of Als's journalistic reduction of the encounter's stakes. But the theoretical space cleared by Himes's silence extends also into the darkly vast otherness of an ongoing history of abjections and abolishings, whose energies and afterlives cannot be managed or accounted for by reigning academic practices of historicism and whose extradocumentary realities are only marginally available to any representational aesthetic logic of realism. The question at Les Deux Magots that evening, while clearly inflected with the kinds of careerist gamesmanship foregrounded in Als's snapshot, has more to do with how to animate novelistically these ancient *and* future realities of black survival and black creativity. The question is complicated in Himes's case by the fact that his literary project seeks to activate an aesthetical-political engagement of a de-legitimated and outcast sensibility, whose ineffable and ineradicable *blackness* is at once anterior to the logic of racialization and, at the same time, augmented, reshaped, and intensified exactly by those dimensions of lived experience unique to the scene of public fascination and public abjection (or exclusion from the zones of thought, value, and history) that is cultural blackness.

Himes's critical tendency toward the necessarily highly reflective figurality of this discarded life and thought has something vital to do with what Theodor Adorno sees as "radical" in all "dark" art after 1945: its reopening of an abyssal "speechlessness" that accompanies and critiques the banalities and horrors of everyday consumerism, administered sameness of social and commercial forms, and the nonstop atrocities on which such art obsessively ignites (*Aesthetic Theory* 39, 40). It is an art whose blackness inheres in its open inability to console or to reconcile its auditor or spectator with such realities, produced and intensified as these realities are by the hyper-capitalism to which they are attendant and by which its spectators are compliantly conditioned. In Himes, however, this immanent blackness moves beyond what might seem the strictly dialectical terrain of Adorno's model and into the question of what Jean-Francois Lyotard later calls the impenetrable "space-time-matter" of language in the moment of working within literature (6). This question, as we will see, forms a great part of the basis of Himes's most incendiary work and seriously complicates, if it does not explode, the customary critical logic by which his work is disposed of as strictly "oppositional." Such a logic presumes Himes's work to be yet only another sounding of the "cry of anguish" of social realism or naturalism that Robert Bone pronounced it to be in 1965.[2] It is suggested here that in both his detective fiction and his novelistic meditations, Himes's work actually produces something much closer to the cry of the real that by necessity escapes every symbolic coding and classification, that breaks every contract of transparent meaning or valuation and undoes every uninterrogated "law of the named" (de Certeau 149).

Not attuned to the radical nonpositionality of this kind of figural irruptivity, Als, throughout his *New Yorker* piece, conflates author and literature. He continually collapses presumably explanatory narratives of class warfare, threatened masculinity, and, most predictably, "black authenticity" into the journalistic conjuring of a one-man Negro Problem—the very ethos that Himes himself weaves and unweaves so athletically throughout each of his nondetective novels and suggests so intensely in the detective works. It is the literary *un*weaving of this ethos in Himes's work that most of his commentators, like Als, leave almost entirely unattended, focusing instead upon what seems the "hardness" of the hard-boiled cadence that characterizes the speech of many of his protagonists and the general style of his narratives themselves. What customarily eludes analysis is the equally palpable parallel track of Himes's style—an imperative of incessant and fluid movement, the continually transformative upheaval of internal vision and thinking by which those same protagonists become more sharply defined in the first place. It is a fluidity within which what is hard is made to boil and dissolve, a technical principle of liquidity by which these characters' masculinist stances and postures are constantly exposed as nothing more than identificatory stops between situational and conceptual crises—which themselves turn out to be as foundational to the stylistic figuration of the novels as they are to the works' thematic premises. As Als claims:

> Himes produced male characters who really were *noir*—in fact and in sensibility. Unapologetic and testosterone-driven, they weren't hard-done-by; they were in love with having done wrong. Turned on by their own bravado, they claimed entitlement and viewed sex as a struggle for power—the only form of intimacy that engaged them. "Race was a handicap, sure . . . but hell, I didn't have to marry it," says Bob Jones, one of Himes's narrators, before describing how he has used his skin color for financial gain . . .
> Undoubtedly, Himes's detachment from the forces that shaped his fellow writers had much to do with his own social entitlement. Unlike Wright or Baldwin, he was a child of the middle class. Privilege doesn't always cushion you from the sting of the lash, but it can act as a balm. Still, Himes was in constant rebellion against his background. . . . In a sense, Himes's entire oeuvre can be read as an attempt to prove how black he really was, and to authenticate, de facto, that abstraction. (90–91)

Just now, it does not seem advantageous to send those stranger effects of Himes's writing into the conceptual lockdown of a merely strategic move of defense against such a psychologizing, even pathologizing account as Als has provided us, though, among other things, the totality of Als's misreading of the cited lines from *If He Hollers* may appear to demand exactly such a direct and immediate rejoinder. For what eludes Als is the radical hollowness at the center of each example of "hard-boiled" Himesian positivity he enumerates; the acutely reflexive and ever-present *absence* of the kinds of self-certitude and self-consistency that such "testosterone-driven" "bravado" as that found in Himes's protagonists would depend upon for all psychic support. Such internal absence characterizes the very first image that Als presents—Himes's own silence before Wright and Baldwin at Les Deux Magots.

Himes's quiet withdrawal from the triangle Als imagines is not an act of aggression or repudiation but is something far less volitional. His concluding line, "they lost me," is in the lexicon of a certain incompetence. It testifies to a frank inability to participate in the exchange as an equal on the field of assertive positing and combat. However, its passivity registers not as a withered impotence but as an educated hesitancy to step into any line of argumentation that might validate primary presumptions of cultural "blackness" or the stasis of subject positionality or identity of any kind. His identification is not with the professional "race-men" that Als all too blithely and reductively suggests Wright and Baldwin to be; nor is it with any flattened, commercial image of "the writer" by which Als can be said to frame the café exchange itself. The signature shifting speeds and intensities of Himes's writerly style, and its general organizational liquidity, all seem to channel Blanchot's channeling of Schlegel: "you can only *become* a writer, you can never *be* one; no sooner are you, than you are no longer, a writer" (61).

Himesian *becoming* permanently disables and scatters the notion of "Himesian" being, and is, for this reason, largely unavailable to instrumentalist or identitarian/ideological concerns of how black, how middle-class, or how rebellious he was or was not. Such typology marginalizes the strangeness to which Himes is attuned, converting the play of his poetics into the flat realism he molecularizes—and thereby reverses. It freezes the divergent energies, tensions, contradictions, colors, and tones that constitute thinking/writing life into a uniform set of narrative ordinances that would choreograph the scripted gestures of some such novelistic "black" subject in the American textual marketplace. Himes's reticence is thus only a withdrawal from the assertive furor of transparency and certitude that is taken so frequently and uníronically to mark his own highly reflexive writing.

For Himes, I argue, the only reality of noir is its dissonant, discordant, always jarring sensibility. What Als puns as noir's social "fact"—the cultural imposition of anthropomorphic "blackness"—is for Himes only one more bizarre code inscribing the matrix of constructed social boundaries, identities, and binaries: top/bottom; in/out; black/white, that alienate thinking life from itself and constitute what Himes views as the absurd aspiration of locating one's place in American culture.

In such work, the question of literature's time, space, and matter, or its figural materiality, as heard and felt within its American twentieth century anyway, is always already cut by the urban sonorities, colors, and movements that, in most of his American literary contemporaries, constitute little more than added flavorings, punctuations, and accents by which to augment an already-established, normative "white" interiority. That is to say that, for most of Himes's contemporaries, forms of vernacular blackness are reduced to modes of black affectivity that are depreciated into the mere instrumentality of seasoning, distorted and imported for the purpose of stereotypic ridicule. What Himes realizes and reworks is the inexhaustible force of this figurality's darkness to itself: the aesthetic shock, to itself, of its very becoming, the ongoing event of its necessary regeneration within the discarded districts of his Harlem, his South Central Los Angeles, his Cleveland, his Jersey City. This figurality's own time, space, and matter, its duration, movement, sound and color, is the surface expressivity of *thinking's* motion. It is a membrane of expressivity as impenetrable as any other; indeed, more so, owing to the thick wall of mythology constructed around its meanings. It is the criminally resistant idiom of an abjected and discarded urban blackness, defined primarily by its being subject to discourses of its utter *non*subjectivity.

While the gestures of such an idiomatic opacity work in part to subvert the "rational" arresting procedures of ideological machineries of comprehension and mastery, in Himes's fiction they also haul themselves in for routine questioning, exposing a reflexive inclination toward self-suspension and self-dissolution in his art that is fundamentally at odds with the conventions of the hard-boiled tradition within which his work is customarily flattened and slotted critically. The dark sensibility that informs the singularities of his work by 1953 is sharply differentiated from the by-then normative protest routes of resistance and advocacy made so pristinely and programmatically respectable and devoid of risk or even surprise, as to be nearly impotent by the midst of the civil rights movement (indeed, so predictably respectable that in novels from *If He Hollers Let Him Go* [1945] and *Lonely Crusade* [1947] to the delirious satire *Pinktoes* [1961], Himes makes a concentrated point of holding what he views as the paralytic middle-class liberalism of the movement up to sustained ridicule, as only another hustle in an American matrix of endless con games).

In other words, the silence that is the breaking of the triad at Les Deux Magots is only another moment of a critique immanent to a wave of untimely and often unknown black artists that includes such figures as Himes and, before him, George Schuyler, as well as younger contemporaries such as Charles Wright, William M. Kelley, the filmmaker Melvin Van Peebles, and Ishmael Reed. Their work, in its radical obsession with the fullness of its own poetic effects and with the rupture of ideological continuum constituted by the very fact of such figural obsession, shows the degree to which it is also calculated to expose the hollowness of the social equilibrium from which it issues.

Disappearance, taking the affective form of reticence during the meeting at Les Deux Magots, is Himes's only logical response to cryptic chords sounded by Wright and Baldwin. Himes hears these chords as part of a pathetic and premodern song demanding the novelistic rehearsal and reprojecting of an essential black humanity and even nobility. The entire life project of such a humanity, as Himes hears it, would be to demonstrate the truth of its claims to the very structure of power and exclusivity that has made the performance of such a plea necessary. In a word, perhaps Himes's favorite, such a project is essentially absurd. That Himes's social nonengagement of this demand might blithely undermine a cultural metanarrative of American "blackness"—that his art undertakes to shatter, rather than to exploit—is theoretically consistent, if affectively incongruous, with the more overtly noisy and aggressive ruthlessness of his writerly aesthetic. As Himes writes in *If He Hollers:*

> The alarm went off again; I knew then that it had been the alarm that had awakened me. I groped for it blindly, shut it off; I kept my eyes shut tight. But I began feeling scared in spite of hiding from the day. It came along with consciousness. It came into my head first, somewhere back of my closed eyes, cold and hollow. It seeped down my spine, into my arms, spread through my groin with an almost sexual torture, settled in my stomach like butterfly wings. For a moment I felt torn all loose inside, shriveled, paralysed, as if after a while I'd have to get up and die. (2)

Abandoned here is the calm self-mastery and effortless resourcefulness of the traditional hard-boiled hero, now collapsed into the involuntary shudders and spasms of a body at the mercy of the unconscious's submerged frequencies. Self-mastery is inverted, self-estrangement is intensified as Bob Jones, protagonist of the first Himes novel, *If He Hollers Let Him Go,* begins to sense, long after the fact, that he is caught up in what Avital Ronell would call an "exploration of the limits of *interiorizing violence*" (93). What comes "along with consciousness" is the noxious return of ideological matter ingested from without. He finds his body to have been no more than a false boundary, powerless to exclude the toxins that so organize and paralyze his movements. He finds, with repeated surprise, that if ideology is indeed ingested like the air we breathe, the racialism that it plugs into is necessarily and incessantly breathed back out into the atmosphere in the next moment with the vengeance of an internally eviscerating virus, returned to the zone of its origin. Himes writes:

> It was the look in the white people's faces when I walked down the streets. It was that crazy, wild-eyed unleashed hatred that the first Jap bomb on Pearl Harbour let loose in a flood. All that tight, crazy feeling of race as thick in the street as gas fumes. Every time I stepped outside I saw a challenge I had to accept or ignore. Every day I had to make one decision a thousand times: *Is it now? Is now the time?* . . .
>
> I carried it as long as I could. I carried my muscle as high as my ears. But I couldn't keep on carrying it. I lost twenty pounds in two weeks and my hands got to trembling. I was working at the yard then as a mechanic and every time my white leaderman started over toward me I drew up tight inside. I got so the only place I felt safe was in bed asleep.
>
> I was scared to tell anybody. If I'd gone to a psychiatrist he'd have put me away. Living everyday scared, walled in, locked up. I didn't feel like fighting anymore. I'd take a second thought before I hit a paddy now. I was tired of keeping ready to die every minute . . . (4)

The detached perspective of the knowing hard-boiled hero is here broken up, folded into a scene that heretofore it would have described and managed as if from a clear-eyed distance. Jones finds himself possessed within the field of social vision, his claustrophobic view limited *only* to the immediate scene of the affective movements before him, his thinking now organized not by the social premapping of any given situation but strictly in terms of his internal responsiveness to the image of "the look," to the suffocating thickness of a crazy, wild-eyed feeling. The reality of this feeling is exposed in its total inability to articulate itself into anything as reassuringly direct as an actual "challenge"; its force is made more palpable and tyrannical by its failure to cohere itself into something like a position, by its utter difference from anything resembling a discourse. Negotiating this passage, like so many in Himes, means abandoning the presumptively given scene of "the racial" and radically re-thinking the contours of the social. For what we observe in Jones are the gradual movements of the opening of an internal vision—not as it reacts to the practical ordering of a situation within culture—as in the narrative progressions of a workday or a trip to the grocery store—but as it reacts to the unfoldings of singularized images, sounds, movements, and textures momentarily disconnected from the principles of "situation." In its dislocation from the narrative logic of situational continuity, the fluidity of Himesian scenography transmaterializes the defining lines of "identity," for we observe here that Jones's sense of a recognizable self-shape is sharply compromised by the fact of his hyper-responsiveness not to "selves" or to types, but to glances, blinks and stares, tonalities and cadences of voice, speeds and arcs of movement. Such fragmentary agents orbit around him as a constellation of blindnesses and deafnesses, insensate and indifferent to any analytic of control or identity, forcing him into an excruciatingly liberatory zone of what Nathaniel Mackey might term a "post-expectant futurity." Within which the redemptive promise of "the human" and its hierarchies of rights and values are abandoned in the experimental practice of life continually exposed to the impossibility of finally determining its own meaning (50–51). What is required is the movement of life into the continual opening of such internal vision and hearing, unburdened from the weight or preemptive conditioning of the baggage of former hope or expectation, of any specific circumstance, disposition, or ending. In this way we observe that Himes's thematizations of racialist American antagonisms function as conceptual vehicles by which not merely to describe, but to detonate and destructure as radically absurd the American ideological nexus of "race," consumerism, and anti-intellectualism that so completely warps his swarming cityscapes. It is in this sense that Himes's fiction and, perhaps most devastatingly, the series of detective novels for which he is best known and most popular does more than eviscerate the "high/low" ideological dynamics that separate such writing from the proper novel. It also disrupts the troglodytic political drives that prop up mythologies of racialism and also support humanist notions of canonicity, literary modernism, and even postmodernism that are formed nowhere near so rigorously as the unsparingly ironic writing that exposes their contradictions and absences.

The sudden popular resurgence of the long-obscured Himes as the grand documentarian of all things "street"—whose customary invocation itself forms only another static substitution for actual engagement of his writing—displaces with the frozenness of journalistic image the aporetic fields of sonic and chromatic breakage and duration that are the real object of Himes's obsession. Each of these fields houses an intrinsic force that Himes maximizes in the motions, tones, and subtones of word and phrase. Each field is the locale for the kind of sensorial engagement that implicates Himes within the tropics of modernism and the surreal, and in exile from the flat realism with which he is still customarily associated. His terrain is the figural, which, as Lyotard reminds us, "is a denial of the position of discourse" (9). The plasticity of the figural improvises and highlights difference, finding its home in paradox and confusion, playing in an aphasic state marginalized by orders of knowledge and imperatives of proper designation.

Stumbling into a new mode of hearing and being during a marijuana stupor at the Blue Note in St. Germain Des Pres, one autumn night in 1961, he awakens to a revelation. "I suddenly realized my slang was ancient; I was inventing a language no one spoke anymore. What makes my books popular was not that they were hip; they were popular because they were absurd" (*My Life* 241). Like Walter Benjamin on hash Himes realizes that language is not his to manipulate but that language *"happens to him* like an outward event" (Ronell 30; emphasis added); he finds himself within its grip and not the other way around. Like Benjamin also, he recognizes this private truth of "self" only through ingestion of something exterior and inhuman.

Where he is lost during drinks at Les Deux Magots in 1953 and again at the Blue Note in 1961 is exactly at the boundary of the inhuman and the re-presentational. For by thinking not in dogma or advocacy but in sound and texture, not in discourses but in discontinuities and intervals, not in positionality but in energies and speeds, he abandons every mapping of the reassuringly human, of the uncomplicatedly "black," and crosses into the poetic nonidentical. In this zone, he relinquishes the notion that the ongoing mutilation of the American racialized can be converted either into an ideological referent or an object of aesthetic manipulation. Himes works within a more profoundly negative zone of art, in which the redemptive tendency to try to equalize or protest the silencing of the abjected via the logic of re-presentation is trashed by the unpresentable reality that haunts it. He realizes that to make the living history of that abjection the object of a cognition, a mere re-presentation by concept is to once again callously "drown out the screams of its victims" (Adorno, *Negative Dialectics* 67). Himes's literature is concerned instead to create worlds of movement, sound, texture, line, and breakage that interact directly with bodies, institutions, laws, and cultures, amplifying the singularity of each, by addressing not its powers of instrumental language but of affective furor, of each field's individual idiom of pure expressivity, its abilities to convey meanings that operate in excess of language. It is work that emphasizes less the presumed content of a discourse than the inscriptive cuts that modes of thinking such as affect and idiom enact on discourse.

The Open Secret of Time

Even in what he thought of as his serious novels, as opposed to the detective series he produced in Paris between 1957 and

1969, Himesian authenticity unfolds not at the levels of the sociological but always within the exquisitely temporal core of the affective; within his refusal to arrogate to a function of identity or "race" thinking the aphasic and suspenseful compulsions of thought, desire, and question that identificatory habituation stops cold and that also cut art loose from any idea of its fixed comprehensibility. Unlike most writers occupying the genre spaces of naturalism or social realism, which allow the image of a more or less stoic subject to stand, racialized, sexualized, gendered, flattened within the political grids of capitalistic modernity's classifications, the proliferation in Himes's work of disjunctive energies and intensities scatters the notion of a self-coherent, unitary protagonist who judges and organizes from without an equally free-standing, external world of meaning. In Himes, thinking is something that calls the thinker from the outside, again, something that takes possession of him from a distance, transfiguring his being, splintering him from an organized unit of coherence and autonomy into a highly volatilized swarm of disjointed affects, impressions, sensations, memories, and constructs. In other words, for Himes, the social reality of reified, racialized life in the States is always already beyond surrealism; the movement of thinking, like that of literature, or music, or the sermon, exposes our actual experience of the passage of time, presenting what Deleuze terms "the pane" through which time is split and "presents pass, replacing one by the next while towards the future, but also of preserving all the past dropping it into an obscure depth" (*Cinema* 87). In the following passage from Himes's 1938 short story "Pork Chop Paradise," the voice of the preacher performs the function of the interconnective pane:

> He rocked his congregations, he scared them, he startled them if by nothing else except his colossal ignorance, he browbeat them, he lulled them, he caressed them. He made hardened convicts want to shout, he made gambling addicts repent and give away their ill-gotten gains and stay away from the games for two or three whole days. He played upon people's emotions. His voice was like a throbbing tom-tom, creeping into a person's mind like an insidious drug, blasting the wits out of the witty, and filling the hearts of the witless with visions of everlasting beauty.
> It had an indescribable range, sliding through octaves with the ease of a master organ. It was like a journey on a scenic railway, dropping from notes as clear and high as Satchmo ever hit on his golden trumpet, like the sudden startling dive of a pursuit plane, to the reverberating roar of heavy artillery.

> You could see hell, in all its lurid fury, following in its wake, and then, with as abrupt a change, the voice took you to green pastures lush with manna. (*Short Fiction* 261)

This voice is the mechanism by which opening fuses itself to opening, by which present disappears itself into a past now gone, displaced by another present now present. The immobility that is the scene of listening is at the same time the scene of this visual pageant's procession—a procession itself borne by the ongoing movement and changing of the voice's sonority. It is a literary playing out of what Eleanor Kaufman describes, in a provocative discussion of time, image, and posed immobility in Klossowski and Resnais, as "a solecism of time, in which past and present inflect one another with a contradictory yet nonetheless sustainable tension." We observe that the friction, or resistance between the fixity of the listening ear and the nonending fluctuation of crescendo and diminuendo projecting from the voice, produces a continual (re)opening of the abundant internal life of visual/sonic forms themselves; the experience of changing images and sounds, which is only the exchange of different presents, is not determined by the organizing narrative of de-scriptions by the speaker, but is motored entirely by the vocative intensity or force of his explorations in the dimension of sonority itself.

Invited by Marcel Duhamel, editor of Gallimard's detective novel series *La Serie Noire*, to start working in this genre in 1956, Himes initially balks, uncomfortable with what he considers his ignorance of the noir novel's conventions. Duhamel appeals to him with an ocular/auralization of literature in which the emphasis is relocated from plot and discovery of meaning or value to the movement of cut and paste, from writing in pathos to thinking in images of a psychovisual and acoustic dream space of endless labyrinths and passages in which colors, energies, and textures appear and shift without warning—writerly effects that are made more forceful, ironically, by way of a certain immobility. Himes describes it thusly in his memoirs:

> "Get an idea," Marcel said. "Start with action, somebody does something—a man reaches out a hand and opens a door, light shines in his eyes, a body lies on the floor, he turns, looks up and down the hall.... Always action in detail. Make pictures. Like motion pictures. Always the scenes are visible. No stream of consciousness at all. We don't give a damn who's thinking what—only what they're *doing*. Always doing something. From one scene to another. *Don't worry about it making sense. That's for the end. Give me 220 typed pages.* ... Keep

the suspense going. Don't let your people talk too much. Use the dialogue for narration, like Hammett. Have your people use the description. You stay out of it." (*My Life of Absurdity* 102; emphasis added)

The apparent refutation of thought argued by Duhamel is in truth only the articulation of thought now unbinding itself from its presumptive obligation to the metaphysical *image* of thought. That dead image is replaced with an emphasis upon exteriority that necessitates a new orientation toward time in which time is no longer that which *connects,* in the illusion of a linear unity, movements, ideas, and bodies, but is instead that which *allows each* of these to open up and unfold with power, independently of each other, according to the inner logic and intensity of each. His indifference is not at all to the notion of thinking, but only to the idea that this question is subordinate to that of who does the thinking. What Deleuze says of Kleist can be thought equally productively of the Himes who produces worlds of such indifference, that in his work "feelings become uprooted from the interiority of a subject to be projected violently outward into a milieu of pure exteriority that lends them an incredible velocity, a catapulting force: love or hate, they are no longer feelings but affects. . . . Even dreams are externalized, by a system of relays and plug-ins, extrinsic linkages" (*A Thousand Plateaus* 356).

At work in Himes is a sensorial labor by which impression is reprojected not simply as expression but more like what Tom Cohen calls ex-scription, in which the inscriptive cut made upon us by the impressions we absorb from the outside creatively marks itself as the trigger of a now-transfigured thinking (17). The cut of the impression that we attempt to narrate or re-present necessarily reconfigures the mechanics *by which* we narrate, thereby guaranteeing the virtual and differential character of the former impression now rendered in another form. Here is an example of Himes enacting Duhamel's formation, in which the presumably descriptive actually opens up an alternative of speed as a way of seeing and thinking matter, in which the value of an image seems to depend upon its relation to other images in the surface of the text and is therefore dependent upon the figuration of that text. By maximizing isolated faculties of description (darkness, speed, uncertainty) Himes forces the relinquishment of this habit of comparison and makes available to us the invasion of nuance or timbre:

> The second shot creased the back of his neck, burned through his fury like a red-hot iron and lighted a fuse of panic in his enraged brain. He was in an awkward position, his left leg

crossed over his right onto the stair below, left arm raised in reflexive defense, right arm groping forward, and his body doubled over in a downward slant like an acrobat beginning a twisting somersault. But his corded muscles moved as fast as a striking snake. His taut legs propelled him in a burst of power across the landing and his right side slammed into the wall, bruising him from shoulder to hip.

Mother-raper! He cursed, gasping through gritted teeth and came off the wall turning, pushing with his right leg and right arm and right hip . . . moving so fast he was around the corner and out of range before Walker's third shot dug a hole in the white plaster wall where a fraction of an instant before, the shadow of his head had been.

He went down the bottom stairs in a somersault. It was started and he couldn't stop it . . . so he took it, catching the third stair with the palms of both hands . . .

Walker chased him, charged down the top stairs teetering as though half blind. He missed the last stair before the landing, slammed sidewise into the wall and fell to his hands and knees.

"Wait a minute, you black son of a bitch!" he screamed unthinkingly.

Jimmy heard him and came up from his squatting position with a mighty push.

The minds of both were sealed, each in its compelling urge, one to kill and one to live, so that neither registered the humor in Walker calling to Jimmy to wait and get himself killed. (*Run, Man, Run* 31)

The differential force of the scene's speed emerges by way of its interspersed stoppages, as the very thinking necessary to movement articulates itself by way of a metaphorical vocabulary of action's necessary breaks. Metaphors of movement and intensity disguise the arresting, cessational function they actually perform; the "red hot iron" that underscores the speed of the bullet that creases Jimmy's neck is itself a rigid solidity possessed of an internal force that leaves the permanent mark of a singe, the "striking snake" that makes visible the danger, speed, and rage that only becomes threatening within the suspended, poised coil of his taut, ready musculature; it is at the same time, however, a solidity, a firm body that while capable of murderously rapid motion, is also there, available to be captured and struck itself by a movement faster than its own. It is the "sealed" quality of each man's thinking—its inflexible indifference to the density of any physical obstacle to the surging of their movements—an unusually and powerfully enabling closure—that separates them hopelessly from any extra-physical dimension of abstraction, such as humor, honor, or justice.

In another passage, from *Yesterday Will Make You Cry,* the customary freneticism of Himes's fiction is shifted from the fissured, entropic cityscape of Harlem tenements, canyons, and unlit streets to the claustrophobic interior of an American penitentiary in the 1930s. Within the immobility of the imprisoned consciousness giving spring to itself, the motion of the unannounced intervals between images articulates the facticity of thinking's weaving and unweaving of its own limits; which is only to say that what we observe in the passage is the conversion of matter's event into matter's reflection by way of an enforced fixity. This conversion provides the means of a certain transport out of lockdown's stasis (state lockdown) into the fluidity of what Deleuze calls "recollection-images," individuated, multiple images that that trigger within us the past in which they are preserved (*Cinema* 87). What emerges in the passage, however, is not simply the life of the boundary at which past collides with the present of its reanimation—but what one sees/hears as an outward movement borne by the very gesture of thinking's rush and the dissolving or collapsing of each of its images into the next—a jumble of movements and shifts whose friction eventuates in the production of images that live and are yet unseen. This materiality of movement within the space of immobility is the historical writing of an utterance unable to assemble itself into a positive statement:

> Those were the days; the moving, living, endless days with legs that dragged but yet kept marching through the stone and steel and five-foot thicknesses of concrete walls. The days with bloody guts filled with the gory slime of degeneracy, enclosed with the gray stone blankness of walls, lashed with bars falling in steady monotonous blows—the bleeding, living, peopled days of convicts doing time . . .
>
> But there were the nights, which were not nights at all but were the moments alone when he escaped the days. The moments when no one was with him, neither the convicts nor the guards, nor the discipline nor the rooted, immovable prison.
>
> The nights of loneliness of which no one knew, which had no past, no future, no hope or perspective or foundations in respectability or beliefs or faith or love or hate, but which were only the times immediately present with thoughts which grew out of nothing and conclusions which grew out of them . . .
>
> All of those confused and not very clear and not very old and too touching thoughts and emotions which grew out of

> those nights out of hackneyed, tear-squeezing stories, out of lying awake when he should have been asleep, or from an old tune in clear notes on some distant convict's mandolin—a sudden lilt of melody across a moment's mood like an eccentric artist's fingers upon the chords of chaotic groping, weaving into romantic confusion or violent rebellion the new and jumbled and not very clear and too touching thoughts and emotions of those nights alone . . .
>
> And those thoughts, like angels' words, like the sidewalks trying to speak, like the mute prayers of the black scared night, weaving fantastic, unsleeping dreams into patterns of girls who were never born, and muted tones that were never played, and poems that were never written; into tense emotional situations wherein he always acted in a brave and noble manner; into horses breaking the barrier at Saratoga while he leaned against the railing, cigarette curling a nonchalant ribbon of smoke into the blue, sunny sky, with fifty thousand dollars on Red Rosebud . . .
>
> Only in his thoughts. The lovely stimulating bittersweet sensations—so utterly unreal. Like something from another world.
>
> And the next day, ashamed of them. Ashamed as if they were the clap or syphilis or cancer. (225–28)

Memory's motion, as it slams against the thick concrete walls and lashing bars of the present, links imprisoned thought to the exterior surfaces and shapes of images and sounds that themselves *live,* embodying an unchecked freedom whose evidence is shown by their very disconnectedness to each other in (their) time and teleology—but not in space—the concretely rigidified space within which they collide without end. This is the scene of radical freedom heard in Mackey's remarkable distillation of the experimental/improvisational in his phrasing of a somehow "post-expectant" (50) futurity, in which the imagining of an elsewhere of unborn girls, speaking sidewalks, unwritten poems, and unperformed music finds the reality of these sounds and their contours, unbound from any purposiveness beyond their own expressivity or articulation. It is a freedom whose first emancipation is from the very hope of its foundation within language or culture. Himes meditates upon the abyss of radical isolation in which thinking *becomes* thinking. The space of nothingness is by necessity one of contingency and purest experimentality in that nothing is returned to its occupant, no correction, no validation, no recognition, no refutation, no discourse of legitimation or even rejection. The materiality of its psychic and linguistic fabric is forced into an obsession with finding and moving beyond its own limits, its boundaries discovering and rediscovering themselves only in the exercise of their own gestures.

Such writing crumples the censoring schemas of genre that would divide surrealism from hyperrealism, modern from postmodern, dismissing the despotic tendencies of those laws of canonicity and racialism that would neutralize into tone-deaf positionalities of either affirmation or repudiation the bodily shudders of horror and guttural cracks of laughter provoked by the laconic athleticism of Himes's expression. Hardly any plunge into a violently nihilistic pool of relativism, Himes's novels are rather an improvisational rethinking of time and event that, in their irreverent defusing of the definitional and in their cinematic poetics of discontinuity, expose and eviscerate the American culture industry that produces "race," "gender," and other categories of cultural identity solely in order to exploit them. In so doing, his work unfolds a strange and darkly impressionistic language in which those closely related dimensions of abjection, the niggered, the noncanonical, and the non-identical can converse openly, demanding an absolutely irreducible form that makes no pretense of strict re-presentationality. This work foregrounds the figural materiality of language in which its accidental, unmotivated timbre or nuance touches that telic, ideologically programmed dimension, a meeting in which the ongoing mutual inscription of these two dimensions clamors for recognition as an event in itself.

What Is Left

Baldwin's informal notion of there being nothing left to introduce or to explore for black writing after *Native Son* automatically implies its opposite, namely, that there exists a something to be left out. In this way he unintentionally announces his subscription to an analytic of propriety and exclusivity that he attacks and dismantles elsewhere throughout his life and career. As he and Wright skirmish on the ideological question of "what is left" for black writing after *Native Son,* Himes checks out, witness once again to the fact that *his* peculiar field of writerly interest—American absurdity—has just now proven itself as fertile as ever. The very articulation of the "nothing left" is enabled by its belonging to a strictly identitarian principle regulating a constellation of issues and pressures unique and proper to "the" project of African American writing. The negatively charged remainder that is everything outside that constellation, or whatever might be "left" in the aftermath of the absolute truth apparently delivered/captured by *Native Son,* is, for Baldwin (at least in this youthful, tense, challenged instance) a marker of impoverishment. But for Himes, the very enunciation of this "nothing left" functions as the commencement of an outward excursion.

"What is left" has everything to do with how to play the membrane dividing and connecting what Himes hears as excess and what Baldwin hears as scarcity in the literary imagining of African American subjectivity in the 1940s and 1950s.

The vicious procedure by which the spectral figure of "blackness" is forced to internalize the rhetoric of otherness that literalizes its subjective distance from its "white" double, unfolds somewhat more subtly but no less fatally in *The End of a Primitive* than in *If He Hollers*. Himes again plays upon the white egoism that creates the phantasmagorical myth of the bestial black Other who is materially conditioned to eventually become exactly the nightmare that race ideology has always already ordained him to be. The protagonist, Jesse Robinson, is acutely aware (and more cynically so than Bob Jones before him) of the transformation and denuding of his chaotic "inside" of possibility, at the hands of an ideologically constricted and racialist "outside."

The terms by which Jesse attempts repeatedly to assert his completeness as a writer and intellectual in racialist culture are not distant from those by which the novel must assert itself formally and aesthetically. It stands not only against its immediate precursors in African American literature such as Ellison's *Invisible Man* (1952) and Wright's *The Outsider* (1953), but also against the grand narrative of literary history itself, as Robinson's habits of quotation and reference from Rabelais to Gorki to Proust represent the tapestry of narratives into which Himes belatedly weaves himself. Jesse's Manhattan is interpretable only in its self-stratification into ontological categories of its own construction. It is a product of presumably stable determinations and oppositions such as black and white, high and low, masculine and feminine, that create for it a readily accessible catalogue of rubrics by which to illusorily define and comprehend itself. In this sense Himes's work addresses a central problematic of literary modernism, this being that the imperative of identity itself assumes the character of law.

The narratives of textual code and sign that the characters must assemble if they are to decipher culture are the same by which they are to assemble themselves into discrete beings. Wresting himself from the last in a series of nightmares structured by the thematic constant of his complete social invisibility, Jesse takes lonely survey of his Harlem rented room. He blearily recomposes himself amid the accumulation of temporal waste that metaphorically underscores his simultaneous superfluousness and fragmentation: dirty ashtray, half-emptied package of cigarettes, half-eaten candy bar, half-emptied milk carton, an alarm clock with a cracked crystal face. Then his eyes meet an ancient mahogany cabinet situated in a corner: "Inside the cabinet, behind the closed doors, were his stacks of unpublished manuscripts, carbon copies, old papers and letters which he always kept nearby, carting them from place to place, hanging on to them year after year, to remind himself that— no matter what he did for a living—he was a writer by profession" (*Primitive* 36). The only avenue into self-actualization for Jesse is textuality, as he has literally written himself into personal subjectivity, staging a rhetorical identity by which to insert himself into the grand narrative of abstracted humanity. Summoning himself into a suddenly coherent self by means of discarded, rejected writing, Jesse inscribes the supposedly secondary function of writing as something else, something generative that doesn't merely document his difference but produces it. Himes narrates this function as a necessary precondition not only of the writer but of subjectivity itself. This is not merely to undermine any presumed dichotomy between subject and object but to demonstrate that anxiety and uncertainty compel the tissues of social narrative and signification that function above all as strategies of resolution, in the forms of codes, traditions, and identities by which culture defines itself to itself.

The cost of such an existence for Jesse is the near absolute indifference of a postliterate culture, or what he terms "all the processed American idiocy" (21). To comfortably situate himself at a remove from the culture of television and waste he so caustically dismisses, he must ignore his own participation within it, discounting the psychedelic possibilities at his immediate disposal in favor of the "higher" responsibilities of a serious writer:

> He was still too drunk for a hangover but his head felt unset and his body unjointed and everything had a double-edged, distorted look like a four-color advertisement with each color slightly out of line.
>
> However his brain was sharp. For the past five years it had never let him down. It was packed with some definite emotion, defined in intellectual terms; futile rages, tearing frustrations, moods of black despair, fits of suicidal depressions—all in terms of cause and effect, of racial impact, and "sociological import"—intellectual horseshit—but nagging as an unsolved problem, slugging it out in his mind, like desperate warriors . . . whatever he did to deaden his thoughts, there was this part of his mind that never became numb, never relaxed. It was always tense, hypersensitive, uncertain, probing—*there must be some goddamned reason for this, for that.* (33)

The deadpan absurdity of the second paragraph's reversal of the first nearly renders the scene comic. Jesse's logo-logical anxiety even penetrates and undercuts the inebriation by which he presumably attempts to obliterate it. But what is actually negated by the admittedly "desperate war" of telos, of "meaningfulness," and the primacy of fixed literary and intellectual conventions, even as they are recognized as the cheapest clichés, is the possibility of self-discovery or invention via actual experience represented here albeit crudely, by the state of drunkenness. Abandonment to radical ambiguity, to the aporetic wonder of "four color," "double-edged" distortion is finally forsaken in the name of "definite emotion" rendered in "intellectual terms," that can access nothing but a heavily commodified, popularly manufactured and conventional representation of blackness, a politically soberized version of black exotica. This commodity is bereft even of the charm of kitsch, for unlike kitsch, this kind of cultural reification takes itself dead seriously. The shattering racism that dictates the vicious reduction of life to what Jesse views as such one-dimensional "intellectual horseshit" is only made possible by an absolute negation of irony and "tense, hypersensitive" uncertainty, all of which might undermine the "'sociological import'" of good protest writing. This genre, true to Himesian fatalism, goes out of style while Robinson is in midcareer—and its demise might seem to create an opening in which he might forge a finer art. But no such opportunity exists; one clichéd fad must be replaced upon its death with another:

> Pope laughed. "You're a hell of a good writer Jesse. Why don't you write a black success novel? An inspirational story? The public is tired of the plight of the poor downtrodden Negro."
> "I don't have that much imagination."
> "How about yourself? You're certainly a success story. You've published twelve novels that were very well received."
> "That's what I mean."
> "I don't understand you."
> "Damn right you don't," Jesse thought. He didn't care to remind Pope that a moment or so back he'd termed the rejected novel as autobiographical. (124)

Himes's wicked burlesque directed at the racialist banality of American publishing and indeed, at the numerous authors who produce such writing, reaches its most penetrating as he permits Jesse to perceive the stupidity of his professional conditions, but also forces him to internalize and accept them. The customary impressionism by which Jesse is able to decipher at the level of the social is brutally repressed at the level of the professional. Sacrificed in his careerist capitulation is the recalcitrant inclination to intertextual distortion and ironic revision that so marks his personality elsewhere. The differential character of his analysis, burdened and burnished as it is by material and political concern, is outlawed by the conventions of a literary market that cannot allow the miscegenation of "black" writing and modernist, impressionistic sensibility:

> From where he stood at the corner of Eighth Avenue—a pesthole of petty thugs where a man could buy a gun, hot or cold, for fifteen dollars up—down to the tricornered, old stone *Times* building in the narrow angle where Broadway crossed Seventh Avenue, was a block of infinite change. Once in the lives of very old men it had been a mudhole; then had come an era of fashion, of furred and diamonded women with their potbellied escorts alighting from lacquered carriages beneath the glittering marquees of plush modern playhouses. Now it was descending into a mudhole again, but of a different kind. The once famous playhouses, lumped together on both sides of the street, were now crummy second- and-third-run movie theaters, contesting with the cheap appeal of a penny arcade with its shooting galleries, mechanical games, flea circus, thimble arena where Jack Johnson had done a daily stint of boxing in his waning years. And in between there were the numerous jewelry stores with fake auctions every night, beer joints, cafeterias, sporting goods stores . . . book stores that dealt principally in pornography, second-class hotels and filthy rooming houses.
> "Poor man's Broadway," Jesse thought sourly, as his searching gaze flitted from the lighted movie signs to the passing faces: then his mind began improving on the commonplace phrase, "Melting pot . . . already melted—rusting now . . . last chance . . . I can get it for you hot—hotter than you think, bud . . . this side of paradise—way this side." (61)

Jesse fades into the loose narrative of images that he imposes on the urban landscape, finally disappearing behind the Fitzgerald reference that maintains its status as forbear only momentarily before it is corrupted by the street suggestion of the leering coda, "way this side." Rather than a mournful elegy to the block's bygone "era of fashion," the passage elucidates Jesse's vision of the inevitability of temporality's rush, of "infinite change," and of the perpetual improvisation made necessary by ongoing impoverishment. Even the deserted past is rendered in imagery of fleeting light and transient beauty, of "diamonded women" passing in "lacquered carriages beneath glittering marquees." The evident waste of the now "crummy" movie houses, "lumped together" into an undifferentiated mass still presents the opportunity of Otherness suggested by the "way this side" of paradise, clearly a "cheap appeal," but still an open invitation into an infinite, anarchic zone of differentiality rather than into a self-evident, solid "state" of ruin.

Himes's identification for the articulation of temporalized sensibilities in writers from Proust to Joyce translates into a precondition for the narrative structure of *Primitive,* in which the language of the interior is identical to that of the social, and in which the horrors of urban reality are staged in the unconscious. *The End of a Primitive* is not so much a naturalistic expression of the futility of relationships "interracial" or otherwise as it is an ironic catalogue of the signifying procedures that expose the oxymoronic status of positive terms like "interracial," that firstly presume a proper "racial" category to be engaged. In the figure of a "white woman" who is devalued and shunned by "her own," because she indulges in sex with "black men," and in the figure of a literary "black man," who privileges his own eccentricity above any collective implication or allegiance, Himes addresses a more comprehensive problem in modernism itself. This problem is the dismantling of the antagonisms of purity and contamination, home and homelessness, origin and absence that continually reproduce themselves as idealizations or abominations and that atrophy into social law.

What enraptures Jesse as he stands on the corner are writerly revisualizations, by which to rediscover the animation of the images that swarm around him without freezing them into the stasis of definition. These gestures, contradictory, unstable, dispersive, constitute the pure point of affect at which articulation itself is revealed as the tissue that substantiates the notion of a self, the point at which expressivity alone materializes the body of thinking. It is a space that in other words, is hopelessly divorced from every discursive principle by which it would organize itself into a re-cognizable positionality. Its occupant's thinking can only determine itself against the nothingness of its boundaries, can only measure itself against the absence of its return or response from without. For Himes, the square cell of imprisonment in *Yesterday* and the Harlem corner of *Primitive* are exactly analogous to the philosophical zone of experiential/experimental *freedom* suggested in Paris by Duhamel and worked out exhaustively in each of the seventeen novels he produced. It is a freedom, following thinkers from Nathaniel Mackey to Jean-Luc Nancy, that is not addressed by any logic of rights or even knowability, but more by a post-Idealist/postexpectant conception of freedom, which abandons every notion of denotation, every claim of truth and propriety, finding itself only in constant confrontation with its utter inability to stabilize the foundations of a solid state calling itself an "I." It is the freedom of writing and of speech, to split from itself and propel itself toward its outside, in the very instant that its sounding opens it to itself forever.

Notes

1. Lawrence P. Jackson, who has authored the first serious biographical study of Ralph Ellison, describes lucidly another transgression of the one-vision-at-a-time rules of engagement that all but completely dominate black literature in the immediate postwar period. Jackson exposes not merely the deeper implication of a nearly fatal myopia in the imagination of African American life and thinking on the part of our culture industry, resulting in the calcification of an aesthetically narrowed canon; more importantly, he throws light on pivotal moments of philosophical and artistic becoming, or discoveries and intensifications of creative vision—divergent and even mutually hostile though these may have been—in the writing lives of Ellison and Himes. While not especially concerned with issues of Himes's stylistic endeavors, and indeed appearing to hurl Himes back into the pre-modernist schema that my essay attempts to complicate, Jackson is one of remarkably few serious critics to note the historical significance of Himes's novels in the thematic expansion of African American writing.

2. Such an approach finds its most perfectly crystallized expression in Bone. He includes Himes's work in what he designates as the "Wright School" of African American writing, a naturalistic arc in which

    > literature is an emotional catharsis—a means of dispelling the inner tensions of race. Their novels often amount to a prolonged cry of anguish and despair. Too close to their material, feeling it too intensely, these novelists lack a sense of form and of thematic line. With rare exceptions, their style consists of a brutal realism, devoid of any love, or even respect, for words. Their characterization is essentially sociological. . . . The white audience, on perceiving its responsibility for the plight of the protagonist, is expected to alter its attitude toward race. (157)

    While most contemporary Himes criticism pushes recognition of the work's tonal dimension beyond Bone's rigidities, Michael Denning is among the very few who appear to see in Himes's figurativeness at least the possibility of a radical literary politics. Restricting his analysis to the detective series, he concludes by writing of one of its later installments, *Blind Man with a Pistol,* that "Here the original comic absurdity is joined to his social vision, and the detective genre is twisted to a postmodernist experimentation that makes this a just contemporary of Ishmael Reed. Here nothing is solved . . . the Harlem of his topography assaults the imaginary Harlems of white America" (Denning 10–18).

Works Cited

Adorno, Theodor W. *Aesthetic Theory.* Trans. Robert Hullot-Kentor. Ed., Gretel Adorno and R. Tiedemann. Minneapolis: U of Minnesota P, 1997.

———. *Negative Dialectics.* Trans. E. B. Ashton. New York: Continuum, 1983.

Als, Hilton. "In Black and White." *New Yorker,* 4 June 2001: 90–96.

Blanchot, Maurice. *The Writing of the Disaster.* Trans. Ann Smock. Lincoln: U of Nebraska P, 1995.

Bone, Robert. *The Negro Novel in America.* New Haven: Yale UP, 1965.

Cohen, Thomas. *Ideology and Inscription: "Cultural Studies" after Benjamin, DeMan, and Bakhtin.* Cambridge: Cambridge UP, 1998.

de Certeau, Michel. *The Practice of Everyday Life.* Trans. Steven Rendall. Berkeley: U of California P, 1984.

Deleuze, Gilles. *Cinema 2: The Time-Image.* Trans. Hugh Tomlinson and Robert Galeta. Minneapolis: U of Minnesota P, 1989.

Deleuze, Giles, and Felix Guattari. *A Thousand Plateaus: Capitalism and Schizophrenia.* Trans. B. Massumi. London: Athlone, 1988.

Denning, Michael. "Topographies of Violence: Chester Himes' Harlem Domestic Novels." *Critical Texts* 5.1 (1986): 10–18.

Himes, Chester. *The Collected Short Fiction of Chester Himes.* New York: Thunder's Mouth, 2000.

———. *The End of a Primitive.* 1955. New York: Norton, 1997.

———. *If He Hollers, Let Him Go.* New York: Thunder's Mouth, 1995.

———. *My Life of Absurdity: The Autobiography of Chester Himes.* New York: Thunder's Mouth, 1976.

———. *The Quality of Hurt.* New York: Thunder's Mouth, 1995.

———. *Yesterday Will Make You Cry.* 1950. New York: Norton, 1999.

Jackson, Lawrence P. "The Birth of the Critic: The Literary Friendship of Ralph Ellison and Richard Wright." *American Literature* 72 (2000): 321–55.

Kaufman, Eleanor. "Deleuze, Klossowski, Cinema, Immobility: A Response to Stephen Arnott." *Film-Philosophy, Deleuze Special Issue* 5.33 (November 2001, 12 July 2004), at www.film-philosophy.com/vol5-2001/n33kaufman.

Lyotard, Jean-Francois. "Gesture and Commentary." *Between Ethics and Aesthetics: Crossing the Boundaries.* Ed. Dorota Blowacka and Stephen Boos. Albany: State U of New York P, 2002. 73–82.

Mackey, Nathaniel. *Atet A.D.* San Francisco: City Lights, 2001.

Ronell, Avital. *Crack Wars: Literature Addiction Mania.* Lincoln, NE: U of Nebraska P, 1992.

CHAPTER 7

"One Is Mysteriously Shipwrecked Forever, in the Great New World"
James Baldwin from New York to Paris

Douglas Field

Language is the only homeland.
—Czeslaw Milosz

In *No Name in the Street* (1972), James Baldwin recollects the moment that propelled him to leave the sanctity of Paris in order to participate in the civil rights movement. In the fall of 1956 Baldwin covered the first International Congress of Black Writers and Artists at the Sorbonne. "One bright afternoon," Baldwin recalls, he was "meandering up the Boulevard St.-Germain on the way to lunch," accompanied by Richard Wright and other unnamed companions (383). The leisurely stroll is ruptured by the image of Dorothy Counts "on every newspaper kiosk." The sight of the fifteen-year-old African American student who was "reviled and spat upon by the mob" as she made her way to school in Charlotte, North Carolina, convinced Baldwin that he "could . . . no longer sit around in Paris discussing the Algerian and the black American problem. Everybody else was paying their dues, and it was time I went home and paid mine" (383).

Baldwin is in fact wrong about the dates: the Congress of Black Writers and Artists took place nearly a year before the photograph of Counts was taken, suggesting the ways in which he would ultimately rewrite—or re-sight—his reasons for leaving Paris for the U.S. South in 1957. Baldwin's first account of the Congress, "Princes and Powers," published in 1957, describes a very different scene from his recollections in *No Name*. Here, the "newspaper vendors seemed cheerful; so did the people who bought the newspapers" (143). Baldwin's mis-memory of the Counts photograph and the 1956 Congress, however, says much about the writer's relationship to Paris. Baldwin recalls seeing Counts's photograph in a "tree-shaded boulevard," in Paris, a safe and genteel environment, far removed from the "strange fruit" on the poplar trees that Billie Holiday evoked so disturbingly or Baldwin's description in "Nobody Knows My Name" of the red soil of Georgia, stained "from the color that had dripped down from these trees" (198). Baldwin's description of "meandering," in Paris and his acknowledgment that he also "dawdled" in Europe (383) is in sharp contrast to the urgency of the movement, where as he recalled in *No Name,* he was "wearily, marching, marching," along with Martin Luther King (435). If Baldwin positions himself as reporter and even *flâneur* at the start of *No Name,* the remaining sections of this long essay seek to show that he marched purposely as a civil rights activist. *No Name* is, in this sense, a carefully constructed rejoinder to mounting criticism that Baldwin was passé, that he had lost his way as a writer.

Baldwin would claim with a disingenuous flourish that he came to Paris by accident. "My journey, or my flight," he recalled in *No Name,* "had not been *to* Paris, but simply *away* from America . . . I ended up in Paris almost literally by closing my eyes and putting my finger on a map" (376). Baldwin's qualification ("*almost* literally") suggests that he may have peeped when placing his finger on the map. Baldwin was no doubt aware of Richard Wright's voyage to Paris in 1947, the year before Baldwin set sail for France. Given the long history of "Black Paris," it is likely that Baldwin would also have associated the French capital at least in part with its black American visitors, among them Countee Cullen, Langston Hughes, and Jessie Fauset. By 1972, Baldwin's description of closing his eyes suggests an acknowledgement that he had become blind to the struggles of the civil rights movement while in France, where his eyes would be reopened by the photograph of Counts.

Baldwin's recollection of waking from his Paris reverie may be inaccurate but it illustrates the writer's complicated relationship to the French capital which I trace through a reading of his "Paris essays": "Encounter on the Seine" (1950), "Equal in Paris" (1955), and "Princes and Powers" (1957) alongside other works where Paris is quietly invoked. Like Richard Wright's oeuvre, few of Baldwin's fictional works are set in Paris, with the exception of his second novel. Here I explore the relationship of *Giovanni's Room* (1956) in relation to wider discussions about black transnational culture and Baldwin's uneasy relationship, not only with Wright and Chester Himes but also with African and black Francophone writers in Paris. Unlike Wright, who played a key role in the 1956 conference, Baldwin was present as a skeptical reporter. In contrast to Paul Gilroy's later call for an understanding of the black Atlantic as a "single, complex unity of analysis," Baldwin repeatedly questions the unity of black transnational culture (15). Tellingly, Baldwin's decision to head to the American South, into the heat and heart of the movement, is precipitated precisely at the moment when Richard Wright, Leopold Senghor, Alioune Diop, the architects of the 1956 Congress, were attempting to define and develop a black transnational artistic and political community. For Baldwin, it seems, this project was less pressing than the material reality of the U.S. movement.

This chapter begins by tracing Baldwin's move from the United States to Paris to show the ways in which he sought exile from the stifling postwar constructions of American identity. In a reading of his essays about Paris, I then explore Baldwin's repeated questioning of the importance or legitimacy of what is now called transatlantic or transnational collaboration. For Baldwin, transnational exchange is fraught with difficulties that arise from cultural and linguistic differences, a feature of his essays that has arguably obscured his significance as a transatlantic writer. Though he was a self-confessed "transatlantic commuter," who not only lived in Paris but also died in the south of France, Baldwin rarely features in works about black transnational culture; for example, he is conspicuously absent from Gilroy's *The Black Atlantic* (*Conversations* 80). My aim here is not to recuperate Baldwin as a key transnational writer but to argue that his writing about Paris nonetheless constitutes a developing and coherent political aesthetic, one that anticipates and feeds into contemporary theories of transnational culture which are attentive to the different structures that make up black internationalism. As I illustrate in conclusion, Baldwin's views on national identity and U.S. imperialism evolved; his later work in particular shows that he was keenly attuned to North America's role in a global context, whether militarily or culturally. Baldwin's writings about Paris and the transatlantic in the 1950s, I argue, do not just trouble the critical romance of transnational culture as an achievable, desirable goal; rather his work adds to and enriches our understanding of the ways in which, as Brent Hayes Edwards notes, "the cultures of black internationalism . . . are equally 'adversarial' to themselves, highlighting differences and disagreements among black populations on a number of registers" (7). If Baldwin's essays about black internationalism articulate what we might call a political aesthetic of difference, his fictional writing about Paris seems even less concerned with black transnational culture. In *Giovanni's Room* (1956), set in a white expatriate Paris community, Baldwin seems interested rather in racial homogeneity and sexual difference. And yet as I argue through a close reading of *Giovanni's Room*, a novel replete with references to the sea, sailors, and nationality, Baldwin was nonetheless drawn to the ways in which black internationalism challenged the concept of national identity in France and the United States as exclusively white. In "Stranger in the Village" (1953) Baldwin concluded that "This world is white no longer, and it will never be white again" (129). Three years later, Baldwin published *Giovanni's Room,* a novel with no black characters. Here, I argue, Baldwin undertakes the risky strategy of employing a white middle-class narrator in order to expose the fabrications of white, heterosexual identity.

From New York to Paris

Baldwin's decision to leave America for Paris on Armistice Day 1948 has become a seminal moment in the writer's literary and political journey. His decision to move abroad afforded the writer distance from the stifling sexual and racial discrimination that he explored so powerfully in *Notes of a Native Son* (1955), what he later described as "five desperate years in the Village" (Conger 557). In "Notes of a Native Son," Baldwin had recalled the painful experience of being refused service at a Princeton burger bar, an episode that nearly cost him his life when he hurled a water mug at the waitress who refused to take his order (70–72).

Baldwin would reiterate in an interview that "I didn't *come* to Paris in 1948, I simply *left* America" and it's important to see his departure from the United States in the context of an increasingly hostile Cold War climate that drove hundreds of North American artists to seek creative refuge in other countries (*Conversations* 84). As Rebecca Schreiber has shown in her study of Cold War exiles in Mexico, the political and cultural climate of the 1940s and 1950s forced large numbers of U.S. writers, artists, and filmmakers into exile. James A. Dievler and other cultural critics have pointed out the ways in which "postwar culture fed the development of rigid identity categories in the postwar period," illustrated by mainstream discussions in existentialism and psychoanalysis about "the self," "identity," and "alienation" (169). For Baldwin, as illustrated by his writing during and about the late 1940s and early 1950s, these rigid identity categories were not only stifling but dangerous, particularly in the ways that mainstream culture created and perpetuated myths about what it meant to be American—a construction that inevitably meant male, white, and heterosexual. The increasing rigidity of sexual and racial categories in postwar New York led Baldwin to note in his 1985 essay "Freaks and the American Ideal of Manhood" (also published as "Here Be Dragons") both that "on every street corner, I was called a faggot," but also that the New York homosexual subculture could not contain or reflect his experience (821). "The queer—not yet gay—world," Baldwin writes, "was an even more intimidating area of this hall of mirrors" (823). Although Baldwin acknowledges that he was "in the hall and present at this company," he recalls that "the mirrors threw back only brief and distorted fragments of myself," an echo, perhaps, of the mirror shattered by the mug in the Princeton diner (823). Finally, as Baldwin recalled in an interview, he had to leave America:

> I no longer felt I knew who I really was, whether I was really black or really white or really female, really talented or a fraud, really strong or merely stubborn. I had become a crazy oddball. I had to get my head together to survive and my only hope of doing that was to leave America. (Cited in Weatherby 62)

Importantly, exile also afforded Baldwin the opportunity to reflect on what he had left behind. It's unlikely that Baldwin would have written his bold essay about masculinity and homosexuality, "Preservation of Innocence" (1949), if he had remained in America—and it is less likely that it would have been published. According to James Campbell, the editors of *Partisan Review*, who were only too happy to republish "Everybody's Protest Novel," a critique of Wright and protest fiction, would not touch "Preservation" "with a ten-foot pole" (*Exiled in Paris* 33).

In the years before his voyage to France, Baldwin had started to make his name as an acerbic and intellectually fearless reviewer; he wrote approximately sixteen book reviews from 1947 to 1949 for a group of left-wing publications associated with the New York Intellectuals, including *The Nation, Commentary,* and *The New Leader.* One of his most damning reviews was a piece on Himes's 1947 novel *Lonely Crusade* ("History as Nightmare") which could only have strained social relations with a future compatriot in Paris. Baldwin's review is a barbed assault on the older writer, who uses "what is probably the most uninteresting and awkward prose I have read in recent years" (11). In a review that reads more and more like a school report (written by a reviewer not long out of school), Baldwin awards Himes "an A for ambition—and a rather awe-stricken gasp for effort," adding that "Himes seems capable of some of the worst writing this side of the Atlantic . . . " (11).

Baldwin's move to Paris may not have endeared him to Himes and Wright but it did accelerate his transition from reviewer to essayist. Welcomed as part of an American expatriate community by the writers and publishers Albert Benveniste and George Solomos (known then as Themistocles Hoetis) Baldwin became, Solomos recalled "a sensation" in the Parisian café society.[1] Toward the end of 1949, Solomos and Benveniste asked Baldwin to contribute a piece to their newly formed avant-garde magazine, *Zero*. In a recent interview Solomos recalls that he asked Baldwin to submit an essay several days before the magazine was ready to go to the printers, and the result was "Everybody's Protest Novel." This famous essay was first published in the inaugural issue of *Zero*, and not, as often attributed, in *Partisan Review*.[2] In *Zero*, Baldwin's essay appeared alongside impressive British and American contributions, including poetry by John Goodwin, William Carlos Williams, and Kenneth Patchen and a short story by Christopher Isherwood. Midway through the magazine, Richard Wright's story "The Man Who Killed a Shadow" sits before Baldwin's "Everybody's Protest Novel." Solomos is adamant that Baldwin was unaware that Wright was contributing to *Zero* and yet the title of the older writer's story seems uncomfortably prophetic.

According to the editorial statement, *Zero* "acts as a raw and basic channel for creative assumptions, affiliating itself to all and to no techniques: conscious and unconscious, erudite and untutored, therapeutic and unpragmatic, right, left." If the editorial veered toward the abstract, claiming allegiance only with creativity, the contributions suggested a leftist political aesthetic. Running for seven issues and published in Paris, Tangier, Mexico, and Philadelphia, *Zero* published poetry, art, fiction, and essays by a diverse range of international writers, including Gore Vidal, Max Ernst, and Paul Bowles. *Zero*, the editorial statement continued, "will apply itself to the introduction and continuation of American writings and art coming most especially from Europe and secondly from America in order to form a double channel of presentation." The "double channel of presentation" was no doubt a reference to the cultural ebb and flow between Europe and North America and yet it unwittingly picks up on the way art was used by the U.S. State Department to win over "the hearts and minds" of Europe during the cultural Cold War, where in Arthur Koestler's words, postwar Paris "was the world capital of fellow travelers" (Saunders 70). Baldwin's early essays were published in magazines that were ideologically opposed to Stalinism. Avant-garde journals such as *Partisan Review* and *New Leader* sought to efface the legacy of the Popular Front, the Communist International's attempt to recruit liberal intellectuals to the Communist Party. If the Popular Front sought to revolutionize society through propaganda, the goal of avant-garde magazines such as *Partisan Review* was to revolutionize literature. In the case of "Everybody's Protest Novel," Baldwin's views on truth, complexity, and the individual fit squarely with the views of the anti-Stalinist left. "Everybody's Protest Novel" was republished by *Partisan Review* and then by *Perspectives USA,* an anti-Stalinist magazine started in the 1950s "to woo European intellectuals to the side of freedom" (Murphy 1034).

"Everybody's Protest Novel" and "Preservation of Innocence" were published in the first and second issues of *Zero.* Baldwin's first essay is concerned with race without mentioning homosexuality, in contrast to "Preservation," a bold essay which discusses homosexuality but does not allude to blackness. As I discuss later on, Baldwin would harness these isolated topics (race and homosexuality) in *Giovanni's Room,* his only sustained piece of fiction set in Paris aside from the short story "This Morning, This Evening, So Soon" (1960), first published in *Atlantic Monthly.* "Everybody's Protest Novel" and "Preservation" share more similarities than their respective themes of protest fiction and homosexual literature. Though neither essay refers directly to the Popular Front, the language in "Everybody's Protest Novel" and "Preservation" is shot through with the rhetoric of the anti-Stalinist left. Baldwin demands representational complexity in both pieces, whether in protest literature or fictional depictions of sexuality. One of Baldwin's central objections to *Uncle Tom's Cabin* (1852) is that it is formulaic: a self-consciously populist novel that Baldwin compares to James M. Cain's *The Postman Always Rings Twice* (1946). For Baldwin, Cain's work is the apotheosis of formula-driven mass cultural artifacts, a concept which he picks up on in "Preservation." Baldwin pillories Cain, like Stowe, because such writers "are wholly unable to recreate or interpret any of the reality or complexity of the human experience." The result, Baldwin concludes, "has now become to reduce all Americans to the compulsive bloodless dimensions of a guy named Joe" (600). Here Baldwin makes a thinly veiled attack, if not on Joseph Stalin, then on what he sees as the limitations of Popular Front cultural forms that ignore the complexity of the individual.

"Everybody's Protest Novel," though an accomplished and incisive essay, is not without its shortcomings. Baldwin never really explains how Stowe's novel is both a pamphlet and "activated by what might be called a theological terror," nor does he explain how this "very bad novel" became such a best-seller (11, 14). And yet one of the strengths of "Everybody's Protest Novel"—and surely one of the reasons that it quickly gained a trans-Atlantic readership—is Baldwin's ability to harness contemporary discussions of the Left with issues of race. In his essay Baldwin combines discussions of protest fiction with wider Cold War concerns, namely the individual, mass culture and ideology. Toward the end of the essay, Baldwin illustrates his understanding of the inter-connections between race and class and the ways in which oppressor and oppressed are imprisoned together. "Within this cage," Baldwin writes,

> it is romantic, more meaningless, to speak of a "new" society as the desire of the oppressed, for that shivering dependence on the props of reality which he shares with the *Herrenvolk* makes a truly "new" society impossible to conceive. What is meant by a new society is one in which inequalities will disappear, in which vengeance will be exacted; either there will be no oppressed at all, or the oppressed and the oppressor will change places (17).

Baldwin dismisses what he sees as the vagaries and romanticism of a "new society" in what reads as an oblique critique of Stalinism. At the same time, his language, though charged with vocabulary associated with class, quietly shifts to a discussion of wider, circum-Atlantic power struggles as Baldwin mentions "the African, exile, pagan" who is taken from the auction block to the church. Baldwin was of course not the only writer to harness discussions of race and social oppression. In *The Revolutionary Answer to the Negro Problem in the USA* (1948), the Trinidadian Trotskyite, C. L. R. James, rejected the Stalinist line that black Americans should subordinate racial issues for the sake of class issues. Baldwin's own writing after "Everybody's Protest Novel" would arguably subordinate discussions of class, focusing on racial oppression. As his references to Africa in his 1948 essay suggest, Baldwin was nonetheless attuned to the transnational structures of slavery, colonialism and imperialism which he would return to in *No Name*.

Baldwin's two essays in *Zero* marked a turning point in the writer's career: from reviewer to a trans-Atlantic commentator and essayist. In 1950 *Commentary* published "The Death of a Prophet," which was a fragmented draft of *Go Tell it on the Mountain* and one of the few stories in the journal that did not deal with a Jewish theme. In the same year, "The Negro in Paris" was published in *Reporter* (the title would be changed to "Encounter on the Seine: Black meets Brown"), followed by several now collected pieces, including a second article for *Partisan Review,* "Many Thousands Gone" in

1951. Not long after Baldwin's first novel was published in 1953 he was starting to command well-paid fees for his articles and work appeared in *Harper's, Encounter, Mademoiselle,* and, by the end of the 1950s, *The New York Times Book Review.* Paris, it seems, enabled Baldwin to transform himself from Harlemite to international writer; and yet, as we will see, his essays on the French capital reveal the extent of his isolation from other intellectual and cultural collaborations taking place there.

Paris Essays

"Someone, some day," Baldwin writes in his essay "Alas, Poor Richard," "should do a study in depth of the role of the American Negro in the mind and life of Europe, and the extraordinary perils, different from those of America but no less grave, which the American Negro encounters in the Old World" (249). Baldwin's essays about the French capital do not constitute such an in-depth study and yet I want to suggest that his "Paris essays"—"Encounter on the Seine: Black Meets Brown" from *Notes of a Native Son;* "Equal in Paris," also from *Notes;* and "Princes and Powers" from *Nobody Knows My Name*—puncture and call into question the myth of Paris as, in Wright's words, the "city of refuge" ("Alas, Poor Richard" 249).[3]

In 1955 *Commentary* published "Equal in Paris," an essay in which Baldwin recalls his early years in the French capital. During this period he "floated, so to speak, on a sea of acquaintances," adding that he "knew almost no one" (103). Baldwin's oceanic metaphor reminds us of Gilroy's focus on the ship as a vessel of intercultural exchange: "the circulation of ideas and activists as well as the movements of key cultural and political artifacts" (14). Yet Baldwin seems to have remained detached from any single cultural or intellectual community in Paris. As I discuss in this section, Baldwin's essays about Paris focus rather on the lack of community among African Americans and black Francophone writers and students, what he describes in "Encounter on the Seine" as the black American's "deliberate isolation" (86). Baldwin's relationship with Wright, for example, was strained, if not tense, something that an FBI report remarked upon in 1955. According to the report (which erroneously describes Baldwin as a student), Baldwin attacked Wright's Franco-American Fellowship Group, set up in 1951 to sponsor young writers. "Wright and his group," the report states, "were the target of attacks from one James Baldwin."[4] Unlike Wright who was on the editorial board of Alioune Diop's famous quarterly *Présence Africaine* and actively involved in Sartre's Rassemblement Democratique Révolutionnaire, Baldwin kept his distance from established intellectual or artistic communities.[5] Although he is often associated with Himes and Wright, as Kevin Bell astutely points out elsewhere in the present volume the triumvirate never formed "an ideological or creative unit" though they are "ever viewed with a certain unitary fashion."

Baldwin's Paris essays focus on the difficulties of developing black transnational culture, anticipating Edwards's observation that the "cultures of black internationalism are formed only within . . . 'paradoxes'" (Edwards 5). In *The Practice of Diaspora*, Edwards revises Gilroy's call in *The Black Atlantic* to consider the Atlantic as "one single, complex unit of analysis," (15) arguing rather that "black modern expression takes form not as a single thread, but through the uneasy encounters of peoples of African descent with each other" (5). In Baldwin's "Paris Essays" in particular, it is precisely these "uneasy encounters" between African Americans and other people of African descent that characterize his writing on transnational culture. Baldwin's writing on Paris counters the suggestion that the French capital is a site of community and cultural exchange. In "Encounter on the Seine," Baldwin makes it clear that African Americans, though they may share the common experience of exile, share little else, a point that he outlined in his resistance to Wright's Franco-American Fellowship Club. For Baldwin, it is only the dwindling black American musicians and singers in Paris who "are able to maintain a useful and unquestioning comradeship with other Negroes" (85). Baldwin's writing underscores his view that exile does not necessarily foster community; black Americans who have fled the ghettos of the United States, Baldwin points out, do not necessarily want to live together.

In "Encounter," it is crucial that Baldwin make sense of the "reality of his being an American," which is the only way that he can "hope to articulate to himself or to others the uniqueness of his experience" (88). And yet there is a high price to pay for becoming American. It is only when he is wrongly imprisoned for theft, an episode that Baldwin recounts in "Equal in Paris," that the French authorities see him as American rather than as a "despised black man" (106). As Baldwin later wrote in "The Discovery of What it Means to be an American" (1959), he left America "to prevent myself from becoming *merely* a Negro; or, even, merely a Negro writer" (137). In "Equal in Paris" Baldwin suggests that becoming American is not just an acquisition, but a painful transformation. In an ironic twist, it is only when he is incarcerated—at "a lower point than any I could ever in my life have imagined"—that Baldwin is liberated from racial interpellation (110).

Baldwin's attention to what he calls the "uniqueness" of the black American's experience is significant, underscoring his reluctance to consider the possibilities of wider black transnational exchanges. Baldwin's discussion of the nameless Africans in "Encounter" (who are not distinguished by gender, class or country) surprisingly makes no mention of the long-established history of African students in the French capital, where he himself had lived since 1948. More surprisingly, however, Baldwin also makes no reference to *Présence Africaine*, which had been founded the year before Baldwin arrived in Paris. During his early years in Paris, Baldwin may of course have struggled to read the articles in *Présence Africaine*, which weren't published in English until 1955. At the same time, it is almost certain Baldwin would have known of the journal, which became the preeminent forum for the cultural and political struggles of pan-Africanism and Négritude. Early issues of *Présence Africaine* contained articles by French intellectuals (Sartre, Albert Camus) but also, on Wright's recommendation, works by Gwendolyn Brooks, Horace Clayton and E. Franklin Frazier.[6]

Baldwin wrote of wanting to "articulate" his experience as a writer in Paris but his audience was clearly not his transatlantic colleagues in Paris. In contrast to the cultural and political exchange signaled by *Présence Africaine*'s inclusion of African American writers, Baldwin writes rather of the cultural and linguistic obstacles in "Encounter": "They face each other, the Negro and the African, over a gulf of three hundred years—an alienation too vast to be conquered in an evening's good will, too heavy and too double-edged ever to be trapped in speech" (89). Baldwin's surprising choice of the colonially inflected verb "conquered" sets the African and the African American at odds, far removed from a notion of transcultural interaction, and in fact echoes back to the start of *Giovanni's Room* with David's musings on his conquering ancestors. For Baldwin, the African and African American, who do not share a common language, are unable to communicate, anticipating his later comment that "we almost needed a dictionary to talk" (Isaacs 324).

Baldwin's repeated references to translation in relation to diasporic encounters in Paris anticipate Edwards's argument that "the cultures of black internationalism can be seen only *in translation*" (7). As Edwards points out, echoing Baldwin's reservations about cultural unity, such encounters between culturally and linguistically removed people of African descent can enable alliances but also call attention to difference. In "Princes and Powers," Baldwin writes of a black transnational culture "which has produced so many different subhistories, problems, traditions, possibilities, aspirations, assumptions, languages, hybrids" (152)—what Edwards calls "unavoidable misapprehensions and misreadings, persistent blindness and solipsisms, self-defeating and abortive collaborations, a failure to translate even a basic grammar of blackness" (5).

Unlike the American participants at the 1956 Congress—among them Wright, Mercer Cook, and John A. Davis—Baldwin as I noted earlier was present as a reporter for *Encounter* (or, as he added wryly, for the CIA) (*No Name* 383). Baldwin's role is significant, illustrating his position as Western observer, not participant, in a conference aimed at unifying people of African descent. The Nigerian poet, M. Lasebikan, who speaks an "extremely strange language," Baldwin writes, was "dressed in a most arresting costume," noting that "he was wearing a very subdued but very ornately figured silk robe, which looked Chinese, and he wore a red velvet toque, a sign, someone told me that he was a Muhammadan" (148).[7] Baldwin's cavalier description and his hazy attempts to describe Lasebikan's national dress (conflated here as oriental, foreign) echo his own earlier discomfort in "Stranger in the Village" (1953), where the local Swiss see him as "a living wonder" (119). Like the villagers, Baldwin's views are based on hearsay: Baldwin wrongly assumes Lasebikan is Muslim because "someone told" him. His own description of Lasebikan outlines what he calls "that gulf which yawns between the American Negro and all other men of color" (146). Observing the participants at the conference, Baldwin writes that it was "quite unbelievable for a moment that the five men standing with Wright (and Wright and myself) were defined, and had been brought together in this courtyard by our relation to the African continent" (147).

Despite his initial distance from the speakers at the conference, he is attracted to Senghor's theories on the harmony in African culture between life and art. Nevertheless, echoing his earlier comment in "Encounter" concerning the gulf between the African and African American, Baldwin believes that "Senghor's thought had come into my mind translated" (150). Baldwin questions Senghor's claim that the heritage of the African American was straightforwardly African. Senghor's conclusion that Richard Wright's *Black Boy* (1945) illustrates the latter's African roots, Baldwin argues, overlooks the specificity of his Mississippi upbringing. To view *Black Boy* as a great *African* autobiography, Baldwin writes, is not to restore Wright's African heritage: "rather it seemed to be taking away his identity" (154).

In "Princes and Powers" Baldwin repeatedly observes how identities are forged in specific historical conditions, illustrated by his probing question, "For what, beyond the fact that all black men at one time or another left Africa, or have remained there, do they really have in common?" (152). At one point, Baldwin concedes that people of black descent *did* have something in common, where again he draws attention to the inexpressibility of this relationship.

Baldwin muses on what he describes as black people's "precarious . . . unutterably painful relation to the white world" (153). This was a comment that he would later redress (153). In an interview eight years after the 1956 conference, he noted that he not only "profoundly distrust[ed]" Négritude but again argued that "oppressions do not necessarily unify so many millions of people all over the world":

> Well, how in the world is this going to connect to so many different experiences? To be born in Jamaica, Barbados, or Portugal, or New York, or to be black, wouldn't seem to me to be enough . . . and the situation of the man in Jamaica is not the situation of the man in Harlem at all (Bondy 16).

In "Princes and Powers" Baldwin is careful to distinguish between the colonial experiences of Africans who wish to overthrow European white rule and the complicated relationship between black Americans and white authority in the United States. "It had never been our interest to overthrow" the dominant white power, Baldwin writes. Rather, "It had been necessary to make the machinery work for our benefit and the possibility of its doing so had been . . . built in" (148). Here as elsewhere in his writing, Baldwin is much more concerned with redefining what it means to be American, than with discarding American identity: he aims not to "overthrow" the concept of a U.S. national identity but to overhaul it. As I argue in the following section, Baldwin would challenge the prevailing constructs of postwar American identity most effectively through his character David, the white middle class protagonist of *Giovanni's Room*.

Paris Fictions

As is true for Wright, little of Baldwin's fictional writing focuses on Paris. Wright, as Richard Gibson points out in this collection, only focused on Paris in his unpublished novel, *Island of Hallucination*. But unlike Wright, Baldwin's literary reputation in France began, in Rosia Bobia's words, "in slow motion," hampered by the late translation of *Go Tell it on the Mountain* in 1957 (13). When Baldwin arrived in Paris in 1948 he was unknown in the literary and intellectual circles and was writing under the shadow of Wright and then later the popular novels of Himes. In one of the earliest articles on Baldwin in France, Jacques Howlett, writing for *Présence Africaine* in 1952, criticized the writer for discussing race in universal terms. Anticipating later criticism of Baldwin by some ten years, Howlett concluded by stating that Baldwin, "although a Black American, is not qualified to discuss racism in the United States" (Bobia 16). Howlett's early article set the tone for Baldwin's uneasy relationship with black Francophone writers that I explored earlier. Although *Giovanni's Room,* published in France in 1958 as *L'Ami de Giovanni,* was favorably received, it was not viewed as a work of political importance. Though Baldwin's literary reputation in France fared better than that of Ralph Ellison, who was published by a small French publisher, it would not be until Wright's death in 1960, and in particular after the publication of *The Fire Next Time,* that "a political Baldwin emerged" (Bobia 25). Baldwin's visit to the American South three years before Wright's death, and his accounts of the trip, illustrate the ways in which he had already become politicized. In France, however, Baldwin's isolation from the communities of black transnational writers meant that he would emerge as "political" only when his essays on the U.S. civil rights movement began to circulate in Paris.

In Baldwin's fictional worlds, characters of different nationalities, often in cameo roles, rub shoulders with the American protagonists in ways that highlight the injustices of American life but also lay bare the fictions of national identity. In his short story "This Morning, This Evening, So Soon," there is the southern African American narrator and his Swedish wife; their son, who has never been to the United States; and Vidal, the French film director who has been imprisoned in Germany during the war and who has a daughter in England. There are unnamed Algerians and the Tunisian prizefighter, Boona, as well as a coterie of young African American students who meet the narrator in a Spanish discothèque that is frequented by Swedes, Greeks, and Spaniards.[8] In *Giovanni's Room,* set in Paris, with forays in America and the south of France, Baldwin's characters are an assembly of displaced, sometimes spectral figures. Giovanni, who has left his Italian village in the south, is an economic migrant who stands in sharp contrast to the wealthy Belgian-born American businessman, Jacques. Many of Baldwin's protagonists, like the author, are frequent travelers in search of a sense of home, characters who confuse the physical displacement of exile with an interiority of belonging. David, in Baldwin's second novel, who has come to "find himself" has never settled, growing up in Brooklyn, San Francisco, Seattle and New York. Although Paris gives David the illusion of freedom ("with no-one to watch, no penalties attached"), the novel begins, as it ends, with David alone. For David has "run so far, so hard, across the ocean even," only to find himself once again confronted with himself (11). As Baldwin suggests in *Giovanni's Room,* freedom is a precarious condition that constantly threatens to slip into isolation.

For Cyraina Johnson-Roullier, *Giovanni's Room* is "modern" in so far as it focuses on Baldwin's "newfound understanding of

'American-ness'" (938). Published during the height of the Cold War and two years after *Brown v. Board,* Baldwin's novel feeds into discussions both about American (and un-American) behavior but also what Benjamin Muse terms the "horror of racial amalgamation" in the 1950s (39). Baldwin is at pains to point out that David, the narrator of *Giovanni's Room,* is tall, blonde and middle-class, described as "a great American football player," and as "American as pork and beans" (34, 87). During the course of the novel, David's white, heterosexual masculinity unravels as he spends time in Paris, suggesting the ways in which Baldwin dismantled and called into question the propaganda of postwar American national identity. Home, whiteness, nationality and sexuality, Baldwin suggests in *Giovanni's Room* and elsewhere in his essays, are not only inextricably entwined but are dangerous and compelling conditions. As he concluded his essay "Encounter," the American search for identity is a "dangerous voyage," one in which white and black Americans will be "in the same boat" (90). If the seafaring images invoke the Middle Passage and transnational exchange, Baldwin's insistence that the passengers are both black and white, complicates such a reading. Baldwin's project is not about separatism but how to recast American, not just African American identity. If postwar American identity is exported as a white, heterosexual construct, *Giovanni's Room* interpolates this fiction through the figure of David.

In "Encounter" Baldwin writes that meeting Africans in Paris "causes the Negro to recognize that he is a hybrid," a position that he expressed rhetorically in *Notes of a Native Son* (89). In "Many Thousands Gone," one of many instances where the pronoun is ambiguous, Baldwin writes: "*We* do not know what to with *him* in life; if *he* breaks our sociological and sentimental image of *him we* are panic-stricken and *we* feel *ourselves* betrayed" (19–20; my emphasis). For critics such as Langston Hughes, Baldwin's views were bastardized; they were, the older writer claimed, "half-American, half-Afro-American, incompletely fused" (Leeming 10). As I argue through a reading of *Giovanni's Room,* a "white" novel written by a black American author, it is precisely this indeterminate space that enables Baldwin to reconfigure American national identity.

Giovanni's Room differs from the clutch of modernist novels by African American writers who also focus on flight from the United States to Europe. As Brent Hayes Edwards has noted, a number of key black American novels from this period use European settings as sites of revelation, illustrating the intercultural ebb and flow of the United States and Europe. Berlin, he points out, is an important setting in James Weldon Johnson's *The Autobiography of an Ex-Colored Man* (1912), Jessie Fauset's novel *Plum Bun* (1929) ends in Paris, Claude McKay's *Banjo* (1929) is set in Marseille and Nella Larsen's *Quicksand*'s (1928) most important scenes are set in Copenhagen. Paris, as Edwards convincingly argues, is frequently represented as "a special place for black transnational interaction, exchange, and dialogue," and yet in *Giovanni's Room* there is no discussion or clear allusion to black characters, let alone a transnational community (5). Unlike *Banjo,* which explores the transnationality of black culture in France, Baldwin's Paris in *Giovanni's Room* is rather the site of the white expatriate community where the black American or African is invisible. *Giovanni's Room,* in other words, seems to follow as much in the tradition of white modernist writing (such as Hemingway's *The Sun Also Rises* [1926]) as the black transnational works that Edwards examines.

Critics have long speculated on whether there are indeed black characters in *Giovanni's Room* and why Baldwin chose not to include or make reference to Paris's black community. Leslie Fiedler, for example, in his review of *Giovanni's Room,* seemed troubled by the novel, concluding that "one begins to suspect at last that there must *really* be Negroes present, censored, camouflaged or encoded" (16). Baldwin himself stated in an interview that the complex entanglement of blackness and homosexuality "would have been quite beyond . . . [his] powers" in 1956, an idea that is reinforced by his inclusion of an African American homosexual character in the unpublished film script of *Giovanni's Room,* written in the 1980s (*Conversations* 239). My concern, however, is not to try and read encoded black characters such as David's lover, Joey, but to argue that *Giovanni's Room* simultaneously converges with and diverges from transnational works such as *Banjo.* Baldwin's focus on a white expatriate community in Paris seems removed from Claude McKay's figuration of black internationalism. And yet *Giovanni's Room* is characterized, not only by the theme of flight, but by numerous references to sailing and water, images that draw attention to Gilroy's mapping of Atlantic culture. Baldwin, though, is not interested so much with connecting black national cultures, but with destabilizing—or unanchoring—white American identity. *Giovanni's Room,* in other words, is not a departure from Baldwin's works that focus on black American culture, but a space from which he explores the complex traffic of whiteness, nationality, and belonging.

From the start of the novel, where David considers his ancestors who "conquered a continent . . . until they came to an ocean which faced away from Europe into a darker past," Baldwin punctuates *Giovanni's Room* with over twenty references to the sea or more generally to water (9). As Magdalena Zaborowska has shown, Baldwin's work more generally merits a closer examination in his "use of the motifs of departure, passage, arrival, acculturation, and the ways in which he shows them embroiled with representations and articulations of racialized identities" (178). Although Baldwin is circumnavigated in *The Black Atlantic*, I want to suggest that the repeated oceanic descriptions in *Giovanni's Room* call attention to Gilroy's persuasive argument that sailing enables the "moving to and fro between nations," what he describes as "crossing borders in modern machines that were themselves micro-systems of linguistic and political hybridity" (12). As I will argue, two of the pivotal moments of the novel which resonate with what Gilroy calls the "discursive slippage or connative resonance between 'race,' ethnicity, and nation" occur with sailors, where, I suggest, we can add "sexuality" to Gilroy's list.

Baldwin's descriptions of the sea, like David, are "too various to be trusted" to one single meaning (11). David's first sexual encounter with a boy begins with swimming in the sea only to be enacted in the shower, an image of purity that is in sharp contrast to the "contempt and self-contempt" of Jacques and Guillaume that "bubbled upward out of them like a fountain of black water" (46). In one of the most troubling moments of the book, Giovanni dismisses women as "like water," claiming that they are treacherous and shallow (77). When David first sees Giovanni, it "was as though his station [the bar] was a promontory and we were the sea" (31), anticipating his later description of how life in their shared room "seemed to be occurring underwater," adding that "it is certain that I underwent a sea-change there" (82). In Baldwin's novel, water represents, not only the literal Atlantic ocean, such as David's reference to "when I took the boat for France" (25), but a liminal space between lands: here the sea functions not only as the site of voyage or exchange but a place of continuous displacement, even sociality itself, something which is both terrifying and liberating.

If water at times suggests the unknown, then it is figured explicitly in David's desire to keep his American heterosexual masculinity *anchored*, a term that Baldwin explicitly uses. In one scene with Giovanni, David "ached abruptly, intolerably to go home" (62). Home, David makes clear, is not his dwelling in Paris but "home across the ocean, to things and people I knew and understood . . . I saw myself, sharply, as a wanderer, an adventurer, rocking through the world, unanchored" (62). David's language at once invokes the rhetoric of pioneers, an echo of the novel's beginning where his "ancestors conquered a continent," and yet his reference to being "unanchored" harks back to his reasons for marrying Hella: to give himself "something to be moored to" (9, 11). Baldwin's choice of the word "moored" suggests, too, the absent North Africans (the

Moors), missing from David's narrative but hinted at through the spectral figure of the homeless man who is "very black and alone, walking alone the river" (47). David becomes "unanchored," like Baldwin's text, which is un-Moored in its conspicuous absence of black characters, whether North African or more generally of African descent. Baldwin, in other words, generates a "discursive slippage" between home and ideas of national rooted-ness, heterosexuality and whiteness. For David to be unanchored from his nation and from Hella, Baldwin suggests, is for him to shade into blackness, suggested by the homeless man who embodies this link between lack of domestic anchoring and blackness, and further suggested by the oblique reference (or notable absence) of the Moors, whose expulsion from Spain underscores the link between blackness and national homelessness.[9]

Baldwin's image of David being "unanchored" with reference to his American and heterosexual identity is further explored through his encounters with a sailor. If Gilroy limns out the ship as both the literal and the figurative vessel of transnational culture, Baldwin's invocation of the sailor queers Gilroy's reading of the significance of "Marcus Garvey, George Padmore, Claude McKay, and Langston Hughes with ships and sailors" (13). In a revealing scene, David gazes at a sailor who is "dressed all in white . . . wishing I were he" (88). The sailor's whiteness is reinforced, not only by his uniform, but by his blonde hair—and this moment of recognition—where David sees the man as a younger, more beautiful version of himself, invokes both nostalgia for home and desire. Though Baldwin does not say where the sailor is from, and despite his peripatetic vocation, David states that "He made me think of home—perhaps home is not a place but simply an irrevocable condition" (88). If home is not a place, but rather a condition, it is the sailor who "who wore his masculinity as unequivocally as he wore his skin" who most acutely reflects this. Untroubled by the questions of masculinity and nationality that preoccupy the narrator, the sailor is in the perpetual present, someone without a past or ties to the present, without "any antecedents, any connections at all" (88). The sailor, whose ship is both a domestic space and a vessel for constant motion, is nonetheless at home in his masculinity and whiteness. That he becomes an object of desire for David suggests, in Baldwin's description of their physical likeness, that his narrator both wants him and wants to be him.

David's gaze shifts from recognition to sexual desire, which the sailor instantly recognizes. In another moment, David realizes that the sailor's response, which is already "lewd and knowing," will "erupt into speech," "some brutal variation of *Look, baby. I know you*" (88). This moment of recognition, which forces David to consider how his body has betrayed his queer desire, is couched in a language recognizable to readers of passing narratives, where the boundaries between concealment and revelation are always precarious. David's anticipation that the sailor will *know* him, in other words, strongly echoes the concerns of the eponymous Ex-Colored Man who watches the woman he has fallen for "to see if she was scrutinizing me, to see if she was looking for anything in me which made me different from the other men she knew" (94). Though Hella suspects David's desire for other men, it is only when she finds him in a gay bar, drinking with a sailor, that she knows for sure, leaving David with the parting words that she would like to drink "all the way to Paris and all the way across that criminal ocean" (156). In Baldwin's second novel, it is tempting to read his own attempts to critique what Gilroy calls "narrow nationalism," not only through sailing, but cruising (12). In *Giovanni's Room,* the sailor represents not just the trade of cultural production and exchange aligned with theories of transnationalism, but gay *trade,* a vernacular term associated with travel and casual sex. If American trade in postwar Europe is associated with the Marshall Plan, where the United States invested in war-torn Europe, Baldwin explores another side of the American identity, one constituted through other kinds of trade. In *Giovanni's Room,* Baldwin exposes the degree to which "narrow nationalism" is linked with compulsory heterosexuality by reminding readers that American national identity is structured around sexual, not just cultural and racial differences.

Conclusion

I want to conclude by returning to *No Name in the Street,* an essay that not only reflects on Baldwin's literal journeys (written in New York, San Francisco, Hollywood, London, and St. Paul de Vence between 1967 and 1971) but also reveals his developing views on America, Paris, and transnationalism. Contrary to the critical consensus that Baldwin had lost his way as a writer by the early 1970s, *No Name* shows the extent to which he continued to evolve as an astute analyst of the U.S. role in international politics. I want to suggest that *No Name* marks a turning point in Baldwin's nonfiction writing where his preoccupations shift from a discovery of what it means to be an American to something approaching what Gilroy defines as the "desire to transcend both the structures of the nation state and the constraints of ethnicity and national particularity" (19).

If Baldwin's "Paris Essays," and *Notes of a Native Son* more generally, can be characterized by his attempts to articulate an experience that is both American and African American, then there is a notable shift in rhetoric in his later work. The "we" Baldwin used in *Notes,* which infuriated and bemused Langston Hughes and other critics, is angrily called into question as Baldwin castigates an old friend in *No Name.* While speaking of U.S. involvement in Vietnam, Baldwin's friend ventures to explain "what I think we're trying to do there." Baldwin narrates his response: *"We?,"* I cried, "what motherfucking *we?"* (364).[10] Thus he violently questions and uproots the pronoun that he had used so interchangeably in his Paris days. For Baldwin, the question of Vietnam, symptomatic of North America's imperialism and thirst for global dominance, forces him to reconsider his articulation of national identity but also revises his early position in "Princes and Powers." If he had initially claimed that the only thing people of color had in common was "their precarious, their *unutterably* painful relation to the white world" (emphasis mine), then his later work suggests that this relation can—and must—be uttered and articulated. Baldwin tells his friend that "America has no business at all in Vietnam; and that black people certainly had no business there, aiding the slave master to enslave yet more millions of dark people" (364).

By the time Baldwin published *No Name,* he had spent an intermittent decade in both Europe and the United States, and, importantly, in Turkey as well. As Magdalena Zaborowska persuasively argues, Baldwin's position at the crossroads of Europe and Asia attuned his thinking, not just to Paris or New York, but to the global ramifications of power. In *No Name,* Baldwin's rhetoric certainly shifts beyond Europe and North America. Gone are the wistful meditations in "Stranger in the Village" to the Swiss illiterati in Loèche-Les-Bains who are related in ways that he is not to "Dante, Shakespeare, Michelangelo, Aeschylus, Da Vinci, Rembrandt and Racine" (121). In an echo of Fanon and Trotsky, as well as the internationalism of the Black Panther Party that he supports in *No Name,* Baldwin writes of how

> the cultural pretensions of history are revealed as nothing less than a mask for power, and thus it happens that, in order to be rid of Shell, Texaco, Coca-Cola, the Sixth Fleet, and the friendly American soldier whose mission it is to protect these investments, one finally throws Balzac and Shakespeare—and Faulkner and Camus—out with them. Later, of course, one may welcome them back, but on one's own terms, and, absolutely, on one's own land (382).

Baldwin's writing here, echoing his comments on U.S. involvement in Vietnam, displays a keen awareness of the ways in which imperialism and globalization are inextricably bound. In "The Discovery" he wrote that Paris enabled him to feel as "American as any Texan G.I.," which now shifts from an invocation of the soldier as a symbol of American nationalism to an awareness of the imperial structures of global power (137).

As Bill Lynne has persuasively argued through a reading of Baldwin's radical trajectory, *No Name* "is the book where Baldwin finally and fully allies himself with this version of what will come to be called 'Third World Marxism'" (29). Lyne rightly points to Baldwin's support of the Black Panthers in his essay, to which it would be useful to add the ways in which both writer and Party, at least in international outlook, "evolved from self-described 'Black Nationalists' to 'revolutionary nationalists,' 'internationalists,' and finally to 'revolutionary intercommunalists' between 1966 and 1972" (Rodriguez 152). Similarly, we might consider Baldwin's praise of Malcolm X in the context of the latter's pronouncement that "the struggle of Vietnam is the struggle of the whole Third World: the struggle against colonialism, neo-colonialism, and imperialism" (Rodriguez 151).

In *No Name*, Baldwin revisits his earlier reasons for his "flight" to Paris which had afforded him a space "where my risks would be more personal," "leaving me completely alone" (376–77). If Baldwin's move to Paris was connected to what Gilroy calls "the association of self-exploration with the explorations of new territories," then in *No Name* he reconsiders what Gilroy also refers to as "the cultural differences that exist between and within groups that get called races" (133). Casting his eye over his years in Paris, Baldwin looks back at the colonial history of France, noting how the "French were still hopelessly slugging it out Indo China when I first arrived in France, and I was living in Paris when Dien Bien Phu fell" (367). In *No Name*, Baldwin seems more attuned to parallels between colonialism and racial discrimination in the United States, such as the link he makes in *No Name* between ghetto "anti-poverty" programs in the United States and "foreign aid" in developing countries (405). Not only is *No Name* his first extended account of the treatment of Algerians in Paris, but his writing now connects the experiences of racial discrimination: "It was strange to find oneself, in another language, in another country, listening to the same old song and hearing oneself condemned in the same old way" (368). In sharp contrast to his earlier distinctions between colonialism and the legacy of slavery, Baldwin writes how 'The Algerian and I were both, alike, victims of this history, and I was still a part of Africa, even though I had been carried out of it nearly four hundred years before" (377).

Paris remains a crucial site in Baldwin's development, from his prophetic title, "Princes and Powers," to his journey, straight from the French capital to the American South in 1957 that he recalled in *No Name*. Visiting the South for the first time and pointing out that he "had come South from Paris," Baldwin recalls that he was "not in my territory now" (394). Though he does not make it clear whether he means Paris or New York, this slippage draws attention to his developing views on nationalism and exile, heightened through his experience of living in France and his drive "to find a resting place, reconciliation, in the land where I was born" (430). While Baldwin had initially found himself a stranger in a European village, in the South, he would become a stranger in his own land, displaced in a "territory [that is] absolutely hostile and strange," where he feels "exactly like a foreigner" (395).

Baldwin's meditation on the Algerians in Paris earlier in *No Name* strongly echoes his own experiences in the South. The North Africans, Baldwin writes, "though they spoke French, and had been, in a sense, produced by France, they were not at home in Paris, no more at home than I, though for a different reason," a comment strongly evocative of his first trip to the South (367). Tellingly, in the South as he surveys the legacy of slavery and the visible "secret" of miscegenation, he sees not only "Girls the color of honey," but eyes "brown like the Arab's" (402). Paris, in other words, becomes not a city for Baldwin but an irrevocable condition that refracted and distilled his writing—a city where, as Baldwin wrote in *No Name*, "Now though I was a stranger, I was home" (387).

Notes

The title quotation is from James Baldwin, "The Price of the Ticket," *Collected Essays*, 842.

1. Interview with George Solomos in London, 14 July 2008.

2. See, for example, *The Price of the Ticket*, where it erroneously states that "Everybody's Protest Novel" was "Originally published in *Partisan Review*, June 1949," 27.

3. Wright may have been referring to Rudolph Fisher's 1925 story, "The City of Refuge," where Harlem is, for King Solomon Gillis, "Land of plenty. City of refuge—city of refuge. If you live long enough—" (73). It's possible that Baldwin did not pick up on Wright's ironic reference to the Fisher story, but the older writer may have been reinforcing his views on the sanctity of Paris echoed in his unpublished 1951 essay, "I Choose Exile."

4. Unlike Baldwin's file, Richard Wright's is available on the FBI's website at www.fbi/gov/. The mention of Baldwin is in Wright's file, section 1b. (There is no pagination but it is on p. 49.)

5. See Baldwin's description of Wright's meeting of the Franco-American Fellowship Club in "Alas, Poor Richard," *Collected Essays*, especially pp. 264–65.
6. See Jacques Howlett, "*Présence Africaine*, 1947–1958," *Journal of Negro History* 43.2 (April 1958): 140–50.
7. See Akin Adesokan, "Baldwin, Paris, and the 'Conundrum' of Africa," for a useful reading of the gaps in Baldwin's report of the conference.
8. In Baldwin's unpublished play, *The Welcome Table*, there is an assembled cast from different countries. See Leeming, *James Baldwin*, who reads the play as a work about "exile and alienation," 373–74. For a useful reading of this short story in relation to migration, see Magdalena Zaborowska, "'In the Same Boat': James Baldwin and the Other Atlantic," *A Historical Guide to James Baldwin*, 177–211.
9. I am indebted to Emily Lordi for helping me to think through this section, particularly the ways in which Baldwin quietly invokes ideas of homelessness and national belonging through the play on "mooring."
10. See also later in *No Name*, when Baldwin writes, "One can wonder to whom the 'we' here refers" (452).

Works Cited

Adesokan, Akin. "Baldwin, Paris, and the 'Conundrum of Africa.'" *Textual Practice* 23.1 (2009): 73–97.
Baldwin, James. "History as Nightmare." Rev. of *Lonely Crusade* by Chester Himes. *New Leader* 30.25 (25 October 1947): 11, 15. Reprinted in *Collected Essays*, 579–81.
———. "Everybody's Protest Novel" (1949). *Collected Essays*. 11–18.
———. "Preservation of Innocence" (1949). *Collected Essays*. 594–600.
———. "Encounter on the Seine: Black Meets Brown" (1950). *Collected Essays*. 85–90.
———. "Many Thousands Gone" (1951). *Collected Essays*. 19–34.
———. "Stranger in the Village" (1953). *Collected Essays*. 117–129.
———. "Equal in Paris" (1955). *Collected Essays*. 101–16.
———. "Notes of a Native Son" (1955). *Collected Essays*. 63–84.
———. *Giovanni's Room* (1956). London: Penguin, 1990.
———. "Princes and Powers" (1957). *Collected Essays*. 143–69.
———. "The Discovery of What It Means to Be an American" (1959). *Collected Essays*. 137–42.
———. "This Morning, This Evening, So Soon" (1960). *Going to Meet the Man*. London: Penguin, 1991. 145–95.
———. "Alas, Poor Richard" (1961). *Collected Essays*. 247–68.
———. "No Name in the Street" (1972). *Collected Essays*. 348–475.
———. "The Price of the Ticket" (1985). *Collected Essays*. 830–42.

———. *The Price of the Ticket: Collected Nonfiction, 1948–1985*. New York: St. Martin's / Marek, 1985.
———. "Freaks and the American Ideal of Manhood" (1985). *Collected Essays*. 814–29.
———. *Collected Essays*. New York: Library of America, 1998.
Barry, Joseph A. "Americans in Paris." *New York Times* (27 March 1949): BR5.
Bell, Kevin. "Assuming the Position: Fugitivity and Futurity in the Work of Chester Himes." "Paris, Modern Fiction and the Black Atlantic." *Modern Fiction Studies* 51.4 (Winter 2005): 846–72.
Bobia, Rosa. *The Critical Reception of James Baldwin in France*. New York: Peter Lang, 1997.
Bondy, François. "James Baldwin, as Interviewed by François Bondy." *Transition* 0.12 (January–February 1964): 12–19.
Campbell, James. *Talking at the Gates: A Life of James Baldwin*. London: Faber and Faber, 1991.
———. *Exiled in Paris: Richard Wright, James Baldwin, Samuel Beckett, and Others on the Left Bank*. New York: Scribner, 1995.
Cassidy, T. E. "The Long Struggle." *Commonweal* 58 (22 May 1953): 186.
Conger, Leslie. "Jimmy on East 15th Street." *African American Review* 29.4 (1995): 557–66.
Dievler, James A. "Sexual Exiles: James Baldwin and *Another Country*." *James Baldwin Now*. Ed. Dwight A. McBride. New York: New York UP, 1999. 161–83.
Edwards, Brent Hayes. *The Practice of Diaspora: Literature, Translation, and the Rise of Black Internationalism*. Cambridge: Harvard UP, 2003.
Fiedler, Leslie. "A Homosexual Dilemma." *New Leader* 39.10 (1956): 17.
Fisher, Rudolph. "The City of Refuge." *The New Negro: Voices of the Harlem Renaissance*. Ed. Alain Locke. Introd. Arnold Rampersad. New York: Touchstone, 1997. 57–74.
Gilroy, Paul. *The Black Atlantic: Modernity and Double Consciousness*. Cambridge: Harvard UP, 1993.
Howlett, Jacques. "*Présence Africaine*, 1947–1958." *Journal of Negro History* 43.2 (April 1958): 140–50.
Isaacs, Harold. "Five Writers and Their Ancestors: Part 2." *Phylon* 21.4 (1960): 317–36.
Johnson, James Weldon. *The Autobiography of an Ex-Colored Man* (1912). New York: Dover Publications, 1995.
Johnson-Roullier, Cyraina. "(An) Other Modernism: James Baldwin, *Giovanni's Room*, and the Rhetoric of Flight." *Modern Fiction Studies* 45.4 (Winter 1999): 932–56.
Leeming, David. *James Baldwin: A Biography*. New York: Knopf, 1994.
Lyne, Bill. "God's Black Revolutionary Mouth: James Baldwin's Black Radicalism." *Science and Society* 74.1 (January 2010): 12–36.
Murphy, Geraldine. "Subversive Anti-Stalinism: Race and Sexuality in the Early Essays of James Baldwin." *ELH* 63 (1996): 1021–46.
Muse, Benjamin. *Ten Years of Prelude: The Story of Integration since the Supreme Court's 1954 Decision*. Beaconsfield: Darwen Finlayson, 1964.

Rodriguez, Besenia. "'Long Live Third World Unity! Long Live Internationalism': Huey P. Newton's Revolutionary Intercommunalism." *Transnational Blackness: Navigating the Global Color Line.* Ed. Manning Marable and Vannessa Agard-Jones. New York: Palgrave Macmillan, 2008. 149–73.

Saunders, Frances Stonor. *Who Paid the Piper? The CIA and the Cultural Cold War.* London: Granta, 2000.

Schreiber, Rebecca M. *Cold War Exiles in Mexico: U.S. Dissidents and the Culture of Critical Resistance.* Minneapolis: U of Minnesota P, 2008.

Standley, Fred L., and Louis H. Pratt, eds. *Conversations with James Baldwin.* Jackson: U of Mississippi P, 1989.

Weatherby, W. J. *James Baldwin: Artist on Fire.* London: Penguin, 1990.

Zaborowska, Magdalena. *James Baldwin's Turkish Decade: Erotics of Exile.* Durham: Duke UP, 2009.

———. "'In the Same Boat': James Baldwin and the Other Atlantic." *A Historical Guide to James Baldwin.* Ed. Douglas Field. Oxford: Oxford UP, 2009. 177–211.

CHAPTER 8

Making Culture Capital
Présence Africaine and Diasporic Modernity in Post–World War II Paris

---

Cedric Tolliver

Out of the ashes of World War II, Moscow and Washington, D.C., emerged with competing claims to be the economic, political, and military capitals of the world, while another world city, Paris, struggled to rebuild itself after the war's destruction. Its power diminished, Paris clung desperately to its status as both the cultural capital of the world and the imperial capital of a far-flung colonial empire. As the historian Robert Gildea notes, "possession of the Empire served as the basis of the French claim to great power status, vis-à-vis Great Britain, the rival colonial power, and the United States, the dominant superpower" (19). That African diasporic writers and intellectuals gravitated to Paris in the years immediately following the war is partly explained by the fact of empire and by Paris's position as the world's cultural capital. In turn, the city proved to be a crucible where anti-colonial writers and intellectuals gathered and organized on multiple fronts to bring about the demise of Paris as an imperial capital. They produced literature, instituted a literary journal, and organized cultural conferences, establishing a cultural front in the struggle to end western imperialism. Through this work these writers and intellectuals created forms of sociality and formed social relations that made culture capital and not merely ancillary to the political in the realization of African diasporic modernity.

Intellectual life for African diasporic writers in Paris, if not always encouraged, was at least tolerated to a degree that contrasted sharply with the suspicion, commercialism, and political domination that asphyxiated writers in the different parts of the African diasporic world. For intellectuals like Aimé Césaire and Alioune Diop, who initially traveled from the colonies to the metropole to complete their educations, Paris offered an intellectual environment significantly less policed than in the French colonial territories. Richard Wright, for example, came to the decision to relocate to Paris from the United States partly out of his avowed need to escape the limits, commercial and otherwise, that restricted the purview of African American literature. Despite their differing places of origins and political circumstances, this group of African diasporic writers shared a conviction in the utility and suitability of culture as both a critique of the existing order and a vehicle for imagining and enacting its transformation. And finally, from a purely professional standpoint, these writers, like others residing there, could avail themselves of the extraordinary concentration of "literary resources" that made Paris "the capital of the literary world, the city endowed with the greatest literary prestige on earth" (Casanova 23–24). This prestige depended on such literary resources as neighborhood cafés, artistic and intellectual networks, sustaining relations with mentors, friends, and acquaintances, access to important journals, and general support for the "creative destruction" of received artistic traditions. In the period immediately following World War II, these institutions were a kind of siren call for African diasporic writers.

Yet, these writers were not simply content to benefit from already existing institutions. In fact, they took a keen interest in creating institutions that might serve their particular audience and needs. The journal *Présence africaine*, founded in 1947, was one such institution. The journal published critical essays, literature, book reviews, as well as notices for events and matters of interests concerning Africa and its diaspora. Drawing work in French from writers such as Léopold Sédar Senghor and Michel Leiris and in English from C. L. R. James, the journal provided a forum that placed culture at the center of the anti-colonial and anti-racist struggles of the day. Through this work writers created and were formed by currents of thought that took the erasure of African diasporic culture in dominant modes of representation as a primary concern and field of engagement. Accordingly, those who participated in the journal linked its presence in Paris and act of documenting that presence to the larger struggles of the world's darker peoples to wrest authority over their own lives away from their erstwhile masters.

For intellectuals like Césaire, Diop, and Wright making culture capital meant providing a critique of the Eurocentric understanding of modernity's history in works that elaborated the histories of modernity contained in African diasporic experience. Their work participated in a tradition of putting African diasporic people at the very foundation of the modern that began in works such as W. E. B. Du Bois's *Black Reconstruction* (1935) and C. L. R. James's *Black Jacobins* (1938). Writing about their inaugural contribution to this long, if understudied, tradition, the literary critic Aldon Nielsen contends:

> James and Du Bois both argue far more than the simple case that black people, whether in the New World or in Africa, have not in fact lived outside the horizon of Occidental modernity . . . [they] trace the emergence of new, modern world-encompassing economies to the rupture of the Middle Passage and the monumental labors of black workers. (19)

In this essay, I approach the life and work of the African diasporic writers who gathered in Paris to "make culture capital" as continuing in the postwar moment the cultural work of linking the African diasporic presence to the very possibility of modernity. Through their work they insisted that peoples of African descent contribute as equals and not as colonial subjects or second-class citizens to the reconfiguring of the world's economies in the wake of World War II. I regard this past moment with a trace of "anti-imperialist nostalgia," which, according to Jennifer Wenzel, "holds in mind hope for changes that have yet to be realized," and "acknowledges the past's vision of the future, while recognizing the distance and the difference between that vision and the realities of the present" (7). The future that Diop, Césaire, and Wright imagined and sought to bring about through their work was guided by their vision of African diasporic peoples as subjects of and not merely just subject to modernity.

Alioune Diop, the founder and director of *Présence africaine*, was born on January 10, 1910, in Saint-Louis, Senegal, a coastal city that was an important commercial hub during the nineteenth century and the capital of the Federation of French West Africa from 1895 to 1902. The inhabitants of the city enjoyed the privileged status of being eligible for French citizenship as residents of one of the "four communes" of French colonial Africa (Coats 207). Diop's family was part of an aristocratic caste in the Wolof ethnicity, which made up more than 75 percent of the population of Saint-Louis. Although he briefly attended a provincial French school directed by his uncle for two years, Diop was fully incorporated into the French colonial world at the age of twelve when he entered the Lycée Faidherbe. His education at Faidherbe, a prestigious school that trained "a significant proportion of the future government functionaries, not only of Senegal but of all of Francophone Africa" (Coats 210), instilled in him a respect for the European Enlightenment and an appreciation for French civilization. After Faidherbe, Diop went on to study classical letters in Alger, before continuing his studies in Paris. After World War II, in 1946, Diop was elected as a Section Française de l'Internationale Ouvrière (SFIO) senator to the French Parliament, a post he held until 1948, when he resigned to devote his energies to *Présence africaine* (Frioux-Salgas 5n1).

The genesis of the *Présence africaine* project has roots in the years of World War II, during the German occupation of Paris. The Vichy regime founded the Foyer des Etudiants Coloniaux to provide students from the colonies with a library and meeting space. Beginning in 1942, Alioune Diop "directed the cultural circle of the colonial students in Paris, which was frequented by nearly all of those who would go on to embrace politics in the setting of the future French Union" (entreprit d'animer le cercle culturel des étudiants coloniaux de Paris que fréquentaient presque tous ceux qui allaient embrasser la politique dans le cadre de la future Union française) (Stadtler).[1] Reprising a role similar to when he acted as tutor to younger students at Lycée Faidherbe, Diop served as a mentor and guide to the students in the center's orbit, some of whom would later assist him in launching *Présence africaine* after the war. One member of this group, Jacques Rabemananjara, reflects on the circumstances surrounding the journal's emergence:

> In Paris, under the German occupation. With the French defeat all of the Western values that we had been taught under colonization to attach ourselves to and that had effectively left their mark were collapsing. We, students from the overseas French territories. Not numerous in the Latin quarter, we enjoyed visiting one another.
>
> A Paris sous l'occupation allemande. Avec la défaite de la France s'effondraient les valeurs occidentales auxquelles sous la colonisation on nous avait appris à nous attacher et qui, effectivement, nous ont tous marqués. Nous, les étudiants d'Outre-Mer. Pas nombreux au Quartier Latin, nous avons pris plaisir à nous fréquenter. (Rabemananjara 17)[2]

Rabemananjara's account points to the centrality of culture ("Western values") to the apparatus of French colonial domination and indexes the space for critiquing that ideology opened by the French defeat. In addition, he draws attention to the pleasure ("we enjoyed visiting") that these students drew from simply communicating with one another about the destruction of Western culture that they were witness to all around them. In this representation, culture also becomes a means of mediating and responding to the dislocations and deprivations provoked by the war.

Little scholarly attention has been given to how colonial subjects experienced the Occupation. As the historian Pap Ndiaye notes, "future works will have to illuminate the everyday life of Blacks during Occupation. But it is fairly clear that, for many, life continued with the usual difficulty" (Des travaux futurs devraient nous éclairer sur la vie quotidienne des Noirs pendant l'Occupation. Mais il est à peu près clair que, pour beaucoup, la vie continuait cahin-caha) (156).[3] According to Rabemananjara, this experience was a crucible for the group's budding anti-colonialism, which was inspired by and crossed with the larger population's resistance to Nazi occupation: "Anti-colonialism was energized from and grew with the rise of hatred for Nazi domination" (L'anticolonialisme s'amorçait et croissait avec la montée de la haine contre la domination nazie) (17). In making the connection between colonialism and Nazism, Rabemananjara makes an argument advanced not only in the works of African diasporic intellectuals such as Aimé Césaire, but also intellectuals of the European tradition such as Hannah Arendt.[4] The *Présence africaine* movement, as Alioune Diop conceived it, was meant to attack at their very foundations the myths used to support colonial regimes and thereby advance the anti-colonialist cause.

Présence africaine nevertheless sought to distinguish its efforts from previous ones by making its primary concern the difficult and elusive concept of culture. Rabemananjara captures a bit of the difficulty of this concept when he states, "of all human activities, culture is the one which knows no boundaries or limits; it is man's permanent face; it is also the base and the condition for man's change and flourishing" (de toutes les activités humaines, la culture est celle qui ne connait ni contours ni limites; c'est la face permanente de l'homme; c'en est aussi la base et la condition de changement et d'épanouissement) (18). Such a definition makes it difficult to establish culture's limits. On the other hand, it is precisely because of its all-encompassing quality that Diop finds culture attractive as a field of operation, gaining in versatility what is lost in precision. Indeed in a 1959 editorial titled "Notre politique de la culture," he declares "the traditional definition of culture proposed and imposed by the West to be neither sufficient nor healthy. And that a capital of cultural experience precious in Asia and in Africa risks being lost for humanity" (la définition traditionnelle de la culture telle que l'Occident la propose et impose n'est pas suffisante. Ni saine. Et qu'un capital d'expérience culturelle précieuse en Asie et en Afrique risqué d'être perdu pour l'humanité) (5). In this statement, Diop offers the capital, or wealth, of cultural experience in Asia and Africa as a challenge to the definition imposed by the West and thus as a source of resistance to European cultural imperialism. This capital, he continues, resides in "the *will* of the peoples [of Asia and Africa] who actualize its value in everyday life" (la *volonté* des peuples qui en actualisent la valeur à travers la vie de tous les jours) (5). Thus, Diop as editor gives voice to the cultural mission of *Présence africaine*, which consists in creating the conditions for and reflecting on the efforts of the masses to realize the value of their culture in the transformation of quotidian realities.

While others in the African diaspora took alternative routes towards this transformation, Diop was ambivalent about embracing other more political orientations such as Pan-Africanism. Although *Présence africaine* articulated a position that sought "to fuse black and European cultural values in a universal humanist civilization" at its inception, as Salah Hassan usefully observes, "the global geopolitical reorganization leading to the end of empire" had its effects in the increasing dominance of "Pan-African nationalism and anticolonialism" in the journal's cultural politics after 1955 (203, 204). According to Rabemananjara, however, for Diop "politics always took on the character of second-rank importance. Primacy remains the privilege of culture; politics is precisely only an aspect and a support of culture" (à ses yeux, la politique a toujours revêtu le caractère d'une instance de second rang. La primauté demeure l'apanage de la culture; le politique n'en est précisément qu'un aspect et un support) (19). Formulated this way, culture comes to mean something closer to a "whole way of life." While attractive, this approach has a disadvantage in that it ignores the complexity and robustness of the political field, flattening out all difference to questions of culture. In making this move, Diop runs up against a limitation similar to the one that Terry Eagleton finds in *Kulturkritik* and modern-day culturalism, which "is a lack of interest in what lies, politically speaking, beyond culture: the state apparatus of violence and coercion" (43). The founders of *Présence africaine*, however, were acutely aware of the French state's interest in their activities and they sought alliances that might protect the journal from the worst abuses of the state's power of violence and coercion.

For members of the circle around Diop, such as the poet Paulin Joachim, there was a compelling and direct objective to their emphasis on culture. In an interview with the cultural critic Bennetta Jules-Rosette, he states:

> We were all in the small group around Alioune Diop, and we had a mission. Essentially, it was to implant African culture in European civilization, to affirm our presence. And in Paris in those years we wanted to launch an African cultural renewal aimed at the white world in which we had been immersed. We wanted to assert our culture and our presence in this world. (*Black* 80)

Joachim makes a very complicated argument here, postulating that despite their total "immersion" in the white world, the intellectuals around Diop retained a culture that predated and was distinct from the one in which they were immersed. In such an example, a group of otherwise alienated intellectuals produce culture that they imbue with the power to bind them to a native population from which they are estranged as a consequence of their education. This was a logical, if compromised, position to take given that following World War II, the world in which these sons of France's colonies had been immersed was undergoing the effects of a globe-altering realignment of forces. By staking such a position, those associated with *Présence africaine* were able to "assert" and lay claim to a "presence" at the very center of the historic struggle of the world's darker peoples to wrest a place for themselves as equals within capitalist modernity.

In 1947, France in particular was caught in the whirlwind generated by this struggle as its colonial authority was being challenged on numerous fronts. At the end of 1946 in Indochina, for example, a coalition of Vietnamese communists and nationalists led by Ho Chi Minh began an insurgency against the French colonialists. Three months later, the Malagasy people rose up in an island-wide revolt against the French colonial administration in Madagascar. The French Army responded brutally, massacring at least 80,000 people. In fact, Jacques Rabemananjara, one of the early collaborators on *Présence africaine,* did not witness the launch of the journal because he had been detained and was facing the death penalty as a result of accusations that he was a lead organizer of the Malagasy revolt. In Paris itself, according to Bernard Mouralis, "the political changes that followed the Resistance and the Liberation brought into question, at least in terms of principles, the traditional relationship that the metropolis entertained with the colonial territories" (3–4). These and other such challenges significantly altered the Parisian scene, making it a suitable base for launching a cultural assault against French colonialism.

Diop's decision to found and base the journal *Présence africaine* in Paris took advantage of the city's new climate. "The Paris of 1947," as Mouralis points out, "was no longer that place of exile that it was for the négritude writers during the 1930s but a place where the African writers belonged, because the city was, from then on, one of the theaters in which the political and cultural future of Africa was being prepared" (3). Thus, by virtue of locating its headquarters in Paris, Diop placed his journal in a prime position to play an eminent role in Africa's future. On a more pragmatic level, the "new journal, by establishing itself in Paris, escaped the risk of marginalization inherent in any attempt to have peripheral voices be heard" (Mouralis 4). In addition, post–World War II Paris was home to a flourishing intellectual scene, perhaps unparalleled at the time in the Western world. At the center of this scene were several journals, such as Jean-Paul Sartre's *Les Temps Modernes* and Emmanuel Mounier's *Esprit*. As both Sartre and Mounier were members of *Présence africaine*'s Committee of Patrons, it inevitably "found itself endowed with the status of those journals that bore witness to the renewal of ideas in the intellectual climate that followed the Liberation, . . . this status [being confirmed in] the circulation that was established . . . between the collaborators of those journals and *Présence africaine*" (Mouralis 4). Indeed, members of the Parisian intellectual elite embraced Diop and his journal with a remarkable amount of enthusiasm and through the journal extended their intellectual and political purview. Increasingly, these intellectuals, who were variously associated with the French Left, began to adopt anticolonial stances. Thus, it was not a unidirectional exchange with *Présence africaine* alone benefiting from its association with the leaders of Parisian intellectual circles, but one with some amount of reciprocity in that the journal became a vehicle through which these intellectuals established their anti-colonial credentials.

That *Présence africaine* enjoyed a close association with the important intellectuals and journals of its time should not, however, be taken as an indication of its ready acceptance by the French authorities. In the days when the journal was still in formation, those associated with it were keenly aware of the risks of their enterprise. Rabemananjara describes them as being "conscious of the riskiness of the stakes. Of the immense hostility that the enterprise could not fail to provoke. From the side of Oudinot Street, where the Ministry of the Colonies is located. From the side of the great interests invested in our countries; they had no wish at all for the awakening of black consciousnesses" (conscients de la hardiesse de l'enjeu. De l'immense hostilité que l'entreprise ne manquerait pas de provoquer. Du côté de la rue Oudinot, Ministère des Colonies. Du côté des grands intérêts investis dans nos pays: ils ne tenaient absolument pas au réveil des consciences noires) (20). While it is difficult to gage the extent to which the journal was perceived as a threat, colonial authorities and their metropolitan counterparts surely had a vested interest in controlling information. The suppression of journals such as L'Etudiant d'Afrique noire, the organ of the FEANF, an African students' federation and the banning of books published by the editor and anti-colonial activist François Maspero (the first publisher of Fanon's *Peau noir, masques blancs*), is a clear indication that the French authorities were keenly aware of the high stakes of the ideological struggle in the fight to preserve their colonial territories.[5] For its part, the *Présence africaine* journal cultivated its close association with the leading French intellectual figures as a form of insurance against repression from the colonial authorities. As Christiane Diop, Alioune Diop's wife and collaborator on the journal, explained in an interview with Bennetta Jules-Rosette:

> [T]hey would have arrested us or stopped us from publishing. So we needed protection by great names—Gabriel Marcel, André Gide. They didn't dare touch us under the protection of these people. They helped us culturally, because we were regarded as subversive. That's very important. (Jules-Rosette, *Black* 45)

While I have yet to establish the extent to which the activities of *Présence africaine* were monitored or not, the Ministry of Colonies did in fact have a special secret police under the direction of the military that was charged with monitoring the activities of certain individuals from the Overseas Territories residing in France. Anecdotal evidence suggests that the police did indeed monitor Diop and his group. For example, Rabemananjara, recalls that during the interrogation related to his suspected involvement in the 1947 revolt in Madagascar, "the chief of Security in Madagascar, the sinister Baron, held against me both my belonging to the Negro movement in Paris that advocated the emancipation of the colonies and my friendship with Alioune Diop, whom he qualified for the circumstance as a dangerous, fiercely anti-French man" (le chef de la Sûreté de Madagascar, le sinistre Baron, me faisait grief de mon appartenance au mouvement des Nègres de Paris qui préconisait l'émancipation des colonies et de mon amitié avec Alioune Diop qualifié pour la circonstance d'homme dangereux, farouchement anti-français) (27). Whether the Ministry of the Colonies' secret police put the *Présence africaine* movement under intense surveillance or not, one might safely assume that the stirrings of anti-colonial revolt in Indochina, Madagascar, and elsewhere provoked the French colonial administration's interest in the activities of colonial subjects residing within the metropole. In fact, since the interwar years the police and the colonial ministry had worked together to develop special brigades charged with monitoring the activities of colonial subjects residing in France, particularly in Paris.[6]

In launching *Présence africaine*, Diop and his circle did not limit themselves to France and the Francophone world; they consciously sought to expand their sphere of influence beyond their immediate context, addressing themselves to the wider world of the African diaspora, particularly the Anglophone section. Reaching out to and including Richard Wright in the Committee of Patrons was the primary means through which the journal initially achieved this goal. When Wright arrived in France in the late summer of 1947, he was probably the most famous literary figure of African descent in the entire world. Those at *Présence africaine* would surely have understood that Wright's success signaled the increased potential for African diasporic cultural products in the literary marketplace. Their association with Wright, who had visited France a year earlier "with his wife and infant daughter as guests of the Cultural Relations Section of the French Foreign Ministry," undoubtedly contributed to reducing anxieties that Diop and his circle might have about reprisals from the Ministry of Colonies (Campbell 6).

The inaugural issue of *Présence africaine* appeared in the winter of 1947, a time when the effects of the recent war were still palpable. As Mouralis notes, "it was an impressive volume of 196 pages which was, in itself, quite a feat in that postwar period when paper was a rare commodity" (Mouralis 3). Despite these deprivations, the journal announced itself with great ambitions: "the first copy," according to Jules-Rosette, "was distributed simultaneously in Paris and Dakar in December of 1947" ("Conjugating" 17). This first issue reflected the multiple aims, audiences, and allegiances of which the journal was a product and which would define its subsequent issues. The first section consisted of what Jules-Rosette characterizes as "pithy confessionals" by French intellectuals, among them Gide, Sartre, Mounier, as well as a salutatory text by Diop (*Black* 38). Confirming the journal's orientation towards the diaspora, the second section was devoted to poems, plays, and short stories by "an international crew of black writers — Léopold Senghor, Bernard B. Dadié, Birgao Diop, Gwendolyn Brooks, and Richard Wright, among others" (Jules-Rosette, *Black* 38). Reviews of works of art, books, and ideas as well as summaries of articles in other journals related to the black world made up the third and final section.

In his introduction entitled "Niam n'goura ou les raisons d'être de *Présence africaine*," Alioune Diop sets the tone for the journal, which has since, over the course of its now more than sixty-year history, "[grown] into a larger publication enterprise, an intellectual group, and a cultural movement" (Jules-Rosette, "Conjugating" 17).

First, Diop draws the title of his essay from a proverb of the Toucouleur people of West Africa, "Niam Ngoura Vana Niam M'Paya," which he translates in a footnote as meaning "Eating in order to live is not eating in order to get fat" ("Mange pour que tu vives" ce n'est pas "mange pour que tu engraisses") (Diop, "Niam" 185 [7]). Diop's use of this proverb is perhaps meant to refer to another French word, "assimiler," which means literally "to take in." This verb connotes not only the process by which food is brought into the body but also the policy of assimilation, the initial governing principle of France's relation toward colonial subjects in its former colonies (and with regard to immigrants today). In this sense, Diop's use of the proverb indicates a program by which *Présence africaine* would accept just enough of European culture and civilization necessary for their own and African culture's survival, but not enough to constitute total assimilation and the replacement of African culture with European culture. In consequence, he rejects overindulgence, which would result in Africans identifying completely with Europe, and thus rupturing all links to African culture.

Throughout the essay Diop figures European civilization as providing the sustenance necessary for a healthy existence within modernity. For example, Diop writes,

> In establishing this magazine, our first and principle aim is to make an appeal to the youth of Africa who has long hungered for intellectual *food*. Few echoes of intellectual life in Europe reach him. His adolescent ardour, abandoned to arid isolation, dooms him to cultural asphyxiation or sterilization. Our hope is that this magazine can constitute itself a window through which young Africa can look out upon the world. (emphasis added)
>
> En fondant cet organe, nous avons songé d'abord et nous nous adressons princaplement à la jeunesse d'Afrique. Elle manque d'*aliment* intellectuel. Peu d'échos lui parviennent de la vie de l'esprit en Europe. Livrée à son isolement desséchant et à sa fougue adolescente, elle court le risque de s'asphyxier ou de se stériliser, faute d'avoir une fenêtre sur le monde. (185–86 [8], emphasis added)

While he does not make the point explicitly, Diop calls attention to the control that colonial authorities exercised over the flow of information in and out of the colonies by reminding his readers that few echoes of intellectual life reach African youth. In such a context, information controls limit the range of Africans' experience of modernity and support the uneven relation of forces that structure capitalist modernity. For Diop, then, *Présence africaine* becomes a vehicle for introducing the life-giving sustenance necessary for the youth of Africa to benefit fully from modernity. These injections are meant to bring about a transformation by which Africans, and more generally those from the overseas colonial territories, would become adapted to modern life and be able to share in the responsibility for improving humanity: "one wishes for the transformation of these overseas men into brains and arms adapted to modern life and sharing the responsibility of thinking out and bettering the lot of mankind" (on souhaite la transformation de ces hommes d'outre mer en cerveaux et bras adaptés à la vie moderne et partageant la responsabilité de penser et d'améliorer le sort du genre humain) (Diop, "Niam" 187 [9]). Clearly Diop expresses a highly problematic idea when he represents colonized subjects as somehow ill-adapted to the exigencies of modern life; a more generous reading, however, might understand Diop as performing a subtle critique of the international division of labor structuring modernity wherein the colonized are conscripted to perform the menial tasks while the thinking and directing is left to the colonizers.

In addition to its concerns with modernity, the first issue of *Présence africaine* also establishes its commitment to building a diasporic community. In his essay "The Uses of Diaspora," Brent Hayes Edwards notes that "at its outset, *Présence africaine* was not primarily conceived as a diasporic project, focusing on issues of connection and collaboration among peoples of African descent. It was more expressly conceived as an African incursion into modernity" (47). Even so, Edwards continues by asserting that "if *Présence africaine* did not initially aim to theorize black internationalism, it represents black internationalism *in practice*, particularly through its translations" ("Uses" 48). The first issue, for example, contains an English translation by Thomas Diop and Richard Wright of Alioune Diop's essay, "Niam n'goura ou les raisons d'être de *Présence Africaine*," as well as French translations of a poem by Gwendolyn Brooks, "The Ballad of Pearly May Lee," and Richard Wright's short story "Bright and Morning Star." It should be noted that Brooks's poem was from her first book of poetry, *A Street in Bronzeville* (1945), which Wright had encouraged Harper & Row to publish. It is probable that he played a similar role at *Présence africaine*.

Yet beyond the translations, Diop's introductory essay provides evidence that the journal conceived its mission, at least in part, as a diasporic project. Diop uses the example of the diaspora to buttress his claim about the value of imparting knowledge of Africa to Europe. In a footnote Diop writes:

> The coloured writers of America have already demonstrated the productive power of their spiritual vitality and its necessity to the world . . . In the near future we shall devote a special issue to coloured non-African writers.
>
> déjà, les Africains expatriés en Amérique—et dont la plupart ont tout oublié des moeurs africaines—ont amplement prouvé que la vitalité spirituelle du nègre et sa puissance créatrice sont désormais nécessaires au monde . . . Nous consacrerons un numéro spécial aux écrivains noirs non africains. ("Niam" 190 [12])[7]

This quote supports the claim that even if *Présence africaine* was not primarily conceived as a diasporic project, as Edwards suggests, it nevertheless founded its claim to relevancy and its hope for success on an engagement with the diaspora.

The journal, however, was only the initial channel for *Présence africaine*'s affiliation with the diaspora through print culture. In addition to the journal, Diop and his collaborators launched a publishing enterprise two years after founding the journal, thereby expanding their operations in the domain of print culture. Given the restricted publishing avenues for works in French about Africa or Africans, *Présence Africaine* as a publishing house opened up critical space for the circulation of ideas about and by Africans and members of the diaspora. These forays into print culture were the foundation of *Présence Africaine*'s diasporic project since diasporas, much like the imagined communities of nations as Benedict Anderson has demonstrated, have relied on print culture for their constitution and sustenance.

Print culture alone, however, did not constitute the whole of *Présence Africaine*'s diasporic activities. In the ten-year period from 1956 to 1966 the group was the principal organizing force behind a series of international conferences that brought together leading artists, writers, and intellectuals to discuss and debate the critical issues facing Africa and its diaspora. While no doubt drawing on the heritage of the Pan-African conferences that W. E. B. Du Bois organized in the first half of the twentieth century, the *Présence Africaine* conferences sought to distinguish themselves by according more attention to cultural matters than narrowly conceived political ones. The title with which the organizers baptized their first conference held in Paris in 1956, "Le 1er Congrès Mondial des Ecrivains et Artistes Noirs" (The First World Congress of Black Writers and Artists), speaks to this effort at distinction. Presenting the congress as the first of its kind, the title also defines the participants as men of culture, "Writers and Artists," and not politicians. In his opening remarks to the conference, Alioune Diop reinforced these claims about the distinctiveness of the congress in relation to previous efforts by declaring that

> Other congresses had taken place following the other war; they did not have the originality of being essentially cultural or of benefiting from the remarkable gathering of such a large number of talents having arrived at maturity, not only in the United States, the Antilles and in the grand and proud republic of Haiti, but also in the countries of black Africa.
>
> D'autres Congrès avaient eu lieu, au lendemain de l'autre guerre; ils n'avaient l'originalité ni d'être essentiellement culturels ni de bénéficier du concours remarquable d'un si grand nombre de talents parvenus à maturité, non seulement aux Etats-Unis, aux Antilles et dans la grande et fière république d'Haïti, mais encore dans les pays d'Afrique Noire. (Diop, "Opening" 9)[8]

If on the one hand Diop sought to distinguish the congress from the Pan-African congresses that had followed World War I, on the other hand he made an effort to associate the congress with the Bandung conference of the previous year, which had brought together leaders from Asia and Africa. Standing before the crowd of participants and spectators assembled at the Sorbonne for the opening ceremony of the congress, Diop claimed that, "if since the end of the war, the Bandung meeting constituted for non-European consciousnesses the most important event, [he] believed [himself] able to affirm that this congress . . . will represent for our people the second [most important] event of this decade [the 1950s]" (Si depuis la fin de la guerre, la rencontre de Bandoeng constitue pour les consciences non européennes l'événement le plus important, je crois pouvoir affirmer que ce premier Congrès . . . représentera pour nos peuples le second événement de cette décade) ("Opening" 9). By drawing this link between the two conferences, Diop initiated the approach according to which the congress is conceived as a kind of cultural Bandung.

Bringing together as it did black artists and writers from all over the globe, this conference and those that followed provided a structure for realizing a diasporic project in the post–World War II period. Out of these conferences black artists and writers created the networks, associations, and groups that sustained diasporic cultural work. By bringing these writers together, these conferences asserted the black diasporic "presence" in modernity, but also allowed for the production of the documents necessary for archiving that presence in a way that recalls the fateful encounter of Wright, Himes, and Baldwin on the terrace of the Deux Magots. These conferences provided African diasporic writers with the occasion to document, while simultaneously instantiating a modern black presence. Similarly, the three African American writers referenced above used the encounter at Deux Magots in subsequent works to document their own presence in a place, which had the allure of being the center of the intellectual world in the West.

It must be noted that the organizing activity that produced these conferences was not, however, an isolated phenomenon; it was shaped by, and it shaped, the larger cultural Cold War being fought between the West and the East. While perhaps not as readily associated with the Cold War as its military, economic, and political aspects, the cultural field was an essential domain, providing "lateral support to the military-political and economic struggle that had set in after 1945" (Berghahn 91). Similar to the black diasporic project, cultural conferences provided the prime site for waging this aspect of the Cold War. As Berghahn notes, "congresses and countercongresses of artists and writers as well as youth festivals and counterfestivals became the most visible expression of this struggle" (129). By 1949 the Soviet Union was at a distinct advantage in this arena, having benefited from several years of offensive operations without any sustained or effective counteroffensive from the West in this aspect of the Cold War struggle. In testament to this strength, the Soviet Union organized two major international peace conferences in the spring of that year, one in New York which drew the attendance of such famous intellectuals as Albert Einstein, Paul Robeson, Leonard Bernstein, and another in Paris attended by the likes of Pablo Picasso, Pietro Nenni, and Frédéric Joliot-Curie. In response, the United States increased its activity, beginning with a counterdemonstration with a sizeable audience in New York and a minimally successful "International Day of Resistance to Dictatorship and War" in Paris (Berghahn 129). Recognizing the centrality of Europe in this cultural struggle, the Americans came together to organize a major event in the "front-line city of the Cold War," Berlin, capped with "a mass rally and the establishment of an 'International Committee for Cultural Freedom.'" The event took place in June of 1950 and concluded with a rally of an estimated ten to fifteen thousand people in attendance (Berghahn 130).

Just one year before the *Présence africaine* congress in Paris, the Congress of Cultural Freedom had begun to rethink its strategy of focusing solely on Western Europe. Convening in 1955, the Milan congress devoted to "The Future of Freedom" had a stronger representation from Asia, the Middle East, Latin America, and Africa, and dedicated, according to Berghahn, "a full day . . . to the problems of nationalism and colonialism"(140). This shift signaled the increasing importance of the Third World in the Cold War, which by the time of the independence struggles of the 1960s would become the major theater of operation.

In the early fall of 1956 when *Présence africaine* opened its 1er Congrès Mondial des Ecrivains et Artistes Noirs in the Sorbonne's Descartes amphitheater, Cold War tensions were running high and were palpable to nearly everyone in attendance. The archive of this historic event is inscribed with the evidence of this tension. For example, in his essay chronicling the conference, "Princes and Powers," James Baldwin writes that "everyone was tense with the question of which direction the conference would take. Hanging in the air, as real as the heat from which we suffered, were the great specters of America and Russia, of the battle going on between them for the domination of the world" (145). That James Baldwin was covering the conference for and published his account in *Encounter*, a journal of the Congress for Cultural Freedom, an organization with established ties to the CIA, only compounds the long reach of this battle.

Describing the opening day's proceedings, Baldwin counts Richard Wright among the "eight colored men" who sat "behind the table at the front of the hall," a place apparently reserved for those intimately involved in organizing the conference ("Princes" 143). It is not without consequence that Wright would position himself alongside the likes of Alioune Diop, Léopold Senghor, Aimé Césaire, Jacques-Stephen Alexis, Dr. Jean Price-Mars, and the other co-organizers of the conference. While on this historic morning Wright was sure to present himself before the world in solidarity, at least for the moment, with his co-collaborators, he had recently sung a quite different tune before a very dissimilar audience at the U.S. Embassy in Paris. In the months leading up to the conference, Wright had apparently presented himself to the Embassy in order to document his distance from the conference organizers who, much to his disapproval, had fallen under the sway of Communists. Perhaps Wright's biographer Hazel Rowley is correct in her suggestion that Wright's visits to the U.S. Embassy were acts of "self-protection" by a writer living precariously in the space between the hospitality of one imperialist nation, France, and the long reach of another nation, the United States, hell-bent on ruining any citizen, especially a black one, who dared not toe the anti-communist line (474). All this serves to highlight the fact that even in his Parisian exile, Wright had not succeeded in escaping the excesses of the Cold War. Performing once again the public ritual of distancing himself from organized Communism, Wright appears in this instance to have made yet another shrewd calculation to preserve his much fought for but hardly secure sense of freedom.

To the extent that the Cold War left its mark on those attending the Paris congress, it likewise had a hand in one very conspicuous absence, that of W. E. B. Du Bois. At this advanced stage of his career, Du Bois was without parallel in intellectual accomplishments in the black world, having been engaged as an activist and scholar for well over fifty years. His world stature notwithstanding, in the United States Du Bois had been ensnared in the McCarthy witch hunt, branded a Communist, and denied a passport; thus he was unable to attend the congress. While barred from being physically present, Du Bois nevertheless addressed the congress via a telegram, which was read aloud during the opening session. According to Baldwin's account, in this telegram Du Bois explained the reason for his absence; he accused "any American Negro traveling abroad today . . . of either not car[ing] about Negroes or say[ing] what the State Department wishes him to say." He also predicted "the future of Africa being socialist," and warned African writers to "not be betrayed backward by the U.S. into colonialism" ("Princes" 146). While Baldwin considered Du Bois' communication as "extremely ill-considered" and as compromising "whatever effectiveness the five-man American delegation . . . might have hoped to have," it nevertheless announced in a very concrete manner the difficulty of trying to disentangle culture from politics ("Princes" 146).

The thirty-some presenters who spoke before the congress addressed from very different angles the African diasporic presence in modernity and culture's essential role in shaping that presence. The organizers of the congress, for their part, had set about to privilege culture as a prime site in the political struggle, decolonization, with which they closely identified. For example, in the essay "Modern Culture and Our Destiny" ("La culture moderne et notre destin") that prefaces the reproduction in *Présence africaine* of the speeches given at the congress, the organizers write that "culture becomes a formidable means of political action at the same time that it has the ambition and vocation to inspire politics" (la culture devient, en effet, pour la politique, un redoutable moyen d'action, en même temps qu'elle a l'ambition et la vocation d'inspirer la politique) (5).[9] Here, *Présence africaine* makes two claims essential to its work: first, that culture work in and of itself is a form of politics; and secondly, that culture, while distinct from the political, exists as a resource for politics. These claims legitimate *Présence africaine*'s work in the cultural field, while also establishing its relevancy for struggles operating within other fields. If the organizers tied their conception of culture to the aims of the conference, their convictions did not result in the censorship of contrary voices. In fact, encouraging different approaches was in line with one of the congress's principles, that "the number, the quality, and the variety of our talents must be the first affirmation of our presence in the world" (Le nombre, la qualité et la variété des talents devaient être une première affirmation de notre présence au monde) ("Modern" 3). Here again the organizers draw attention to the important work of simply affirming a presence. The critical import of this position is painfully evident when one considers that "our histories in [the] progress of modernity and modernism have generally been written as if black people had little to do with the subject other than be subject to it" (Nielsen 26). By presenting a number of voices, these conferences became sites for African diasporic writers to present themselves to the world as subjects in modernity. Indeed, many of those who made presentations during the three days would eventually come to be recognized as the African diaspora's most distinguished and well-known intellectuals and writers, in no short part due to the critical insights on modernity to be found in their work.

While undoubtedly less well known than many of his collaborators on the organizing committee and those who addressed the congress, Diop's contribution was crucial. Although not the congress president, this honor having been bestowed upon Dr. Price-Mars, Diop was unquestionably the central driving force behind the congress. In fact, he closed his opening remarks to the conference with a somewhat embarrassed acknowledgement of his role in bringing about the conference: "I will not finish this rapid evocation of our problems without expressing my joy to all those, artists, thinkers, and writers who helped me to fulfill the wish that had inspired me to serve black culture for over fifteen obstinate years" (je n'achèverai pas cette rapide évocation de nos problèmes, sans exprimer ma joie à tous ceux, artistes, penseurs, écrivains qui m'ont aidé à combler le vœu qui m'inspira plus de quinze années d'obstination au service de la culture noire) (Diop, "Opening" 17). In addition to his organizing activities, Diop also used the occasion of his opening remarks not only to assess the situation facing those artists committed to realizing a future for African diasporic peoples free from colonialism and second-class citizenship, but also to make a critical intervention into the debates that he anticipated animating the conference over the following three days.

In the context of his speech, Diop provides us with many critical reflections on debates concerning black culture, but his thoughts on the relationship between politics and culture are most relevant to the present discussion. James Baldwin writes that "in speaking of the relation between politics and culture [Diop] pointed out that the loss of vitality from which all Negro cultures were suffering was due to the fact that their political destinies were not in their hands" ("Princes" 144). By putting the question of political independence at the forefront of the congress and relating it to culture Diop articulates a position central to the anticolonial struggle. This position recognized that the nation-state was "the prime political form of modernity" and that "cultures are intrinsically incomplete, and need the supplement of the state to become truly themselves" (Eagleton 57, 59). Diop broached the subject in the context of his discussion of the "scandalous question of peoples without culture," "a myth created expressly by those truly responsible for colonization" (la scandaleuse question des peuples sans culture . . . les vrais responsables de la colonisation ont sciemment forgé ce mythe) ("Opening" 12). Here Diop makes a clear and poignant argument about the role of culture in politics, in this case providing the ideological justification for colonization. Diop's categorical refusal of the existence of peoples without culture must be understood as an anti-colonial position, as it rips away the mythical foundation on which the edifice of colonization was built. Diop attributes the circulation of such a myth to "the often overlooked and all too natural link, which [he feels] obligated to invoke in order to remain loyal, between the political and the cultural" (ce que l'on perd de vue assez souvent, c'est le lien tout naturel et que je suis obligé d'évoquer pour être loyal, entre le politique et le culturel) ("Opening" 12). That the link between politics and culture is often overlooked points to the centrality of culture to politics. Culture operates to smooth over the fissures and antagonisms that are the occasion of politics, while also being a means of bringing these same antagonisms into relief.

It is this operation of culture that gave *Présence Africaine* and the various black men of culture gathered at the congress their raison d'être. Looking across the contemporary political landscape, Diop saw the desperate and urgent need for cultural intervention:

> If political authority (the State) can exercise a deadly pressure on culture and if dictatorship has become more dangerous today than centuries ago, then it is certain that it is the responsibility of culture, for people's safety and equilibrium, to inspire politics, to think and animate it.

> Si l'autorité politique (l'État) peut exercer sur la culture une pression mortelle, et si la dictature est devenue aujourd'hui plus dangereuse qu'il y a quelques siècles ; alors il est certain qu'il appartient à la culture, pour le salut et l'équilibre des peuples, d'inspirer la politique, de la penser et animer. ("Opening" 13)

Faced with this urgent reality and awesome responsibility, Diop both critiques the idea that "politicians alone could create works that fulfilled the people's aspirations" (les seuls hommes politiques comme tels puissent formuler or créer des œuvres qui comblent l'attente totale des peuples) and outlines the unique role of writers and artists "to translate for the world the moral and artistic vitality of our compatriots and at the same time to communicate to them the sense and flavor of foreign works or world events" (de traduire pour le monde la vitalité morale et artistique de nos compatriotes, et en même temps de communiquer à ceux-ci le sens et la saveur des œuvres étrangères ou des événements mondiaux) ("Opening" 17). Thus, in his opening remarks Diop not only analyzes the centrality of culture in resolving the world's pressing political problems, but he also defines the unique role of black men of culture as political subjects, with the agency to bring about a much needed transformation of the modern world.

The role of artists and intellectuals as political agents would be revisited in varying degrees throughout the remainder of the congress. The most forceful and penetrating treatment would close the second day of the congress, when Aimé Césaire gave his address entitled "Culture and Colonization," which, "wrung . . . the most violent reaction of joy" from the audience, according to Baldwin ("Princes" 157). In this text, Césaire assigns to artists and intellectuals the important, if limited, role of "announcing the coming and preparing for the arrival" (d'annoncer la venue et de préparer la venue) of "[their] people and their creative genius finally rid of that which constrains and sterilizes" ([leurs] peuples et leur génie créateur enfin débarrassé de ce qui . . . contrarie ou . . . stérilise) them—political oppression in the guise of colonialism (205). Other delegates addressing the congress—Richard Wright, George Lamming, and Frantz Fanon among them—would also take up similar questions, if not in the same polemical vein as Césaire. By doing so these delegates initiated a conversation on the relationship between culture and politics and the political role of artists and writers, a conversation that *Présence africaine* would have a pivotal role in animating over the course of the next ten years. These conversations provided the cultural imperative for the anti-colonial struggles that advanced the still incomplete political project of a radical restructuring of capitalist modernity.

The foundation for this radical restructuring had been laid in modernity's past, during Paris's reign as the "capital of modernity." In his important historical-geographical study, David Harvey establishes Paris as the central site in the birth of modernity, growing from the "moments of creative destruction" that were the rebellions of 1848 and the governmental response to them, which culminated in Louis Napoleon's coup d'état and Haussmann's transformation of the city (Harvey 1). That officers such as "Louis Cavaignac, a bourgeois republican general with much experience in colonial Algeria," led the army that "ruthlessly and brutally put down the revolt" inextricably links this history of modernity and Paris's reign as its capital to the history of colonial expansion and its consequences (Harvey 6).[10] If the historic struggles of the Parisian proletariat behind the barricades in 1848 announce the birth of modernity, then the Algerian people's encounter with the imperial forces charged with breaking resistance to the expansion of global capitalism calls for a politics of culture attuned to the silences of the vanquished. Attending to these silences makes visible the links that bind the conquest and subsequent colonization of Algeria to the same historical forces that produced what Marx saw as the "farce" of Louis Bonaparte's rise to power (594). By bringing what Diop calls the "capital of culture experience" to politics, the development of such a culture of listening amplifies the farcical elements of the current tragic order.

Notes

1. For a discussion of the inception of *Présence Africaine*, its "original hopes and the structural conditions that governed their realization," see Miller.

2. All translations from this work are Julie-Françoise Kruidenier Tolliver's and mine.

3. Equally, all translations from this work are Julie-Françoise Kruidenier Tolliver's and mine.

4. This is one of the central arguments of Césaire's *Discourse on Colonialism*. For a discussion of Arendt's thesis on this question see Richard King's *Race, Culture, and the Intellectuals: 1940–1970*, particularly pages 100–110.

5. For a discussion of FEANF see Ndiaye, *La condition noire*, p. 327. For a larger discussion of the editing and anticolonial activities of François Maspero see his *Les abeilles & la guêpe*, Paris: Éditions du Seuil, 2002.

6. For a fuller description of these efforts see Clifford Rosenberg, *Policing Paris: The Origins of Modern Immigration Control between the Wars* (Ithaca: Cornell UP, 2006), particularly chapters 5 and 6.

7. It is interesting to note in passing that the translators Richard Wright and Thomas Diop elided the phrase "et dont la plupart ont tout oublié des moeurs africaines" (and who for the most part have forgotten everything of African mores).

8. All translations from this work are Julie-Françoise Kruidenier Tolliver's and mine.
9. All translations from this work are Julie-Françoise Kruidenier Tolliver's and mine.
10. In *The Eighteenth Brumaire of Louis Bonaparte*, Marx refers to these generals as "the heroes of Africa" (598). The editorial note states that "this refers to the generals distinguished for their savage deeds in Africa during the conquest of Algeria" (599n4).

Works Cited

Baldwin, James. "Princes and Powers." *Collected Essays*. Ed. Toni Morrison. New York: Library of America, 1998. 143-69.
Berghahn, Volker R. *America and the Intellectual Cold Wars in Europe*. Princeton: Princeton UP, 2001.
Casanova, Pascale. *The World Republic of Letters*. Trans. M. B. DeBevoise. Cambridge, MA: Harvard UP, 2004.
Césaire, Aimé. "Culture et Colonisation" (Culture and Colonization). *Présence Africaine* (Jun.-Nov. 1956): 190-205.
Coats, Geoffrey. "From Whence We Come: Alioune Diop and Saint-Louis, Senegal." *Research in African Literature* 28.4 (1997): 206-19.
Diop, Alioune. "Niam n'goura or *Présence Africaine's* raison d'être," trans. Richard Wright and Thomas Diop. *Présence Africaine* 1 (Oct.-Nov. 1947): 185-92. The French original appears in the same issue, 7-14.
———. "Opening Remarks" (Discours d'Ouverture). *Présence Africaine* (Jun.-Nov. 1956): 9-18.
Eagleton, Terry. *The Idea of Culture*. Oxford: Blackwell Publishers, 2000.
Edwards, Brent Hayes. *The Practice of Diaspora: Literature, Translation, and the Rise of Black Internationalism*. Cambridge, MA: Harvard UP, 2003.
———. "The Uses of Diaspora." *Social Text* 66 (Spring 2001): 45-73.
Frioux-Salgas, Sarah. "*Présence Africaine*: une tribune, un movement, un réseau." *Gradhiva* 10 (2009): 5-21.
Gildea, Robert. *France since 1945*. 2nd Ed. Oxford: Oxford UP, 2002.
Gilroy, Paul. *The Black Atlantic: Modernity and Double Consciousness*. Cambridge: Harvard UP, 1993.
Harvey, David. *Paris, Capital of Modernity*. New York: Routledge, 2003.
Hassan, Salah D. "Inaugural Issues: The Cultural Politics of the Early *Présence Africaine*, 1947-1955." *Research in African Literature* 30.2 (1999): 194-221.
Jules-Rosette, Bennetta. "Conjugating Cultural Realities: *Présence Africaine*." *The Surreptitious Speech*. Ed. V. Y. Mudimbe. Chicago: U. of Chicago Press, 1992. 14-44.
———. *Black Paris: The African Writers' Landscape*. Urbana: U of Illinois Press, 1998.
King, Richard. *Race, Culture, and the Intellectuals: 1940-1970*. Baltimore: Johns Hopkins UP, 2004.

Marx, Karl. *The Eighteenth Brumaire of Louis Bonaparte*. 1852. *The Marx-Engels Reader*. Ed. Robert C. Tucker. 2nd Ed. New York: Norton, 1978. 594–617.
Maspero, Francois. *Les abeilles & la guêpe*. Paris: Éditions du Seuil, 2002.
Miller, Christopher. "Alioune Diop and the Unfinished Temple of Knowledge." *The Surreptitious Speech*. Ed. V. Y. Mudimbe. Chicago: U of Chicago Press, 1992. 427–34.
"Modern Culture and Our Destiny" (La culture moderne et notre destin). *Présence Africaine* 1 (Jun–Nov. 1956): 3–6.
Mouralis, Bernard. "*Présence Africaine:* Geography of an 'Ideology.'" *The Surreptitious Speech*. Ed. V. Y. Mudimbe. Chicago: U of Chicago Press, 1992. 3–13.
Ndiaye, Pap. *La Condition Noire: Essai sure une minorité française*. Paris: Calmann-Lévy, 2008.
Nielsen, Aldon Lynn. "The Future of an Allusion: The Color of Modernity." *Geomodernisms: Race, Modernism, Modernity*. Ed. Laura Doyle and Laura Winkiel. Bloomington: Indiana UP, 2005.
"Notre politique de la culture." *Présence Africaine* N.S. 24–25 (Fév.–Mai 1959): 5–7.
Rabemananjara, Jacques. "Alioune Diop, le cenobite de la culture noire." *Hommage à Alioune Diop, Fondateur de Présence Africaine*. Rome: Éditions des amis italiens de présence africaine, 1977. 17–36.
Rosenberg, Clifford. *Policing Paris: The Origins of Modern Immigration Control between the Wars*. Ithaca: Cornell UP, 2006.
Rowley, Hazel. *Richard Wright: The Life and Times*. New York: Henry Holt, 2001.
Städtler, Katharina. "Genèse de la literature afro-francophone en France entre les années 1940 et 1950." *Mots Pluriels* 8 (1998). Web. 17 June 2011. http://motspluriels.arts.uwa.edu.au/MP898ks.html.
Wenzel, Jennifer. "Remembering the Past's Future: Anti-Imperialist Nostalgia and Some Versions of the Third World." *Cultural Critique* 62 (Winter 2006): 1–32.

CHAPTER 9

Richard Wright's "Island of Hallucination" and the Gibson Affair

Richard Gibson

The Gibson Affair was a scandal that rocked the African American community in the Paris of late 1957 and provoked tremors that continued long after. As the affair bears my name, I must accept or at least share responsibility; however, this is neither a confession nor an apology. This is an attempt to provide clarification of the mystery that still surrounds this incident, which some believe to have destroyed or diminished a certain cozy easiness of life in Paris for African Americans, dating back to the mid-nineteenth century. But the Algerian War of Independence, which began in November 1954 and ended in 1962, effected profound changes in that seemingly innocent relationship. *Les événements,* as the ambushes and scattered attacks were euphemistically called at the onset, became a full-scale colonial war in Algeria, which revealed the complex realities of French racial attitudes growing out of colonial expansion and the steady increase of African and Asian immigrants in France since the First World War.[1]

Hundreds of African Americans today live permanently in the French capital without having to confront the vagaries of commonplace, everyday racism that they might still have to cope with in the United States. If of course they have sufficient financial means. Millions of North Africans and Africans from south of the Sahara and even those born in France are coping with French racism that differs greatly from the Anglo-Saxon variety of separation and segregation. Whereas the French Jacobin tradition proclaims "republican values" and the universality of humanity, it just as effectively excludes ethnic, cultural, and religious differences.

My awareness of these French realities began only at the end of 1954 when I was being frequently stopped by French police and asked for my papers. Because of my light skin and frizzy hair, they would mistake me for an Algerian or some other North African but when I presented my U.S. passport or *carte de séjour,* I often received an apology. Nowadays, I add, I make, without any difficulty, visits to Paris and even to the Charente-Maritime, where an African American cousin rediscovered distant French cousins of ours, descendants of the African American painter Henry Ossawa Tanner, who had been unable to live with his white American wife and their son in the racist America of his day, but lived comfortably in France from 1898 to his death in Paris in 1937 (Alexander-Minter 23–33). But there was no visible Algerian problem in those years. In the 1950s there was.

Michel Fabre produced what has become the standard account of the Gibson Affair. Although emphasizing the influence of the Cold War on those involved, Fabre has reluctantly admitted that the Affair was really about the question of Algeria. This is what he wrote in his biography of Richard Wright in 1973:

> In the spring of 1958, Wright was forced to go to the French police apropos of a curious matter which had actually started several years earlier and was then referred to in the American black colony as the "Gibson affair."
>
> In 1956, Wright's friend Ollie Harrington, a former NAACP public relations officer and a well-known cartoonist for the *Pittsburgh Courier,* rented his Paris studio while he was away on the Cote d'Azur to Richard Gibson, a young black novelist in Paris on a Whitney scholarship. Harrington was disagreeably surprised on his return to find that Gibson not only refused to vacate the apartment, but claimed to own the furniture, paintings and personal belongings that he had left behind. The argument continued for almost two years. Gibson made violent attacks which verged on the psychotic, while Harrington resigned himself to living elsewhere rather than call in the police, fearing that the American Embassy might intervene on account of his status as an expatriate with Communist sympathies. Meanwhile, the Afro-American novelist William Gardner Smith, who was working for Agence France-Presse, had helped get Gibson a job and would not disavow his friend, with the

result that the black community had slowly taken sides in the struggle. Wright naturally supported Ollie Harrington, who had been his good friend since his arrival in 1955, although he did not share all his political opinions.

In 1957, one of the letters to the editor of the October 21 issue of *Life* magazine bore Harrington's signature and, replying to a September 30 article, violently condemned French policy in Algeria. Similar letters were also sent to *The Observer* in London, in reply to articles by M. Kraf and John G. Weightman that appeared on January 20 and January 30, 1958. Harrington, however, had not written these letters. Since the French policy was to deport any foreigner who got involved with French domestic politics, someone must have used this maneuver to compromise him, and he accordingly initiated an investigation with the support of the well-known criminal lawyer Jacques Mercier. Both the French and American police found conclusive evidence that Gibson had written the letters. A memorable fight ensued in the Café de Tournon, where Harrington thrashed his opponent so thoroughly that he had to be taken to the hospital; Gibson signed a confession, but the American Embassy intervened with the Sureté Nationale to hush up the affair.

Wright became involved because he was asked to testify along with the mathematician Joshua Leslie, his wife, who was an American cancer researcher, and William Gardner Smith, but he was also an indirect victim of the affair. Personal vengeance could account for Gibson's desire to get Harrington deported, but was he not also helping to discredit certain Afro-American exiles in Paris by associating them with the F.L.N. only a few weeks before the Algerian question came up for discussion in the Security Council of the United Nations? Could he be working for an organization like the CIA, which certainly had enough reasons to dislike the idea of Blacks like Wright being reluctant to support American propaganda while living in Europe?

These questions haunted Wright, who was not this time exaggerating the ramifications of the affair. The entire fabric of his life in Paris was affected. . . . Wright actually spent weeks assembling a file of documents to protect himself if need be. He also made a list of questions designed to reveal Gibson's real motives and William Gardner Smith's true position. He wisely got in touch with Gibson himself, who wrote back denouncing Smith as a "false brother," and reassuring Wright that he was too big a figure for anybody to harm without an extraordinary amount of maneuvering. But there was no way of knowing the truth or that Smith, who was ostensibly acting as a friend, was actually attacking him, and while it was also rumored that Wright was an FBI agent, he was convinced that the CIA itself was the source of all these machinations (461–63).

Containing several errors of fact or appreciation,[2] Fabre's 1973 version was nevertheless closer to the truth than his 1985 version presented in the original French text of *La rive noire: De Harlem à la Seine*, a survey of African American writers in France from 1840 to 1980. In the French text, he claims that I had been arrested by the French police and convicted of forgery, which never happened. He imagined that of my own accord I had slipped away to the United States in the hope of being forgotten. Yet in the very next paragraph, he reported that I was among those quoted in the notorious *Time* magazine article of 12 November 1958 about African American writers and artists in Paris, "Amid the Alien Corn." In that article, *Time* even welcomed my return to the United States and correctly reported that I was working for CBS News in New York. A furious Richard Wright denounced the article, linking it with the forgery of the Gibson Affair, claiming that he had never been interviewed by the magazine, and vehemently denied the magazine's assertion that he had declared: "The Negro problem in America has not changed in 300 years." He considered this another instance of "forgery." *Time* replied that his photographer friend Gisèle Freund, whom he had allowed to take the photo that appeared in *Time* magazine with the article, had also interviewed him while doing so. Wright threatened to sue *Time*, which he never did, but rather forced Freund to write a statement denying that she had "interviewed" him, although they must have chatted while she was taking his picture, and could not understand what all the fuss was about (Rowley 496–97).

I never considered suing Fabre, especially since the publication of the 1993 edition of his biography of Wright, in which he made some corrections in two footnotes. He reveals his sources in Wright's papers and adds that he had received "the evidence of several people who wish to remain anonymous."[3] Nevertheless, some persisting errors that he had promised to correct (see note 2) were published again in the 1999 reprint of *La rive noire*.[4] Fabre quickly apologized and made a vigorous effort to ensure that Hazel Rowley, who was working on her biography of Richard Wright, knew that his previous assertions were untrue.

I was able to meet Fabre thanks to the efforts of his student LeRoy S. Hodges Jr., who had contacted me when writing his biography of William Gardner Smith. Until then, no author writing about African Americans in Paris in the 1950s had made such an effort. I pointed this out to Tyler Stovall when we met in Paris after the publication in 2001 of his own survey of the African American community in Paris, noting that he had faithfully parroted Fabre's early errors.

The English translation of Fabre's *La rive noir*, published in 1991 as *Black American Writers in France, 1840–1980*, did not contain the obvious untruths in the original French text. Although Fabre presented the Gibson Affair as a minor cold war skirmish rather than a real argument among African American expatriates about France's colonial war in Algeria and the racist treatment of Algerians in France, he rightly pointed out that the plot of the unpublished "Island of Hallucination" is quite close to the intrigues of the Gibson Affair and its characters are an amalgam of those who were involved in it (*La rive* 159).

"Island of Hallucination" was the second novel of an intended trilogy that began in Mississippi with *The Long Dream* (published in 1958). Wright surprisingly planned to set the final novel in Algeria, although he seemed to know nothing about the country and the struggle of the Algerian people for independence. He certainly neither said nor did anything to help them. Instead, Fabre reports:

> In one of the rare interviews he gave on the Algerian war . . . Wright showed that he could distinguish between racism and French nationalism. He believed the Algerian war had nothing to do with race but with the awakening of French nationalism "now employed to forcibly convert Muslims who are religious fanatics, to Western civilization": "My feelings in such circumstances are ambiguous. Frenchmen tell the Muslims at the point of their submachine guns 'You are French.' We, American Negroes, might wish to be forced in a similar way to consider ourselves as American." (*Black* 185)

With such a gross misunderstanding of both Islam and the historical, social, and political realities behind the national liberation struggle of the Algerian people, it is no wonder that Wright chose to visit the Gold Coast, a British colony that was moving peacefully (because, unlike Algeria, there were no white settlers there) toward independence and transformation of the colony into the African state of Ghana under the leadership of the American-educated Kwame Nkrumah. Wright also was prompted to visit Ghana because he had a personal introduction to Nkrumah through a Trinidadian friend living and working there, a fellow ex-Communist turned Pan-Africanist, George Padmore, author of *The Gold Coast Revolution*.[5]

Moreover, the Gold Coast was not French, and he felt that nothing he might say about it would upset the French government (Campbell, *Paris* 205-233).[6] From that trip he produced *Black Power: A Record of Reactions in a Land of Pathos* (1954) in which he bemoaned African primitivism and tribalism, extolled Western civilization, and concluded the book with an open letter to President Nkrumah, telling him sternly: "AFRICAN LIFE MUST BE MILITARISED! . . . not for war, but for peace; not for destruction, but for service; not for aggression, but for production; not for despotism, but to free minds from mumbo-jumbo" (Wright 347). The book was understandably not well received in Africa.

Wright's trilogy was never finished. He forgot the Algerian project and abandoned the manuscript of "Island of Hallucination," which had received a cool reception when it reached his publishers in New York. Just before his death he began working on a new novel called "A Father's Law," about the guilty feelings of a man who abandoned, as Wright himself had done, a woman whom he was about to marry when he discovered she was suffering from congenital syphilis. The unpublished "Island of Hallucination" is Wright's only work set in Paris. It follows from *The Long Dream* (1958) in which Tyree Tucker, a black undertaker and community leader in Mississippi, profits from betraying his own people and is nevertheless killed by white racists jealous of his success. His son, Rex Tucker, nicknamed Fishbelly, is able to flee after being briefly imprisoned and then released.

Book One of "Island of Hallucination" opens with the ex-convict Fishbelly—carrying six thousand dollars cash in his wallet—sitting in seat 17 of flight 409 to Paris, observing his fellow passengers, all white. He is accosted by a friendly French couple, Jacques and Nicole, at the Shannon, Ireland, refueling stop common to transatlantic flights in those days, and enticed by the young woman and her partner into handing over two thousand dollars of his cash upon arrival in Paris, which he hopes to get back along with her love. Their crude scam is obviously used by Wright to point out that French people, who profess not to be racist, could easily cheat gullible black Americans like Fishbelly. The young man subsequently learns in little time from wiser African Americans whom he meets in Pigalle that the City of Light is full of criminals, pimps, and spies, some of them black. He also comes across sexy French women, many of whom are prostitutes. "Island of Hallucination" is drenched with paranoia and fear, misogyny and homophobia, and lots of raunchy sex.

Whatever Wright planned for the future, there is no mention of Algeria in this novel, in which he carefully sets the action three years before the beginning of the Algerian War on 1 November 1954, and rather during the Korean War and the riots by the French Left against the visit to Paris at the end of May 1951 of General Matthew Ridgway who had been the American military commander in Korea. The scene of the terrified Fishbelly being chased by a mob of angry demonstrators because he is wearing an American hat is one of the best in the novel. He throws away the hat and is hailed by the mob for doing so. On the last page of "Island of Hallucination," Wright leaves Fishbelly, walking home in the morning sun after a dramatic night, promising to change his dissolute life and swearing to himself never to leave France.

Begun early in 1958, the final draft of the typescript of "Island of Hallucination" was completed by February 1959. Wright seems to have written furiously and crudely as though trying to exorcise the demons who were transforming his supposed haven in Paris into such a hell that by the time of his sudden death at the age of 52 on 28 November 1960, he had been desperately trying to resettle in London, but he was destined to become a permanent Parisian.

Because of the reluctance of the U.S. State Department to issue him a passport in 1947, Wright sought and obtained a formal invitation from the French government to visit France with his wife as official guests. They remained several months before returning to New York, determined to return and settle permanently, which they did in August 1948. Their return was greeted by many French intellectuals on the Left, led by Jean-Paul Sartre, and some on the Right welcomed them back as well, because he was considered an anti-Communist. Both Left and Right seem to have grown weary of Richard Wright's political vacillations in the years to come as Paris became the cockpit of the cold war (Saunders 69).

Wright had walked out of the Communist Party of the United States because he believed that the Party was neither helping him enough as a black writer nor for African Americans in the fight against white racism. He did not reject Marxism-Leninism or the Soviet Union. And he did not consider himself an anti-Communist, though his powerful denunciation of Communism nevertheless was a featured contribution to *The God that Failed,* a collection of essays by former Communists who had quit the Party, edited by British Labour Member of Parliament Richard Crossman. Wright's moving essay deeply offended Communists and their sympathizers everywhere, including his friend Ollie Harrington. Wright later sought to assure people whom he knew at the American Embassy in Paris that Harrington was not a member of the Party. He had gone previously to the Embassy to ask their assistance in preventing certain prominent left-leaning African Americans, such as Paul Robeson and

Dr. W. E. B. Du Bois, from attending what was planned as a "Second Bandung" conference, bringing together non-aligned writers of color to an International Congress of Negro Writers and Artists, organized in September 1956 by the French African review *Présence africaine*. Wright was a member of the Executive Committee and seemed to have been extremely fearful that if the wrong people attended the conference might fall under Communist influence. The State Department heeded his plea, although he must have felt some secret embarrassment when the conference opened with the reading of a blistering message from Dr. Du Bois condemning the U.S. government for not granting him a passport to travel abroad. Somehow the news of Wright's visits to the American Embassy got out, and he bitterly complained that he was being called "an FBI informer." His friend Kay Boyle, who lived in Connecticut, wrote in 1956 to confirm that he was being accused of "working with the State Department, or the FBI, I don't know which, and that you give information about other Americans in order to keep your passport and be able to travel" (Campbell, *Paris* 221–22).[7]

Wright himself had indeed traveled to the Bandung Conference of nonaligned nations held in Indonesia in 1955 on tickets and expenses paid for by Michael Josselson, a CIA agent, who was the executive director of the Congress for Cultural Freedom, which the CIA covertly funded. Wright returned from Indonesia after the conference in the company of the former German Communist leader Ruth Fischer, a personal friend who lived in Paris from the 1950s until her death in 1961 (Warner). When she was a German Communist leader before the Nazis came to power, she had been in a face-to-face quarrel in the Kremlin with Stalin, and had managed to survive by fleeing eventually to the United States and recanting Communism. She was one of the founders of the Congress for Cultural Freedom, whose CIA connection Wright claimed not to have known until 1960, although many others around the world were well aware "who paid the piper." One such person was British theater critic Kenneth Tynan, who freely admitted to James Baldwin and me at a party in New York in 1959 that the Congress's British literary publication *Encounter* was CIA funded, but added that he would continue to contribute articles to it because it was "a fine magazine and not filled with American propaganda."

Whatever Wright's political contradictions, it is quite understandable that Harrington, who remained his friend until his death in 1960, was furious when in 1977 his widow, Ellen Wright, allowed a French professor, Michel Fabre, to publish and write an afterword to the suppressed final section of Wright's autobiography, *Black Boy* (1945) with the title *American Hunger*. Harrington said that he had believed that Wright had destroyed the manuscript, containing anti-Communist views he had supposedly abandoned, and declared that its publication by his widow and Michel Fabre "amounts to a mugging of a dead genius." He then went on to link Wright's "mysterious death" in Paris to "the murders carried out by the secret armies of the FBI and the CIA." He said, "Paris, particularly its centuries-old center of intellectual activity, the Latin Quarter, seemed to have been selected as a vital target by these 'patriotic' criminals" (Harrington 4–5). Harrington himself died at the age of 84 in East Berlin in 1996 after the Wall had been torn down, which in Harrington's view had let into the former German Democratic Republic the rats of capitalism, racism, and fascism from the West. Although the decades since have proved that he may not have been altogether wrong, Madeline Murphy, a relative of mine from Baltimore, felt differently then. When she visited Harrington and his family at their home in East Berlin when attending the World Peace Conference Special Session in 1979, she felt sufficiently at ease to tell him that she had noticed "a quiet hostility" against blacks in what was then the German Democratic Republic and told him that she had heard of racist "spitting incidents against blacks, carefully and surreptitiously acted out to avoid punishment." No denial was made by Harrington, and Madeline said she "realized much must still be done to educate the German people to rid themselves wholly of this racism, undoubtedly stemming from the Nazi past" (Murphy 376–85).[8]

Hazel Rowley's biography of Richard Wright has been criticized harshly by some, but I am grateful for her painstaking research into the causes of Wright's sudden death. Following Harrington's lead nearly a decade later, another American in Paris, the journalist Schofield Coryell, revived the mystery in 1986, claiming that "on the afternoon preceding the author's death, a close female friend of Richard Gibson visited Wright. The combination of circumstances was enough to start the rumor among Wright's circle of intimates that his death was in fact the final death blow dealt by his political enemies" (13–15). Rowley found that the truth was that Wright had indeed been visited by a woman on his last day of life in the Clinique Gibez in the Paris suburb of Neuilly. According to Rowley, she was a prostitute bringing him the proceeds of an exchange into French francs of dollars that Wright had left with a well-known moneychanger in Paris before entering the clinic. Shortly before entering the clinic, Wright had received a postcard that I had sent him from Cuba while on an official visit as the President of the New York Chapter of Fair Play for Cuba Committee, which I later headed nationally as Acting Executive Secretary until a rather hasty departure from the United States in 1962 to avoid wasting the organization's resources to defend me from unfounded allegations that I was an unregistered Cuban agent.

During their stopover in New York from Havana on their way home to Paris early in 1960, Jean-Paul Sartre and Simone de Beauvoir were guests of honor at a reception given by Fair Play for Cuba Committee. Knowing of their friendship with Wright, I discussed inviting him to join with other African American writers and artists that Fair Play was planning to send on a delegation to see the New Cuba. They thought it a good idea, but doubted Wright would accept. According to Rowley, Wright was distressed to receive my postcard from Cuba and considered it a provocation, which it was not, but I never followed up with an invitation. As for Wright's untimely death, Rowley ascertained that it was caused by his doctor's persistent dosage of bismuth, a dangerous drug, which had given him liver poisoning. Ellen Wright had not asked for an autopsy into the cause of his death, listed by his doctor as a heart attack, before the cremation of his body at Père Lachaise Cemetery on 3 December 1960.

As for the manuscript of "Island of Hallucination" in which Wright had lashed out in frenzy and hatred at these "false brothers," as he called the African Americans in Paris and elsewhere who he believed were bent on destroying him, Ellen Wright decided also to consign it to obscurity. Having become an active literary agent in Paris, thanks in part to the support of Simone de Beauvoir, the widow may have feared the legal consequences of publishing its vitriolic characterizations even posthumously along with the seven other works left by her husband.

Excluded from the public because of this fear, the manuscript was held for many years in total darkness at Yale University's Beinecke Rare Book and Manuscript Library and no one was allowed to examine even the title page until 1996. And then for some years, only a favored few were permitted to consult the manuscript and attempt to describe its tangled, fantastic melodramatic plot.[9] This explains why even the book's title has so frequently been mistakenly given as *Islands of Hallucinations* or *Island of Hallucinations*—such as recently in September 2004 in a thought-provoking paper by Rebecca Ruquist, in which she observes that it "read in part like a thinly disguised *roman à clef* of the African American expatriate community in Paris" (290). Of course that is exactly what the novel is, and the keys can be easily deciphered by those who were around at the time as habitués of the small but lively Café Tournon on the Left Bank near the Luxembourg Palace. There is only one hallucination, as Wright explains through one of the few sympathetic characters, Ned Harrison, an expatriate black lawyer, probably based in my view more on Noel Torres, who was an African American lawyer working for the U.S. Army at its logistics base in Chateauroux, than on Ollie Harrington or Wright himself.

The hallucination is that which afflicts the main villain, Charles Oxford Brown, who accepts the nickname of Mechanical, a bisexual provocateur who lives with a woman, but is described by Wright as ready to go off with any other woman or man he fancies. When they meet, Fishbelly immediately realizes Mechanical is an informer and thereafter calls him a "robot." Ned confirms that Brown is indeed an informer, and says he works for both the Americans and the French, hiding under the cover of a journalist working for an obscure African American news agency. This character is based in part on William Gardner Smith and most certainly on James Baldwin—as Wright has him recount as his own experience Baldwin's celebrated "Equal in Paris" (1955), the true story of his arrest at Christmas 1949 by French police for inadvertently taking a sheet from a Paris hotel.

According to Ned, Mechanical is himself being spied on by another black American, Bill Hart, who says he is from Cleveland, but actually has been living in Rome and admits to harboring sympathies for Italian fascism. In the last issue in Spring 1955 of the Paris-based little magazine *Merlin,* I contributed a short article on my Italian friend the controversial author Curzio Malaparte, a founding member of the Fascist Party who was to join both the Communist Party and the Roman Catholic Church on his deathbed and bequeathed his famous villa on Capri to the Chinese Writers Guild. I had met him in Rome when I worked briefly for the English language publicity office of Italian Films Export under American writer Bill Murray, who was much later to work for *The New Yorker,* and for Edmund Stevens, former Moscow correspondent of *The Christian Science Monitor,* who had taken over their Mediterranean News Bureau in Rome after Stalin had expelled Stevens with his Soviet wife and family from the USSR. My Roman days no doubt prompted Wright's tagging me in "Island of Hallucination" as the "superspy from Rome who spied on spies," but strangely enough not as the forger and chief villain.

The motor of the book's plot comes straight from the Gibson Affair as Wright has Mechanical forge a letter in Ned's name, which, when he is exposed as the forger, brings the novel to its melodramatic end when he hangs himself from a Gargoyle on one of the towers of Nôtre Dame—in a pastiche scene from Victor Hugo's far greater nineteenth-century novel of that name. As a priest hastily cuts down Mechanical's body from the rope, Ned comments that he "lived and died in a hallucination that was his own" and adds that "in well-knit society . . . hallucinations are shared, are the collective extensions of a people's vision of life, of a meaningful outlook upon the world." In the words of Ned, Mechanical was simply "a *person rejected* by other *persons"* ("Island" 512). Hence, he only had one hallucination, his own.

James Baldwin and William Gardner Smith were both my friends. Baldwin's essays "Everybody's Protest Novel" (1949) and "Many Thousands Gone" (1951) had stung Wright as unjust and a betrayal of his past support of Baldwin's career as a young writer. My own brief outburst against the protest novel, "A No to Nothing," first appeared in the *Kenyon Review* and was reprinted in the Winter 1953 issue of *Perspectives USA,* edited by Lionel Trilling, next to Baldwin's "Everybody's Protest Novel."

When I first met him at the Tournon, Wright remarked, "So you're the boy who wrote them nasty things about me." He nevertheless shook my hand and bought me a coffee, which he was not known to do often. After the storm broke in October 1957, he maintained contact with me and invited me several times to lunch, giving me questions to answer and taking copious notes. I thought he was only trying to help Ollie Harrington, who needed no further help, as the French DST, the security service, were well aware that Harrington had not written the letter with his name that had been published in *Life* on 21 October 1957. The forged letter said, referring to an article on Algeria published in a previous issue:

> Sirs:
> LIFE maintains there will be political and economic chaos in Algeria when France gives up her colonial holdings ("Hopeful Plan for Algeria," LIFE, Sept. 30). The chaos LIFE forgets to mention is right here in France. Any American who thinks that France of her own will, will grant Algeria, if not independence, at least some liberal status where seven million Algerians will not be crushed politically and economically by a million Europeans is mad.
> OLLIE HARRINGTON
> Paris, France

My friend, Philadelphia-born novelist and journalist William Gardner Smith, who rose eventually to become chief of the English-language service of the Agence France-Presse, was especially detested by Wright although he had never written a line against him or the protest novel as a genre, as Baldwin and I had. Wright wanted me to confirm his strong suspicion that Bill Smith was the person who had really forged the letter and was behind a plot against Harrington, himself, and other African Americans in Paris, perhaps aided by the Jamaican-born Joshua Leslie, another Tournon regular, who had studied at the University of Chicago and was then working on a Ph.D. in Mathematics at the Sorbonne. I had not realized that

Wright was collecting material for a new novel that was to become "Island of Hallucination" in which Leslie is unflatteringly caricatured by Wright under the name of Juggler, a loud-laughing Trinidadian Communist graduate student at the Sorbonne.

In "Island of Hallucination," Mechanical is more than a simple observer. He is an informer who plays at being a Communist, but is also acting under orders from an older charismatic militant black leader of a Trotskyist organization, the CTR, called Cato, "a black white man," grey-haired in his 60s, who knew Trotsky personally and is a super-revolutionary looking forward to World War III, which he believes the Communists will win, and on to World War IV, which he is convinced that the Trotskyists will win. Cato is clearly based on C. L. R. James, known to friends and comrades as Nello, who had migrated from Trinidad to the United States and was later deported to Britain during the McCarthyite years because of his militant leftwing political activities. He died much respected in Hackney, East London, where his name today honors one of the local public libraries. Richard and Ellen Wright first met James and his wife, Constance Webb, a former photographer's model and Communist organizer, when they were living in New York. She was to write the first biography of Wright published after his death. Wright knew that William Gardner Smith had visited James in New York, not long before Smith left for France, although he never joined James's Correspondence group or any other political organization.

The publication of Smith's spare, beautifully written first novel, *Last of the Conquerors,* made him a celebrity in Philadelphia. Based on Smith's experience of American racism and love for a German woman when he was a young black G.I. in West Germany in the early years of the Allied occupation after the end of World War II, the book was a critical success and earned him some money and many admirers among members of the fractious leftwing groups that greeted him when he returned to his home town. He mixed easily with Communists of strict Muscovite obedience and various denominations of Trotskyists—the Socialist Workers Party, the Shachmanites and members of the Correspondence Group in which C. L. R. James was a leading figure. They all seemed eager to recruit him to their ranks. Smith confessed that he found James's writing brilliant, enjoyed his love of literature and his choice of beautiful white women.

I met Bill Smith thanks to Irene Rose, a charming white woman, a grandmother who shared with me her own bemused experience of the arts and the micropolitics of the American Left. Living in Philadelphia because of her husband's business there, she had become a good friend of African American painter Beauford Delaney when living earlier in New York. Having read admiringly of Beauford in Henry Miller's essay "The Amazing and Invariable Beauford Delaney," I exchanged letters with him and eventually met him when he came to Philadelphia to accept a prize for his paintings exhibited at the annual art show of the Pyramid Club composed of local African American gentry, and he discovered I was only 16 years old. He introduced me to Irene and she invited me often to her home in a small eighteenth-century house in the Society Hill section of Center City Philadelphia.

I was fascinated by Bill and his young bride, Mary Sewell Smith, who came from a prominent black family and worked as a social worker. Before setting off for Europe in 1951, I spent long hours with them in their West Philadelphia apartment, discussing literature and politics and how to get out of the United States. My friendship with Bill was to last until we were both living and working as AFP subeditors, a job that he had got for me a few months after I arrived in Paris following my discharge from the U.S. Army in Germany at the end of 1954. I was well aware that neither of us at that time would have been able to hold a comparable position in the United States. I had gone into the Army in Trieste, Italy, and spent only a few months in the United States before finagling a transfer to Germany, where I remained until the end of my two years of service. Then I headed straight to Paris, looking for my friends Bill Smith, Beauford Delaney, and James Baldwin. When I had first visited Paris from Rome in 1952, Bill had introduced me at the Café Tournon, announcing jokingly to friends and acquaintances that I was his separated wife's lover.

Probably thanks to my connections with the *Kenyon Review*, I received a John Hay Whitney Fellowship for Literature in 1951, but left for Rome rather than Paris on the advice of Eleanor Clark, whom I met through Robert Penn Warren and whom she later married. Warren had urged me to talk to her about my impending European trip as I was about to spend a month at the Yaddo writers and artists' community in Saratoga Springs, New York, where Eleanor was finishing up her *Rome and a Villa* (1952), a book that became very popular and boosted the attractions of the Eternal City for Americans planning to go abroad. When I finally got to Paris, Mary had left Bill to return to Philadelphia and he was living alone at the Hotel Tournon on the corner of rue Saint-Sulpice, where he found me a room. Later when the hotel was closed for conversion into apartments, Bill was offered the vacant room just above the nearby café—in which the refugee Austrian novelist Joseph Roth had lived until his death just before the Second World War.

William Gardner Smith was certainly not the first writer to frequent the Tournon, but he was, as far I know, the first African American, whereas Wright favored the Monaco, which was even closer to his home on the rue Monsieur-le-Prince. Among the others who spent time at the Tournon were the writers and editors of the *Paris Review* and its mainly British rival *Merlin*. The Americans were led by George Plimpton, Bob Silvers, Max Steele, and Peter Mathiessen, who later admitted that he had been working for the CIA as well.[10] The only African American woman writer around, Vilma Howard, dropped in occasionally until her marriage to Christopher Scott, a British man working at UNESCO. Closest to the black American writers were *Merlin's* mainly Brit pack, led by novelist Alexander Trocchi, the poet Christian Logue and joined by American writer and later distinguished editor and publisher Richard Seaver and the famed translator into English of the works of the Marquis de Sade, Austryn Wainhouse, whose father was then a high-ranking U.S. State Department official but whose son stayed far away from our heated political discussions. Logue on the other hand had boldly argued with George Padmore one evening when Wright brought his visiting friend to the Tournon. The innovative French novelist Georges Perec (1936–1982), known to us only as a chess player and film buff, also frequented the Tournon on afternoons, when Wright occasionally played the pinball machine by the door. The Tournon was obviously not just a "black church" as Wright maintained in "Island of Hallucination." However, so well known were the political inclinations of many of its habitués that the French *série noir* novelist Jean-Patrick Manchette uses it as a setting for intrigue and plotting of the assassination of a Third World leader in his very successful French thriller of 1971, *L'affaire N'Gustro,* based on the kidnapping and murder in Paris, with French police assistance, of the Moroccan leftist leader Mehdi Ben Barka, who had been lured to Paris from exile in Switzerland.

The Tournon is their hangout, but the real meeting place of the conspirators in "Island of Hallucination" is further down the road at 31 rue de Seine, a building owned by Raymond Duncan, brother of dancer Isadora Duncan, who dressed in a Greek toga and sandals and ran his Akademia Duncan on the ground floor and was the landlord. On the top floor, there were two adjacent studio flats connected through a hidden door/closet through which one could pass from one to the other. Harrington lived in the one on the left, which he sublet to me. Living in the other was an American woman of British origin named Pamela Oline, who had been red-baited while working for the U.S. government in Morocco, but managed to clear her name and return to New York, where she eventually became a prominent psychotherapist and artist. Although she was certainly neither a Trotskyist nor a Communist, Pamela served Wright as model for Nellie, a devout white woman follower of Cato whose "secret cell of Trotskyists" meets in her flat. It is there, in the absence of Cato, but the presence of others, that Mechanical flamboyantly forges a long far-fetched letter in the name of Bill Hart, denouncing Ned Harrison as "a commy!" and commenting gleefully to those watching, "Presto! Ned's expelled from France" (385).

In the real world, no one would have been expelled from France for Wright's fictional letter, whether forged or not. Nor was I for a much more effective one that was not intended to prompt anyone's expulsion, and certainly not my own, although Bill Smith clearly hoped that I would leave the country. Bill was indeed the instigator of the letter, but its real inspiration came from a colleague working at AFP named Jean Chanderli, a senior editor and political commentator. Bill had been introduced to Chanderli at the Place de la Bourse headquarters of the French news agency by François Fejtö, a Hungarian refugee and well-known commentator on Eastern European affairs, whom we both knew. I saw Fejtö frequently, but was not introduced to Chanderli, whose name was given to me by Bill, but I only met him in 1959 when he was then known as Abdelkader Chanderli, the militant Algerian nationalist who headed the Algerian National Liberation Front Observer Mission at United Nations headquarters in New York. I was surprised to discover when we met how much he already knew about me and not only from Bill Smith. In fact, Chanderli said he had heard nothing from Bill Smith since their meetings before he left France shortly after Bill had promised to do everything possible to publicize the Algerian national liberation struggle in the United States at a moment when the Algerians felt American sympathies were starting to turn away from the French, and when American oil companies started looking closely at the vast new oil field discovered under Algeria's Sahara Desert. Eventually, Chanderli, joined in New York by FLN leaders Mohammed Sahnoun and M'hammed Yazid, and aided by a Tunisian journalist at the United Nations, Simon Malley, and his American wife, Barbara, seized this opportunity and was able in 1961 to persuade the young Senator John F. Kennedy to make a speech in the U.S. Senate in favor of Algerian independence from France.

But in Paris in 1957, all I knew was that we African Americans had to do something drastic to help the Algerian fighters, and Bill came up with the idea of a letter-writing ring in which we would write American and British newspapers and magazines denouncing French colonial rule in Algeria. Each of the letters would be signed in someone else's name so that, if need be, the real person could go to the French police to protest legitimately about the forgery and misuse of their name in support of the Algerian cause. But why, I asked, did he want me to sign a letter on behalf of Harrington? Bill said because Harrington was well known at the Tournon for loudly trumpeting the French Communist line of that time, that the Algerian insurrection was "a petty-bourgeois nationalist phenomenon" that had nothing to do with the international revolutionary movement headed by the Soviet Union. And he added cheerfully, "Because if you're caught, everybody will think this was only because of your fight over the apartment." I did not think much of that, especially as my young family and I were no longer living in the studio flat on rue de Seine, but in a much larger apartment near the Porte de Clignancourt, and a British woman colleague from AFP had taken Harrington's old flat when he could not or would not pay the large rent arrears that he had left behind without telling me when he left for Sweden and I took over as sub-tenant.

Learning that I had moved in when Harrington left, Raymond Duncan threatened to have me evicted. I was able to convince him that I had moved in without any knowledge of the rent arrears, which I could not afford to pay, but assured him I would keep up the rent while I was there. He agreed to let me stay only when I gave him a written undertaking not to allow Harrington to return until he had obtained Duncan's permission to do so, and I stuck to that agreement when Harrington returned, to his obvious displeasure.

Bill did not write the letter to *Life* magazine. I did, and gave him a copy which he was to post to *The Observer,* the British Sunday newspaper. Although I still have the original issue of *Life* of 21 October 1957, I have never seen the letter that is said to have been published in *The Observer.* Within days after the publication in *Life,* Smith announced that the situation had changed drastically and that he was not going to ask Joshua Leslie or anyone else to join us in the letter-writing ring and that he had not written the letter he had promised. I began to smell a rat, but I was still not prepared for the visit of the French security police, the DST, to my home early on the morning of my day off. They took me away with my small Olivetti portable typewriter for questioning at their headquarters.

Rather than questioning, however, they began by informing me that they knew all about me and showed me a written statement by William Gardner Smith, stating that he had become aware of my crime of forgery in which he had not been involved in any way. I could see that he had provided them with samples of my handwriting that proved that I was the culprit, but I noted that Bill had not given them the copy of the letter to *The Observer* that he was to have posted. I was pleasantly surprised to learn that no charges would be laid against me and that I was not under arrest, but might be if I did not sign a statement of apology to Ollie Harrington and pay his legal fees, which I agreed to do with alacrity. I was allowed to leave after about three hours and a lunch of sandwiches and beer with a severe warning to me that I would be in big trouble if I were to contact Bill Smith or make any publicity about the case, which they repeatedly insisted was not of a political nature but strictly personal. I would be allowed to remain freely in France as long as I stayed out of French politics and did not get into any further trouble. No one mentioned the American Embassy.

I was astounded and returned home to calm my anxious wife and my mother-in-law, who was visiting from London, where awaiting me as well was a *pneumatique* from AFP, which asked me not to return to work the next day, but assured me that I would remain on full pay until further notice. There was no mention of the matter of forgery; however, I learned through friends that Bill Smith had raised a petition among AFP staff, demanding my dismissal, but the *Syndicat national des journalistes* (SNJ), the journalists union to which I belonged, had pointed out that this would be a breach of my contract as I had never been arrested, formally charged with or convicted of any crime. AFP had no choice but to negotiate my voluntary departure with a year's salary, which helped us clear the mortgage on the small *pavillion* that we had bought in Rosny-sous-Bois just outside Paris. When my mother-in-law returned to London, the room she vacated was taken by a cousin from Maryland, Benny Waters, whom I was lucky to run into one evening at Leroy Haynes's soul food restaurant. I had first met Benny, a veteran jazz musician, in New York when he was playing with Jimmy Archie's band at Ryan's 57th Street. Like many other African American jazzmen, he had come to Paris because it was still easy to find work and he was at that time playing at La Cigalle in one of those "Negro bands" mentioned by Richard Wright in "Island of Hallucination." Benny remained in my life and in Paris until he returned to Maryland at the age of 90 to live with a nephew because of failing sight and died two years later.

My novel, *A Mirror for Magistrates,* was published early in 1958 by Anthony Blond, Ltd. in London. Later in the year, I received news of the serious illness of my 84-year-old maternal grandmother in Philadelphia, Sadie Thomas. She had raised me alone after the death of my mother, her only child, when I was five years old, and, although she was alone in Philadelphia, she had urged me to get away to Europe when I had the chance. From her and her brother, Frederick King, I had first heard of our distant French cousins. Since I still had some cash from the AFP settlement, I was able to purchase a cheap Sabena air ticket to fly to New York via Brussels and Montreal and took the train from New York to Philadelphia. Because my grandmother had never seen any of her grandchildren, my wife allowed me to take my two-year-old daughter, Dominique, with me, expecting that we would not stay long because my grandmother had been reported on the verge of death. Fortunately, she was alive when we arrived in Philadelphia and able to announce that God had answered her prayers when she saw me and her grandchild enter her hospital ward. Mary Smith proved to be a loyal friend and helped me care for my young daughter, and I was put up by various friends, including briefly writer/journalist Joe Hunter and his novelist wife, Kristin Hunter, who remained friends although they could not understand what had happened between their friend Bill and me.

While in Philadelphia, I heard through a friend that the Urban League in New York was looking for me for a job being offered by CBS News for the post of their first permanent African American newsman. After some rather intensive interrogation and tests over three days, far worse than the DST, which also touched on my slight Algerian FLN connections, but clearly of interest to CBS News, I was hired and asked to establish contact with Chanderli, who I had not known until then was in New York, and I quickly got in touch with him. I was also introduced to Robert Taber, a veteran photoreporter, newswriter and expert on guerrilla warfare who had been yanked out of Cuba when the State Department protested that he had hurt American interests by revealing that Fidel Castro was alive and well in the Sierra Maestra when President Fulgencio Batista's American-backed government claimed that he and all his followers had been wiped out.

My Algerian contacts were to be of no use to CBS News. Taber and I were assigned to work together on the night shift at WCBS and talked a lot during the quiet hours of the similarities between the Algerian and Cuban revolutions, and in time I found myself in another scandal when we set up the Fair Play for Cuba Committee to rally liberal American opinion in support of the Cuban Revolution. The network was obviously not happy with us, and Taber had to quit his job and spend a few years in Havana, while I was eased out, paid off, and given a CBS Fellowship at Columbia Graduate School, which left me free to act as a part-time correspondent at the United Nations for *Revolución,* the newspaper of Castro's 26th of July Movement, and to hang out at the UN with Simon Malley and our Algerian friends and to liaise with them to bring together African Americans with Cubans living in the United States and Arab students and various American liberals and radicals in mass demonstrations against French colonial rule in Algeria and in support of the Cuban Revolution. It was I who suggested that Fidel move from the unwelcoming Hotel Commodore on 42nd Street to the Hotel Theresa in Harlem. On our arrival, I found Malcolm X, whom I had met while working for CBS News, waiting in the hotel lobby to welcome Fidel on behalf of the black community. Subsequently, I was twice subpoenaed before the Senate Internal Security Sub-Committee, accused of being an unregistered foreign agent, and when I decided that my continuing in the top post at FPCC was endangering the organization's continuing existence, made secret preparations and left the country via Canada for England to stay temporarily in London with the family of my British wife, Sarah, whom I had married in Paris with Bill Smith as my best man.[11]

Chanderli provided us in 1962 with an official invitation to now independent Algeria, where we were immediately given jobs on the new weekly publication of the Party of the FLN, *Révolution africaine*. Bill Smith did do something for Algeria. He wrote the only novel by an African American author in support of the Algerian Revolution, *The Stone Face* (1963), which was not published until a year after Algeria had won its independence. It was not translated into French. He left AFP to go to Ghana to teach journalism and work for Ghana radio, thanks to an invitation from his old friend Shirley Graham Du Bois, the wife of Dr. Du Bois. There he again met Wright's older daughter, Julia, who was working in Ghana with her French husband. According to yet another roman à clef, *Agenda,* written by French lawyer Jacques Vergès, my old boss in Algiers, Lausanne and again in Paris in 1963 and 1964 at *Révolution africaine,* when it acquired notoriety by establishing offices next door to the Balmain fashion house on the rue François Ier, my own dubious reputation was following me. In Vergès's novel, a character said to be the son-in-law of a famous black American writer, meets the narrator and says that the newly arrived African American journalist, *"Le correspondent d'USP"* (rather than CBS), had been somehow involved in the mysterious death of his famous father-in-law (46–50). In 1991, Julia Wright made a surprise visit to see me in London, and I lent her Vergès's novel to photocopy the passage. Most of her questions were about her father's sexuality, perhaps because of allegations of homosexuality made by Margaret Walker in her biography of Wright.[12] When I saw Julia again with her mother at the African Americans and Europe Conference organized by the Sorbonne in February 1992 by Michel Fabre, her mother, Ellen Wright, allowed me to embrace her when I greeted her on the stage where we were to discuss the Tournon Group with the widow of Chester Himes, Lesley Packard Himes, the famous African American artist Edward Clark, poet and lawyer Sam Allen (who was once involved with the CIA-funded Society for African Culture), and a very subdued Ollie Harrington, who had just arrived from East Berlin. It was rumored that he been attacked by neo-Nazi skinheads in East Berlin. Julia sat behind the panel and closer to Harrington than to her mother next to me, and during the discussion she almost denied visiting me in London. I apologized to Harrington for any unintentional damage that I might have done him but tried to point out that it had indeed been Bill Smith who had set me up for reasons I still could not understand. I pointed out, moreover, that if Smith had not urged him to do more than deny authorship of the forged letter, which could have been easy to do, there would have been no Gibson Affair at all. Harrington made no contribution to the conference except to tell some old jokes. It was obvious that he was not interested in talking about the Gibson Affair. Later at the Café Select in Montparnasse, he told me in passing that he had little time left him and he had to go soon to the United States to Detroit to make some money to leave his German wife and their son. When I suggested that we ought to get together to compare my various files and his Stasi files, he replied he was no longer interested in anybody's files. Both he and I were interviewed separately on camera by Madison D. Lacy for a Mississippi Educational Television/BBC television film on Richard Wright. He died four years later at home in East Berlin after two books of his were published in the United States.

As for William Gardner Smith, the mystery remains. Michel Fabre confirmed that Smith never wrote anything nor spoke to anyone about his role in the Gibson Affair, except to say that I was dangerous and should be avoided. Yet when CBS News was considering hiring me, he had allowed Bernard Redmont, another American journalist working for AFP, to write a glowing official letter of recommendation for me without any mention of the Affair, which CBS already knew about. Bill was accused repeatedly of being an American or French agent, or both. If French, of which there is yet no proof, he was at least well rewarded by being appointed chief of AFP's English-language Service shortly after being expelled from Ghana when Kwame Nkrumah was overthrown by a coup d'etât in 1966. He died of lung cancer in 1974 at the age of 47. LeRoy S. Hodges Jr., his faithful biographer, with whom I had a long exchange of letters, could not bring himself to believe what I had told him about Smith's role in the Gibson Affair. Unfortunately, the likeable Hodges died before I could tell him what I thought of his otherwise excellent biography of Smith. At least he and his mentor, Michel Fabre, had the decency to seek me out to ask for my side of the complex story. Although some of his errors of fact persisted despite his efforts, I am grateful that Fabre did try to correct them.

As for other false assertions concerning me, I need only point out that a Statement in Open Court was read out in 1985 at London's High Court of Justice Queen's Bench Division between myself, the Plaintiff, and Penguin Books Ltd, Defendants, who withdrew untrue allegations made in a book published by them, entitled *Inside BOSS* by Gordon Winter, a self-confessed South African secret agent, announcing the withdrawal of the book and declaring that "Mr Gibson has never worked for the United States Central Intelligence Agency," as well as refuting its other insinuations, such as being "traitor to the causes he espouses" and "agent provocateur" and so on. I received a substantial sum in damages and all my costs, tax-free, and the judge pointed out that their repetition of such misinformation would constitute aggravated libel.

However, I am nevertheless quite certain that this long-awaited act of justice will not put paid to all untruths circulated about the Gibson Affair. And while I do not think that "Island of Hallucination" is a great book, it is a very important document about Richard Wright's state of mind at the end of his life and reveals as in a cracked mirror the tensions and the sad delusions that moved some leading figures in the African American community in Paris in the 1950s, torn apart by the cold war and above all by their contrasting attitudes to the sudden eruption of the Algerian national struggle against French colonial rule. Therefore, I strongly urge Julia Wright, who must now control the copyright, to take courage and let her father's strangest book, "Island of Hallucination," be published at last.

Notes

1. See Fabre, *Black American Writers in France, 1840–1980,* especially pages 1–8, where he traces succinctly the evolution of the African American presence in France.

2. Among these errors are: 1) Harrington went to Sweden and not to the South of France; 2) I arrived in Paris in December 1954 immediately after discharge from the U.S. Army in Germany to study French on the G.I. Bill; 3) Harrington left behind no paintings or personal belongings; 4) I made no attacks, psychotic or otherwise, on Harrington; 5) while Harrington certainly bested me in the fight outside the Café Tournon, it was he who provoked the brawl, but I suffered only a black eye and was not hospitalized; 6) there is no evidence of any intervention by the U.S. government.

3. Fabre's revealing footnotes are as follows:

    1. Richard Gibson to M. Fabre, November 18, 1987. What were Gibson's motives? In a June 26, 1977, letter to LeRoy Hodges, he claimed that the whole thing had been the result of a scheme he and Smith had concocted. A left-winger, he

Richard Wright's "Island of Hallucination" and the Gibson Affair 245

had acquired pro-Algerian sympathies because, being light-skinned, he was often mistaken for a North African by the French police and treated as such. Smith had joined him in doing something to help the Algerians by denouncing French colonialism in English-language publications. Signing the names of others would serve as a protection, and if questioned by French authorities, each in turn could deny having written the letter. Smith was to get the approval of other black Americans and reportedly suggested that the first letter be sent in the name of Harrington. Assuming Smith later provided the police with proof that Gibson was the forger, Smith's motives for betraying him are unclear. Did he act out of sexual jealousy? Was he under pressure from the French DST or police, who were uneasy about anyone meddling with French policy in Algeria, and did he use Gibson as a scapegoat in order to protect himself?

2. Gibson to Wright, August 22, 1958. In his letter of August 11, 1958, to Wright, Gibson intimated that Smith had double-crossed him. Among a list of thirty-one questions which Wright drew up, presumably for Gibson, appear, for example, the following: "Why were Ollie and I linked as targets of Smith? Ollie as an alleged Red and I as an alleged FBI man? . . . Could you have any idea why a girl with whom Smith was sleeping would come to my apartment on three occasions and ask to use my typewriter when she had one and could have used Smith's or could have borrowed Ollie's, since Ollie lived next door to her?" Wright also made a floor plan of Harrington's apartment, showing how the girl, Pamela, could have entered via a closet; and for the benefit of several of his friends he also had Xeroxes made of the documents of the investigation, including the March 24, 1958, letter in which Gibson admitted to Harrington that he had sent the letter to *Life Magazine* and the two letters to *The Observer* with the manifest intention of compromising him with the French authorities. Gibson apparently thought this was his only chance to save himself from expulsion from France. Wright eventually used most of these details in "Island of Hallucinations."

"My sources for the Gibson affair are Wright's correspondence and papers, and the evidence of several people who wish to remain anonymous. In 1960, Richard Gibson sent Wright a postcard from Cuba, suggesting that he come and see the achievements of Castro's regime as if he really was in favor of it, but the Maoist magazine *Revolution,* of which Gibson had been on the editorial board for a time, openly denounced his 'counterrevolutionary' activities, in its April, 1964, issue" (Fabre, *Unfinished Quest* 613–14). Actually, my activities consisted mainly of demanding that Vergès pay his mounting bills when he failed to obtain Chinese subsidies for the glossy review. After that last issue, he returned to Algeria and then left his Algerian wife and was not heard from for seven years. Asked where he had been, he would only say he had been "behind the looking-glass."

4. The reprint was published by André Dimanche Éditeur, Paris, 1999.

5. Wright heartily recommended Padmore's subsequent work, *Pan-Africanism or Communism?*

6. The U.S. edition of James Campbell's *Paris Interzone* is titled *Exiled in Paris.*

7. See also Campbell's "Black Boys and the FBI," 1290–98. Based on documents released under the Freedom of Information Act, Campbell discusses Wright's direct line to the embassy and the U.S. government surveillance of African American writers in Paris, including numerous mentions of James Baldwin, but whose own FBI file was begun only when I persuaded him later in New York to become involved with the Fair Play for Cuba Committee.

8. Harrington was shocked to learn from me in Paris in 1992 that Madeline Murphy was related to me by marriage to my cousin, Judge William H. Murphy Sr. of Baltimore, and that she had described in detail her visit to his East Berlin home. She wisely had not mentioned my name to him.

9. Wright would not have been pleased to find himself among the keys in Chester Himes's roman à clef, *A Case of Rape,* written in Paris in 1956–57 and published in French as *Une Affaires de viol* in 1963 and for the first time in English in 1980. His death is exploited in John A. Williams's *The Man Who Cried I Am* (1967).

10. Harry Mathews also dropped by rarely and recently has caused some deliberate confusion in his novel *My Life in CIA* (2005), whose main character is Harry Mathews, who is believed to be in the CIA but may not be.

11. For a detailed history of the Fair Play for Cuba Company, see Van Gosse 137–73.

12. The subject of homosexuality comes up numerous times in Walker's text. See pages 88–89, 91, 92, 155, and 310.

Works Cited

Alexander-Minter, Rae. "The Tanner Family." *Henry Ossawa Tanner.* Ed. Dewey F. Mosby and Darrell Sewell. Philadelphia: Philadelphia Museum of Art, 23–33.

Campbell, James. "Black Boys and the FBI." *Times Literary Supplement,* 30 Nov.–6 Dec. 1990: 1290–98.

———. *Paris Interzone.* London: Secker and Warburg, 1994.

Coryell, Schofield. "Updating a Myth." *Passion* 44 (1986): 13–15.

Fabre, Michel. *Black American Writers in France, 1840–1980*. Urbana: U of Illinois P, 1991.
———. *La rive noire*. Paris: Lieu commun, 1985.
———. *The Unfinished Quest of Richard Wright*. Trans. Isabel Barzun. New York: Morrow, 1973.
Gosse, Van. *Where the Boys Are: Cuba, Cold War America and the Making of a New Left*. London: Verso, 1993.
Harrington, Ollie. "The Mysterious Death of Richard Wright." *People's World, World Magazine*, 17 December 1977: 4–5.
Hodges, LeRoy S., Jr. *Portrait of an Expatriate: William Gardner Smith, Writer*. Westport, CT: Greenwood, 1985.
Manchette, Jean-Patrick. *L'affaire N'Gustro*. Paris: Gallimard, 1971.
Matthews, Harry. *My Life in CIA: A Chronicle of 1973*. Normal, IL: Dalkey Archive, 2005.
Miller, Henry. *The Air Conditioned Nightmare*. New York: New Directions, 1945.
Murphy, Madeline. *Madeline Murphy Speaks*. Columbia, MD: Fairfax, 1988.
Padmore, George. *Pan-Africanism or Communism?* London: Dobson, 1955.
———. *The Gold Coast Revolution*. London: Dobson, 1953.
Rowley, Hazel. *Richard Wright: The Life and Times*. New York: Holt, 2001. 496–97.
Ruquist, Rebecca. "*Non, Nous Ne Jouons Pas La Trompette*: Richard Wright in Paris." *Contemporary French and Francophone Studies* 8.3 (2004): 290.
Saunders, Frances Stonor. *Who Paid the Piper? The CIA and the Cultural Cold War*. London: Granta, 1999.
Smith, William Gardner. *Last of the Conquerors*. New York: Strauss, 1948.
Stovall, Tyler. *Paris Noir African Americans in the City of Light*. Boston: Houghton, 1996.
Vergès, Jacques. *Agenda*. Paris: Simoën, 1979.
Walker, Margaret. *Richard Wright: Daemonic Genius*. New York: Warner, 1988.
Warner, Michael. "The Cultural Cold War: Origins of the Congress for Cultural Freedom, 1949–50." *Studies in Intelligence* 38.5 (1995). 12 September 2005, at www.cia.gov/csi/studies/95unclass/Warner.html.
Webb, Constance. *Richard Wright: A Biography*. New York: Putnam, 1968.
Wright, Richard. *Black Power*. New York: Harper, 1954.
———. "Island of Hallucination." Ts. 3.34.472. Beinecke Rare Book and Manuscript Library. Yale University, New Haven, CT.

CHAPTER 10

Entering the Politics of the Outside
Richard Wright's Critique of Marxism and Existentialism

Jeffrey Atteberry

> But if a selfish West hamstrings the elite of Asia and Africa, distrusts their motives, a spirit of absolutism will rise in Asia and Africa and will provoke a spirit of counterabsolutism in the West. In case that happens, all will be lost. We shall all, Asia and Africa as well as Europe, be thrown back into an age of racial and religious wars, and the precious heritage—the freedom of speech, the secular state, the independent personality, the autonomy of science—which is not Western or Eastern, but human, will be snuffed out of the minds of men.
> —Richard Wright, *White Man, Listen!*

Richard Wright issued an invitation to the Western world to enter a political terrain that it has historically and ideologically foreclosed, in one way or another, as outside politics. His invitation went unheeded. The West today, if not the world, can only hope that such an invitation will be extended once again, but will we know how to read the invitation if and when it arrives? Do we even have the cour-

Richard Wright's Critique of Marxism and Existentialism 249

age to read it, much less accept it? Perhaps the best preparation for facing such questions would be to revisit the original invitation. In 1956 Wright addressed the First International Congress of Black Writers and Artists, an event sponsored by *Présence Africaine* and organized by Alioune Diop.[1] The invitation in Wright's lecture, "Tradition and Industrialization" (later published in *White Man, Listen!*), appears near the end and was printed originally in all caps as if to avoid the possibility of being overlooked: "The West, in order to keep being Western, free, and somewhat rational, must be prepared to accord to the elite of Asia and Africa a freedom which it itself never permitted in its own domain" (100). The force of this "must" may, even still today, not sound like much of an "invitation," but political invitations of this sort, especially when coming from the disenfranchised, are rarely festive affairs; they are "invitations" in contrast to the fearful alternatives. Wright knows perfectly well, however, that, for these very reasons, the invitation will be ignored, if not scornfully rejected. "Oh, I'm asking a hard thing and I know it," he confesses (100). The hard things still bear asking.

That such an invitation would be issued by Wright in Paris in 1956 is far from a coincidence. Paris during the mid-twentieth century was the cultural and political capital of the black Atlantic. Colonized peoples from across the globe for some time had been arriving at the metropole and were fashioning in Paris itself the very political space that Wright was inviting the West to enter. Against the backdrop of the Algerian War for Independence, international congresses were being held, conferences were organized, and journals were published. Such an environment should be considered "political" in both a practical and theoretical sense. Recently, Jacques Rancière has suggested that "The essence of politics is *dissensus*. Dissensus is not the confrontation between interests or opinions. It is the manifestation of a distance of the sensible from itself. Politics makes visible that which had no reason to be seen, it lodges one world into another" (par. 24). The increasingly physical appearance of the colonized world in the space of Paris at the heart of the metropole may be considered just such a lodging of one world within another. The colonized world made itself manifest, began to appear, quite materially to the world of the colonizer which had heretofore carefully controlled the form of that appearance by policing the "distance of the sensible from itself." Rancière's recent description, however, is only a tenuous sign that the metropole has begun, perhaps, to recognize the political space that Wright had invited it to enter, forty-five years earlier.[2]

Much of Wright's lecture was devoted to describing the space that the West was being invited to enter, for he knew that the West would not recognize this space, even though it had been forcefully shaping that space, materially and ideologically, for hundreds of years. This lecture was not, however, his first attempt at such an endeavor. A few months before, Wright published *The Color Curtain,* an extended commentary on the Bandung Conference of 1955. In March of that year, representatives from twenty-nine African and Asian countries met in Indonesia in an effort to advance decolonization and to confront collectively the attendant problems of such a process. Among these problems was how to avoid becoming inscribed within the emerging dichotomies of the Cold War period. As such, the Bandung Conference laid the groundwork for what would become the Non-Aligned Movement. The first and longest chapter of *The Color Curtain,* entitled "Bandung: Beyond Left and Right," serves as an introduction to the colonial world. The chapter uses a common questionnaire to construct biographical and political profiles of a number of individuals from across Africa and Asia. The text performatively acts as the kind of personal introduction that often accompanies invitations. The subtitle to the chapter, moreover, already gestures toward the geopolitical positioning of these "outsiders," for they are situated "beyond" or outside the hegemonic dichotomies that were shaping the global political space. Wright emphasizes that the identities of these "outsiders" are political in their very formation. Similarly, Wright begins "Tradition and Industrialization" by outlining the social and historical forces behind the formation of his own identity. In doing so, he explains the political tenor of his own subject position as it intones his invitation. Wright presents himself as a black American who, as such, is in a unique position to issue this invitation which is, in fact, directed specifically to the *white* West. Wright explains that "my position is a split one. I'm black. I'm a man of the West. These hard facts are bound to condition, to some degree, my outlook. I see and understand the West; but I also see and understand the non- or anti-Western point of view. . . . Hence, though Western, I'm inevitably critical of the West" (78–79). Recalling Du Bois's notion of double-consciousness, Wright avers that his position as an African American places him in a position that affords him knowledge of both the West and its "outside." Wright implicitly argues throughout the lecture that African Americans, as in the West but not of it, are well situated to act as guides into the emerging political space because, historically, their subject positions have long been shaped by the very same forces that are currently producing these spaces on a global scale.

Indeed, throughout his lecture, Wright describes a world that has been Westernized through colonialism and imperialism and which remains, nonetheless, not of the West. The political space of a decolonized world is one in which regions that had previously been designated by the West as "outside" the political, economic, and juridical spheres come to exert an immanently transformative pressure on those very spheres. As the distance between metropole and periphery began to collapse, it became increasingly difficult for the metropole to pretend that the peripheries were not integral to the economic, social, cultural spaces of the center. Today, as globalization and neoimperialism continue, this recognition has taken the form of a political and economic integration that positions these outsides as "excluded interiors." Economically, these former outsides appear simply as particular markets within the ostensibly universalized circuits of global exchange. Politically, they have been incorporated within the body of the United Nations as placeholders in the General Assembly, while remaining outside the chambers of the Security Council where true executive power is wielded. In short, a total subsumption of the outside has occurred that has in no way altered the basic structural relationship between inside and outside. On the contrary, Wright had invited the West to enter the politics of the outside, and the movement of this entrance would require an opening on the inside that would fundamentally alter the very relationship between inside and outside.

An open and revised relationship between inside and outside powers Wright's politics of the outside. In the years before "Tradition and Industrialization" and *The Color Curtain*, Wright had begun to clear the way in *The Outsider* for entering the politics of the outside by interrogating the basic framework structuring the relationship of inside and outside. When it was initially published in 1953, *The Outsider* was widely read as reflecting Wright's critical turn from communism to existentialism. A few decades later, however, once critics began to examine closely Wright's engagement with existentialism, the ambivalence of that relationship began to emerge, and *The Outsider* increasingly seemed to be a somewhat implicit critique of existentialism as well.[3] In what follows, I will argue that both of these critiques are intimately related in Wright's *The Outsider*. In particular, the rigor of Wright's critique of Communist Party practice leads directly and necessarily to a theoretical critique of existentialist philosophy insofar as existentialism reproduces, on a fundamental level, the basic ideological structures that underwrite and program the political practices of the Communist Party. The specific ideological structures that bind communism and existentialism together are articulated in the philosophical tradition through the categories of "the particular" and "the universal." Just as the political space of Bandung was situated "beyond left and right," the politics of the outside have to be situated beyond the particular and the universal.

By 1953, Wright's criticisms of Communism were no secret, having been publicly aired nine years early with the publication of "I Tried to Be a Communist" in *The Atlantic Monthly,* and anyone who had read the earlier piece would inevitably recognize the fictional recreation in *The Outsider* of its more emblematic scenarios. In both works, Wright dramatizes the dictatorial power of the Communist Party over the human concerns and personal affairs of its members. Through the experiences of the protagonist Cross Damon, as well as those of Bob Hunter, Wright hones his criticism of Communist practice by focusing on the relationship between African Americans and the Communist Party. In doing so, Wright's novel highlights the tensions between African Americans and the Party, a relationship that had been historically and politically structured according to the theoretical relationship between tactics and strategy. The politics of race as they played out within organized Communism, however, do not constitute an isolated theme in the novel. The race politics of Communism appear in *The Outsider* as a symptom of more fundamental structures and racialized features of western ideological culture. Consequently, in his critical portrayal of the political relationship between African American and the Communist Party, Wright's critique opens upon the fundamental categories of western thinking as they were being taken up and redeployed by the most prominent European thinkers of his day, the existentialists.

In *The Outsider,* the protagonist Cross Damon is introduced to the Communist Party by Bob Hunter, a Pullman porter who has been trying to unionize the other porters. During the lengthy scene of this initial encounter, Hunter is firmly informed by Jack Hilton, a white member of the party establishment, that he must immediately cease his organizing activities. Dismayed, Hunter inquires as to why, and the only answer that he gets is, "The Party is not obliged to justify its decisions to you or anybody" (247). A heated argument ensues, and the attitudes of the party toward questions of race are quickly clarified. Hilton demands that Hunter obey the party's decision and proceeds to threaten him if he doesn't do so. Hilton flatly declares,

> If you don't, then the Party will toss you aside, like a broken hammer, and seek another instrument that will obey. Don't think that you are indispensable because you are black and the Party needs you. Hell no! The Party can find others to do what it wants! Is this asking too much? No. Why? Because the

Party needs this obedience to carry out its aims. And what are those aims? The liberation of the working class and the defense of the Soviet Union. (248)

In this speech, the basic tenets structuring the relationship between the party and its African American members are expressed in the clearest of terms. Hilton tells Hunter that he is no more than "another instrument," a "hammer," for doing the work of the party. Moreover, the ultimate aims of the Party are the "liberation of the working class and the defense of the Soviet Union." Racial justice per se is clearly not understood as a stated objective. Rather, issues of race politics are conceived as means to these declared ends. Precisely because Hunter's racial identity makes him an ancillary instrument, a mere means to an end, the party declares that he is far from "indispensable"; other means can and will be found, as Hilton's abrupt termination of Hunter's organizing activities already indicates.

In Wright's presentation of this scene, questions of race politics are understood as tactical problems that are systematically and strategically subordinated to class and Soviet politics. While it is true that the Communists were one of the few political organizations of the time interested in "the negro question," that investment was understood by the Communists themselves as purely tactical. Ever since the Fourth Congress of the Communist International in 1922 and its adoption of "Theses on the Negro Question" at the behest of the Negro Commission, the Communists openly recognized the tactical importance of race politics, particularly as it involved blacks in the New World, in the struggle against capitalism. The first thesis clearly stated, "The Fourth Congress considers it essential to support all forms of the black movement which aim either to undermine or weaken capitalism and imperialism or to prevent their further expansion" (Adler 331). The practical subordination of race politics to class politics is grammatically inscribed into this proclamation by the restrictive clause qualifying that "forms of the black movement" are to be supported. The thesis does not proclaim unconditional support for all forms of "the black movement"; rather, the proclamation declares party support for only those movements that are deemed to advance the fight against capitalist imperialism. The adoption of this position is in line with the historical trend of the Third International to organize political activity across the globe under the strategic control of the Soviet state, in contrast to the isolated and relatively uncoordinated tactics of the Second International. As a historic and political document, "The Theses on the Negro Question" is truly quite significant insofar as it politically recognized the connections between colonialism and racialism and cleared the way, in the United States and elsewhere, for the active involvement of the Communist Party in the political struggle for racial justice. As long as the relationship between tactics and strategy was open to constant negotiation, the Communists' recognition of the struggle for racial justice afforded blacks their own tactical opportunity to form alliances with the Communists in the pursuit of their own political objectives.

Under Stalin, however, the subordination of tactics to strategy became an ever more rigid buttress for the party dictatorship. Negotiations over how the relationship between tactics and strategy should direct political action were increasingly suppressed; correspondingly, politics within the Third International became progressively more depoliticized. On the international level, the activities of Communist Parties around the world became tactically secondary to the strategic aims of the Soviet Union, which held itself forward as the point at which the most decisive blow to global capitalism was being delivered. Moreover, because of the racialized structures of power within each nationalist party, this trend further manifested itself in the instrumental domination and subordination of blacks and their political concerns. While the Communists presented blacks with a political opportunity, it remained "a *white* man's Party," as Bob Hunter's wife forcefully declares (257). As a white man's party, the concerns of blacks were tactically taken up, in accordance with the first thesis on the "negro question," only when they were understood to serve the larger strategic interests of the white industrial working class, which was understood to be the authentic and universal political subject. These dynamics directed the racial politics of the Communist Party in every western nation, and it is within this context that Wright's opposition to the party must be understood, for his position reflects a larger political struggle within and around the Communist Party. Within the racialized domain of western Communism, the tactics/strategy paradigm dictated that the political concerns of the white, industrialized worker constituted the party's central concern, while the political struggles of blacks were deemed to be outside that core interest.

Examples of protest and resistance from black activists are legion. In 1933, for instance, Claude McKay would express his "concern about the Communists capturing the entire colored group by cleverly controlling such organizations as the so-called National Negro Congress" (228). This charge is especially pointed when one recalls that Claude McKay, as one of the more prominent members of the Negro Commission at the Fourth Congress, was largely responsible for the adoption of "The Theses on the Negro Question."

McKay forcefully asserted the need for black independence in any alliance with the Communists on the political basis of the theses, writing that "Experience since the Emancipation should have taught the various colored leaders that it is a mistake to deliver the colored people over to any one political party" (229).[4] While McKay had always maintained some distance between himself and the party establishment, others such as Aimé Césaire had aligned themselves with the party in the most official manner possible. Césaire not only had great institutional prominence with the Communist Party, as the mayor of Fort de France and as a deputy of the French Parliament, but he also had had a close association with Richard Wright since their collaborative founding of *Présence Africaine* in 1946. Césaire's famous 1956 "Letter to Maurice Thorez," in which he passionately explained the reasons for his resignation from the Party, helps frame the theoretical stakes at work within this general struggle and Wright's own stance within it. Indeed, the timing of the letter's publication must be marked here, for it was originally published on October 24, 1956, just over a month after Césaire had participated in the International Congress of Black Writers and Artists where Wright delivered his lecture "Tradition and Industrialization."

In his letter, Césaire lays out a stringent critique of the tactic/strategy paradigm as it determined the political position of blacks within the Party. From the very beginning, Césaire contrasts his struggle with the privileged struggle of the French Communist Party. He writes, "the fight of colonized peoples against colonialism, the fight of colored peoples against racism, is much more complex—indeed, it's of a completely different nature than the fight of the French worker against French capitalism, and it cannot be considered a part or a fragment of that fight" (8–9).[5] On the one hand, Césaire makes absolutely no distinction between the fight against racism and colonialism, underscoring the way in which these two social and ideological structures have become mutually supportive. On the other hand, he insists that this fight differs in nature from that of the French proletariat and, therefore, cannot and should not be reduced to "a part or a fragment of that fight." In refusing to be "a part or a fragment," Césaire rejects the racialized logic of tactical subordination to strategy, a point that he makes even more explicit when he describes his political activity as guided by "a will that does not confuse alliance with subordination" (10). Through the dominance of their strategic concerns, which remain racialized in their Eurocentric orientation, the Communists systematically perverted a political alliance into a relation of subordination. As such, Césaire declares, "the very anticolonialism of the French Communists bears the mark of the colonialism which it fights" (13). The structures of subordination on which colonialism is based are reproduced within the structures of the party itself, through the political theory of strategy and tactics. On this basis, both European colonialism and western Communism alike have systematically constructed a racialized ordering of the inside and the outside.

The reproduction of these structures occurs so readily because, at a fundamental level, the ideologies of both colonialism and communist strategy, as historical products of the West, depend on the same basic conceptual apparatus. A key component of that apparatus has been the concept of the "universal" as it has been structurally opposed to the "particular." Césaire anticipates and forestalls the reactionary implementation of this very specific apparatus of capture when, at the end of his letter, he affirms, "I'm not entombing myself within a strict particularism. Nor do I want to lose myself in a fleshless universalism. There are two ways of losing oneself: through walled segregation in the particular or through dissolving into the 'universal.' My conception of the universal is one of a universal rich with all that is particular, rich with all the particulars, the deepening of all particulars in their coexistence" (15). The relationship between the particular and the universal constitutes an integral component of Western thought as an ideological apparatus of capture. It has long programmed the global hegemony of western capitalism, whether it takes the historic form of colonialism or its present "globalized" form. Quite simply, the racialized deployment of these categories by the West has systematically determined the concerns of the white West as "universal," while those of the nonwhite periphery are taken as "outside" the universal in their "particularity." With the Communists, the racialized subordination of the particular to the universal is simply filtered through the tactic/strategy paradigm.

During the Stalinist regime, this subordination became increasingly rigid in its practical application. It was also explicitly theorized by Stalin in order to justify his own political maneuvering. In his formulation of relationship between tactics and strategy, Stalin repeatedly emphasizes the particularity of tactics as opposed to the implicitly universal dimension of strategy. He explains that "Strategy strives to win the war, or to carry through the struggle, against tsarism let us say, to the end; tactics, on the contrary, strive to win *particular* engagements and battles, to conduct *particular* campaigns successfully, or *particular* operations, that are more or less appropriate to the concrete situation of the struggle at each given moment" (169; emphasis added). By emphasizing the particular character of tactics, Stalin was able to consolidate the power of his own strategic position as General Secretary of the Central Committee. Césaire foresees the deployment of the particular as a category against him, and he can anticipate this maneuver so well because of its ideological consistency and its programmatic predictability. As Césaire knows, the party response would inevitably be that his adherence to his "particularistic" racial concerns are the result of strategic shortsightedness that reveal a more general failure to grasp the political struggle on a more "universal" level. His concerns for racial justice are considered, precisely as racial, matters of purely "particular" interest to the party and the "universal" political struggle in which it is engaged. In responding in advance to such a charge, Césaire aims to disable the machinery behind it by refusing to accept the binarism of the particular/universal pair. Rather, in entering on an alternative political course, he proclaims the need for a thorough reconceptualization of their relationship.

Contemporary political theory is still grappling with the problem laid out by Césaire. Within recent years, the category of the "universal" has been a central topic for many political theorists from all across the political spectrum. On the one end, there are those, such as Jürgen Habermas and John Rawls, who variously continue within a Cartesian tradition and thus posit "rationality" as the universal basis for political order. On the other end, there are those, such as Judith Butler, Ernesto Laclau, and Étienne Balibar, who seek to reconceptualize the basic structures of political subjectivity itself through a rigorous and dynamic rearticulation of the relationships between particularity and universality.[6] These latter theorists participate in a larger trend on the left that takes the overcoming of the metaphysics of subjectivity as the necessary theoretical condition for an effectively resistant mode of political thinking. In this context, for instance, Hardt and Negri's recent proposals to replace the categories of particularity and universality altogether with those of singularity and commonality attest, if nothing else, to a desire within contemporary political theory to transfigure its basic ontological ground.[7] At this level, Heidegger arguably constitutes the horizon of contemporary political theory insofar as it was Heidegger who, with *Being and Time,* introduced *Dasein* as that being in terms of which the basic categories of human subjectivity are to be rethought. Of course, Heidegger's engagement with National Socialism has raised many legitimate concerns among some theorists and philosophers, who accept the central importance of radically rethinking subjectivity but question the viability of Heidegger's philosophy and its terms to accomplish that task in a politically responsible way.

The trenchant critiques of Aimé Césaire's "Letter to Maurice Thorez" were, in many ways, anticipated by Richard Wright's *The Outsider.* Moreover, Wright articulates his critique within a conceptual framework of existentialism that is plainly Heideggerian.

As such, Wright's work merits much more attention from contemporary political theorists. Given the intellectual milieu of Paris in which Wright wrote *The Outsider,* it should come as no surprise that he would approach the practical and theoretical issues raised by Communist politics through a narrative discourse that is marked by existentialism. In addition to his active involvement with *Présence Africaine,* Wright, as is well known, had a prominent position in the existentialist circles of Jean-Paul Sartre. As early as 1945, the inaugural issue of *Les Temps Modernes,* for example, included Wright's short story "Fire and Cloud" as its very first piece of literature. It was preceded in the layout only by Sartre's presentation of the journal. *Les Temps Modernes* would later publish a serialized translation of *Black Boy* in 1947. During this same period, *Les Temps Modernes* was also introducing Heidegger to the French public through essays by Sartre, Simone de Beauvoir, Maurice Merleau-Ponty, and Emmanuel Lévinas.[8] The intensity of Wright's intellectual engagement with existentialist philosophy during this period is legendary. According to Wright biographer Michel Fabre, Wright's existentialism was based largely on his reading of Heidegger, and he discussed Kierkegaard, Nietzsche, and Heidegger with Heidegger's renowned student, Hannah Arendt.[9]

Nevertheless, for many critics, Wright's engagement with existentialism has been judged as "ill-digested" and this judgment serves to justify many of the negative evaluations that have been passed on the novel.[10] Unfortunately, such negative judgments have tended to be made in the absence of any rigorous examination of Wright's relationship to existentialist discourse. As such, these evaluations seem hasty if not ill-conceived. In general, these assessments problematically presume that any deviations from existential orthodoxy attest to some degree of misunderstanding. Moreover, these judgments are grounded in the implicit positing of European existentialists as the authoritative model by which the supposedly inauthentic novelist on the outside must be judged. This model of judgment, which is basically the classical form of judgment in the western philosophical tradition, is once again supported by the same categories of the particular and the universal.[11] Judgments that the existentialist features of Wright's narrative are "ill-digested" entirely miss the point that Wright is concerned with undermining the very structures that underwrite such judgments, especially in their racialized formulations.

In Wright's work, as Paul Gilroy understands it, "the tension between the claims of racial particularity on one side and the appeal of those modern universals that appear to transcend race on the other arises in the sharpest possible form" (147). Wright's work—

and *The Outsider* specifically—should be taken as a thorough critique of the very structures that make such tensions appear to be irresolvable or, rather, a critique of the ways in which the categories of the particular and the universal program a cultural and ideological resolution of their fundamentally aporetic structure through racialized mappings of the inside and the outside. In engaging existentialist discourse, especially in its Heideggerian guise, Wright avails himself of the most rigorous attempt within the rarified confines of European philosophy to undertake a similar project. In this regard, it is worth repeating, with Gilroy, that Wright "was not straining to validate African-American experience in their European terms" (171). If anything, Wright's use of existentialism may strike some as "ill-digested" precisely because he refuses to incorporate this discourse in its entirety since, in Wright's estimation, it ultimately fails to carry out its critique in a fashion that is sufficiently radical.

Recalling Césaire's statement that "there are two ways of losing oneself," the story of Cross Damon represents the dangers presented in the path of "walled segregation in the particular." If Cross's encounter with Communism stages the dangers of "universalism," his solitary "outlaw existence" and his ultimate fate highlight the dangers that haunt any retreat into particularism (224). The form that Cross's particularism takes should be understood against the background of Heidegger's *Being and Time*. Cross's personal library replicates the existentialist cannon, and District Attorney Ely Houston tells Cross in the end that "Your Nietzsche, your Hegel, your Jaspers, your Heidegger, your Husserl, your Kierkegaard, and your Dostoevsky were the clues" (560). The inclusion of this list at the end of the novel explicitly confirms that Cross is to be read as an existentialist figure. The specifically Heideggerian character of his existentialism is dramatized through the central plot device of the narrative. Cross fakes his own death in a way that can be read as an allegorical treatment of what Heidegger calls an "authentic being-toward-death" (§53, 260).[12] Throughout most of the novel, Cross Damon acts under the assumed identity of Lionel Lane, an identity that he comes to adopt after it is mistakenly believed that Cross has died in a subway accident. Immediately on hearing his reported death, Cross "felt dizzy as he tried to encompass the totality of the idea that had come so suddenly and unsought into his mind, for its implications ramified in so many directions that he could not grasp them all at once." In confronting his "death," Cross has an "intuitive sense of freedom" that is rooted in the fundamentally open possibility that is his existence (105). This rush of possibilities that seize Cross and that Cross decides to seize on resonates quite dramatically with Heidegger's description of the pure possibility of Dasein to which authentic being-toward-death is attuned. In *Being and Time,* "being-toward-death" names the immanent possibility of death as that which discloses Dasein as an open field of possibilities.

An "authentic" being-toward-death, however, does not grasp this open field of possibilities as being lost in the world of chance, but understands death as essentially and always its "ownmost possibility [*eigenste Möglichkeit*]." Dasein thus grasps itself in its "non-relational" and essential solitude, thereby freeing itself for its own death in a way that frees it from "clinging to whatever existence one has reached" (§53, 263). In much the same way, Wright's character understands and takes the possibility that has been freed for him through the "possibility" of his own death. What's most important to mark here, however, is simply the fact that Wright's narrative quite clearly situates Cross Damon within a trajectory that is mapped out by Heidegger's *Being and Time.* The path that Cross assumes, with its violent decisions and tragic end, resounds as a critique of Heidegger's being-toward-death as the primordial means by which existence relates to itself. At the very beginning of the book the reader is told that Cross's "problem was one of a relationship of himself to himself," which is nothing more than the problem or the question which Heidegger says Dasein essentially is (10).[13] The manner in which both Cross and Heidegger pursue this problem forms the fundamental object of Wright's critique in *The Outsider.*

Much like Hardt and Negri today, Heidegger begins *Being and Time* by offering his existential analytic of Dasein as a radical displacement the category of the "universal" in approaching the question of self-relation. Dasein does not, Heidegger promises, relate itself to itself through the mediation of the universal. In the opening section of *Being and Time,* Heidegger clearly establishes that the "'universality' of being" is the basic metaphysical "prejudice" that needs to be dispelled in order to retrieve the question of being (§1, 3). Here Heidegger frames his project as the radical overcoming of metaphysics through the proper retrieval of the question of being, a question that has been obscured by the simultaneous assertion that "'Being' is the most 'universal' concept," and Aristotle's recognition that "The 'universality' of being 'surpasses' the universality of genus" (§1, 3). In short, the category of the "universal" as it applies to the question of being makes being "the most obscure concept of all." As such, Heidegger abandons the category of the universal immediately. The being of Dasein is not to be approached through any 'universal' concept of being; rather, "we shall call the very being to which Dasein can relate in one way or another, and somehow always does relate, existence [*Existenz*]" (§4, 12). Heidegger thus situates the "truth" or "essence" of Dasein not in any form of "universal" being, which would be the classic metaphysical gesture, but in "existence," which has traditionally been conceived as pertaining to the domain of the particular. In positing Dasein as the being whose analytic properly retrieves the question of being, Heidegger replaces the "universal" as a category for the analysis of being with the category of existence. Heideggerian existentialism, then, as an attempt to find another terrain on which being itself is to be understood, may be taken as an anti-universalism that is not necessarily an anti-essentialism. Heidegger's Dasein is essentially characterized as having its essence, not in some universal being that would transcend its being-there, but in its very existence.

Although Heidegger's analytic of Dasein attempts to overcome the universal/particular relationship as a fundamental ontological structure, the categories surreptitiously return to encode his distinction between the "authentic" and the "inauthentic." After introducing the "universal" as a category pursuant to the classical metaphysics that his "fundamental ontology" strives to overcome, Heidegger avoids using the term. It returns, however, in his crucial analysis of "the call," the interpretation of which provides the basis for determining whether or not Dasein has assumed an "authentic" existence. The call, according to Heidegger, is not to be confused with the "conscience" of the "they," which "pretends to recognize the call in the sense of a 'universally' binding voice" (§57, 278). The appeal to the "universal" here is the mark of inauthenticity. The use of scare quotes around the word "universal" here is, of course, meant to suggest its usage by the "they." On this level, Heidegger himself is not using the term, but mentioning it. Nevertheless, the force of the universal as a concept cannot be so easily contained or distanced. Heidegger's deployment of the universal and the particular to structure the distinction between the inauthentic and authentic understanding of the call comes to the fore when he writes that "the call does not give us to understand an ideal, universal potentiality-of-being; it discloses it was what is actually individualized in that particular Dasein" (§58, 280). The call is not offered as evidence of any universality; to the contrary, it underscores the primordial particularity of Dasein in its nonrelational existence. The authentic relation to the call discloses Dasein as isolated or "segregated," as Césaire might say, within the walls of its particular existence. The authentic experience of this nonrelational solitude takes the existential form of "guilt."

The foregoing sketch outlines those elements of Heidegger's existentialism that inform Wright's narrative at many of its most crucial moments. While Heidegger eschews the terms "universal" and the "particular," it is far from clear that he has not merely inverted their hierarchical relationship and then reinscribed them under the sign of the "inauthentic" and the "authentic." Moreover, the racialized inscriptions of the "authentic" and "inauthentic" have proven to be just as pernicious as those of the "universal" and the "particular." Wright's turn to existentialism may well have been motivated in part by his rejection of Communism, but existentialism is by no means embraced in *The Outsider* as a simple, viable alternative. As early as 1949, in fact, Wright had already declared that "I am not an 'existentialist'" ("Richard Wright" 137). Indeed, through Cross Damon, the existentialist particularism of Heideggerian Dasein is revealed to be no less dangerous than Communist universalism. Throughout the novel and against the backdrop of a menacing politics of universalism, Wright contests the political implications of Dasein's authentic individuation as nonrelational by opposing guilty-being and being-toward-death with a thought of the promise that resounds with a fundamental affirmation of innocence.

Cross Damon's assumption of his own being-toward-death is, in an appropriately Heideggarian manner, immediately accompanied by a sense of guilt. The sense of endless possibility that is unleashed in his being-toward-death overwhelms him, as mentioned already, and "he suddenly felt like a criminal" (105). Before Cross has actually committed any crime, the sense of being a criminal seizes him, much in the same way that being-guilty precedes any factical guilt of Dasein. This sense of being a criminal colors Cross's new relationship with himself, a relationship marked by a complete dissociation from his previous social existence. Cross's own being-toward-death confronts him with the nonrelational character of his existence. In assuming this path, he is thrust into an isolating particularism that ultimately will alienate himself from himself more completely than ever. Cross quickly realizes that "He had to break with others and, in breaking with them, he would break with himself. He must sever all ties of memory and sentimentality, blot out, above all, the insidious tug of longing. Only the future must loom before him so magnetically that it could condition his present" (114). The break with others that is required by seizing on his "death" results in a break with himself because, as Cross is beginning to realize, the self is nothing when secluded within the total particularism of being-toward-death. From this point on, Cross struggles with "his non-identity which negated his ability to relate himself to others" (195). The criminal extent of this inability to relate to others, the violent force of its strict impossibility, forces itself on Cross in the most factical of ways when he kills Joe Thomas, an old friend whom Cross unexpectedly encounters and who recognizes Cross, thus threatening to ruin his plans. The murder of Joe Thomas merely confirms the degree to which, because of his resulting inability to relate to himself and others, "he had been deprived of the will to make decisions" (149). Rather than discovering a new-found freedom, as Cross had hoped, his severance from society results in the most servile subjection to the contingent necessities of his existence.

Cross had, in resolutely seizing on his own being-toward-death, hoped to "work out a new destiny" (108). Instead, through his non-identity and his self-alienation from others, Cross finds himself exposed to the constraints of what Heidegger would call his thrownness. In beginning to craft his new identity, Cross quickly realizes that to "begin his new life he would relive something he knew well, something that would not tax too greatly his inventive powers. He would be a Negro who had just come up fresh from the Deep South looking for work" (111). The new identity that Cross desires to craft, if it is to be believed by others, must adhere to the highly racialized codes of behavior that are enforced by society. Before Cross assumes the identity of Lionel Lane, he has to perform various stereotypical roles. While his death might have liberated him in an immediate sense from his previous identity, it also subjects him ever more rigorously to the constrictions of his social existence. Indeed, it highlights the degree to which his identity as "Cross Damon" had always already been shaped in response to those very same prescriptions. These conditions are dramatically staged in the scene where he gets Lionel Lane's birth certificate from the clerk's office. To ensure his success, Cross decided that he would approach the clerk in "the role of a subservient negro" (214). The shining success of this performance leads Cross to reflect that he now

> knew exactly what kind of man he would pretend to be in order to allay suspicions if he ever got into trouble. In his role of an ignorant, frightened Negro, each white man—except those few who were free from the racial bias of their group—he would encounter would leap to supply him with a background and an identity; each white man would project out upon him his own conception of the Negro and he could safely hide behind it. (217)

Stripped of any identity of his own, being cut off from any meaningful social relations to others, Cross finds that his possible identity becomes determined by the structure of social relations as they are shaped by racialized hierarchies of power. Initially, here, Cross believes that the projection of this identity on him will provide a kind of cover behind which he "could safely hide." This cover, however, also outlines the surface of his fundamental exposure to his being with others. His search and need for a cover is precisely what will deliver him over to the Communist maneuverings of Gil Blount. In being told about Gil, Cross reflects that in "all his cudgeling of his brain to find some disguise for his outlaw existence, he had never seriously considered Communism. But why not?" (224). The cover that he believes will be offered by the Communists turns out, however, to be the cause of his very undoing.

Cross believes that he can use the Communists, just as they will attempt to use him, because he adheres to his belief in an identity that can be crafted in and through the withdrawal from his social relations with others. His hope that he can hide behind the Communist cover reveals his existentialist belief that his death has freed a self to hide in the first place, a "self" whose immediate relationship to itself as self would form the core of his authentic identity. Here, Cross, once again, proves himself to be a faithful Heideggerian, for Dasein is introduced as "always mine [*je meines*]" (§9, 41). This character of always-being-my-own-being or *Jemeinigkeit* is precisely what is assumed in the authentic being-toward-death. The extreme particularism of the self that results from such a withdrawal, however, hands Dasein over, like Cross himself, to "a possibility that it inherited and yet has chosen" (§74, 384). Heidegger's existentialist particularism, in brief, becomes socialized as a fatality in which the individual is given over to the historical destinies of a community. At the crucial moment in which Heidegger rearticulates Dasein with the "universal" realm of the they, Dasein's ownmost possibility immediately becomes that of the community itself. At this moment, Heidegger argues that "if fateful Dasein essentially exists as being-in-the-word in being-with others, its occurrence is an occurrence-with and is determined as *destiny*. With this term, we designate the occurrence of the community of a people.... The fateful destiny of Dasein in and with its 'generation' constitutes the complete, authentic occurrence of Dasein" (§74, 384).[14] Having decided not to address directly the articulation between the particular and the universal, Heidegger's thinking at this pivotal point of articulation finds itself divested of the means to forestall the metaphysical mechanism by which the "universal" of a "community" is filled with a particular content.[15] In positing a nonrelational moment in the individuation of the particular, the particular content that is "fated" to fill the universal continues, moreover, to be determined by historical and social forces that remain unaffected by this moment of articulation.

As evidenced both in the "strategy" of the Comintern and in Heideggerian existentialism, this moment of articulation is the moment of the political itself that both the party and Heidegger depoliticize, which of course is the most reactionary political maneuver of all. The former immobilizes the dynamics of this articulation through a strict logic of subordination, while the latter short-circuits those dynamics by insisting on the nonrelation between authentic Dasein and the inauthentic Mitsein of the community. The unthought relation of the "between" in this "non-relation" produces the depoliticized character of this political (re)articulation. Thus, Cross Damon repeatedly asserts that Communism and Fascism are only superficially different. These similarities are situated, according to Cross, on "pre-political ground" (488). In describing this ground as "pre-political," Cross is not conceding the "de-politicizing" gesture of both, but articulating an important distinction between the depoliticized and the prepolitical. The fundamentally relational structure of being is its prepolitical ground, strictly speaking, insofar as relation itself is the very ground of the political. The depoliticizing gesture of disarticulation, on the other hand, disavows this prepolitical ground. It thus forecloses terrain on which the formation of particular identities takes place and posits, instead, a nonrelational identity that preexists the moment of articulation. Wright's parable instructs its readers, however, that the formation of effective political identities does not take place independently of the moment of articulation between the self and society. The effective identity of political agents is formed along the edge, the clifflike margin, of this articulation.[16] Their individuation, precisely as political agents, takes place through the activity of this articulation, a dynamic process which characterizes politics as such and which, consequently, engages both the agents and the society in a reciprocal transformation.

In experiencing the unfolding of his own fate and seeing how, in taking the path that he has chosen, his fate is intimately linked to the destiny of men like Bob Hunter, Cross Damon comes to realize that his position as an "outsider" is by no means isolated and nonrelational. During the brief interval in the narrative when Cross Damon is between identities, when he has adopted the transient and ungrounded identity of "Addison Jordan," Cross hypothesizes that "Maybe man is nothing in particular. . . . Maybe that's the terror of it. Man may be just anything at all" (175). Such a declaration is practically an existentialist cliché, no doubt, and it encapsulates quite succinctly the "being-the-ground of a nullity" which Heidegger calls the being-guilty of Dasein (§58, 285). The force of Cross's experience as Lionel Lane will lead him to revise, however, or at least supplement, his hypothesis. With his dying words, Cross attests to the insufficiency of his prior formulation; he testifies that "Alone man is nothing. . . . Man is a promise that he must never break." (585). By the end of the novel, Cross has come to realize that he, in fact, had broken a "promise" in assuming his death and thus isolating himself from the network of social relations. Wright, throughout the final chapter of *The Outsider,* offers the illocutionary speech act of the promise as a performative model for thinking the political moment of articulation between personal identity and a community, between the particular and the universal.

In faking his death, Cross had necessarily broken his ties to others. The moment of recognition comes when he learns that District Attorney Ely Houston knows Cross is guilty of four murders, but cannot prove it and decides to let him go free. At this moment, Cross realizes that he "had broken all of his promises to the world and the people in it, but he had never reckoned on that world turning on him and breaking its promise to him too! He was not to be punished! Men would not give meaning to what he had done!" (573). Cross had broken off his relations with the world, but even in severing all relations, he had counted on his retreat having some meaning. His insistence on attaching a meaning to his protest depended all along on the one-sided nature of his withdrawal, but now the "ludicrous nature of his protest came to him and he smiled wryly at his self-deception" (573). His protest would have meaning only insofar as the world kept its promise to him, the simple promise to give meaning at all. What binds the individual and society together, what they have in common, is meaning or sense. They do not share a given or particular meaning, however; nor does this promise proclaim the content of any "universal" meaning. Rather, the promise of sense itself conditions the possible positing of any such meaning. The communicability of meaning holds forth the very promise of the political.

The promise, therefore, continually lays out the prepolitical ground; and, in this sense, by extending his invitation, Wright was also making a promise. Thus, Wright's lecture "Tradition and Industrialization" begins with an attempt to reopen communication and to clear the way, once again, toward politics. The first sentence, in fact, describes a political world in which "a legion of ideological interests is choking the media of communication of the world today" (74). When the media of communication become saturated with ideological interests, the possibility of an effective political position—a position whose relationship to the political field would not be determined in advance—becomes increasingly difficult to articulate. The first necessary gesture for entering the politics of the outside, according to Wright, would be to recover the prepolitical ground which has been depoliticized through the ideological positing of "absolute objectivity of attitude." "First of all," as Wright says, "let us honestly admit that there is no such thing as objectivity" (77). Objectivity, here, names the relation between a subjective position and events or objects which are, in some sense, deemed to be "outside." Absolute objectivity would posit the existence of a transcendent outside which is determined as being absolved of all relation. The fate of Cross Damon stages the tragically illusory character of understanding the outside in such terms. Rather than being outside all relation, the "most rigorously determined attitude of objectivity is, at best, relative" (78). Wright is not simply advocating an absolute relativism in place of absolute objectivity. He is articulating the most rigorous conception of objectivity by emphasizing its relational character. Absolute objectivity paradoxically negates the essentially relational character of objectivity by positing an outside that is absolved of all relation. Objectivity, in its most rigorous determination, is determined in relation to the outside. The outside with which it enters into relation, however, cannot be determined absolutely, which is the mistake of absolute objectivity. While absolute objectivity is the error of determining the outside absolutely, there is an absolute outside. What makes the outside "absolute" is not its lack of a relation, but the sheer impossibility of determining it absolutely.

The outside is that which can never be completely enclosed; nor can it be completely expelled, insofar as such an expulsion would denegate its relation to the inside. These have been the historical errors of neoimperialism and colonialism, respectively, in relating to the outside. Rather, the outside is an immanent field of difference among which determined positions emerge. The outside is not a determined space or position, but the positionality of position as such. The universal and the particular, along with their political doppelgangers, strategy and tactics, serve as structural indices of thought that coordinate conceptual positions. Entering the politics of the outside, as Richard Wright would have us do, not only requires an engagement with those spaces, both geopolitical as well as biocultural, which have been positioned as "outside." It entails a restructuring of the relationship to the outside as such so that the "outside" represents neither any particular political position nor even the universal space of politics itself. In the politics of the outside, the "outside" represents nothing other than that which cannot be represented within politics. Entering the politics of the outside would expose politics to the force of difference, the resistance of the outsider, which the politics of representation remains unable and unwilling to recognize.

Notes

1. For a detailed discussion of this particular congress, in addition to a highly informative discussion of the general historical context, see Bennetta Jules-Rosette.

2. The sign is "tenuous" because Rancière, like so many others, still never mentions the historical period of decolonization as an example, preferring to stick with the "classic" examples from ancient Greece and the European Marxist tradition.

3. See, for example, Michael Fabre ("Richard Wright") and Amritjit Singh.

4. For more on the historical and biographical context of these statements by McKay, see Cooper 330–33.

5. All translations of this text are my own.

6. The bibliography here would be extensive. A few of the key texts in the past decade would include Butler et al.'s *Contingency, Hegemony, Universality,* Laclau's *Emancipation(s),* and Balibar's *Politics and the Other Scene.* It should also be noted that the trends that I outline in the remainder of this paragraph extend not only to the "poststructuralists" of this list, but also to "postcolonialists" such as Gayatri Spivak and Dipesh Chakrabarty. See the former's *A Critique of Postcolonial Reason* and, particularly, the latter's *Provincializing Europe,* which is explicitly indebted to Heidegger in exploration of themes that "could be considered 'universal' to structures of political modernity" (19).

7. Hardt and Negri develop this argument throughout *Multitude,* which attempts to address the many questions, raised by their book *Empire,* concerning their conception of political agency and subjectivity. The difficulties posed by such a "substitution" are too complex to examine in depth here. Nevertheless, it should perhaps be pointed out that such a substitution cannot take place simply through a change in vocabulary. The philosophical challenge behind such a substitution can be measured, however, by the stubborn persistence of this vocabulary. Throughout *Empire,* for instance, as they are beginning to formulate the features of what they call "the common" in *Multitude,* they have recourse to a very Hegelian vocabulary of the "concrete universal" (362).

8. For an in-depth history of Heidegger's reception in France, see Dominique Janicaud.

9. See Fabre (*The Unfinished Quest* 299, 374).

10. James Tuttleton has written that "In Paris he became a spokesman for the American colony of blacks (and for African blacks in Paris), and he founded and joined many literary and liberal political organizations. The Existentialism of Sartre and Camus was then all the rage, and Wright began to read in the philosophy of Heidegger, Husserl, and Jaspers. This Existentialism, in ill-digested clumps, unfortunately mars his novel *The Outsider"* (169). Tuttleton's assessment continues a line of critical reception that began with the initial appearance of *The Outsider* in 1953 and Arna Bontemp's casual dismissal of Wright's "roll in the hay with existentialism" (106).

11. For Antonin Artaud's rigorous demolition of these categories, especially as they pertain to the structure of judgment, see my "Reading Forgiveness and Forgiving Reading: Antonin Artaud's *Correspondance avec Jacques Rivière.*" Here would be a crucial site for exploring Robin D. G. Kelly's suggestion that "it is hard to comprehend some of his [Richard Wright's] most radical political impulses without surrealism" (181). Incidentally, Wright donated a manuscript to a benefit auction held for Antonin Artaud in 1946 on his release from the psychiatric facility at Rodez, where he had been institutionalized for nine years.

12. All citations of *Being and Time* will be given by section number followed by the number of the German pagination, which is reproduced in the margins of most available English translations.

13. "Dasein is a being that does not simply occur among other beings. Rather it is ontically distinguished by the fact that in its being this being is concerned *about* its very being. Thus it is constitutive of the being of Dasein to have, in its very being, a relation of being to this being" (§4, 12).

14. The historical and political interpretation which the National Socialist would give to the destiny of the German community finds itself inscribed most immediately within Heidegger's thought at this specific moment. First published in 1927, Heidegger's thinking in this passage would assume a historically more ominous tone in his 1935 lectures published as *An Introduction to Metaphysics* where he writes, for example, that the German nation "is the most metaphysical of nations. We are certain of this vocation, but our people will only be able to wrest a destiny from it if *within itself it* creates a resonance, a possibility of resonance for this vocation, and takes a creative view of its tradition" (38).

15. Although this is not the place to do so, a rigorous examination should be done here of how a dialectical maneuver reminiscent of Hegel's dialectic of sense-certainty discernibly at work in Heidegger's disarticulation surreptitiously returns to program this moment of re-articulation. In addition to attending more closely to section 51 of *Being and Time,* such an analysis would also have to work through Heidegger's lecture course *Hegel's Phenomenology of Spirit.*

16. The phrase "clifflike margin" is from Wright's *White Man, Listen!,* which is dedicated to "the lonely outsiders who exist precariously on the clifflike margins of many cultures."

Works Cited

Adler, Alan, ed. *Theses, Resolutions and Manifestos of the First Four Congresses of the Third International.* London: Ink Links, 1980.

Atteberry, Jeffrey. "Reading Forgiveness and Forgiving Reading: Antonin Artaud's *Correspondance avec Jacques Rivière.*" *Modern Language Notes* 115 (2000): 714–40.
Balibar, Étienne. *Politics and the Other Scene.* London: Verso, 2002.
Bontemps, Arna. "Review of the Outsider." *The Critical Response to Richard Wright.* Ed. Robert J. Butler. Westport: Greenwood, 1995. 105–107
Butler, Judith, Ernesto Laclau, and Slavoj Žižek. *Contingency, Hegemony, Universality: Contemporary Dialogues on the Left.* London: Verso, 2000.
Césaire, Aimé. *Lettre à Maurice Thorez.* Paris: Présence Africaine, 1956.
Chakrabarty, Dipesh. *Provincializing Europe: Postcolonial Thought and Historical Difference.* Princeton: Princeton UP, 2000.
Cooper, Wayne. *Claude McKay: Rebel Sojourner in the Harlem Renaissance.* New York: Schocken, 1987.
Fabre, Michel. "Richard Wright and the French Existentialists." *The Critical Response to Richard Wright.* Ed. Robert J. Butler. Westport: Greenwood, 1995. 111–21.
———. *The Unfinished Quest of Richard Wright.* Trans. Isabel Barzun. 2nd ed. Urbana: U of Illinois P, 1993.
Gilroy, Paul. *The Black Atlantic: Modernity and Double Consciousness.* Cambridge: Harvard UP, 1993.
Hardt, Michael, and Antonio Negri. *Empire.* Cambridge: Harvard UP, 2000.
———. *Multitude: War and Democracy in the Age of Empire.* New York: Penguin, 2004.
Heidegger, Martin. *An Introduction to Metaphysics.* Trans. Ralph Manheim. New Haven: Yale UP, 1959.
———. *Being and Time.* Trans. Joan Stambaugh. Albany: State U of New York P, 1996.
———. *Hegel's Phenomenology of Spirit.* Trans. Parvis Emad and Kenneth Maly. Bloomington: Indiana UP, 1988.
Janicaud, Dominique. *Heidegger en France.* 2 vols. Paris: Albin Michel, 2001.
Jules-Rosette, Bennetta. *Black Paris: The African Writers' Landscape.* Urbana: U of Illinois P, 1998.
Kelly, Robin D. G. *Freedom Dreams: The Black Radical Imaginary.* Boston: Beacon, 2002.
Laclau, Ernesto. *Emancipation(s).* London: Verso, 1996.
McKay, Claude. *The Passion of Claude McKay: Selected Poetry and Prose, 1912–1948.* New York: Schocken Books, 1973.
Rancière, Jacques. "Ten Theses on Politics." Trans. Rachel Bowlby and Davide Panagia. *Theory & Event* 5.3 (2001): 33 pars. 21 Feb. 2005. http://muse.jhu.edu/journals/theory_and_event/v005/5.3 ranciere.html.
Singh, Amritjit. "Richard Wright's *The Outsider:* Existentialist Exemplar or Critique?" *The Critical Response to Richard Wright.* Ed. Robert J. Butler. Westport: Greenwood, 1995. 123–29.
Spivak, Gayatri Chakravorty. *A Critique of Postcolonial Reason: Toward a History of the Vanishing Present.* Cambridge: Harvard UP, 1999.

Stalin, Joseph V. "Concerning the Question of the Strategy and Tactics of the Russian Communists." *Works.* Volume 5. Moscow: Foreign Language Publishing, 1953. 163–83.
Tuttleton, James W. "The Problematic Texts of Richard Wright." *The Critical Response to Richard Wright.* Ed. Robert J. Butler. Westport: Greenwood, 1995. 167–72.
Wright, Richard. *The Outsider.* 1953. New York: Perennial, 1993.
———. "Tradition and Industrialization." *White Man, Listen!* New York: Doubleday, 1957.
———. "Richard Wright, the Black Dostoevski." Interview with Ramuncho Gomez. Trans. Kenneth Kinnamon. *Conversations with Richard Wright.* Ed. Kenneth Kinnamon and Michel Fabre. Jackson: UP of Mississippi, 1993.

FROM NÉGRITUDE TO MIGRITUDE

CHAPTER 11

René, Louis, and Léopold
Senghorian Négritude as a Black Humanism

Michel Fabre—Translated by Randall Cherry and Jonathan P. Eburne

I had the great privilege of working with Léopold Senghor—through correspondence, at least—in 1963, while I was doing research for a biography of Richard Wright, and between 1980 and 1982, when we served on the thesis defense committee for Martin Steins's dissertation on the origins of Négritude. I was struck, on this second occasion in particular, by how he returned, insistently, to the theme of cultural *métissage* (hybridity) with a near-prophetic tone. To help shed light on the important place of this theme in his writings, I would like to discuss a number of documents I acquired from what remained of René Maran's private library after he had bequeathed portions of it to the University of Dakar. Essentially, I would like to consider the relationships forged between the young Senghor, then a student at the Sorbonne, and some of the slightly lesser-known figures who were present at the start of the Négritude movement in Paris.

And where better to begin than with Senghor's association with Maran himself, to whom he dedicated his 1956 book, *Ethiopiques,* in the following words: "To René Maran, who prepared the way to Négritude for us, in honor of our friendship."[1] What, we might ask, did Senghor mean by "prepared the way" (*ouvrir la voie*)? A letter from Senghor, dated June 6, 1945, thanking Maran for his favorable appraisal of his first book, *Chants d'Ombre* (Shadow Songs), offers some clues:

> You know how much I admire your work. Because of your dual French-African cultural background, you were better qualified than anyone else to evaluate "Songs," in which I have tried to express myself fully and authentically, and have tried to express the "harmonious reconciliation" that I strive to achieve between my two cultures. . . . Most importantly, you said I was "on the right path" (*dans la droite voie*). Far from resting and being self-satisfied, I want to move forward, through hard work and without being self-complacent. (Letter)

In 1965, in a volume published by Présence Africaine paying homage to Maran, Senghor is even more explicit: "He was the first in the French-speaking world to be summoned to choose sides as either a 'French Writer' or a 'Black Man.' Out of sheer *moral and intellectual integrity,* he was the first to refuse this choice—by choosing to assume fully the responsibility of being both at the same time" ("René Maran" 11).

Senghor admits that Maran's poetry was susceptible to "the delights of the finely turned phrase," but adds that it also uncovered "Negro gifts for imagery and rhythm, as well as a form of lyricism that is the true source of poetry—Négritude." This style is authentically Negro by virtue of "the force of images that give poems their physicality and 'African' novels their dynamism. That is what makes René Maran, in the French-speaking world, the Forerunner of Négritude" (12). What is more, Senghor maintains that the entire tradition of the Francophone black novel, or the *roman nègre,* originated with him: "After Maran, no one could ever make Negroes live, love, work, cry, laugh, or speak like Whites again. No longer would Negro characters speak pidgin French; instead, they would speak *wolof, malinké,* and *éwondo* in French. For it was Maran who first gave expression to the black soul [*l'âme noire*] in French, in a Negro style" (13).

The first critiques of the colonialism were voiced in Maran's 1921 novel *Batouala*. While they appear in the book's preface and not in the text itself, Maran nonetheless referred to his novel in a letter to his friend Mercer Cook, the African American professor of French at Atlanta University, as "a damning indictment against colonial methods" (Letter). Be that as it may, his criticisms dealt only with the dysfunctions of the colonial system, without addressing the principal aim of the colonial enterprise itself. Nor did Maran's novel depict a truly flattering image of primitive life, even if the novel did set off a new wave of interest in all things African, and even if blackness was soon to be all the rage. When, thanks in large part to Maurice Delafosse, the methods of French ethnographic analysis were applied to African culture and colonial theory, they served as a counterbalance to the assimilationist ideals, dating from the French Revolution, that were so dear to Maran. As a consequence, Maran found himself somewhat at odds with the new indigenous policy that sought to preserve native customs and yet revived the myth of the noble savage. Maran would find support from the Left, whose "colonization against colonialism" campaign strove to topple the old regime. It should be noted that W. E. B. Du Bois's efforts at the Pan-African Congresses of 1919 and 1921 to turn the entire world's attention to the problem of colonialism and Marcus Garvey's efforts to forward a platform of race-first nationalism were each to fail in France: the black elite, overwhelmingly reformist, saw colonialism as primarily a national concern. Maran himself worked in association with Maurice Satineau to publish the pan-Africanist journal *Les Continents* (1924), which served as a forum for contesting the positions of the Inter-Colonial Union, Ho Chi Minh's political stronghold, whose members broke with the bourgeoisie and the colonial enterprise. Also, at that time Lamine Senghor was the chair of the first exclusively black-run organization, the Committee for the Defense of the Negro Race, whose party line consisted of an unsteady mixture of race and class. However, the Paris-based Antilleans (Maran, Satineau, Gilbert Gratiant, and others) did not subscribe to this territorial protonationalism. They were for political integration but felt that that their contributions could best serve the interests of all civilization. And so began to take shape a form of cultural relativism founded on the genius of ethnic groups.

While the Paris-based Africans demanded reforms, the assimilated Caribbean community, which considered itself to be the vanguard of the black race and the instigator of the evolution of Africa, wanted to work with the powers that be toward altering colonial policies. It was at this point, between 1925 and 1928, that their contacts with Haitians (and especially writer Jean Price-Mars) and African Americans (including writers Langston Hughes, Countee Cullen, Claude McKay, and, above all, Alain Locke) led them toward a form of black cultural internationalism: their watchword, "Afro-Latinism," carried an implicit challenge to the supremacy of an Anglo-American worldview. French civilization was now seen from a black perspective. Attitudes on African heritage were divided, and *métissage* was seen as a cultural ideal.

Senghor arrived in Paris in 1928 to prepare for his entrance exam to the *Ecole Normale Supérieure,* at the prestigious high school, *Louis-le-Grand,* which is also where Aimé Césaire in September 1930 began the first year of his two-year preparatory course, or *hypokhâgne,* while Senghor was still enrolled there. Senghor received his degree in literary studies in 1931, whereupon he spent the next three years living at the *Cité Universitaire* residence halls, preparing for the highly competitive teaching qualification known as the *agrégation*.

In 1927, the socialist party leader Léon Blum announced his desire for the colonial legislation to move further toward instituting self-government, after the example of the British Commonwealth. Senghor joined the Socialist Student Movement in 1930, under the influence of Georges Pompidou, and would always remain faithful to the principles of socialism even after his rupture with the S.F.I.O., the French socialist party, ten years later. But the black students of his generation were intent on thinking for themselves. They did not want to imitate either their elders or whites. Having different national origins and ideological mindsets, they neither formed a unified school of thought, nor ever had a leader; yet they often thought along the same lines. The time of purely passive assimilation had passed. Now it was time to "assimilate so as not to be assimilated," as an antidote to colonialism (Senghor, "Vues").

The 1931 Colonial Exposition at Vincennes had an enormous impact on black students in Paris, most notably the Martiniquan Nardal sisters—Paulette, Jane, and Andrée—and their cousin Louis Achille, who participated in the exposition along with a number of black Americans, including the sculptor Elizabeth Prophet. It served as the backdrop for the publication of the *Revue du Monde Noir*, the bilingual journal the Nardal sisters and Achille had founded in 1930, as they sought to bring about a new awareness of the cultural contributions of the diaspora. The *Revue du Monde Noir* tended to depoliticize the question of blackness, and the idea of the colonial Empire as a multicultural reality appealed to the Antilleans, who wanted to promote dialogue between blacks and whites, and who held out hope for future fraternity.

The influence of African Americans was quite palpable, too. Among the complementary and contradictory impulses that animated the Harlem Renaissance, Alain Locke's stances were most readily embraced by the Antilleans, as Locke seemed to be the very embodiment of the mixed-race establishment: in short, he stood for the notion that modern Negro art was not to be viewed as merely an extension of African art, but, rather, as an expression of contemporary racial temperament and talent, without any return to origins.

Whereas Locke's embrace of cultural *métissage* appealed to Senghor and the *Revue du Monde Noir* circle alike, Senghor and his friends were less swayed by the more politicized group that had formed the League for the Defense of the Negro Race (namely, Lamine Senghor and Emile Faure). Notably, Léopold Senghor was a distant cousin of Lamine Senghor, but he did not share the latter's communist-based ideology that prioritized politics over culture. Indeed, if Senghor underwent any direct influence, it was that of the *Revue du Monde Noir* circle, especially Paulette Nardal and Dr. Price-Mars, not to mention the impact of Alain Locke's anthology, *The New Negro* (1925), and the writings of Hughes and McKay. Senghor had studied English for roughly ten years, and could translate their works. He was much more inclined to embrace the literary examples of the African Americans because their work was not as primitivist as that of Garan Kouyaté or Emile Faure, the leader of the League for the Defense of the Negro Race. American writers, he felt, drew on the past to fuel a Harlem Renaissance that was forward-looking. For Senghor, what some African nationalists called instinct amounted to no more than intuitive reasoning; and, like Maran, he shunned the black Zionism of Garveyism. The influence of Haitian intellectuals was principally historical, insofar as it helped him ensconce himself in the values of black cultural heritage.

But there was still the thorny question of *métissage*. Students of color in Paris generally looked down on the mixing of the races—but on cultural and not biological grounds. Having been assimilated, the mixed-race bourgeoisie, they argued, had lost its Negro soul in adopting a white worldview, only to suffer from an inferiority complex in return. What is more, Senghor and his friends felt that the black elite should not marry in France and thereby abandon the struggle for black culture. Senghor himself had been smitten with the prettiest of the Nardal sisters, Andrée, but her family did not consider this too-black African a good match for a "proper" Martiniquan lady like Andrée. And so he was to marry the sister of his friend Félix Eboué, instead.

Primitivism, which intellectuals of W. E. B. Du Bois's generation had shunned, succeeded in exerting a certain appeal over young readers of Claude McKay's *Banjo* (1929)—especially in this new, modernist primitive reconfiguration. Some Antillean students wanted to break with culture of the West and look to Africa as a racial fatherland: race was thus conceived of as a way to affirm the survival of African traditions in mixed-race cultures. In this way, the cultural *métissage* of the Antilles only enhanced the value of Africa's cultural contribution, in keeping with the notion of indigenism expounded by Price-Mars. The indigenism movement would take two forms: one political, under the communist Jules Roumain, the other cultural, encouraging a return to a society modeled on Africa.

By 1930–31, Senghor's and Césaire's emergent opinions on the existence of an independent black culture, valid on its own terms, began to diverge from the stances adopted by Antillean communists like Etienne Léro, who would found the journal *Légitime*

Défense in 1932. The two men, unlike their communist counterparts, saw cultural autonomy as the prerequisite for attaining independence of any kind, even political independence. *Légitime Défense*, for its part, dealt largely with the dilemma faced by Antillean students, who had to choose between communism and racial solidarity, and it singled out the assimilationists for censure. The great merit of the *Légitime Défense* circle was, in Senghor's view, that it drew attention to the astounding imagery of surrealist poets. Although the surrealists certainly broke no new ground in terms of the portrayal of blackness, they were attuned to the Negro aesthetic, at least symbolically, in that they turned their backs on reality, rationalism, and accepted conventions. What Senghor considered unfortunate, though, was that most of them overlooked Negro melody and rhythm, lavishing attention on the attendant image.

A new dimension of the language of racial identity, marking a crucial step toward "Négritude," can be found, I wish to suggest, in an article by Louis Achille published in the *Revue du Monde Noir*. The son of a high-school principal in Fort-de-France, Martinique, and a cousin of the Nardal sisters, Achille had lived in Paris before taking a position as an instructor, then professor, of French at Howard University, between 1932 and 1943. Like his cousin Paulette, he represented a major link between black Americans and the *Revue du Monde Noir*, in which he published "The Negroes and Art." That article would prove to be the most significant piece to appear in the journal foreshadowing Négritude before the term itself existed. Achille's assessment of Modern Negro Art may be seen as something of a prologue to Senghor's later exposition on the same subject. To be sure, Jean Price-Mars had already dealt with the idea that rhythm was a distinctive attribute of the Negro, but Achille, in this essay, sought to explain how music and dance affected the Negro's very psychology. Achille writes,

> Negroes are essentially artists. Since American Negro music and dance and African sculpture have been made known all over the world, this can no longer be questioned. In no other human race, indeed, is the aesthetic sense so general a gift and does it so often interrupt the activity of each individual. This is because, in the whole race, in its purest elements as well as in such half-breeds as have kept the distinctive racial features, there occurs what never happens in other races, except in very few privileged persons. (Achille 57)

The black race, for Achille, possesses supreme natural gifts that predispose it toward aesthetic creation. Art is not a matter of taste; it emanates not so much from the intellect but from instinct, procuring a sense of satisfaction that is as much physical as spiritual. Artistic creation is not a pastime, but a fundamental form of expression that engages the body as a whole, and is as natural as drinking and eating (54). Achille even declares that the black race, by nature, is more predisposed to artistic creation and emotive expression than to manual production, which explains why the Negro excels particularly at dance, which he considers the most spontaneous form of artistic creation.

Achille concedes that it would be difficult to imagine that an entire race might possess a superior faculty of emotion and artistic creativity, as other races might possess a capacity for wonder. Nonetheless, he adds:

> [This faculty] . . . can radiate beauty, by the attitudes and movements it inspires, as soon as a succession of rhythms is heard. . . . For a congenitally artistic race evinces its gift in all the branches of its activity. The aesthetic emotion thus always kept alive in it, endows each individual with a continuous mood of happiness which deters him from pursuing other satisfactions. Hence the large careless laughter of the Negro which endures from his birth to his death, and extends from Africa to America. (59-60)

In 1934, in *l'Etudiant martiniquais,* a newsletter for the Association of West African Students, which Senghor headed up, Senghor stated that he wished to assimilate European culture but also wanted to remain close to his own people. In short, he was seeking to reconcile his ancestral heritage with the exigencies of the modern world. In that search for a synthesis, Négritude began to come into being. What he labeled "black humanism" was a cultural movement that "aimed to explore the black man's identity using Western reason and the Negro soul as investigative tools, since both reason and intuition are required." Senghor did not refer here to a biological expression of race, but to the "Negro soul" (*l'âme nègre*), that is, Negro culture.

Thus, in the years before 1935, a number of black students in Paris had worked out the basic premises of Négritude without actually formulating them into concrete concepts. In 1935, in the first issue of their journal *l'Etudiant Noir,* Césaire published his essay "Négreries," and Senghor published "Humanism and Us: René Maran," in which he made no mention of the word "Négritude" (whose coinage he credited to Césaire). The group did, however, affirm the existence of a black culture while simultaneously extolling its distinguishing characteristics; so, ironically, in resisting the colonizer, their writings borrowed some of colonizer's weapons.

L'Etudiant Noir, the Martiniquan student journal, also betrayed some contradictions in the writers' positions: Césaire abandons *métissage* in favor of black people in his article "Négreries." His notion of a "spirit of the bush" emerges from a biologically based definition of culture as the expression of race (Césaire 326). Césaire rejects the idea of cultural *métissage*, whereas Senghor endorses it, praising the humanism of the assimilated René Maran. While *L'Etudiant Noir* gave only slight consideration to social issues, the Guyanan writer Léon Damas took an avid interest, recommending that the indigenous elite and the colonial powers work in association. In the context of the Popular Front, Damas declared himself in favor of political and cultural regionalism. Damas's own notion of the *l'âme nègre* barely went beyond a supposed intuitive sense for surviving in the tropics (see Kesteloot 113–29). Torn by the duality of being a mulatto, he rejected biologically based definitions of blackness.

By about 1936, the intellectual debate was gradually displaced toward the reformism expounded by the Sudanese writer Garan Kouyaté in his journal, *Africa*. Africans no longer pinned their hopes on cultural assimilation and instead advocated a Franco-African culture, which fit in with the discourse of colonialists like Robert Delavignette. But in the end, the African component of this dualism seemed symbolic at best.

After 1936, Senghor's and Césaire's discourse on blackness was increasingly informed by their discovery of the French translation of German ethnologist Leo Frobenius's *History of African Civilization* (1936). Their close reading of the text affected their thought in important ways: Senghor was particularly marked by the theory of cultural circles (*Kulturkreise*); the characterization of black civilization as sober and severe, compared to the Asian esthetic; and the vindication of the cultural heritage of black Ancient Egypt. Henceforth, Senghor would use the term "culture" to mean civilization, and would argue that the spiritual held primacy over technical and material progress. However, his concept of culture remained anchored in Paul Rivet's teachings at the *Institut d'ethnologie de Paris:* culture was to be seen as the symbiosis between a longstanding movement of race, geography, history, and society; the races arose from the interaction of genetic mutation and environment, meaning environmental factors of all kinds. Race is defined by the general environment (geographical, historical, societal). The great civilizations sprang from a double *métissage*, at once biological and cultural, with the second element being the most determinant. The "genius" of the black race became apparent after examining Negro-African civilization, because, in spite of the diversity of migrations and *métissages* black cultures share common characteristics across the five continents.[2]

In a talk he gave in September 1937 at the Dakar Chamber of Commerce, "Le problème culturel en A.O.F." (The Cultural Problem in French West Africa), Senghor spoke of culture as a "racial reaction . . . tending toward a moral and intellectual equilibrium between man and his environment" (Senghor, *Liberté 1* 11). By culture he meant the spirit of civilization, the latter being its aggregate cultural heritage. Hence, Négritude was not to be seen as an ideology of cultural separatism. Rather, Négritude's supporters were still under the spell of the idea of a colonial empire, which carried an implicit acknowledgement of cultural and ethnic pluralism within a larger whole. This would lead Senghor to the idea of a federation.

In that 1937 speech, Senghor posited the notion of a black, multi-continental civilization as the basis for the evolution of culture as a whole. Frobenius's upending of accepted beliefs about technological complexity as the measure of culture, which served as the inspiration for Senghor's own theory of culture, permitted him to sidestep the cultural domination of the West without calling into question the notion of civilization itself. Senghor was indebted as much to the ethnological studies, if not the colonialist-related political ideas, of administrators like Maurice Delafosse, a professor of Negro-African languages and civilizations at the Colonial School (which became the National School for Overseas Territories when Senghor himself taught there beginning in November 1944). It would take a Negro-African reading of ethnological literature to identify the black soul—that is, blackness—beyond the facts and material achievements of civilization. But he would continue to base his gnosiology on emotion: the black soul is endowed with a mission aimed to redeem Western Civilization. He wanted to help humanize the human race and the modern world, through the black soul. And it is important to bear in mind that his idea of Négritude does not reject discursive reason but, rather, rationalism, that is, the supremacy or primacy of discursive reason: the "we" of Aristotelian philosophy is seen as consisting not merely of the intellect but of the entire spirit, in a synthesis of discursive reason and intuition.

Now, after this slight detour, let us turn to the question of whether it is possible to speak of a kinship between Senghor and Maran. After all, Maran had never been torn between French culture and a heart left in Senegal; Senghor was a French-speaking African and Maran was a Frenchman of color. It was out of Senghor's friendship for Maran that he made him out to be blacker than he was, for the purposes of his ideology. Nonetheless, he found his style to be authentically *"nègre,"* even more so than Maran had perhaps intended it to be. Senghor felt that one had to be black to come upon such new and forceful images. In Senghor's view, Maran used all the techniques—alliterations, onomatopoeias, repetitions, and linguistic reduplications—that were the hallmarks of so-called primitive writers.

It should be pointed out that in his cultural activities, too, Senghor's thinking on *métissage* as a symbiosis of values never lost its intensity. If he sought to root himself solidly in the values of Négritude, it was so that he might open himself up to complementary values, starting with Arabo-Berber and European influences. Faithful to the teachings of Paul Rivet, the ideology of Négritude would repose on the idea that the black race is grounded in realities that are as much cultural as they are biological. Whereas the notion of a subjective Négritude might describe a form of individual racial consciousness, even this notion precludes the sense of superiority that characterizes racism. Objective Négritude, the aggregate features of the world's black civilizations, bears an existential authenticity and also falls within the category of being.

When *Chants d'ombre* appeared in 1945, Senghor rushed a dedicated copy to René Maran, as Césaire had done with his *Cahier d'un retour au pays natal* in 1939. Maran prepared a review, as had become his common practice, but this was an exceptionally long one, entitled "L'écrivain noir Léopold Sédar Senghor et son oeuvre" (The Black Writer Léopold Sédar Senghor and his Works). This 1946 essay has come down to us today in the form of carbon copies and forms part of the collection of Maran's papers at the l'Université Cheikh Anta Diop in Dakar. Maran begins by stressing the overriding importance of linguistic studies for an ethnologist, and adds that we "will never get to the bottom of the secrets, treasures, qualities and defects of the black soul unless we rely on an educated Negro trained in the European style" ("L'écrivain noir"). He notes that André Breton had praised Césaire's *Cahier* as being "the greatest lyric monument of our times" (Breton xiii). *Chants d'ombre* deserves the same praise, Maran argues, and goes even further because it "conveys a message . . . inviting men of good will to work together on a common project where French culture and African culture would merge into a totally harmonious whole, marked by dignity and reserve, nobility and greatness" ("L'écrivain noir").

In Maran's eyes, it was because Senghor, "this Senegalese man of the finest black who loves France with the same fervor as for his native country," held an *agrégation* degree, that he seemed to be best suited to "bring about this marriage between reason and emotion" ("L'écrivain noir"). Senghor himself, in *La Communauté impériale française,* a brochure Maran saw as rich in profound insights and new ideas, affirmed that the ultimate goal of colonization was to "bring to pass an active assimilation which would, in turn, prepare the way for a fruitful association." Here, assimilation should be understood as the mastery of European ways of thinking and working. And the fruitful association aimed toward advancing the work of the Imperial colonist community would result from the contributions of not only "black souls" but also the labor of "black toilers of black lands" (Senghor, *Liberté 1* 45).

Maran closely followed the intellectual development of this young man who, by all appearances, was "destined to one day utter the right watchwords to bring about the joining of the races" (Maran, "L'écrivain noir"). Maran takes race here in its cultural sense. That is, Maran sees Senghor as a reformer, in stating that "The social writer, who heretofore pursued questions of justice and logic with the keenest interest has now given way to the poet, and has asked him to translate his deepest thoughts into rhythms and images that speak to the spirit and heart" ("L'écrivain noir"). Maran then cites Senghor's elegy, "Nurse Emma Payelleville" (1945), commenting on its impact, more than on its style:

> This threnody—this hesitant and sustained trembling, this pure burst of friendship, this gift of thanks from a race never fooled by the conquering race that misunderstood it far too long, this communion of souls in loyalty and gratitude—expresses the harmonious reconciliation that this French writer of color, endowed with the rarest of gifts, has achieved, while appealing to the prestige of surrealism, in synthesizing his French culture and his African culture, without renouncing anything of either. ("L'écrivain noir")

For Maran, the most beautiful poem in *Chants d'ombre* is "Que m'accompagnent kora et balafons" (To the Music of Koras and Balafongs), in which France and Sub-Saharan Africa embark upon a "true marriage of genuine love. With amazed joy, we witness a journey that takes us from African dusks where space is nothing but music, those veiled tom-toms that chant *the distant breathing Night,* to the river, *blue in the cool September meadow, to the Somme, and the Seine, and the Rhine, and the wild Slavic streams that flow red under the sword of the Archangel*" ("L'écrivain noir").[3]

Maran concludes his unpublished 1946 review with a statement that pertains more to Maran himself than to Senghor: "Only a black Frenchman, with French education and training, could undertake the task that Léopold Sédar Senghor has taken on. It says a lot for France that it has a writer who has already paid it the greatest tribute, and who may soon astonish the world" ("L'écrivain noir").

Maran continued to sing Senghor's praises the following year in the weekly left-wing journal *Les Lettres Françaises*. He states that, under the influence of the French writers they admire, but also under the still greater influence of a talented black elite in America,

French intellectuals of color were actively engaged in vindicating and glorifying their race. Senghor was all too conscious of the debt he owed to black Americans, to France, and, above all, to "the race from which he sprang—which is why he put his heart and intellect at their service." As Maran insists, Senghor's 1939 essay "*Ce que l'homme noir apporte*" (The Black Man's Cultural Heritage) and "the admirable poems in *Chants d'ombre*" each "attest to a pure musicality; and both are testimony to this dual, insistent passion." He affirms "the unbreakable ties that bind him with his homeland, Black Africa, and with the Civilization of the Earth," but he has also embarked upon the noble pursuit of reconciling the virtues of the black and white races. Maran sees Senghor as the leader of a new generation of young talents, including Birago Diop and Paul Hazoumé, because of his "radiant authority" and his "communicative prowess," which will give their writings "the most rational output." Maran, seeing great promise in Senghor's writings on Negro-African civilization encouraged him to develop them, in the hope that they would one day take form in a completed work ("Léopold Sédar Senghor et l'Afrique noire" 4). What work could Maran have been referring to if not the then-unpublished *Anthologie de la nouvelle poésie nègre et malgache de langue française,* which would appear in 1948? In a review of that work, which is still among Maran's unpublished manuscripts, Maran asserts that a revolution has taken place, constituted by "Black humanism's entry into French arts and letters, even though the most well-informed of them have yet to suspect this, with the exception of Jean-Paul Sartre."[4] For once, Maran lashed out against the stereotypes long nourished by a paternalist mentality that had not as yet progressed beyond the stage of black dance and the stereotypical, big-lipped smile of the black character from Banania advertisements: "When will they see that the black world has been steadily making strides since the end of the World War and, since then, that it has continually grown in self-awareness and come to recognize its great self-worth?" (Maran, Review).

In the same review, Maran argues that black people carry inside them secrets that have remained intact since the dawn of time. Their witchdoctors, griots, and traditional storytellers are the heirs of civilizations dissipated by the effects of slavery—a situation which must be called into question. "They are Africa. And Africa always has new things to reveal to any man who has eyes that see and ears that listen" (Maran, Review). Black Americans have cleared a path to freedom. But whereas they continue to be a race turned inward, so as to avoid reprisals from their white countrymen, "Frenchmen of color, sustained by the France of Abbé Grégoire and Victor Schoelcher, have made a commitment, once and for all, to continue on the path they have embarked upon (dans la droite voie), and they are preparing to wage a battle that will not end until the day the last racial barriers are but a dream within a dream" (Maran, Review).

It would seem that Maran has in mind a cultural battle that would extend beyond a solely nationalist viewpoint. But, whoever may have been, as Maran puts it, "the forerunners of this humanism endowed with staggering riches" (Review), it was only recently that this humanism's self-consciousness had fully come into being. Maran cites Etienne Léro, Césaire, and Senghor as the intellectuals responsible for this transformation. He saw Senghor as the great theoretician of this black humanism and Césaire as one of its distinguished practitioners. But, whereas Césaire "always swims far out to sea," with Senghor, "even in his lightest and most ethereal poems," surrealism never makes him "lose sight of reality" (Maran, Review). Both, by turns and sometimes simultaneously, served as intellectual springboards for him. The black humanism that he illustrates and defends is not merely a game of the intellect. That is why his essays in *La Communauté impériale française* (1945) and in *Les plus beaux écrits de l'Union française* (1947) now stand, in retrospect, as manifestoes (Maran, Review).[5]

The *Anthologie de la poésie nègre et malgache*, featuring the famous preface by Jean-Paul Sartre, is also a manifesto: "In its quality, in its breadth, and in the will that has presided in choosing the works it includes, everything about it is significant, and has its own singular emphasis, color, and meaning." Indeed, "the cries of revolt shouted by the people of color in the Antilles, in Guyana, in Black Africa and in Madagascar are as legitimate as those uttered by Black Americans" (Maran, Review).

At that time, Maran himself subscribed to this notion of Négritude: he stated that the poems of Damas (citing Damas's recent anthology, *Poètes d'expression française* [1947]), Léro, Césaire, Senghor, Roumain, Birago Diop, David Diop, Jean-Jacques Rabéarivelo, Jacques Rabemananjara, and many others

> were possessed by this secret rhythm, this divine delirium, which are two forces of . . . the black race. It is this rhythm and this delirium that give their sarcasms, their sadness, their humor, their accusations, their demands, their blasphemies, their panicked outbursts, and the dances and songs, set to tom-toms and balafons, that imbue everything with their sound-filled light, an incantory beauty and magic that is not yet all of Africa, but is already Africa (Maran, Review).

At a contemporary conference titled "A travers l'âme et le folklore nègres" (Inside the Black Soul and Black Folklore), Maran revisited the notion of a soul common to Negro-Africans, in spite of the "tribal differences due to racial mixing [*métissage*] from invasions and the influence of geological environments." Among the numerous customs illustrating and emphasizing such communality, the most evident was dance. Having assailed the cliché of "dancing Africa," he stresses that "it is impossible not to talk about dance, the moment you talk about Black Africa. It is through dance, as much as through music and song, that the European first encounters the black world" ("A travers l'âme").

Maran cites the Baron de Wimpffen, Abbé Grégoire, R. P. Labat, and even Gobineau himself, who had conceded: "The source from which the arts sprang is hidden in the blood of blacks. This overarching imaginative power that we witness enveloping and penetrating into primitive civilizations resulted from nothing other than the still growing influence of the Melanin Principle." He mentions the *calenda, boshimen* dances, the blues, and spirituals. He also emphasizes the importance of orality and asserts: "These fables, proverbs, and stories emanate directly from the black humanism both 'heralded' by Aimé Césaire and Léopold Sédar Senghor, two of the most remarkable products of French universities . . . and manifested in the artistic creations produced by the long-disappeared black civilizations, which Europe and scientists are in the process of resuscitating" ("A travers l'âme"). In twenty years, things had come full circle: while talking of black humanism, Maran, the assimilationist, was employing the language of Négritude, which had gained currency, thanks to Senghor.

Notes

1. This inscribed edition now forms part of the Maran collection at the Bibliothèque Centrale de l'Université Cheikh Anta Diop, Dakar, Sénégal. Michel Fabre's own collection of Maran's books is now housed at the Manuscript, Archives, and Rare Book Library at Emory University, including inscribed copies of Senghor's earlier books of poetry, *Chants d'ombre* (1945) and *Hosties noires* (1948). (Translators' note)
2. See Senghor, *De la Négritude: Psychologie du Négro-Africain*.
3. Maran cites lines from "To the Music of Koras and Balaphons," in italics. See Senghor, *Collected Poetry*, 17–24.
4. See Sartre's preface to Senghor's 1948 *Anthology*.
5. See also Senghor, *Liberté 1*, pp. 39–69 and 70–82, respectively.

Works Cited

Achille, Louis. "L'Art et les Noirs/ The Negroes and Art," *La Revue du Monde Noir* 1 (1931), 53–56. Rpt. Jean-Michel Place, 1992. 57–60.
Breton, André. "A Great Black Poet." Introduction. Césaire, *Notebook* ix–xix.
Césaire, Aimé. "Négréries." *L'Etudiant Noir 1*. 1935. Georges Ngal, *Aimé Césaire: un homme à la recherche d'une patrie.* Paris: Présence Africaine, 1994.
———. *Notebook of a Return to the Native Land.* Trans. Clayton Eshleman and Annette Smith. Middleton, CT: Wesleyan UP, 2001.
Kesteloot, Lilyan. *Histoire de la littérature négro-africaine.* Paris: Editions Karthala, 2001.
Maran, René. "A travers l'âme et le folklore nègres." Ts of a lecture. René Maran papers. Bibliothèque Centrale de l'Université Cheikh Anta Diop, Dakar, Sénégal.
———. "L'écrivain noir Léopold Sédar Senghor et son oeuvre." Ts. René Maran papers. Bibliothèque Centrale de l'Université Cheikh Anta Diop, Dakar, Sénégal.
———. "Léopold Sédar Senghor et l'Afrique noire." *Les Lettres françaises* (Paris), 10 Sept. 1947: 4.
———. Letter to Mercer Cook. 25 December 1938. Mercer Cook Papers, Moorland-Spingarn Research Center Library, Howard University.
———. Review of Senghor's *Anthologie de la nouvelle poésie nègre et malgache de langue française.* Ts. René Maran papers. Bibliothèque Centrale de l'Université Cheikh Anta Diop, Dakar, Sénégal.
Nardal, Paulette. Letter to the author. 12 March 1972.
Sartre, Jean Paul. "Black Orpheus." *What Is Literature? and Other Essays.* Cambridge, MA: Harvard UP, 1988. 291–330.
Senghor, Léopold Ségar. *The Collected Poetry.* Trans. Melvin Dixon. Charlottesville, VA: UP of Virginia, 1991.
———. *Ethiopiques.* Paris: Editions du Seuil, 1956.
———. "L'humanisme noir." *L'étudiant martiniquais* 1 (March 1935). Typed transcript in Fabre papers. Atlanta: Emory University.
———. *Liberté 1: Négritude et Humanisme.* Paris: Seuil, 1964.
———. Letter to René Maran. 6 June 1945. René Maran papers, Bibliothèque Centrale de l'Université Cheikh Anta Diop, Dakar, Sénégal.
———. *De la Négritude: Psychologie du Négro-Africain.* 1962. *Senghor: Prose and Poetry.* Trans. John Reed and Clive Wake. Oxford: Oxford UP, 1965. 29–34.
———. "René Maran, précurseur de la négritude." *Homage à Maran.* Paris: Présence Africaine, 1965. 9–13.
———. "Vues sur l'Afrique noire, ou Assimiler, non être assimilé." Senghor, *Liberté 1* 39–69.

CHAPTER 12

Nos Ancêtres, les Diallobés
Cheikh Hamidou Kane's *Ambiguous Adventure* and the Paradoxes of Islamic Négritude

---

Marc Caplan

Though famously home to a variety of diasporic black writers, musicians, and artists, Paris is significant to Black Atlantic thought in an institutional, ideological sense as the birthplace in the 1930s of Négritude. As an aesthetic movement, Négritude was the first effort by black artists, primarily poets, to create an aesthetic that was both explicitly black, pan-African, and at the same time modernist. Négritude aspires to express a specifically black sensibility in terms that derive from cosmopolitan, ostensibly universal sources at the heart of Western, specifically French, culture. It is as such the first effort by a collective of African intellectuals to assert control of the cultural apparatus of colonial modernity, and thus stands as a historically crucial and artistically provocative development in the struggle against colonialism. As an ideological program Négritude offers at the same time the most intense and influential example of how black Atlantic literature has interacted with modernism and the metropole.

Though the founders of Négritude intended for their movement to be pan-African, uniting black people from Africa and the

New World in a new creative spirit, the ideology in fact developed in parallel directions during the 1940s and 1950s among Caribbean and African intellectuals. It is necessary to acknowledge this divergence because in so doing one comes to understand how Négritude, the primary term in an ostensibly unified Black Atlantic cultural lexicon, came to signify quite distinct aesthetic and political perspectives; this leads the critical reader in turn to question the notion of the Black Atlantic as a singular historical entity. Moreover, a focus specifically on African Négritude helps to reintegrate African literature into a historical discourse about the Black Atlantic that has tended to focus exclusively on the African diaspora.[1]

As a fundamentally synthesizing position between traditional Africa and modern France, Négritude articulates an ambivalence toward its simultaneous nationalist and cosmopolitan aspirations, situating its protagonists—whether actual ideologues or fictional characters—between allegiance to their native culture and a supposedly universal humanism. For example, Alioune Diop, founder of the central Négritude journal of the independence era, *Présence Africaine*, writes, "As for Western civilization, it is definitely murderous—even towards itself. But it is the seat of the most powerful institutions to support democracy, justice, and love . . . We all need the West. We also need it to master . . . an all too powerful appetite on its own part for domination—so that we may live harmoniously . . . with other human civilizations" (Diop xvi). Diop in this statement simultaneously differentiates African culture from the West, yet announces the continued dependence of Africans on the West both in a political sense and in a sense of cultural affiliation; Africa's interaction with the world at large can only be achieved, according to Diop's logic, through the mediating intervention of the West. This reasoning is in fact essential to the rhetorical and political strategies of African Négritude generally.

Indeed, in the context of Négritude, literature in Western forms becomes for African intellectuals a means to create a separate cultural formulation between the systems of power organized around the polarities of native tradition and colonial modernity; moreover, creating this literature in a colonial language provides a singular opportunity for anti-colonial intellectuals to address a genuinely international audience. The space cleared by this literature is, however, often as much a no-man's land as a room of one's own. The author's autonomy, to the extent that it exists at all, is dependent on the sufferance of social institutions, such as publishing houses, school systems, and political organizations typically controlled by the power structures from which the writer seeks to liberate himself or herself.[2] For a Francophone writer, particularly during and immediately after the colonial era, such institutions were generally located—as Alioune Diop knew firsthand—in Paris rather than Dakar or Bamako. Literary narrative, as opposed to the lyric poetry that characterizes the first flowering of Négritude creativity, provides, among other merits, a means to analyze the complex interaction between African and French cultures, and among these power formations and the individual African subject. To begin this process of analysis, this essay focuses on the ideological and aesthetic affiliations of the first novel by Cheikh Hamidou Kane, *L'Aventure ambiguë*.[3]

As Emmanuel Obiechina has described it, Kane's novel is "a storehouse of Négritude in prose" (82). More than a passive receptacle for a static, reified ideology, however, the narrative is simultaneously an assessment of Négritude's directives for the African intellectual, as well as a dramatization of the conflicts affecting traditional African elites on the eve of decolonization. Though a writer from the second generation of Négritude who came of age nearly thirty years after Léopold Sédar Senghor had first coined the term, Kane was nonetheless part of the first generation of Francophone African novelists. Moreover, Kane's novel articulates his generation's ambivalence toward the concept of Négritude itself, and therefore of the mediated, ambiguous position of the colonial intellectual. As the novel's protagonist states, "I confess that I do not like the word [Négritude], and I don't always understand what it would be meant to cover" (142). Despite Kane's resistance toward the term, this work scrutinizes—as Obiechina and others have noted—the central themes of the movement.

Kane (b. 1928) was born in Senegal, and after receiving a quite rigorous traditional Koranic education he studied philosophy and law (with equal rigor) at the University of Paris. He then returned to Senegal, where he made his career primarily in bureaucratic and diplomatic services. *L'Aventure ambiguë* created a *succès d'estime* when it was published in France, and received the 1962 *Grand prix littéraire de l'afrique noir*. The novel tells the story of Samba Diallo, a child of the traditional African elite, and opens with an image of him nobly enduring the obligatory poverty and harsh—indeed, sadistic—teaching methods of the traditional Koranic academy. As a young boy, Samba Diallo is still required to learn the sacred text of the Koran by rote memorization—that is, as an oral narrative. Immediately preceding the ceremony of his initiation into manhood and more intellectually engaged study of the Koran, the Islamic equivalent of the bar mitzvah referred to in the novel as the "Night of the Koran" (71), Samba Diallo is withdrawn from the Koranic academy and placed in a French colonial school. From there, he is launched on the ambiguous adventure of the book's title, traveling, like the author, to Paris, where he falls in with a young French communist woman (Lucienne) and an old man from the Caribbean (Pierre-Louis). On his return to Africa, he finds the master who taught him the Koran has died, and the only person who preserves his memory is "the fool" (*le fou*), an old, mentally disturbed man who, like Samba Diallo, has returned from Europe. When this man takes Samba Diallo to the master's grave, the protagonist finds himself no longer able to pray. In reaction to his apparent apostasy, the fool murders him, and the novel concludes with Samba Diallo's dying thoughts.

During the African episodes of the novel Kane schematizes the relationship between his protagonist and the community by presenting Samba Diallo typically in socially isolated situations, either in dialogue with one person or communing with the dead in his memories. This tendency is inversely underscored by the autobiographical detail that Cheikh Hamidou Kane's own name in the Peul language is Samba, a name traditionally given to second sons. If Samba Diallo is, like the author, a second son, why is there no reference anywhere in the novel to his siblings? Indeed, perhaps the greatest distinction between *L'Aventure ambiguë* and the great neo-realist classics of African literature—such as Chinua Achebe's *Things Fall Apart* and Camara Laye's *L'enfant noir*—is the virtual absence of anthropological detail in its description of traditional African life. In lieu of ritual ceremonies, family dynamics, culinary customs, or life cycle events, the study of the Koran, a tradition by no means associated exclusively with Africa, is the only representation of the tradition juxtaposed against the modern world. This is a curious synecdoche indeed, one that reduces the difference between Africa and the West to exclusively ideological and religious terms.

As a critical exposition of Négritude ideology in narrative form, *L'Aventure ambiguë* emphasizes both the paradoxes of this ideology and the ambivalence that calls it into being. Négritude in its African manifestations seeks to affirm in metaphysical and artistic terms a unifying black essence—a *négritude,* to coin a phrase—and yet, this essence inherits the assumption of an immutable racial identity from the white supremacist doctrines propounded by colonialism during the nineteenth century. As one of Senghor's most famous epigrams states, *"L'émotion est nègre, comme la raison hellène"* ("Emotion is negro, just as reason is Greek") (my translation) (24). Négritude thus shares with previous pan-African ideologies the racialist double bind:[4] simultaneously accepting the belief in fixed, biologically determined racial identities and rejecting the power imbalances that these racial categories were created to justify. As significant as Négritude is as an aesthetic movement and an anticolonial ideology, it is equally relevant insofar as it demonstrates the contradictions of colonial thought, and the impact these contradictions exerted on the colonized intellectual.

For example, the universalism that Senghor advocated is characterized and compromised by its attitude toward language. Thus Senghor writes in his essay, *L'Art négro-africaine:*

> The French always feel the need to comment and explain the meaning of images by abstract words. For the Negro poet this is rarely necessary. His public has this second sight spontaneously, because it is initiated . . . gifted with inner eyes which see through walls. . . . There is no need to explain that the young girl who has just seen her fiancé triumph in athletic games is flooded with joy as she sings: I shall not sleep; I shall watch on the open square/The tom-tom of me is decked in a white necklace. (qtd. in Kesteloot 88)

Although Senghor's idealization of the "spontaneous," unmediated rapport between the African poet and his audience invests his Francophone poetry with imagistic concreteness and specificity, the actual audience for whom he writes is far removed from the African traditions he invokes. After all, how many African people of his generation were actually capable of reading poetry in French?[5] Moreover, his decision to write in French—a decision both determined by his status as a French citizen,[6] and compelled, as Alioune Diop states, by the reality of intellectual life under colonialism—prompts him to adopt a system of reference quite removed from his ostensibly authentic African aesthetic; his appeals to authority in this essay, for example, aren't African griots, they are La Fontaine and Baudelaire. Négritude declares its identification with the folk, in a language only a self-conscious minority could understand.

With Négritude's focus on the universal, the decision to articulate African "authenticity" in French becomes indicative of the Négritude writer's estrangement from his native culture—an estrangement that is a central preoccupation of Kane's novel. In practical terms, French is the *only* language for modern literary expression under the pan-African terms of Négritude. Thus, Senghor writes, "We express our message in French since French has a universal vocation and since our message is also addressed to French people and others. In our languages the halo that surrounds the words is by nature merely that of sap and blood; French words send out thousands of rays like diamonds" (qtd. in Ngugi 19).[7] It may be noted that the opposition between the hardness, polish, and dazzle of French "diamonds" and the organic, earthy functionality of African "sap and blood" replicates a dichotomy that recurs throughout the literature of Négritude: Africans are closer to the earth, the spirit, and the life force of an authentic creativity—their indigenous culture is more natural and vibrant than the cold, technological symmetry of the West. But the French have the diamonds. As Christopher Miller states,

> The inventors of Négritude ideology . . . were educated in the French colonial system and were more accustomed to expressing themselves in French than in Martinican Creole or Senegalese Wolof. The birthplace of black francophone literature is more Paris than Fort-de-France or Dakar, and it is now easy to recognize in Négritude . . . the signs of alienation from the author's native past: nostalgia, so to speak, the desire to coincide again, to bring the past back. (16)

Though writing in French is a necessary anticolonial gesture, one that alerts both other black intellectuals as well as the colonizer of the African writer's condition, this gesture reinscribes the alienation that colonialism had created between the intellectual and his native community in the first place. However "authentic" these authors portray themselves, they are always implicated with the modern, imperial culture—with Paris.[8]

Unlike Senghor, for whom French is both the "natural" language of a new, pan-African black poetry as well as the object of the poet's mystification, French for Kane is identified as part of the apparatus of colonialism, and thus a source for the colonial subject's ambivalence. Describing his newly discovered antipathy toward colonialism, a hostility awakened only while living in Paris, Samba Diallo states,

> My hatred is a re-inhibition . . . an annulment of love. I loved them too soon, unwisely, without knowing them well enough. . . . Perhaps it was because of their alphabet. With it, they struck the first hard blow at the country of the Diallobé. I remained for a long time under the spell of those signs and the music of their language. When I learned to fit them together to form words . . . my happiness knew no further limit. (158–59)

Where French in Senghor's poetics is the vehicle through which the poet transubstantiates the magic of African existence into a cosmopolitan work of art, connecting the African writer with the wider world, the colonial language for the second-generation novelist is understood as the primary means by which the colonized African is torn away from the only home he or she would ever know. French, it may be noted, still retains the quality of magic for Samba Diallo—he is under the spell of its signs and its music—but Kane is more intent to make explicit the political consequences of this mystification than a previous generation of poets had been. His work therefore extends and focuses the political project of Négritude, and provides a literary complement to the contemporaneous process of decolonization.

In *L'Aventure ambiguë,* the automatic assumption of French as the obvious or natural language for the Francophone African writer begins to be questioned through a series of inversions and erasures. For example, the name of Samba Diallo's native language, Peul, is never mentioned, though it is clear that most conversations in the first part of the novel take place in this language, not in French. Thus, in the first chapter, the (African) teacher of the colonial school tells Samba Diallo's father and the Koran instructor that his school "only teaches men to join wood to wood—to make wooden buildings." Kane explains, "Pronounced in the language of the region, the word 'school' means 'wood.' The three men smiled with an air of understanding and slight disapproval of this classic play on words in connection with the foreign school" (9). Kane does not pretend that these characters would be speaking French in this situation, but he also does not go so far as to translate their conversation from the unnamed African language. He instead leaves the reader to struggle in the gap created by a colonial situation that is inherently multilingual and a literary culture that is rigidly, repressively monolingual; the best the Francophone reader can hope for is to have the colonial teacher's wordplay explained, *evoked,* but therefore *absent* in the discourse of the novel itself.

The psychological and ideological conflicts at the heart of *L'Aventure ambiguë* find expression on the level of the novel's discourse through generic, as well as linguistic, ambiguity. In formal terms, Kane suggests here that the difference between white and black, between outside and inside, between modernity and tradition is the difference between comedy and tragedy; the triumph of modernity is a *commedia,* in Dante's sense of a tale with a happy ending, for those with access to power, a tragedy for its colonized victims. For example, when Samba Diallo first enters the colonial school, the perspective shifts from him to the children of the white colonial administrator:

> The story of Samba Diallo is a serious story. If it had been a gay recital, we should have told you of the bewilderment of

the two white children, on the first morning of their sojourn among little Negroes, in finding themselves in the presence of so many black faces. . . . But nothing more will be said of all that, because these memories . . . would bring gayety to this recital of which the profound truth is wholly sad. (50-51)

Likewise, when Kane introduces the communist Lucienne's parents, M. and Mme. Martial, in the Parisian section of the novel, he describes them as behaving like comedians (110-11). The shift in perspective between black and white, tragedy and comedy, suggests that Kane himself, like his protagonist, is capable as an *évolué* of seeing both viewpoints,[9] but as a consequence he is suspended between these polarities.

The tendency to portray situations from alternating, self-canceling perspectives establishes a vacillating structure to the conflicting ideologies that inform this novel. Kane provides a metaphor for understanding this structure of ambiguity when he writes, "I walk. One foot before, one foot behind, one foot before, one foot behind: one-two, one-two. No! I must not think: one-two, one-two. I must think of something else. One-two, one-two" (128). Both the footsteps and Samba Diallo's self-consciousness in observing them bespeak an irresolvable tension between before and after, past and future, tradition and modernity, Africa and France. Samba Diallo's resistance to the tyranny of binary thinking demonstrates his efforts to break free not only of the various dialectics in which he is enmeshed, but also of the lockstep, marching conformity demanded by colonial modernity of the *évolué,* and by Islamic tradition of its adherents. Significantly, however, the place where this self-consciousness manifests itself is the Boulevard Saint-Michel; the protagonist comes to Paris, as he says earlier in the novel, because it is "the itinerary which is most likely to get me lost" (113). Similarly, at the moment when Samba Diallo discovers his estrangement from his own body, on the Boulevard Saint-Michel, he compares himself to Rilke's character Malte Laurids Brigge, so that Paris itself becomes in this passage not only a physical landscape, but also an intertextual one. That the novel as a whole incorporates this structural ambiguity can be seen in its formal designation as a *récit,* which Abiola Irele notes is a term Kane took from André Malraux, and which suggests either a written, journalistic account or an oral "recitation" (Irele 167).[10]

The suggestion that the conflict between black and white is ultimately an opposition between an oral recitation and a written one calls attention to an additional conflict in the book between two "logi": the Word of French modernity against the Word of African Islam.

To interrupt the irresolvable contest between Africa and Europe that initiates Négritude, Kane portrays Islam as a cultural presence in Francophone Africa that is as significant as "Blackness" and "whiteness," but which identifies with neither. Because Négritude derives much of its intellectual dynamism from the dialectical opposition of Africa and Europe, as a formal ideology it has surprisingly little to say about Islam, a religion that arrived in Western Africa as part of a colonizing mission from the North that precedes European colonialism by several centuries, and yet which quickly became an integral and highly adaptive fixture of Western African life. Islam is, for example, the religion of over 90 percent of the nation of Senegal, but not the religion of Léopold Senghor, its first president (a Catholic), who belatedly formulated the concept *Arabité* as a complement to Négritude not as an extension of his thinking about the role of Islam in his native culture, but as a form of Realpolitik.[11] Nonetheless, the most pronounced and enduring effects of Négritude on African literature, particularly the African novel, can be found in the work of Muslim authors, of whom Kane is both the most orthodox and, perhaps paradoxically, the most representative.

At the heart of the novel's ambiguous structures is a crisis in religious faith and cultural identification—a crisis between Islamic faith and secular disbelief that Kane suggests is fundamental to the lived reality of African Négritude. Samba Diallo's negotiation of this crisis leads him to embrace an impossible goal, as he admits by the grave of his childhood friend, the old woman Rella:

> For a long time, near his dead friend, the child reflected on the eternal mystery of death, and, on his own count, rebuilt Paradise in a thousand ways. When sleep came to him he had grown entirely serene again, for he had found the answer: Paradise was built with the Words [of the Koran] that he used to recite, the same glowing light, the same deep and mysterious shadows, the same enchantment, the same power. (42–43)

The crisis can thus only resolve itself in Paradise, through the transcendence of strife itself, metonymically connected at the grave with death and a retreat to the past. As Kane describes Samba Diallo's quest, it is a means of escape from the difficulties and anxieties that both impending adulthood and the modernity of the French school have rendered inevitable. The quest itself is therefore doomed to failure by time, in both a temporal and historical sense. The Paradise that Samba Diallo pursues in his mystical search is the stasis, alternately, of childhood or of death; although adulthood demands the abandonment of this fantasy, the apostasy that adulthood, travel to Paris, and modernity engender in him creates the pretext for his premature death—at the hands of the fool, the only adult in the novel who refuses to abandon this dream of paradise. As Victor Aire states, Samba Diallo's anxieties toward adulthood provide a metaphor for the Diallobé's anxiety toward modernity: "Here [in the Night of the Koran] Kane sings the swan song not only for his protagonist's childhood but also for an era in the history of his people" (756; my translation).

Kane is not only aware that his novel elegizes the lost autonomy of his native culture; his protagonist makes this point explicit by stating, "I am not a distinct country of the Diallobé facing a distinct Occident, and appreciating with a cool head what I must take from it and what I must leave with it by way of counterbalance. I have become the two. There is not a clear mind deciding between the two factors of a choice. There is a strange nature, in distress over not being two" (150–51). In this context, fusion becomes a source of anxiety over a death of sorts for the distinct cultures being fused. The ambiguity of being two means, of course, no longer being one—that is, identical with nature, God, and the other abstractions that Négritude valorized as essential to African culture. Samba Diallo, having become one with the West, is now, in Woody Allen's formulation, "two with nature," and as such he contrasts with his father, who remains in Africa, and therefore maintains his equilibrium in precisely the manner no longer available to Samba Diallo's generation. By the standards of the previous generation, Samba Diallo has grown too close to the West, and, like Icarus, is consumed, like a sacrifice to the sun, by the blinding rays of the Enlightenment. In commenting on the ending of the novel, Kane, though not contradicting the interpretation of Samba Diallo's death as a sacrifice to the struggle between Africa and the West, nonetheless emphasizes its spiritual significance over politics. He states:

> In my view this is not a hopeless ending. The death of Samba Diallo is only the proof that there is a real conflict. You understand, if there had not been the initial civilization in which Samba was rooted, there would have been no problem when he was introduced to Western civilization; he would have thrived in it. On the contrary, he dies because of it. Why?.... It means: 1) That we do have permanent values ... and we therefore must nurture them. ... 2) By not recognizing that, we reach the point of negating ourselves and our specific val-

ues; this will destroy us. . . . Western values inculcated indiscriminately can lead to the destruction of the African who is unable to assimilate them. (qtd. in Mortimer 64)

Moreover, the fact that Samba Diallo has lost a sense of identification with his native, precolonial culture is a consequence of the triangular competition of power structures—traditional African, Islamic, and Western—that define the protagonist's cultural predicament, and determine its characteristic ambiguity. Whereas in a typical Négritude formulation, the West contrasts with animist Africa to the exclusion of Islam, in most respects *L'Aventure ambiguë* depicts a conflict between Islam and the West, to the exclusion of the animist tradition long suppressed by Islam.[12] As Nouréini Tidjani-Serpos points out, "the Diallobé are forced by the vicissitudes of history to forget their original religion in order to adopt Islam, which over the course of centuries at last gives the impression of being a 'natural' faith, to such an extent had it infused the life of the Diallobé" (195; my translation).[13] On an intertextual, or even metatextual, level, therefore, there is no African epic behind or beneath *L'Aventure ambiguë* the way the *Sunjata* epic—the most celebrated and influential traditional narrative in West Africa—informs and animates the symbolism of Camara Laye's *L'Enfant noir*. *L'Aventure ambiguë* relegates the animist or syncretic tradition commemorated in epics such as *Sunjata* to the unspoken cartography of the face of *la Grande Royale*, the powerful older sister of the Diallobé chief: "[I]t was like a living page from the history of the Diallobé country. Everything that the country treasured of epic tradition could be read there. . . . Islam restrained the formidable turbulence of those features, in the same way that the little veil hemmed them in" (20-21).[14] For Kane, the Koran takes the place that *Sunjata* holds for contemporaneous works of African literature such as *L'Enfant noir* as the ancient mythic subtext for the ambiguous adventure of modern, written, colonized culture.

In this regard, it is worth recalling that the Koranic study depicted in this novel is an almost completely oral undertaking. As Tidjani-Serpos states, the rote memorization of the Koran "was perhaps adapted . . . to the oral character of African text production; however, this sort of memorization, without any accompanying explanation, corresponded perfectly with another trait of African culture: science is never more appreciated than when it is secret and when it demands years of wandering and suffering before it can be properly acquired" (189). Tidjani-Serpos' observations therefore connect the conflict between Africa and the West not only to orality and literacy, but also to further distinctions between secrecy and openness, the community and society, inside and outside, and, at its cosmic extreme, death and life. As Tidjani-Serpos states explicitly, "The foreign school, as *life,* is, so to speak, the antithesis of the Koranic school, which is apprenticed to *death"* (192).

Nonetheless, the pre-Islamic African tradition does reassert itself, surreptitiously, in apparent alliance with the West, when *la Grande Royale* persuades the people to send their prize pupil, Samba Diallo, to the colonial school. Indeed, *la Grande Royale* acknowledges that her advocacy violates the public submissiveness demanded of women by traditional Islam, even as her arguments ultimately serve to subvert the power of Islam among the Diallobé: "I have done something which is not pleasing to us and which is not in accordance with our customs" (45). On the surface, the *Grande Royale*'s speech is an act of "defensive modernization"[15]—to save the tradition, one has to destroy the tradition; to save the next generation, one must force them to forget their heritage.[16] And yet, as a woman, *la Grande Royale* violates the tradition in a specifically gendered way. If her face, as Miller writes, is a "map" of the pre-Islamic Africa repressed by the Fundamentalist Diallobé, this speech is her revenge.

But the consequent assertion (cf., Tidjani-Serpos 195), that the Koranic Teacher and Samba Diallo's father represent the conservative wing of the Diallobé elite, with *la Grande Royale* representing the liberal, is an over-simplification that leads to an unfortunate condemnation of the male characters in the novel along reductive ideological grounds. Tidjani-Serpos writes of these male characters that they "are the collaborators who wish to ameliorate the system by infusing it with more spirituality" (202). In fact, given the subaltern status of the Diallobé as a whole, the sympathetic reader can understand both sides of this struggle within the Diallobé as attempts to reconfigure and preserve a sense of power for themselves in the face of colonialism's overwhelming force. For the Koranic Teacher and his allies, preserving power means resisting colonialism's efforts to remake the Diallobé in its image; for *la Grande Royale,* preserving power means making a strategic alliance with colonialism, in effect subordinating the native aristocracy to the more powerful hegemony of the French. Seen from this perspective, *la Grande Royale* advocates political accommodation of imperialism. By contrast, the Koranic Teacher more actively champions the minority culture, thus transforming the tradition from a reactionary force to an implicitly revolutionary one—provided that such an antimodern movement is coupled with humanistic values, as demonstrated here by the Knight's sympathetic familiarity with Western philosophy, and the general absence of racist animosity in the novel. By staging this conflict between the two spiritual leaders of the Diallobé, Kane's novel presents Senghorian Négritude's synthesis of accommodation and resistance as two mutually exclusive ideological positions. What Senghor stages as a dialectic, the Diallobé experience as ambiguity.

At the same time, *la Grande Royale* is, symbolically, a reminder of a previous act of repression among the Diallobé, and it is significant that her campaign in favor of the colonial school sets her directly at odds with an Islamic tradition that had excluded her, as an animist and a woman, to begin with. In this context, what Philip Curtin has described as the difference between "neo-traditionalists" and "defensive modernizers" is particularly useful; nonetheless, the conflict between these "neo-traditionalists" and "defensive modernizers"—the Koranic Teacher and *la Grande Royale*, respectively—serves to critique Curtin's opposition of tradition with modernity in the African context, and illustrates that both "neo-traditionalist" and "defensive modernizers," though each derive from a weakened tradition's negotiation with modernity, perpetuate conflicts from *within* the tradition (235–38).

After all, *la Grande Royale* coordinates a "conspiracy" between herself and the colonial school against the Islamic tradition, a "conspiracy" that aligns these two forces against the Koranic school in a struggle, cosmologically, between life and death. As *la Grande Royale* tells Samba Diallo, "The teacher is trying to kill the life in you. But I am going to put an end to all that" (22). Seen from this cosmological perspective, only the Koranic school, as presented here, properly appreciates the inevitability, and therefore the significance, of death as the counterpart to a meaningful life, and perhaps this understanding is the only explanation for the attraction this austere regimen holds for Samba Diallo, and the only way to understand the novel's transfigured conclusion as a victory, both for the Koranic Teacher and Samba Diallo.

Although the conflict between modern France and traditional Africa is presented as a struggle between existentialist secularism and orthodox Islam, it's noteworthy that Kane's use of French, characteristic of Négritude aesthetics, prevents him from integrating not only Peul into the discourse of his novel, but Arabic as well. Indeed, it's not clear how many of his devout characters even understand the language of their faith; as a Catholic nun writing in *Présence Africaine* states of Samba Diallo's father, known as *le Chevalier* [the Knight], "The words, which he [*le Chevalier*] doesn't understand, for which he suffers martyrdom, he loves for their mystery and somber beauty" (Soeur Marie-Céleste 220; my translation). It is significant, in this regard, that not only is the Koran never quoted, translated, or paraphrased in the novel, but the study of this Holy Book is confined to the Koranic school, a narrative space that is not only separated emotionally from the modern world that engulfs the novel's protagonist, but indeed becomes the victim of what Mikhail Bakhtin, in a radically different religious and historical context, describes as the "agitated and cacophonous dialogic life" that renders both the Koran itself and the values it represents "simply an object, a *relic, a thing*" (344).[17] For Samba Diallo, like Kane, the tradition must be elegized because, having been to France and back, he believes that it *is* a relic, one that is in imminent danger of disappearing, along with the purity of the values associated with it.

Nonetheless, the drastic, self-effacing rejection of African Islamic culture that *la Grande Royale* advocates is justified not only by the hegemony of French cultural power, but also by the economic depredation of colonialism itself: The sacred words of the Koran have not dried up only because of their removal from the sphere of everyday life, but also because colonialism has undermined their social authority. For Kane, however, acquiescence to the material poverty of the tradition is a value instilled at the Koranic school that is *not* directly challenged in the narrative. As Samba Diallo's father states in the first debate over whether to send him to the colonial school, "We have nothing left—thanks to them—and it is thus that they hold us. . . . The woodcutters and the metalworkers are triumphant everywhere in the world, and their iron holds us under their law. . . . But we are among the last men on earth to possess God as He veritably is in His Oneness" (10).

Part of the spiritual value that Kane perceives in the material poverty of the tradition derives from the doctrines of Sufi mysticism in which he was raised and which his novel reflects.[18] Another aspect, however, is the fact that for Kane, the modern world that was introduced to Africa by colonialism, and that represents colonial power in its technological, intellectual, and cultural aspects, is not an abstract concept but an open and intimate component of daily life. As Kane writes,

> The new [colonial] school shares . . . the characteristics of cannon and of magnet. From the cannon it draws its efficacy as an arm of combat. Better than the cannon, it makes conquest permanent. The cannon compels the body, the school bewitches the soul. . . . From the magnet, the school takes its radiating force. It is bound up with a new order, as a magnetic

stone is bound up with a field. The upheaval of the life of man within this new order is similar to the overturning of certain physical laws in a magnetic field. (49-50)

In this context, poverty itself acquires a spiritual and political value as an expression of resistance to the material domination of the colonial order.

This linking of the colonial school with the cannon and magnet emphasizes that the modernity introduced to the Diallobé via French education—characterized by the colonialist slogan *"nos ancêtres, les Gaulois"* invoked in the title of this essay—is not only an outside imposition, but ultimately a function of imperial domination; modernity in *L'Aventure ambiguë* is not just an alien presence, it is also a system that degrades the traditional culture and disempowers the superseded culture's leaders and adherents. By the same token, however, if the value of the tradition can be measured by its poverty, how can it hope to sustain or perpetuate itself? Even the Koranic Teacher admits, "dire poverty is the enemy of God" (82). Indeed, everywhere in this novel, the tradition is equated with night, infirmity, asceticism, and death; by contrast, modernity and Paris, the City of Light, are associated with daytime, material plenty, and technology. The observation, noted amid a decisive debate between Samba Diallo's father and the colonial administrator, that "[a]t this moment Lacroix had to fight the temptation to push the electric light switch which was within the reach of his hand," therefore assumes significance in representing not only the conflict between Africa and France, but also the ambivalence toward imposing the material, antispiritual values of the West too suddenly on African culture (79).

The death of Samba Diallo—the character who embodies the hazards of "electric light," the sudden, artificial illumination of French culture on the African soul—at the novel's end can thus be interpreted, simultaneously, as the point of epiphany at which his struggle with tradition and modernity can be resolved, but also as a kind of child sacrifice in the tradition's ongoing struggle *against* modernity and, as the novel's title suggests, against ambiguity. Indeed, if *la Grande Royale*'s motivation in sending the protagonist to the colonial school was to kill the Islamic tradition in his character, then his death constitutes an act of retribution, a return of the repressed; at the same time, his own inability to pray at the Teacher's grave fulfills the logic of his religious education, which instilled in him only the belief that genuine faith was incompatible with sustained immersion in the modern world. Similarly, Mongo Beti, the Cameroonian novelist and ferocious critic of Négritude, describes his *évolué* (or rather, failed *évolué*) protagonist, in the novel *Mission terminée*, as a sacrifice: "Without being aware of it, I was no more than a sacrifice on the altar of Progress and Civilization. My youth was slipping away, and I was paying a terrible price for—well, for what? Having gone to school, at the decree of my all-powerful father? Having been chained to my books when most children of my age were out playing games?" (63). It should be noted that Kane, a student of Négritude, portrays the dissolution of Négritude's efforts at synthesis in more tragic and definitive terms than one of its chief opponents.

As a modernist worldview, Négritude is simultaneously premised on an existential attitude of estrangement and despair, as well as a Promethean effort to expand the limits of the possible imposed by the strictures of tradition and the indifference of the new regime. As Jean-Paul Sartre describes the underlying pessimism of Négritude, with surprising lyricism,

> It is from the shock of the white culture that his [the writer's] Négritude has passed from immediate existence to the state of reflection. But by the same token he has more or less ceased to live it. In choosing to see that which he is, he has split himself in two, he no longer coincides with himself. And reciprocally, it was because he was already exiled from himself that there was this duty to declare himself. He begins thus by exile; the exile of the body offers a striking example of the exile of his heart. (18)

Despite the well-known problem of Sartre's insistence on speaking for black people and Négritude alike, this passage expresses a genuine insight. Indeed, this remark not only provides a rejoinder to the Nigerian author Wole Soyinka's oft-quoted remark that "a tiger never has to proclaim his tigertude" but also speaks eloquently to the absence of an uninterrupted relationship with Africa, and with the self, that calls Négritude into being.

Although only a few chapters of the novel take place in France, Paris functions in *L'Aventure ambiguë* as both the polar opposite of Samba Diallo's unnamed home and the ideological birthplace of his existential ambivalence; *L'Aventure ambiguë* is thus as much a Parisian novel, written in the philosophical spirit of contemporaneous French fiction, as it is an African one. Moreover, because Samba Diallo's birthplace remains unnamed, Paris is the most tangible place in the narrative. With its tragic ending and its persistent tone of elegy, *L'Aventure ambiguë* can be seen as Négritude's swansong—and not just, as Aire writes, the swansong of the Diallobé (756)—even as it offers the most sophisticated exposition of Négritude values anywhere in the African novel. As Kane himself writes, "It may be that we shall be captured at the end of our itinerary, vanquished by our adventure itself. It suddenly occurs to us that all along our road, we have not ceased to metamorphose ourselves, and we see ourselves as other than what we were. Sometimes the metamorphosis is not even finished. We have turned ourselves into hybrids, and there we are left" (112–13). The novel's resolution in ambivalence and death ultimately suggests the failure of a previous generation's concept of African authenticity—a concept that equates race with culture. Indeed, in a quest for authenticity, what could be more unsettling and discouraging than ambiguity? The consequence of ambiguity for Samba Diallo is the simultaneous retention and exhaustion of Négritude's project, the celebration of racial authenticity as a form of cultural, rather than biological, essentialism: "I am like a broken balafong, like a musical instrument that has gone dead" (150). Here the balafong, a central Négritude symbol of African authenticity, is rendered defunct and silent.

For Kane, this dilemma can truly be resolved only in death—at least this is the implication of the literary silence he maintained for nearly 35 years after the publication of his first novel.[19] Following Kane, subsequent generations of African writers, in both English and French, have moved beyond the critique of colonialism and the essentialist opposition of black against white that characterizes Négritude. Kane in the era after *L'Aventure ambiguë* turned his energies toward building the African state and strengthening its ties with the developed world. Subsequent writers have devoted their energies to critiquing the inability of the African state to provide or recover both physical and spiritual sustenance for the majority of its citizens, a generation after independence. They have migrated, intellectually, away from Paris as the birthplace of their post-colonial ambivalence—even as historical circumstances in the neo-colonial era have often driven them into exile from their native lands. Fate and history have thus made the nationalist writers in the era of independence, along with countless less privileged refugees, as cosmopolitan as the Négritude writers of the colonial period. As such, the novelists of Négritude offer a model and a lesson to everyone who experiences home as exile, and exile as home.

Notes

1. Even Paul Gilroy's seminal work, *The Black Atlantic: Modernity and Double Consciousness* focuses exclusively on African Ameri-

Cheikh Hamidou Kane's *Ambiguous Adventure*   307

can, Caribbean, and black British culture and invokes Africa as such only as a point of origin—that is, as a point of departure *after which*, in the context of slavery, immigration, and travel, black modernity becomes possible. This critical stance suggests, unwittingly, that Africa is an absence in Black Atlantic culture to be filled with modernity; sub-Saharan Africa's own encounter with modernity tends to be effaced from most discussions of the Black Atlantic—and, indeed, from most models of postcolonial theory.

2. "Herself": on the subject of gender, it is necessary to note that there is *no* female exponent of African negritude in the realm of prose narrative. The first Francophone African female writer began publishing a decade after the era of independence began: see Kuoh-Moukoury. For a theoretical discussion of the belated entry of women into Francophone African literature, see Miller 246–94.

3. My translations depart slightly from the published English translation, but for the reader's convenience I cite its page numbers.

4. For a thorough examination of the racialist contradictions affecting pan-African thought, see Appiah, particularly chapters 1 and 2: 3–46.

5. In this regard, Christopher Miller writes,

    UNESCO statistics on francophone countries show literacy rates ranging from less than 1% in Niger to 6% in Senegal (in 1961), 19% in Cameroon (in 1962), and 30% in Zaïre (in 1962). Literacy in all these cases means literacy in French; illiteracy is defined by UNESCO in these terms: "A person is illiterate who cannot with understanding both read and write a short simple sentence on his everyday life." . . . On the other hand, in certain small areas of certain countries, the rate of enrollment in school and therefore of literacy is significantly higher: of children 7 to 12 years old in the Ivory Coast, fifty percent are estimated to be in school. (69–70)

    One can only add that, however low literacy rates were in the era of independence invoked in this citation, they were lower during the colonial era, when Senghor formulated his negritude polemics.

6. As G. Wesley Johnson explains, as early as 1915, natives of the "four communes," Dakar, Goree, Rufisque, and Saint-Louis—Senegalese settlements that by virtue of their longstanding history of interaction with the French empire were counted, like Martinique and Guadeloupe, as part of Metropolitan France—"could vote in French elections, stand for public office, travel freely within the French empire and in France, but in matters of marriage, inheritance, and certain family arrangements they could, if they chose, follow customary law. . . . They were in fact full French citizens . . . whereas relatives or friends born outside of the communes or living in the Protectorate . . . were simply . . . subjects without status and with limited rights under the French colonial regime" (141). Senghor and other natives of these four communes, unlike virtually every other black person in French West

Africa, were born as French citizens, a condition that explains, at least in political terms, the importance he ascribes to the French language as a vehicle for African creativity.

7. Ngugi's source is the *postface* to Senghor's 1956 collection of poems, *Ethiopiques*. For the original, see Senghor's *Liberté 1* 225–26.

8. Hence V. Y. Mudimbe writes, "The product of a singular moment in European history, more particularly in French thought, it [negritude] carries these marks. Nonetheless, the fact that its promoters had appealed to a Western 'technician', J. P. Sartre, to establish it theoretically, according to a distinguished and rigorous philosophical tradition, provides evidence for the existence of a quite particular intellectual line of descent" (*L'autre* 101; my translation). Note, of course, that Mudimbe sees negritude as the African response to a particular moment in French thought—and not African culture.

9. In this respect, one should note that the narrator refers to Samba Diallo's father exclusively as "the knight" (*le chevalier*) after the colonial official Jean Lacroix—whose name *(la croix!)* suggests that the conflict in this book between Africa and the West extends symbolically back to the medieval struggle between Islam and Christianity—describes him as such. Through this change in perspective, this estranged way of describing the protagonist's father, the narrator begins to tell Samba Diallo's story from a western point of view. Kane as such seems to use the technique of *style indirect libre* to underscore the *foreignness* of the novel as a literary form in Africa. Or adapting Kane's tendency to view circumstances through alternating perspectives, one can see the adoption of a white man's description of a black character as the author's acknowledgment that most of his readers will similarly view this book, given that it was published in France, through the eyes of white people.

10. It's worth considering, therefore, Kane's use of the term when describing the surprise of the white children: "Mais il ne sera rien *dit* de tout cela, parce que ces souvenirs en ressusciteraient d'autres . . . et égaieraient ce *récit* dont la vérité profonde est toute de tristesse" (62; emphasis added). It may be noted that Kane uses the verb *dit* and not *écrit* in this passage.

11. Hence George Lang writes of Senghor's *Les Fondements de l'africanité, ou negritude et arabité*, "It is hardly surprising that Senghor's *Fondements* was conceived as an address delivered in the presence of Gamal Abdel Nasser, or that as the Catholic president of a nation over 90 percent Muslim, Senghor found good reasons of his own to attribute an important role for Islam in his Universal Synthesis of cultures" (306). It should be stressed that *Arabité* as an afterthought to negritude figures Islamic culture in racial terms rather than religious ones; unlike Kane, Senghor invokes Islam as a further manifestation of his binary thinking,

rather than a complication of the racialist dialectic.

12. Mildred Mortimer explains this historical context by writing, "Among the Toucouleur of Senegal, Kane's ethnic group, Islamization took place in the eighteenth century; the *torodbe* (religious aristocracy) drove out the animist Peul dynasty in 1776. In the past two centuries, the Toucouleur have felt themselves to be the carriers of Muslim civilization and from the time of their conversion began to launch holy wars on neighboring groups. . . . For Kane, Islam is a powerful spiritual force that must be used in the struggle to resist Western materialism" (54).

13. One may add that Kane's identification of Islam as a "natural" African religion parallels Senghor's identification of French as a "natural" African language, even as his novel complicates and critiques the assumption that either of these *cultural* apparatuses, or perhaps any other, is in fact *natural*.

14. For an illuminating discussion of this description, see Miller 9–10.

15. I derive the term "defensive modernization," along with its counterpart "neo-traditionalism," from Curtin, 235–38.

16. *La Grande Royale* states, "The school in which I would place our children will kill in them what today we love and rightly conserve with care. Perhaps the very memory of us will die in them. . . . What I am proposing is that we should agree to die in our children's hearts and that the foreigners who have defeated us should fill the place . . . which we shall have left free" (46).

17. Understood in historical terms, Bakhtin's remarks about religion betray a humanist's anguish over the increasingly stultifying effect of a totalitarian regime on the dialogic life so essential to him. The target of Bakhtin's complaint here is as much Stalin as the Patriarch of the Orthodox Church.

18. On Kane's incorporation of Sufi principles in *L'Aventure ambiguë*, see Harrow 261–97. See as well Victor O. Aire, 152–60.

19. Though Kane's literary reputation rests almost exclusively on *L'Aventure ambiguë*, he has in the last decade returned to writing with a second novel, *Les gardiens du Temple*. A synopsis of the novel on the back cover states:

> Cinq ans après son indépendence, un pays africain (qui resemble fort Sénégal) est déchiré entre traditions et progrès, affirmation de soi et influence occidentale. Aussi, n'est-ce pas un hasard si la révolte éclate dans la communauté qui défend le plus farouchement ses coutumes ancestrales, les Sessene. Les Sessene n'enterrent pas leurs morts, ils les recouvrent d'une mince couche d'argile avant de les placer, debout, dans un baobab creux. Le gouvernement décide de les punir de leur comportement 'réactionnaire'. Mais le contrôle de la situation lui echappe, bientôt la grève générale se déclare et le pays entier est gagné par l'insurrection.

> Five years after its independence, an African country (which strongly resembles Senegal) is divided between tradition and progress, self-assertion and western influence. It is not by chance, therefore, that a revolt breaks out in the community that most fervently defends its ancestral customs, the Sessene. The Sessene don't bury their dead; they cover them in a thin layer of clay before placing them, upright, in a hollow baobab tree. The government decides to punish their "reactionary" behavior, but it loses control of the situation and soon a general strike is declared and the entire country is consumed by insurrection. (my translation)

Works Cited

Aire, Victor O. "Mort et devenir: Lecture thanato-sociologique de *L'Aventure ambiguë.*" *The French Review* 55.6 (1982): 752–60.
Appiah, Kwame Anthony. *In My Father's House: Africa in the Philosophy of Culture.* New York: Oxford UP, 1992, 1993.
Bakhtin, M. M. *The Dialogic Imagination: Four Essays.* 1981. Trans. Caryl Emerson and Michael Hilquist. Austin: University of Texas P, 1987.
Beti, Mongo. *Mission Terminée.* 1957. Paris: Buchet, 1999.
Curtin, Philip, ed. *Africa & the West: Intellectual Responses to European Culture.* Madison: University of Wisconsin P, 1972.
Diop, Christiane Yandé. Foreword. *The Surreptitious Speech:* Présence Africaine *and the Politics of Otherness 1946–1987.* Ed. V. Y. Mudimbe. Chicago: University of Chicago P, 1992. xvi.
Gilroy, Paul. *The Black Atlantic: Modernity and Double Consciousness.* Cambridge: Harvard UP, 1993.
Harrow, Kenneth W. "Camara Laye, Cheikh Hamidou Kane, and Tayeb Sali: Three Sufi Authors." *Faces of Islam in African Literature.* Ed. Kenneth W. Harrow. Portsmouth: Heinemann, 1991. 261–97.
Irele, Abiola. *The African Experience in Literature and Ideology.* 1981. Bloomington: Indiana UP, 1990.
Johnson, G. Wesley, Jr. "The Senegalese Urban Elite, 1900–1945." *Africa & the West: Intellectual Responses to European Culture.* Ed. Philip Curtin. Madison: University of Wisconsin P, 1972.
Kane, Cheikh Hamidou. *Ambiguous Adventure.* 1963. Trans. Katherine Woods. Oxford: Heinemann, 1972. Trans. of *L'Aventure ambiguë.* 1961. Paris: Éditions 10/18, 1998.
———. *Les Gardiens du Temple.* 1995. Paris: Roman Éditions, 1997.
Kesteloot, Lilyan. *Black Writers in French: A Literary History of Negritude.* 1963. Trans. Ellen Conroy Kennedy. Washington, D.C.: Howard UP, 1974, 1991.
Kuoh-Moukoury, Thérèse. *Essential Encounters.* Trans. Cheryl Toman. New York: MLA Texts and Translations, 2002. Trans. of *Rencontres Essentielles,* 1969.
Lang, George. "Through a Prism Darkly: 'Orientalism' in European-Language African Writing." *Faces of Islam in African Literature.* Ed. Kenneth W. Harrow. Portsmouth: Heinemann, 1991.

Miller, Christopher L. *Theories of Africans, Francophone Literature and Anthropology in Africa.* Chicago: University of Chicago P, 1990.
———. *Mission to Kala.* Trans. Peter Green. Portsmouth: Heinemann, 1964.
Mortimer, Mildred. *Journeys through the French African Novel.* Portsmouth: Heinemann, 1990.
Mudimbe, V. Y. *L'Autre face du royaume: une introduction à la critique des langages en folie.* Paris: L'age d'homme, 1973.
Mudimbe, V. Y., ed. *The Surreptitious Speech:* Presence Africaine *and the Politics of Otherness 1946–1987.* Chicago: University of Chicago P, 1992.
Ngugi wa Thiong'o. *Decolonising the Mind: The Politics of Language in African Literature.* 1986. London: James Currey, 1988.
Obiechina, Emmanuel N. *Language and Theme: Essays on African Literature.* Washington, D.C.: Howard University P, 1990.
Sartre, Jean-Paul. "Black Orpheus." Trans. S. W. Allen. Paris: Présence Africaine, n.d.
Senghor, Léopold Sédar. *Liberté 1: Négritude et Humanisme.* Paris: Editions de Seuil, 1964.
Senghor, Léopold Sédar, ed. *Anthologie de la nouvelle poèsie nègre et malagache de langue française.* [Anthology of the new Black and Malagacy poetry in French]. Paris: Presses Universitaires de France, 1948, 1997.
Soeur Marie-Céleste, S.C. "Le mysticisme chez Cheikh Hamidou Kane." *Présence Africaine* 101–102 (1977): 216–26.
Tidjani-Serpos, Nouréini. "De l'école coranique à l'école étrangère ou le passage tragique de l'Ancien au Nouveau dans *L'Aventure ambiguë* de Cheikh Hamidou Kane [From the Koranic School to the Foreign School, or the tragic transition from ancient to modern in Cheikh Hamidou Kane's *L'Aventure ambiguë*]." *Préscence Africaine* 101–102 (1977): 188–206.

CHAPTER 13

Redefining Paris
Transmodernity and Francophone African Migritude Fiction

Pius Adesanmi

I met you in the elevators of PARIS.
You were from Senegal or the Antilles
And the seas traversed surfed on your teeth,
Permeated your smile,
Sung in your voice like waves in the hollows.
Midday on the Champs Elysées
I suddenly encountered your tragic faces:
Your expressions attested secular grief.
And yet at the Boule Blanche
And under Montmartrian colors,
Your voice, your breath, your whole being exuded joy.
You were music, you were dance.
—Jean Brierre, "New Black Soul"

**On Transmodernity:
Paris and Foundational Black Internationalism**

Three scenarios—two obvious, the third less so but far more important—emerge from Haitian writer Jean Brierre's poem that serves as the epigraph to this essay. The first relates to the universally acclaimed status of early-twentieth-century Paris as the crucible of black intellection, a site for the articulation of polyvalent cultural expressions in all areas of the arts; the second, a corollary of the first, underscores the geographical position of the French capital at the heart of a centripetal nexus that consolidated the nascent black internationalism of the period by bringing together black cultural luminaries from Africa, the Caribbean, and the United States.[1] In this complex but felicitous interweaving of black politics and culture, Négritude movement encountered Harlem Renaissance; avant-garde "white" Paris of Dada and Surrealism encountered *l'art nègre,* laying the foundation, much later, for cubism's so-called discovery of primitivism via Pablo Picasso;[2] white musical Paris encountered African American jazz. The expression of Paris's desire for black otherness reached its ultimate consecration in the aestheticization and consumption of the body of African American model and actress Josephine Baker.[3] What these two scenarios foreground is the emergence of "Parisianism"[4] and "Black Paris," two hermeneutic categories that have entered critical/cultural discourse as a means of engaging the totality of black cultural and textual practices informed by the matricial ontology of Paris.

The third scenario borders on the centrality of Paris to the discursive fashioning of a transnational black modernity at once deconstructive of and resistant to the dominant post-Enlightenment narrative of Euromodernity the space of which it problematically inhabits. It is no longer news, as Enrique Dussel reminds us in his Frankfurt lectures, that the project of modernity, narrativizing itself as the reason, rationality, technology, and liberal democracy of the Western white male, circumscribed the black subject as an alterity defined and instrumentalized solely within the political economy of slavery and colonialism. By denying agency and even coevality to its constructed others, Euromodernity set the stage for the emergence of alternative modernities that, as Dussel claims in another context, are "trans-modernities" because they lie beyond the truth claims of the European episteme, constantly undermining its will to universalism: "To repeat: the thesis advanced in this essay is that modernity's recent impact on the planet's multiple cultures (Chinese, Southeast Asian, Hindu, Islamic, Bantu, Latin American) produced a varied 'reply' by all of them to the modern 'challenge.' Renewed, they are now erupting on a cultural horizon 'beyond' modernity. I call the reality of that fertile multicultural moment *'trans'-modernity* (since 'post'-modernity is just the latest moment of Western modernity)" (World System 221).

Of particular interest to our discussion is Dussel's description of the other's voice as a form of rebellious modernity. For Africa and its Atlantic diaspora, the rebellion against the tropological claims of modernity and its subalternizing symbologies came in the form of a veritable textual revolution for which Paris served as a confluence. From the 1920s to the 1940s, African American, Caribbean, and African intellectuals met and fraternized in Paris. In the process, they founded a plethora of journals and newspapers such as *Les continents, La voix des nègres, La revue du monde noir, La dépêche africaine, Légitime Défense* and *L'Etudiant noir*. Although these journals, reviews, and newspapers did not always reflect monolithic ideological positions and varied considerably in the degree of their militancy vis-à-vis the European ur-text of representational modernity they aimed to undermine, the point remains that they combined to inscribe not only a black aesthetic countermodernity in a space defined and inhabited by the texts of the colonial library but equally and, more importantly, they constructed epistemologies of subjecthood and agency through which the revalued voice of the black man did not only speak the truth to the power of modernity but also became transmodern in the sense of placing the black subject beyond the epistemic claims of Euromodernity.

Because narrative was central to the long process of dehistoricizing the black subject,[5] prose narrative easily became the vector of black transmodernity in early-twentieth-century Paris. Two novels, Claude McKay's *Banjo* and René Maran's *Batouala* became celebrated icons of Parisian transmodernist black resurgence. Given this constellation of black energies and epistemologies, the question needs to be asked at this point what specific role Africa and Africans played in the transnational nexus of Black Paris. Beyond Paris's ontology as the geographical matrix of the constitutive texts of Black Paris, how did African actors in the equation evolve idioms of continental self-fashioning informed by the Parisian experience? Broadly speaking, it is possible to identify two "African modes of self writing"[6] as having defined the foundational status of African textual inscription in the Black Paris equation.

First is the initial African contribution to the elaboration of Négritude poetics and imagination and second is the emergence of the journal, *Présence Africaine*. The poetry of Léopold Sédar Senghor and David Diop were especially crucial to the construction of Black Paris as a Dusselian transmodernity. Apart from the fact that the Caribbean and African American interlocutors of Senghor in Black Paris encountered in his "royaume d'enfance" (kingdom of childhood) of poetry the flora, fauna, rhythms, and landscapes of an "African world"[7] they could only imagine as a "site of memory,"[8] it is equally through Senghor's famous strategy of inscribing the symbologies and enunciative modalities of tradition within the interstices of the dominant western text that the rupture of modernity is initiated and an African textual transmodernity emerges. Senghor's poem "Totem" provides one of the most illuminating examples of the emergence of an African transmodernity within the discursive praxis of Black Paris. Against the backdrop of an ambient catholic modernity, the poet persona introduces his animist totem to protect him in Paris from "the arrogance of lucky races" (14). Drawing on a concatenation of images, the poem produces a powerful visual effect through the flow of a panegyric diction that projects the totem and all it represents—the totality of the poet's traditional/spiritual weltanschauung—in a manner that unsettles the poem's circumambient catholic/Euromodernist space.

Apart from Négritude poetics, the emergence of the journal *Présence Africaine* as the most important cultural voice of the black world in the twentieth century also doubles as the crystallization of African participation in the deconstructive textual enterprise of black transmodernity. Beyond the role and personal pragmatism of Alioune Diop, the journal's Senegalese founder, what needs to be underscored is the fact that a great deal of the prose writings that were later to form the corpus of Francophone African literature, especially short stories, novellas, and novel excerpts, first appeared in *Présence Africaine.*

Epistemologies of Difference:
Paris in the Francophone African Novel

If African discursive rupture of post-Enlightenment modernity emerged in the form of black political transnationalism and textual resistance epitomized by the journal *Présence Africaine* and Négritude poetry, it is in the early Francophone African novel that the voice of Black Paris acquired a discernible agency and the historical process of the master's gaze, always trained on non-western peoples, is reversed. Paris and its people are not only subjected to a counter-orientalist maneuver by being narrativized by the Francophone novelist but, more importantly, the recreated black subject becomes the author of the agential gaze. Like the Négritude poets, a significant number of early-twentieth-century Francophone African novelists had long spells as students in Paris. Most of them ultimately returned to their respective countries as vanguards of the nascent cultural nationalism or arrowheads of independence movements. What this trajectory of expatriation and repatriation produces in the early novel is a deracinated migrant hero who, as an

African outsider to the modernity of Paris, trains his gaze on the city and through a narrative process of introspection begins to articulate a deconstructive transmodernity.

This phenomenon, which Fredric Michelman celebrates as the emergence of "the hybrid hero" (35) in Francophone African fiction, equally marks the inscription of Paris as a site of alienation and deracination in which the African subject is forced to negotiate terms of engagement and identity spelled out in the idiom of race and other cultural markers. Whether an admirer of France or a disenchanted observer, the hero of the early Francophone African novel is in many ways the ancestor of the postcolonial, transnational, diasporic subject of contemporary cultural theorizing. Ousmane Socé's *Mirages de Paris,* Ake Loba's *Kocoumbo l'étudiant noir,* Ferdinand Oyono's *Chemin d'Europe,* Bernard Dadié's *Un Nègre à Paris,* Charles Nokan's *Violent était le vent,* and Cheikh Hamidou Kane's *Ambiguous Adventure* are all representative of this trend.

Although an entrenched critical tradition tends to condemn early Francophone African novels informed by the Black Paris experience, such as Bakary Diallo's *Force-Bonté* and Socé's *Mirages de Paris,* as enacting an "almost worshipful praise of France" (Michelman 34), what is often underestimated by those meritorious critiques is the fact that the hero of early Francophone novels was the first to reverse the gaze of modernity by moving, albeit problematically, to the subject position, occupying spaces of enunciation, and subjecting Paris to the representational modalities of the native/outsider gaze. These initial African narrativizations of Paris also provide a necessary theoretical counterfoil to current Black Atlanticist narratives, offshoots of Paul Gilroy's work such as Michelle Wright's *Becoming Black,* which agree that the production of "blackness" was an effect of eighteenth- and nineteenth-century discourses of modernity and that the twentieth century witnessed the emergence of black countermodernities, but refuse nevertheless to accord Africa its proper place as the foundation of those Atlanticist forms of blackness.

Dadié's *Un Nègre à Paris* and Hamidou Kane's *Ambiguous Adventure* offer some of the most informing insights into the subjection of Paris to the transmodernist gaze of the African subject. Traveling in Paris with a clearly defined aim of observing, recording, and commenting on French people, culture, history, and civilization, Dadié's hero offers a hark back to the masterly voice of the hero of Montesquieu's *Lettres persanes* (1721), who brings the voice and the gaze of the Orient to bear on the peoples of Paris. Only this time, the narrative and the gaze belong to an African subject undertaking a critique of modernity. It is however in Kane's novel that we encounter the most famous African engagement of the psychic and psychological split that is often inscribed as the basis of post-Enlightenment non-western identities spawned by the trauma of contact with Europe. This split famously theorized as "double consciousness" by W. E. B. du Bois and echoed by Frantz Fanon in *Black Skin White Masks* as a "self-division," which is "a direct result of colonialist subjugation" (17), constitutes a thematic leitmotif in Francophone African fiction with Paris serving as its geographical inflatus.

The trajectory of Samba Diallo, the tragic hero of *Ambiguous Adventure,* overlaps with the real life odysseys of most of the Francophone African novelists of the first half of the twentieth century: early education in their respective West African colonies where insertion into modernity occurs as a material effect of the credo of assimilation, with its insistence on the superiority of French culture, language, and civilization; relocation to Paris for advanced studies and the subsequent experience of French racism which exposes the hypocrisy of the doctrine of assimilation; a crisis of consciousness ensues, occasioning the psychological split; the subject returns "home" to Africa in the hope of resolving the identity crisis only to find himself/herself alienated from an originary culture now also in transition. The textual effects of this archetypal trajectory are shifting plots woven around a departure motif: departure of the hero from the colonized margin to the imperial center and his return to Africa as a disgruntled subject.

What Samba Diallo brings into this scenario is a deep understanding of French post-Enlightenment philosophy and the alienating effects of the modernity it spawned and into which he has been inserted. This accounts for the extraordinary perspicacity with which he engages the dilemmas of that psychological rift:

> It still seems to me that in coming here I have lost a privileged mode of acquaintance. In former times the world was like my father's dwelling: everything took me into the very essence of itself, as if nothing could exist except through me. The world was not silent and neuter. It was alive. It was aggressive. It spread out. No scholar ever had such knowledge as I had then, of being . . . here now the world is silent, and there is no longer any resonance from myself. I am like a broken balafong, like a musical instrument that has gone dead. I have the impression that nothing touches me anymore. (149–50)

Samba Diallo loses in Paris what the critic Harry Garuba calls the "animist materialism" (266) of his African space where the de-secularization of social space allows for an organic connection between man and his natural environment. This supposedly warmer, more humanized telos is often contrasted in black internationalist writing with the cold, capitalist materialism of the western socius.[9] Paris may be cold, secular, and capitalistic, its modernity may now have to contend with the alternative modernities of the texts of Black Paris, the African may have become the subject of his own dissident counter-narratives, but the dominant culture nevertheless is organic and sediments easily into the worldview of the African, occasioning the psychological split, the double consciousness and its attendant saga of the hybrid identity. Samba Diallo puts this dilemma brilliantly: "I am not a distinct country of the Diallobé facing a distinct Occident, and appreciating with a cool head what I must take from it and what I must leave with it by way of counterbalance. I have become the two. There is not a clear mind deciding between the two factors of a choice. There is a strange nature, in distress over not being two" (150–51).

For the African subject in Black Paris—as opposed to African Americans and Caribbeans in the same context—the inevitability of *métissage* as a resolution of the latent identity crisis comes at a greater risk: the African American and the Caribbean have an incipient, always present western-ness as part of their being that the African lacks. Consequently, contact with Paris is fraught with the danger of the psychic split lacking any originary western-ness to sustain it and this eventuates in an alienation that operates at a deeper level: "The West had become involved in his life insidiously, with the thoughts on which he had been nourished every day since the first morning when he had entered the foreign school in the town of L. The resistance of the Diallobé country had warned him of the risks of the Western adventure" (151).

For this subject, home becomes the solution to a fundamental crisis of existence and identity. The hero of the Francophone African fiction returns home to Senghor's *royaume d'enfance* (kingdom of childhood) bearing the sign of Paris and the modernity he encountered and engaged rather ambivalently. Re-insertion into the African world becomes a mirage for two reasons: the traditional Africa of the hero's expectation no longer exists in its imagined fixity. It is also involved in its postcolonial negotiations of a modern identity and the registers of this transition are lost on the returnee hero who, like Samba Diallo and other fictional protagonists of the period, are condemned to tragic ends.

When *"nous pas bouger"* Leads to *"le bruit et l'odeur"*: The Transmodernity of Migritude

If the transmodernity of early Francophone African fiction was one that undermined the dominant truth claims of western modernity by subjecting Paris to the gaze and the commentary of the black African outsider, thereby appropriating the mechanism of representation for the subaltern, the terms of this deconstructive African novelistic practice were to change very dramatically as from the 1980s. A new generation of Francophone African novelists emerged but unlike their predecessors, they were not prepared to construct a Black Paris from the perspective of the transient, transitory outsider. The new generation positioned themselves along the lines theorized by Obioma Nnaemeka in a now classic essay as "inoutsiders" (86). Two popular cultural events in the 1990s can be evoked to conceptualize this shift in the novelistic representation of Paris in Francophone African writing. Salif Keita, a famous Malian musician released an album containing a hit song, *"Nous pas bouger"* (we won't budge!). The song, which is primarily about the experience of African immigrants in France, especially under a draconian dispensation that came to be known as *"les lois Pasqua"*—stringent immigration rules mostly targeted at sub-Saharan Africans and North Africans, associated with then French Interior Minister Charles Pasqua—soon became something close to a defiant Black Atlanticist anthem, chanted by African immigrants all over Europe and North America. The song talks about racism, problems of integration and the brutality of French police in dealing with African immigrants but ends defiantly in the repeated refrain, *"nous pas bouger!"*—we won't budge! This refrain is indicative of the new African immigrant's relationship to Paris, which s/he now claims as home. First generation African subjects in Paris rarely self-fashioned as immigrants because there was always a concrete notion of home to which they envisaged an eventual return, hence the self-conceptualization as transient exiles and/or deracinated, alienated intellectuals. The new immigrant lacks this escapist recourse. He was most probably born in Paris and has never been to Africa. Yet, Paris denies him the strategic identity of the autochthonous subject and this initiates new mappings of the struggle for social and political agency.

The move from outsider to inoutsider by the black African subject in Paris does not fail to attract a response from the autochthonous voice. In the early 1990s, French President Jacques Chirac, who was then Mayor of Paris, complained openly at a public event about *"le bruit et l'odeur"*[10] (the noise and odor) of African immigrants, which he claimed were driving real French citizens crazy. The attack was especially targeted at North African immigrants and caused a scandal in the French public space of discourse. Zebda, a rap music group composed of North African street youths from Toulouse, released an album entitled *"Le bruit et l'odeur."* The hit song of the same title included a direct clip of Jacques Chirac's infamous tirade and the defiant rap lyrics advised the autochthonous French citizen to learn to live with "my noise and my odor" because "this city was built on my back."[11]

What these scenarios indicate is the implication of Black Paris in the new global idioms of transnationalized diasporic identities. Scholars across a broad range of disciplines agree that these fluid global dynamics are not new, only the scale and the ease with which people move are unprecedented and so are the cultural dynamics that devolve from such movements. Arjun Appadurai's description of this new global configuration as involving "interactions of a new order and intensity" (1) becomes pertinent for literature to the extent that it has crystallized in the emergence of what Liselotte Glage and Rüdiger Kunow call "a new international and intercultural space of representation" (7) governed by the thematics of home and exile, of deterritorialization and deracination, of diasporic subjecthood and identity. Scholars such as Avtar Brah in *Cartography of Diaspora* and Iain Chambers in *Migrancy, Culture, Identity*, also agree that the new cultural issues and identities thrown up by these dynamics need to be viewed from the perspective of their politics of refusal: refusal of antecedent identitarian fixities, refusal of neat, temporally linear narratives purporting to map the trajectory of immigrant and diasporic subjecthood from a point of departure to a point of arrival and back. In Anglophone postcolonial fiction, a certain critical mapping of the new international space of representation has carved a spatial nexus linking Britain, the United States, and Canada as the sites of diasporic novelistic discourse. Consequently, novelists based in these countries such as Zadie Smith, Hanif Kureishi, Kazuo Ishiguro, Ben Okri, Salman Rushdie, Jhumpa Lahiri, Rohinton Mistry, Micheal Ondaatje, and Edwige Danticat have acquired notoriety for being read as migrant/diasporic authors.

In France, this new international and intercultural space of representation has been occupied since the mid-1980s by two sets of novelists with different trajectories but whose idea of Paris and politics of self-imagining are best captured in the scopic regime of the songs *"nous pas bouger"* and *"le bruit et l'odeur."* First are the novelists of Maghrebian origin, children of first generation Maghrebian immigrants, mostly born in France but who are still rejected and placed under stereotypical signs of Otherness: Arab, Islam, terrorism. The corpus of novels produced by these writers comes under the critical tag, *littérature beur, beur* being the sound derived in French when Arab is inverted. Novelists such as Leila Sebbar, Azouz Begag, Hocine Touabti, Ramdane Issaad, Jean-Luc Yacine belong to this tradition.

Second are novelists from sub-Saharan Francophone Africa

who are also children of first-generation immigrants or who moved independently to Paris as teenagers and now have very vague memories of Africa. These writers, now referred to as the third generation of Francophone African writers, have thematized identity and otherness as conditioned by their location in the diasporic and/or exilic space. Abdourahman Ali Waberi, a novelist and one of the most visible members of this new generation of African writers based in France, has recently suggested that the new novelists be called "*les enfants de la postcolonie*" (children of the postcolony) (8). Waberi's suggestion is informed by the fact that most of the novelists in question were born after 1960, the emblematic year of Africa's political independence from Europe. These diasporic, "exiled,"[12] and/or displaced writers have produced a novelistic corpus that is expansive enough to merit critical attention as an important shift in African construction of Black Paris. This shift can better be understood within the discursive context of post–Cold War reconfigurations in global political economy.[13]

Although the list of young France-based Francophone African novelists producing Black Paris novels is now very broad, mention must be made of Calixthe Beyala, Fatou Diome, Kossi Effoui, Bessora, Daniel Biyaoula, Aboubacar Diop, Simon Njami, Blaise N'Djehoya, Marie Ndiaye, and a host of others. Of the critical taxonomies that have evolved around these writers—the critic Bernard Magnier has called them "black beurs," "negro-gallic" or "negro-politan" writers in an essay (102)—their recent characterization by critic Jacques Chevrier as "migritude" (14) writers is particularly pertinent for our discussion of how their works constitute a transmodernity on the one hand and how they break with antecedent African textual practices within the ambit of Black Paris on the other hand. Migritude—a contraction of migration and Négritude—evokes two mutually reinforcing ideologies as well as a negation. Migration of course implies the location of these new writers in the diasporic space of Paris while Négritude evokes the deconstructive black politics of the texts vis-à-vis the dominant narratives of their context. But migritude negates the return to source philosophy of Négritude. For the migritude writer, Paris is home and it is the context in which s/he seeks to articulate a resistant black identity that refuses to construct Africa as a site of salutary return.

Loukoum and the Struggle for Meaning

From the foregoing, it is clear that a struggle for meaning resides at the center of the textual politics of migritude fiction. Against the unitary narratives of a neat post-Cartesian identity that Paris seeks to impose, the alienated migritude subject inscribes resistant notions of ontology that are informed by his/her multilayered, multi-accented experiences. Calixthe Beyala's novel *Loukoum*, a bildungsroman of some sort, is significant in its complex thematization of the politics of migritude transmodernity in Paris. First is the presence of those transgressive modes of migrant ontology that riled Jacques Chirac to the point of blanketing immigrants as a malodorous lot: the presence of the crowd. Second is the inversion of the space of the evolution of the African child: Paris as opposed to the romanticized African village of early Francophone African fiction.

Against what obtains in much of migritude fiction where the hero or heroine is usually a young adult, Beyala presents the vicissitudes of Parisian migritude existence through the "innocent" observations of Loukoum, her seven-year-old itinerant protagonist. This strategy allows the author to weave an aura of false detachment and objectivity around the underlying identity nuances of the narrative. It is through Loukoum's eyes that we are introduced to the culturally bifurcated universe of the migritude persona. This bifurcation starts from Loukoum's opening statement: "My name is Mamadou Traore according to my birth certificate; in everyday use it is Loukoum" (1). This is the first hint of the split between the two identities of the hero: African and Parisian. Born into an African migrant family living in Paris, he is given an African name that ties him to his roots, but in the public sphere of Paris he must shed this name for the less African-sounding but more pronounceable Loukoum that, unfortunately, is not wholly European. Loukoum pursues the tensions between his two opposed codes of meaning when he avers further that: "On official documents I am seven years old, but in Africa I would be ten seasons old" (1). This hiatus between the African and Western temporal epistemes vitiates the being caught between them.

While the heroes of antecedent African novels have a concrete Africa to return to in their attempt to resolve the existential crisis, the protagonist of the migritude novel lacks that strategic advantage: s/he is permanently entrapped in the site of deracination and is therefore locked up in an unending struggle against alienation. In the case of Loukoum, it is in the streets of Belleville (a real Parisian suburb) that we come to grips with the reality of his social disability. Conforming to the migritude tradition of a highly sequential story line woven around the quotidian, Beyala takes us into the oscillating world of Loukoum between a transgressive domestic context and a racist school setting. It is in the handling of Loukoum's domestic situation that Beyala reaches the transgressive peak of the narrative by placing the Islamic and polygamous family of the hero in the heart of Paris. This represents a fundamental unsettling of French monogamist monoculturalism. Abdou Traore, Loukoum's father, is a former member of the French colonial regiment. After his demobilization, he remains in France and is entitled to family subsidy provided by the state.

This marks the beginning of his problems with the French state and its secular, monocultural ethos, for he scandalously keeps two wives and several children under the same roof. What is more, the family subsidy is calculated based on the number of individuals in a given household. Loukoum's innocence constantly provides the prism through which the transgressive modernity of the novel is foregrounded. Hence, the complex issue of polygamy in Paris is introduced quite off-handedly by the hero:

> The Mothers? Right! I have two of them, and they are the cause of this whole row! Of course you know about it! It was in the newspapers. A nigger with two wives and a slew of kids just so he could receive family benefits for his dependants. It created a whole scene! . . . How was I supposed to know that everyone else only has one wife and that kids only have one mother? I thought, of course, that the children at school also had two of them but I never asked any questions since there wasn't any need to discuss it. (2)

Loukoum's ignorance of the fact that his father's polygamy constitutes a transgression of the dominant culture into which he was born does not, however, blind him to a more fundamental crisis of identity that he confronts in school and, as usual, discovers quite innocently. It takes him little time to realize that he is not quite wanted in school: he does not fit in, being always at the receiving end of cruel jokes and snide remarks from his white classmates. And his teacher's belief in his congenital lack of intelligence reinforces his unease. His quest to understand the hostility of his classmates and teacher leads him to the question of his identity. He gradually realizes that he may not quite be as French as he had thought himself to be. Somehow, his own Frenchness lacks a certain quality associated with that of his white classmates. His racialized interpretation of his identity predicament is soon confirmed by the scandal that breaks out when his relationship with Lolita, a white girl, is discovered. Lolita is removed from school and sent away for psychiatric evaluation. The only rational explanation the dominant culture offers for the travesty of a white girl dating a black compatriot is to conclude that she has mental problems. Meanwhile, the authorities have had enough of Abdou Traore's polygamy. He is arrested and his indigent family breaks up. Loukoum and all the other children consequently undergo the trauma that such situations bring about.

Place des Fêtes and the Credo of Fragmented Being

Like *Loukoum,* Sami Tchak's *Place des fêtes* is one of the most significant novels in the migritude tradition. It equally departs from the tradition of such first-wave Francophonic Black Paris novelists as Hamidou Kane, Bernard Dadié, and Ferdinand Oyono, who explored immigrant motifs by deploying the classic plot of a centrifugal flight from Africa (site of diminished opportunities/failure) to the Occidental El Dorado. France, in Tchak's novel, is not a locus of salutary arrival. It is a fait accompli, a totalized site of diasporic ontology. The Africa of the hero of a migritude text like *Place des fêtes* bears close resemblance to the mythical, romanticized Africa of African Americans and Caribbeans that we encounter in such plays as Lorraine Hansberry's *A Raisin in the Sun* (1961). It is an imagined space of ancestral anchorage, gleaned from the memory of parents who originally departed.

The considerably constrained identity choices of the hero—as opposed to his parents who have the comforting illusion of a stabilized African identity—take the reader into the fatalisms which ultimately eventuate in a hostility towards the identity myths of the hero's parents. Lacking an African way of being, alien to the familiar sights, smells, and sounds of Paris, the city of his birth, which continues to apprehend him as an Other and a problem, the hero embarks on a course of self-validation which he articulates by claiming Paris as an inoutsider and manifesting a programmatic hostility towards Africa.

This ontological impasse accounts for the hero's constantly shifting temperament and impacts on the plot and narrative structure of the novel. The chapters are sequenced like cinema clips and every single chapter bears the significant title, "*putain de . . .*" (Whore of . . .). Every character he describes—including his parents, sisters, and all African immigrants—every situation he evinces, is introduced using the vulgar interjection. The cinematic mode throws us into his life in the streets of Paris and we witness the familiar life situations of immigrant and diasporic populations in a western city. The hero's language never departs from the curse-laden, vulgar street slang of Paris. He has no compunction in furnishing lurid details concerning his two sisters who are now prostitutes in Holland, his sexual romps with his voluptuous cousin, his participation in the gang rape of the cousin of his Malian friend, his incestuous relationship with one of his own sisters and, finally, his latent desire to sleep with his own mother whom he calls a whore.

The quasi-Oedipal hostility of the hero to the person of his father is also another indication of the abdication of the roots motif. For his father represents Africa, a constant reminder of why his own Frenchness will never be complete. He has no patience with his father's obsession of returning to die in an Africa he has all but lost. He condemns the hypocrisy of African immigrants who cling to romanticized reminiscences of home while downplaying the atrocious conditions of poverty that occasioned their flight in the first instance. He condemns their compulsive evocation of race whenever they confront official French policies deemed hostile to immigrants and defends the right of France to adopt measures against invasion by immigrants. Yet on other occasions, France becomes the target of his acerbic, vulgar recriminations. In the end, no one escapes the hero's verbal darts, not even himself. He thus succeeds in sustaining an aura of physical and psychological discomfort throughout the text, a condition which *Place des fêtes,* like all migritude texts, metaphorizes as the inescapable foundation of Black Paris subjecthood.

Conclusion

The last century witnessed two major dynamics in Francophone African novelistic representation of Paris. The first half of the century witnessed narratives in which Paris figured as a temporary site of illumination, subjected for the first time to the gaze of the outsider who has no illusions about his nonbelonging and constantly entertains dreams of a final return to Africa. That last two decades of the century, on the contrary, produced narratives in which the children of yesterday's passing outsiders now lay claim to an inclusiveness that constantly escapes them. Because of their investment in the African immigrant milieu of Paris, the latter works are essentially narratives of race, otherness, and entrapment in the margins of society. They present us with the familiar fare of cultural and identity issues faced by immigrant communities in the West.

It is, however, in their deployment of history as background that the two representations of Paris unite. Migritude novels may refuse to evoke the possibility of an eventual return to Africa; there is however no mistaking their latent historical referent: colonialism. The Africans we come across in *Loukoum* and *Place des fêtes* are not dehistoricized characters constructed in a vacuum. The narratives constantly insist at a subtextual level that these characters are effects, in the present, of the historical event of colonialism. Taken collectively, the novels of the migritude tradition are fictionalized theoretical discourses on the colonial trajectory of the geolinguistic space we now refer to as Francophone Africa. Beyala's and Tchak's heros in *Loukoum* and *Place des fêtes* respectively are second-generation children of Malian and Senegalese immigrants. Born in France, neither character has ever been to Africa. But it is through their eyes that the novels establish a cause and effect linkage between colonialism and the diasporic condition in Paris.

If they are in Paris, it is because France once exercised authority over their parents in the colonial dispensation. If they are in France, it is because colonial rape and plunder have produced economically impecunious postcolonial formations that would not be able to guarantee them dignified, meaningful existence were they to return. Those who insist on a physical return, like the hero's father in *Place des fêtes,* ultimately die in penury. Flashback, allusion, and other textual devices abound in these works to keep the image of a dysfunctional Africa constantly in the background. It is precisely in the inability of the new immigrants to envisage or entertain a permanent return to a postcolonial space bereft of agential possibilities that Paris, ironically, regains a problematic status as a site of redemption in migritude narratives.

Notes

1. The expression *"internationalisme noir"* belongs to Jane Nardal, one of the often unmentioned "founding mothers" of the negritude movement along with her sister, Paulette Nardal, and Suzanne Césaire. Jane used the expression in an article of the same title published in the journal, *La Dépêche africaine,* 1928. It has recently found currency in the work of Brent Hayes Edwards, who deploys it in his significant book, *The Practice of Diaspora.*

2. The literature on primitivism and Picasso's encounter with African art is, obviously, vast. However, mention must be made of Simon Gikandi's excellent essay, which examines the racial/racist undertones of the expansive literature on Picasso and Africa.

3. For more on these processes of (de)valuation of the black Other in early-twentieth-century Paris, see Petrine Archer-Straw. See also chapter 10 of Michel Fabre's excellent study.

4. Parisianism is a much more recent term and is lesser known than Black Paris. It refers more to the ubiquitous referentiality of Paris to the plot, setting, and themes of Francophone African novels since the mid-1980s. For more on the notion, see Bennetta Jules-Rosette's study, *Black Paris: The African Writers' Landscape.*

5. Although Edward Said's *Orientalism* has become the classic citation for the role narratives played in the Occident's construction and representation of its historical others, a more appropriate text in the case of Africa would be Alta Jablow and Dorothy Hammond's.

6. I borrow the phrase from the title of Achille Mbembe's celebrated essay, "African Modes of Self-Writing." For a critique of Mbembe's theses in the said essay, see my "Nous les colonisés: Reflections on the Territorial Integrity of Oppresssion."
7. I am thinking of Wole Soyinka's deployment of this term in his book of the same title.
8. This is a reference to Pierre Nora's celebrated essay, *Les Lieux de Mémoire* (*The Site of Memory*).
9. Indeed, Samba Diallo's statement harks back to Senghor's famous poem "New York," where the black warmth of Harlem is contrasted with the cold, calculating materialism of Manhattan.
10. For details on this event and excerpts from Chirac's speech, see http://chiraquie.free.fr/verbatim.htm
11. For a full text of the lyrics of "Le bruit et l'odeur," see www.paroles.net/chansons/33196.htm
12. I use the taxonomy of exile here advisedly because of the sensitivity of a good number of African intellectuals (especially the Anglophones) to it. While some contest it, others reject it outright, as Wole Soyinka does in his essay "Exile: Thresholds of Loss and Identity." From his base in Ithaca, New York, Soyinka's much younger compatriot, the poet Ogaga Ifowodo, also rejects any attempt to describe him as an exile. As I am yet to come across any Anglophone or Francophone African intellectual in my generation who wouldn't rather be home if conditions were right, I consider the resistance that any of them articulates against the label of exile to be totally misguided.
13. These reconfigurations, whose disparate manifestations are now loosely referred to as globalization, have not only facilitated an unprecedented movement of people from the Global South to the metropolitan sites of the West but have also generated an increased awareness in the presence of the Other and the politics of Otherness. As traditional boundaries crumble under the dual advance of migration and the immediacy of the information age, theory is forced to undertake a radical re-examination of its categories. The border as a physical locus of division is refigured as a site of contact and continuity capable of generating novel forms of identity. It becomes an independent territory, a borderland, as Gloria Anzaldua puts it. Mary Louise Pratt encourages us to reflect on the possibilities of contact zones, while Arjun Appadurai suggests five scapes that regulate flows in an essentially borderless, transnational space.

Works Cited

Adesanmi, Pius. "Nous les colonisés: Reflections on the Territorial Integrity of Oppression." *Social Text* 78 (2004): 35–58.

Anzaldua, Gloria. *Borderlands: The New Mestiza.* San Francisco: Aunt Lute, 1987.
Appadurai, Arjun. "Disjuncture and Difference in the Global Cultural Economy." *Public Culture* 2.2 (1990): 1–24.
Archer-Straw, Petrine. *Negrophilia: Avant-Garde Paris and Black Culture in the 1920s.* London: Thames and Hudson, 2000.
Beyala, Calixthe. *Loukoum: The Little Prince of Belleville.* London: Heinemann, 1995.
Brah, Avtar. *Cartography of Diaspora: Contesting Identities.* London: Routledge, 1996.
Brierre, Jean. "New Black Soul." *Black Poetry of the French Antilles.* Trans. Seth Wolitz. Berkeley: Fybate Lecture Notes, 1968.
Chambers, Iain. *Migrancy, Culture, Identity.* London: Routledge, 1994.
Chevrier, Jacques. "Afrique(s)-sur-Seine: Autour de la Notion de 'Migritude.'" *Notre Librairie* 155–156 (Juillet–Decembre 2004): 13–17.
Dadié, Bernard. *Un Nègre à Paris.* Paris: Présence Africaine, 1959.
Diallo, Bakary. *Force-Bonté.* Dakar: Les Nouvelles Editions Africaines, 1985.
Dussel, Enrique. "Eurocentrism and Modernity (Introduction to the Frankfurt Lectures)". *Boundary 2* 20.3 (1993): 65–76.
———. "World-System and 'Trans'-Modernity." *Nepantla* 3.2 (2002): 221–44.
Edwards, Brent Hayes. *The Practice of Diaspora: Literature, Translation, and the Rise of Black Internationalism.* Cambridge, MA: Harvard UP, 2003.
Fabre, Michel. *From Harlem to Paris: Black American Writers in France, 1840–1980.* Urbana: U of Illinois P, 1991.
Fanon, Frantz. *Black Skin, White Masks.* New York: Grove, 1967.
Garuba, Harry. "Explorations in Animist Materialism. Notes on Reading/Writing African Literature, Culture, and Society." *Public Culture* 15.2 (2003): 261–85.
Gikandi, Simon. "Picasso, Africa, and the Schemata of Difference." *Modernism/Modernity* 10.3 (2003): 455–80.
Glage, Liselotte, and Rädiger Kunow. *The Decolonizing Pen: Cultural Diversity and the Transnational Imaginary in Rushdie's Fiction.* Trier: WVT Wissenschaftlicher Verlag Trier, 2001.
Jablow, Alta, and Dorothy Hammond. *The Africa That Never Was: Four Centuries of British Writing about Africa.* New York: Twayne, 1970.
Jules-Rosette, Bennetta. *Black Paris: The African Writers' Landscape.* Urbana: U of Illinois P, 1998.
Kane, Cheikh Hamidou. *Ambiguous Adventure.* New York: Collier, 1969.
Loba, Ake. *Kocoumbo, l'étudiant noir.* Paris: Flammarion, 1960.
Magnier, Bernard. "Beurs Noirs a Black Babel." *Notre Librairie* 103 (1990): 102–7.
Maran, René. *Batouala.* Paris: Albin Michel, 1938.
Mbembe, Achille. "African Modes of Self-Writing." *Public Culture* 14.1 (2002): 239–73.
McKay, Claude. *Banjo.* San Diego: Harcourt, 1957.
Michelman, Fredric. "The West African Novel since 1911." *Yale French Studies* 53 (1976): 29–44.

Nnaemeka, Obioma. "Feminism, Rebellious Women, and Cultural Boundaries: Rereading Flora Nwapa and Her Compatriots." *Research in African Literatures* 26.2 (Summer 1995): 80–113.
Nokan, Charles. *Violent était le vent*. Paris: Présence Africaine, 1966.
Nora, Pierre. *Les Lieux de Mémoire*. Paris: Gallimard, 1984.
Oyono, Ferdinand. *Chemin d'Europe*. Paris: Julliard, 1960.
Pratt, Mary Louise. *Imperial Eyes: Travel Writing and Transculturation*. London: Routledge, 1992.
Senghor, Léopold Sédar. "Totem." *The Collected Poetry*. Trans. Melvin Dixon. Charlottesville: U of Virginia P, 1991.
———. "New York." *The Collected Poetry*. Trans. Melvin Dixon. Charlottesville: U of Virginia P, 1991.
Socé, Ousmane. *Mirages de Paris*. Paris: Nouvelles Editions Latines, 1964.
Soyinka, Wole. *Myth, Literature and the African World*. New York: Cambridge UP, 1976.
———. "Exile: Thresholds of Loss and Identity." *Anglophonia* 7 (2000): 61–70.
Tchak, Sami. *Place des fêtes*. Paris: Gallimard, 2001.
Waberi, Ali Abdourahman. "Les Enfants de la postcolonie: esquisse d'une nouvelle génération d'écrivains francophones d'Afrique noire." *Notre Librairie* 135 (1998): 8–15.
Wolitz, Seth. *Black Poetry of the French Antilles*. Fybate Lecture Notes, 1968.
Wright, Michelle. *Becoming Black*. Durham: Duke UP, 2004.

CHAPTER 14

Interurban Paris
Alain Mabanckou's
Invisible Cities

Dawn Fulton

Dans la rue Têtes-de-Nègres, la population défèque partout, de jour comme de nuit, surtout dans le ruisseau qui coupe la ville en deux et que notre actuel maire, pour gagner haut les mains les élections, deux ans plus tôt, avait baptisé avec tambours et maracas la « Seine ». Il avait expliqué aux habitants que la vraie Seine, en France, coupe aussi la ville de Paris en deux : d'un côté il y a la rive gauche, de l'autre, la rive droite.... Il nous avait fait comprendre que c'était plus qu'un honneur pour nous de nous identifier à cette ville de rêve, de sorte que nous nous sentirions à Paris, et ce n'était pas donné à n'importe quel pays du tiers-monde de posséder un cours d'eau qui coupe une de ses agglomérations en deux.

     In Heads-of-Negroes Street, the population defecates everywhere, by day as by night, especially in the stream that cuts the city in two and that our current mayor, in order to win the election hands down two years ago, baptized the "Seine" with much fanfare of drums and maracas. He explained to the inhabitants that the real Seine, in France, also cuts the city of Paris in

two: on one side is the left bank, on the other the right bank. . . . He had us understand that it was more than an honor for us to identify ourselves with this dream city, so that we would feel as if we were in Paris, and that it was not given to any ordinary third-world country to have the chance to have a body of water cutting one of its urban areas in two.
—Alain Mabanckou, *African Psycho*

Je sais que la France n'est ni l'Amérique du *Black Power*, ni l'Afrique du Sud. Mais la France a été habitée par l'Afrique, et l'Afrique hantée par la France.

I know that France is neither the America of Black Power nor South Africa. But France has been inhabited by Africa, and Africa haunted by France.
—Yambo Ouologuem, *Lettre à la France nègre*

In March 2007, Alain Mabanckou was one of 44 writers to sign a manifesto published in the French newspaper *Le Monde*, "Pour une 'littérature-monde' en français" (For a "world literature" in French), which called for a rethinking of the field of Francophone literary studies and highlighted Mabanckou's preoccupation with how the shifting categories of geography and language affect the way his fiction is read and marketed.[1] In the essay he contributed to the anthology associated with the manifesto, *Pour une littérature-monde* (*For a World Literature,* Le Bris 2007), Mabanckou remarks in particular on the "literary geography" of the publishing world, noting the politics that govern how—and more importantly where—his works are displayed on bookstore shelves, more often than not, he claims, assigning him the status of "foreigner" because he is a writer from the Republic of Congo.[2] His assertion of a stronger affinity with the French writer Louis-Ferdinand Céline than with the Nigerian writer Wole Soyinka accords a controversial privilege to language and history over geography, but seems to do so out of an accumulated frustration with the particular bias of a geographical reading that conflates all writers from an entire continent: "such a 'continental' understanding of literature for a long time hindered the intelligibility and independence of art. Africa is such a vast continent, made up of so many entangled cultures, and exhibits such a tremendous complexity that one would have no trouble digging up two writers from the same country who would be 'strangers' to each other!" (147). Mabanckou closes his essay with a reflection on the importance of travel in the concept of a "world literature in French," suggesting that it is by "imagin[ing] the writer in his *mobility*"

(149, emphasis in the original) that the Francophone literary readership can get beyond the taxonomic shelving strategies of the current marketplace. Decoupling the writer from a single fixed point in space, he implies, might offer a means of releasing that writer from preconceived or stereotyped notions of culture and geography while at the same time—perhaps paradoxically—promoting a more nuanced vision of the globe's peripheral spaces.

Given this call for "a broader, expanded, explosive framework" (149) for conceptualizing literature written in French, the varied geography of the author's own fiction seems to offer a parallel meditation on the potential collusion between mobility and geocultural specificity. Indeed, the settings of Mabanckou's novels suggest a writer who does not wish to be pinned down geographically: whereas *Les Petits-fils nègres de Vercingétorix* and *African Psycho* are set in unnamed or fictional central African countries, *Verre cassé* and *Mémoires de porc-épic* evoke urban and rural settings in the Republic of Congo, *Et Dieu seul sait comment je dors* looks at the African diaspora in Guadeloupe, and the 2009 commercial success *Black Bazar* anchors its narrative around a bar in the center of Paris. The resonance between this last novel and *Verre cassé* is such that the two works form a kind of transnational duet, with Jip's bar in Paris's Les Halles neighborhood acting as a metropolitan response to *Verre cassé*'s Le crédit a voyagé, each bar brought to life by a droll and incisive customer-narrator. But it is in the novel that will be the focus of this essay, *Bleu-blanc-rouge* (*Blue-White-Red*), that Mabanckou delves most extensively into the conceptual exigencies and ramifications of movement between Africa and Europe, specifically between the Congolese city of Pointe-Noire and Paris. In this wry and poetic portrait of a group of young male migrants who trace a repeated oscillation between these two urban spaces, Mabanckou explores the persistence of colonial-era mythologies that posit the French capital as a cultural and economic pinnacle, while at the same time asking whether these mythologies might not be susceptible to alternative forms of reading and economic exchange. This essay argues that the particular migrant practice of these characters finds a parallel in Mabanckou's exploration of their informal trade lines in his fiction and in his literary worldview more generally, suggesting a means of mitigating Paris's cultural and economic dominance through an appropriation of its symbolic power that revises the map of interpretive authority in the Francophone world.

Bleu-blanc-rouge presents the first-person narrative of Massala-Massala, a young Congolese man hoping to make his mark in life by completing a journey of initiation to Paris. As he embarks on this potentially transformative journey in a tradition already established by other young men from his city of Pointe-Noire, the novel offers Mabanckou a platform for the exploration of a form of underground migratory trade called *la sape*. This practice, the subject of extensive study by anthropologists and sociologists, stages a dynamic interplay of masculine migrant economies, Occidental mythology, somatic transformation, and political resistance.[3] *Sapeurs* (the acronym "sape" designates the *Société des Ambianceurs et des Personnes Elégantes*, the word "ambianceur" being a neologism—denoting one who brings ambiance to a party or gathering— that has just recently begun appearing in dictionaries), young men primarily from Brazzaville and Kinshasa, travel to Paris to acquire high-end designer clothing which they bring back home in an ostentatious display of inside knowledge of the fashion world.[4] Thanks to its naïve and hapless narrator, Mabanckou's novel shows us both the socio-economic advantages achieved by the successful *sapeurs* and the duplicity and criminal activity necessary to acquire that success. Massala-Massala, unable to adapt quickly enough to these unforeseen demands, is apprehended by police in the act of selling metro passes on the underground market, jailed for eighteen months, and ultimately deported in shameful failure back home to Pointe-Noire. Structured in two parts, his narrative is one of admiration for his fellow *sapeurs* and hope that he might one day join them ("Le Pays," or "Home / The Country") followed by disillusionment and failure in the French capital ("Paris").

As anthropological studies of the practice have noted, *la sape* constitutes an important example of underground or "second" economies that do not figure in recorded accounts of global trade.[5] In this sense Mabanckou's novel complicates the prevailing global economic picture by bringing to light an unsanctioned transfer of goods between Paris and Congo in a network of global trade where the emphasis on links between and among First World urban sites increasingly overshadows the viability of "lesser" cities and surrounding national areas.[6] But even as he foregrounds the economically subversive strain of this migratory exchange, Mabanckou points to the concealment of this practice—indeed, of the migrants' very presence in Paris—as a crucial element in the successful *sapeur*'s migration. While *la sape* is fundamentally performative in that the ostentatious display of newly clothed bodies back home in Congo secures the profit that drives the migratory exchange, the young men must maintain their invisibility and anonymity at all costs while acquiring the tools of their self-transformation in the French capital. This tension between necessary camouflage in Paris and exaggerated self-display in Pointe-Noire foregrounds the particularity of Paris's representation in Mabanckou's novel. For while the *sapeurs'* strategy of socio-economic transformation undoubtedly taps into familiar modernist conceptions of Paris as a singular site of artistic freedom and universalist self-invention, the fact that these migrants maintain an underground existence in the city of light highlights the crucial question of recognition and legitimacy in such conceptions of the French capital. As I will explore later in the essay, the authoritative power of Paris—the relentless dominance of this urban center particularly in the Francophone world—forms a common concern in Mabanckou's literary portrayal of *la sape* and in his critical reflections on the Francophone publishing market. The intricate ways in which the French capital figures in Mabanckou's novel—both as a potentially transformative (and profitable) mythology and as a counterfeit lure—suggest that the ready and widespread global consumption of Paris subtended by its connotative power may ultimately offer the possibility of de-centering the city's authoritative hold on the terms of that consumption.

Sub-Urban Literacy: *Bleu-blanc-rouge* and the Paris Underground

The urban mythology at the heart of Mabanckou's *Bleu-blanc-rouge* is one that is far from unfamiliar to readers of Francophone literature of migration, positing Paris as an idealized, magical, transformative city. In the novel's first part, set in his native Pointe-Noire, Massala-Massala functions as a kind of straight man in this process of mythologization, naively endorsing its premise and thereby representing the heartfelt belief of many in his community:

> It was that faraway country, inaccessible even if its fireworks sparkled in every one of my dreams and left me with the taste of honey in my mouth when I woke up. . . . Who in my generation hadn't visited France *by mouth,* as we say back home? One single word, *Paris,* was enough to transport us as if by magic to the Eiffel Tower, the Arc de Triomphe, or the Champs-Elysées. (36)[7]

Paris, standing in for and interchangeable with France, is literally a city of dreams for Massala-Massala, who consumes and contributes to the impassioned construction of this narrative through a repeatedly replenished vocabulary of fantasy, Paris "par la bouche."[8] As critics have noted, this representation of Paris by the *sapeurs* is part of a "mythe occidental" (western myth) fed by and feeding into repeated migration to the *métropole* from Francophone Africa.[9] Many of the novels that treat this phenomenon forcefully tear apart the mythology of Paris as promised land, insisting instead on the cold welcome and harsh economic conditions of metropolitan migration, and, as Pius Adesanmi explores in his contribution to this volume, positing an implicit salutary return to Africa. But Mabanckou's novel diverges from this literary tradition not only in its refusal to idealize the African space as an alternative to the demythologized European one, but also in its trenchant assessment of the enduring power of the very Parisian mythologies that its narrative belies.

Mabanckou's strategy of demystification in *Bleu-blanc-rouge* is to reveal, through his ingénue narrator's eyes, the concrete conditions behind the scenes of the successful *sapeur* economy. His emphasis is on the poverty and precariousness that characterize their metropolitan existences: the *chambres de bonne* (maid's rooms) where they sleep crowded together on the floor and the false papers and illegal trade undertaken in order to acquire their status-defining wardrobe. Massala-Massala's shock upon his arrival in Paris is such that he initially remains in a kind of daze, trapped in the seventh-floor walk-up apartment in the condemned 14th arrondissement building where he has been deposited by his *sapeur* connection. He describes sharing this tiny maid's room with more than a dozen other Congolese, sleeping on top of each other "like corpses brought together by fate in a mass grave" (136),[10] and resolves to write lengthy letters to his family at home detailing the conditions of his new life in Paris and denouncing the unconscionable gap between the life of glamour and luxury that was described to him in Pointe-Noire and what he is currently experiencing.

Yet Moki, the man who served as the exemplary *sapeur* in the novel's first part, quickly convinces Massala-Massala not to send these revelatory letters. Instead, he is to describe only the wonders of Paris, as all of the other would-be *sapeurs* have done and will continue to do. Indeed, there is a template letter on the wall of the maid's room describing a luxurious apartment with a view of the Montparnasse Tower and numerous purchases of clothing and gifts for those awaiting the writer back home. Observing wryly that using the letter required only changing the name of the addressee and sending it off, Massala-Massala notes that this reproduced text "was clear and summed up our desire to perpetuate the dream" (133).[11] His cynical assessment underlines the extent to which the *sapeurs'* project of migratory self-transformation is fundamentally bound up with the perpetuation of this Parisian mythology: the "audience" waiting in Pointe-Noire anticipates and expects the carbon-copy narrative communicated in the generic letter, just as they expect the return of the *sapeur* to follow a familiar script of luxury and cultural triumph.

The existence of these reproduced letters thus underscores the power of this time-honored narrative of "Parisianism" in the successful execution of the *sapeurs*' transnational exchange. Indeed, this mythologizing power offers the young men, many of whom, as Rémy Bazenguissa-Ganga and Janet MacGaffey maintain, are out of work or have dropped out of school, a significant means of resistance to their socio-economic condition. Along these lines, Didier Gondola points out that the illusion of *la sape* effects a transformation that conceals the social failure experienced by many of these young men in their African homes (31).[12] The *sapeurs* return home not as they left but as "Parisiens" or "mikilistes" endowed with a privileged familiarity with this otherwise inaccessible place and visibly marked by their experience.[13] The expensive clothing they wear is the primary component in an entire system of corporal manipulation meant to signal a profound shift in their identity and thereby their social status; many of the *sapeurs* return to Congo not only with Paris metro maps and designer clothing but also with pharmaceutically-induced weight gain and skin lightened by creams. They are men made anew, "Parisians with a capital 'P'," as the reproduced letter exclaims, broken free from the constraints of their previous socio-economic status in Congo.

As much as the mythical status of Paris may be firmly implicated in the circumstances of their poverty, then, the *sapeurs* fully exploit the connotative value of the French capital, mining its spectacularity and exhausting its potential for self-invention and myth-making. Their Paris is in many ways the modern Paris enjoyed, explored, and critiqued in intellectual circles of the interwar and postwar periods, but the fact that the capital acquired from this contact is anchored to the all-important set of clothing upon which their exported narrative will be based also illuminates the importance of Paris as arbiter of fashion. For them, this conception of Paris engages not only Baudelairean notions of fleeting temporality but also the production of a particular urban literacy: fashion as lexicon. As Dominic Thomas has cogently observed, the practice of *la sape* demands a certain reading of the *sapeur*'s body by the relatively exclusive audience of fellow *sapeurs* and enthusiasts who must recognize the name brands and fashion trends being displayed as well as by the wider audience of friends and family waiting at home who read the accumulated signs of the *sapeur*'s "Parisianism."[14] Moki, expounding at length on his latest trip to Paris to his avid audience in Pointe-Noire, notes that the term "sapeur" is in fact being supplanted by the word "Parisian," as if to solidify the link between this form of literacy and the city itself: "Clothing is our passport. Our religion. France is the land of fashion because it is the only place in the world where clothing still makes the man" (78).[15]

The recuperation of this proverb ("c'est l'habit qui fait le moine" in French)—more often used in the negative to protest the notion of superficial character judgment—as a foundational creed for the *sapeurs* points to an intriguing nexus between the fluidity of self-invention offered by the capital of modernity and the commodification of clothing offered by the capital of fashion. Thanks to the particular urban literacy of Paris, where the lexicon of style has the currency to transform the self or "make the man," the young Congolese migrants are able to rewrite their place in society with a set of clothes. Strikingly, in this configuration of the Parisian encounter, it is the immaterial wealth of the *sapeurs*' "Parisianism"—the cultural capital acquired by their supposed proximity to Montparnasse and their invented integration into French society—that forms the counterfeit piece of their transaction, while the material goods acquired then stand in as concrete referents to the nonexistent experience. Mabanckou's focus on the industry of *la sape* in his novel of Parisian migration thus introduces an encounter with the capital of modernity that, while clearly invoking established patterns of intellectual migration, necessarily modifies the consumption of Paris in light of the exclusion of these migrants from mainstream Parisian society as well as from exogenous intellectual communities.

Shifting Capital: The Global Economy of the *Sapeurs*

The urban encounter inscribed by Mabanckou's *sapeurs* is not, of course, confined to the French metropolitan landscape, and this too accounts for the distinctiveness of *Bleu-blanc-rouge*'s vision in the corpus of Francophone literature of immigration. For the system of interpretation the novel establishes is more precisely an *inter*urban system, based not solely on mappings of a Parisian cityscape but on a repeated trajectory between two urban sites.[16] Rather than telling a tale of *enracinement* (taking root), of immigrants carving out a definitive space for their communities in a new land, Mabanckou selects a migration narrative that is defined precisely by its continuous displacement: the *sapeurs* elaborate a practice that is fundamentally relational in that it depends upon a continuous exchange between a French metropolitan economy and a Congolese one. Without the performance of their Parisianism at home in Pointe-Noire, and without the continued production of the Parisian mythology that underwrites that performance, the transactions of Mabanckou's *sapeurs* would have, in effect, no currency.

The placement of Paris as one pole in a bilateral exchange thus points to the possibility of an unaccustomed relative status for the *métropole* in this particular practice of urbanism: even as it feeds on the familiar mythologies of French universalism, *la sape* connotes a potential shift in the conceptual positioning of Paris on the global stage. Rather than being the universal center inscribed by the geography of colonialism, as evoked in Pascale Casanova's monumental study *The World Republic of Letters*, Paris figures in the *sapeur* economy as a kind of backdrop, an almost incidental terrain providing the series of reproduced objects and images with which the *sapeurs* construct their performance. As Jaime Hanneken puts it, the *sapeurs* don't migrate to Paris so much as they migrate "to *sape*" (381). The locality of Paris is thus displaced by the migratory practice itself, and the proverbial city of light is relegated to secondary status as a site whose connotative value provides merely an ingredient in the production of the *sapeur* identity. Indeed, as we have seen, it is paradoxically the Parisian mythology itself that the *sapeurs* use to defy the economic inequities of their condition. In this sense, it could be argued that Mabanckou's intervention in the corpus of Francophone literature of migration falls somewhere outside the binary between validation and demystification of the "mythe occidental" by making the myth the very fabric of a new hierarchy between Paris and its former colonies.

Along these lines, critics have proposed *la sape* as a kind of reverse colonization because of the forgeries and illegal trade tied up in the practice that suggest the defiant collection of a debt the French state refuses to pay formally.[17] But Mabanckou's novel also points out the ways in which colonial models of representation are imbricated in the exchanges effected by the *sapeurs*. Their reversal of colonial hierarchies amounts to a kind of "exotisme à rebours" (reverse exoticism), a strategy of consumption that posits and exploits a Paris mythology in much the same way that colonial ideologies invented and reproduced a series of images and myths about the African continent.[18] Intriguingly, framed in this way, the form of migration effected by the *sapeurs* is perhaps closest to that of the tourist: the *sapeurs* begin with a set of postcard images produced by a collective (Congolese) imaginary, travel to Paris to confirm this mythological construction, collect a set of relevant "objects of interest," and return home, where the objects and accompanying mythology will be consumed and perpetuated.[19] Mabanckou's *sapeurs* thus upend the conventional economic hierarchy of tourism, casting the African migrant in the role usually assigned to the wealthy first-world visitor and the Paris sojourn in the role of the tropical island tour—or African safari. Through the performative dimension of *la sape*, moreover, the spectacle of Paris is transferred to the body of the migrant, who engages, as we see in the first part of Mabanckou's novel, in a prolonged act of self-spectacularization upon his return to Congo.[20]

Mabanckou's portrayal of tourism in reverse suggests a means of demolishing a colonial mythology not by refuting it out of hand but instead by appropriating and converting it in a transnational exchange that enables a reversal of socio-economic structures in Congolese cities. The narrative of Paris as a space of privilege, wealth, and cosmopolitanism is broken down into its salient parts for a selection of key objects and attributes (photos, postcards, metro passes, clothing) whose value is refigured in the currency particular to the community of the *sapeurs*. This Franco-African exchange thus posits Paris as a kind of distorted commodity, a source of derivative value acquired through a process of cultural translation that strips the *métropole* of any intrinsic value. In the context of literature of metropolitan migration, Mabanckou's novel again presents a unique vision, in that it imagines the postcolonial immigrant's "conquest" of the colonial capital accomplished not via cultural acceptance and social integration by the "host" country but through a successful exploitation of mythology and material goods.

It is important to note, however, that while that social acceptance by the dominant culture is not an aspect of the *sapeur*'s experience in Paris, it does form a key thread in the fabricated narrative the migrants bring back with them to Pointe-Noire. In the first part of *Bleu-blanc-rouge*, Moki's triumphant return from Paris entails a lengthy description of his exploits punctuated by avid questions from a breathless admiring crowd; but one voice from the back of the room dares to shed doubt on the *sapeur*'s dominance of the city of light, citing precisely the question of recognition: "So all of Paris knows you?" (73).[21] Amidst the general shock and disdain for the "imbecile" who dared question Moki's performance, the seasoned *sapeur* responds that, to him, Paris is like a village: "Everyone knows me in Paris and everyone calls me by my name when I walk down the street: Charles Moki" (74). Adding that anyone in the crowd who is lucky enough to visit Paris one day will be unable to do so without his help, Moki seals the authority vested in him as an irrefutable reciprocity: having been recognized and approved by Paris, he now has Paris "in his pocket" (75), as currency that is his to distribute as he sees fit.[22]

As we have seen, of course, the metropolitan exchange is anything but reciprocal in this sense for the successful *sapeur*, social recognition being antithetical to the concealment of their underground economy. While this is only one aspect of the cultural capital they manufacture in their exchange, it is a component of their Parisian narrative that has striking consequences for the dynamics of authoritative power in the Francophone world. For even as the cultural superiority of Paris is fundamental to the *sapeurs*' trade system, it is nonetheless in Pointe-Noire that the value of the capital acquired is realized. For Massala-Massala and the community of *sapeurs*, "le pays" remains the point of reference before, during, and after their stay in Paris; their European sojourn is framed as an explicitly temporary project whose meaning is ultimately articulated upon their return. As Moki puts it, "the final judgment is at home" (136).[23] Mabanckou thus effects an important *authoritative* shift in his vision of Paris's place on the Francophone stage, maintaining the French capital's mythological purchase but suggesting that, in the unseen "second-economy" conversions of the *sapeurs*, the power to legitimize such narratives may emerge elsewhere than in the colonial-era center.

Points of Origin: Remembering African Cities

In light of Mabanckou's effort to pit mobility against a "continental" world vision, it is worth noting that the foregrounding of this interurban exchange has the important corollary of addressing the geographic and cultural specificity of the *sapeur* community. For the centralization that asserts the priority of Parisian space also underwrites a homogenizing conception of the outsider, placing the immigrant into the generalized category of the postcolonial other, or, in the more vitriolic language of right-wing nationalist politics, the foreign invader. As Massala-Massala discovers upon his expulsion from France, for example, when the policemen who are to escort him onto the plane impatiently attempt to count and classify the group of African deportees before them, his national identity is incidental, subject to the logistical constraints of implementing the state's immigration policy:

We have to be counted. Like merchandise.
They count. They mess up. They start over. They mess up again. They start over again. They divide us up into little groups. No, by country is better. It's more practical, it seems. To keep the ones who don't speak or understand French from ending up in the wrong country. (219–20)[24]

Massala-Massala's presence in fact generates a logistical blip in this absurdist calculation in that he is the only one of the deportees from Congo-Brazzaville, provoking a debate between a policeman who served in the *AEF* (French Equatorial Africa) and another whose grandfather was an administrator during the "blessed days of the colonies" (220)[25] concerning whether or not Lingala is spoken in both Congo-Brazzaville and Zaïre. The French-accented Lingala greeting in which this debate culminates, "stripping the language of all its elegance" (220),[26] underlines the colonially inflected purview in which Massala-Massala's identity is still saturated in this critical instance of Franco-African relations. The administration of French immigration policy occurs through the lens of a nostalgic—and approximate—colonial epistemology, and the protagonist's position as a would-be *sapeur*, a postcolonial tourist making his own assessments of metropolitan merchandise, seems to fade to invisibility. In the politics of interpretation so critical to *la sape*, the underlying gesture of this expulsion is ultimately the assertion of an opposing system of literacy, one that pulls the clandestine *sapeur* out from underground and reads him as an "undesirable" (219) hangover from a vaguely differentiated colonial past.

The visibility of Brazzaville on the map of metropolitan immigration is a concern Mabanckou raises in his book-length essay *Lettre à Jimmy* (Letter to Jimmy), an homage to and reading of James Baldwin's work and life. The essay follows a primarily biographical trajectory, but gives emphasis to the years Baldwin spent in Paris and particularly to the writer's critical work on race relations in the French capital. Indeed, Mabanckou's gesture in addressing his subject in the second person (which he does throughout the essay) posits the text as a dialogue between a Congolese writer and an African American one, thereby highlighting the vexed questions around translation and collectivity in the black community that, as Douglas Field points out in this volume, so profoundly marked Baldwin's "Paris condition." The epigraph Mabanckou selects for his essay, taken from a 1961 interview with Baldwin, evokes the friction between the Parisian experience of the Francophone African and that of the African American; here Baldwin acknowledges the considerable privilege accorded him by his American passport as an undeniable aspect of his life in Paris: "If I were an African, [Paris] would have been a very different city to me . . . " (Standley 14).

In a chapter entitled "Du Noir américain et de l'Africain: l'incompréhension" ("Of the Black American and the African: Incomprehension"), Mabanckou further explores these challenges to black internationalism, noting not only the uneasy encounter between histories of American racism and French colonialism but also the tensions within the black Francophone community. He decries the conception of this latter community as a homogeneous one, citing both the hierarchies between black Antilleans (from the Overseas Departments of Guadeloupe and Martinique and thereby holding French citizenship) and black Africans and, from his personal experience, the use of Senegal to stand in for the African continent:

> And how many times, dear Jimmy, during my long stay in France, was I asked if I was Senegalese? Over time the col-

lective imagination has constructed this generic character that we inherited from our participation at France's side in the First and Second World Wars. Responding that I was Congolese, I would have to clarify, with patience and pedagogy, that there are two Congos, even though the border between ex-Zaïre (today the Democratic Republic of Congo) and my country (the Republic of Congo) was marked out by the Europeans! Perhaps I should have added that my capital city, Brazzaville, was the capital of the Free French movement during the Occupation? (94–95)[27]

Mabanckou's impatience with the "generic" figure of the *tirailleur sénégalais* into which he is automatically absorbed as an African man in France rails against the persistence of colonial categories, against the unwanted pedagogical role imposed on him by this ignorance, and above all against the invisibility of his own national history in metropolitan epistemologies. But the passage is also a protest against the reductive logic that so quickly forgets even the colonial-era mappings of African space where his capital city had a critical role. As Massala-Massala's encounter with French immigration policy reveals, even the lines drawn by colonial geographies have congealed into thick approximations, framing Paris as the center to a vague mapping of a colonial elsewhere. Reading this commentary on the postcolonial African diaspora through the lens of *Bleu-blanc-rouge*'s inscription of underground interurban trade lines suggests that Massala-Massala's demythologizing narrative can also be seen as an effort to review the map of global cities, to bring precision and nuance to African topographies by remapping their overlooked urban centers.

In fact, Mabanckou's literary representation of the *sapeur* economy, while it certainly resonates with the sociological work that maps networks from Brazzaville to Paris and from Paris to Kinshasa, putting these African cities "back on the map," goes further in that it lodges itself not in the capital city of Brazzaville but in Congo's second-largest city—and former capital—Pointe-Noire.[28] Massala-Massala's disgraceful return to Congo underlines the secondary status of his home in Paris-centered global mappings, as he learns that the deportation flight will make stops in Bamako, Dakar, and Kinshasa before landing in Brazzaville, where he will be left to his own devices: "in this last city, which is in my country, I will be left to my own fate, I am told, with a few French francs in my pocket. I don't know Brazzaville. From there I'll take the train, then an all-terrain vehicle will take me to my neighborhood, several kilometers from Congo's coastal city of Pointe-Noire" (214).[29] The protagonist's destination comes at the end of a long list of stops as if to underline its distance from the metropolitan center: his home is external to an already decentered city, situated even beyond the end of the rail lines that already indicate an insignificant position outside the airport hub system. The wry claim of unfamiliarity, "I don't know Brazzaville," thus suggests a statement of defiance against the epistemological shorthand of the French state: against the assumption that African capitals are essentially interchangeable, against the notion that Brazzaville can stand in for the entire Republic of Congo, and against the presumption of universal currency behind those French francs in his pocket.

Toward a Literacy of Migration

Alain Mabanckou's take on the geography of literary publication in French marks a protest against a marketing logic that makes the African continent invisible by making it homogeneous. At heart, his is a critique of the formidable centripetal force of Paris in the Francophone literary world. In his essay, "Le Chant de l'oiseau migrateur" ("The Song of the Migrating Bird"), he points to the enduring role of Paris as the "unchallenged centre, the standard against which everything was compared and measured" (145), leaving peripheral literatures written in French compelled to "gravitate around this centre" (145). For him, this problem is not restricted to literature from Africa or from other areas formerly colonized by France: "French 'provincial' writers are no better off than their 'francophone' counterparts, and for the Parisian establishment that considers them 'local,' 'pastoral' authors, they are a source of derision" (145). The vortex of Paris in the literary marketplace, then, would seem to have the same exoticizing effect on writers from France's secondary urban spaces as it does on writers from former colonial cities. Paris, to the extent that it stands in for France, also eclipses anything outside its periphery, as is clearly expressed in the sentiment of Mabanckou's would-be *sapeur* in *Bleu-blanc-rouge:* "France was not Marseilles or Lyon, and certainly not cities we've never heard of like Pau, Aix, or Chambéry. France was Paris" (88).[30] Mabanckou thus points out in both his critical work and his fiction the spatial particularity of the postcolonial Francophone context: that the unrelenting hierarchies of empire articulate an opposition not just between "the West and the rest" but more accurately between Paris and the rest.

Mabanckou's essay, much as the collection *Pour une littérature-monde* does as a whole, stages an implicit dialogue with Pascale Casanova's work on literature, capital, and space. In tracing Paris's rise as the "capital of the literary world, the city endowed with the greatest literary prestige on earth" (24), Casanova notes in particular the power of what she calls "consecration" that assures Paris's incontestable centrality in the world of literature: "Consecration in Paris is indispensable for authors from all dominated literary spaces: translations, critical studies, tributes, and commentaries represent so many judgments and verdicts that confer value upon a text that until now has remained outside world literary space or otherwise gone unnoticed within. . . . By virtue of its status as the central bank of literature . . . Paris is able to create literary value and extend terms of credit everywhere in the world" (127). Moreover, Casanova attributes a unique, if tragic, status to Francophone writers in this context because of the coincidence of this imposing capital of world literary space and the site of political dominance in the Francophone world. As she aptly notes, the very ethic of universalism that subtends Parisian mythologies makes consecration virtually impossible to achieve for Francophone writers:

> [T]he power of Paris is still more domineering and more keenly felt by Francophone writers for being incessantly denied in the name of the universal belief in the universality of French letters and on behalf of the values of liberty promoted and monopolized by France itself. How can one hope to found a new literary tradition that will be free from the influence of the world's most prestigious literature? No other center, no other capital or authority, can really offer a way out from this impasse. (124)

The incidence of French colonial history thus generates a separate category of the outsider from the Francophone world, one that cannot benefit from the consecrating machinery of Paris, paralyzed by the very mythology of universalism that created it.

Returning to Mabanckou and his literary *sapeurs,* the gesture of demythologization in *Bleu-blanc-rouge* suggests an important ideological complement to the effort to decentralize Paris: that the counterfeit narrative of universalism must be inscribed simultaneously as a deceptive lure and as a fully viable means of economic profit and social advancement. To uncover the underground trade of the *sapeurs* is to belie the collective mythology of Paris, but it is also to shunt into visibility the unsanctioned ways in which that mythology can be repackaged and sold abroad. More importantly, these narratives of metropolitan migration suggest that the "impasse" of non-recognition in the French capital evoked by Casanova might paradoxically effect a shift in consecrating power to "other centers" outside the *métropole.* Thanks to the persistence of the very colonial-era hierarchies that hijack the maps of cultural dominance in the Francophone world, the capital ventures of the *sapeurs* succeed precisely because their constructed narratives have purchase in Pointe-Noire. As we have seen, the "final judgment" of the *sapeurs'* self-transformation occurs in Congo, effectively negating the social exclusion to which they were subject abroad. The consecration impossible to achieve in Paris (or to verify for those outside the trade lines of mobility) seems, at least in Mabanckou's formulation, to have a new home in the Congolese "second city" of Pointe-Noire.

Similarly, in his essay Mabanckou refrains from making a call to bypass the indomitable Parisian center by rejecting the geographical paths drawn by French colonial history. Rather, he suggests that it is by acknowledging the lines of affiliation in French letters—by recognizing the common tool of the French language, "this tool that many inherited in problematic ways, others by choice, and others even because their ancestors were Gauls" (149)—that the reductive effects of Paris-centrism might be countered. It is, in other words, by embracing the linguistic and historical ties that link Paris to Bamako and Saint-Malo and Marseille that literature written in French might be internationalized. And that global vision of French-language literary production might, in turn, pull writers—and centers—from the overshadowed "rest" of the Francophone world into a state of culturally nuanced visibility. Much as the French language remains the problematically inherited tool for many a Francophone writer, *Bleu-blanc-rouge* suggests that the same mythologies that keep Paris firmly fixed as a cultural and economic center can also feed surreptitious mappings that reorient the capital city in terms of specific exterior points of origin. Mabanckou has recently dedicated himself to a new cultural project, moreover, that shifts the terms of access and exchange in a way that exceeds what may be possible in the world of paper publishing as it is currently configured: he maintains an interactive blog where writers, critics, and sometimes anonymous readers from throughout and beyond the Francophone world weigh in on the latest publications in French.[31] Even as the arbitrative force of Paris is palpable in the selection of topics and texts on the blog, the plurality of voices represented by its contributors suggests that the models of transnationalism offered by new digital technologies may offer a means of fostering the emergence of new authoritative centers in the world of literary production and consumption.

Notes

1. My thanks to Joe Keith, Greg Mann, and Vinay Swamy for their helpful readings of early drafts of this essay. Unless otherwise noted, translations are my own.

2. "In 'literary geography' and on the shelves of bookstores, I often share space with 'foreigners' such as Luis Sepúlveda, Mario Vargas Llosa, Orhan Pamuk or Arturo Perez-Reverte" (147).
3. See MacGaffey and Bazenguissa-Ganga, Gandoulou, and Gondola. Dominic Thomas explores the understudied importance of gender in the practice of *la sape* in *Black France* (165–68).
4. The verb *se saper* in French is a slang term for "to dress" or "to dress up."
5. Bazenguissa-Ganga and MacGaffey prefer the term "second economy" to "informal economy" to designate "activities that are unmeasured, unrecorded, and, in varying degrees, outside or on the margins of the law, and which deprive the state of revenue" (4).
6. On links between urban centralization and the ever-widening gap between wealthy cities and poor cities, see for example Davis, Holston, and Sassen.
7. "C'était ce pays lointain, inaccessible malgré ses feux d'artifice qui scintillaient dans le moindre de mes songes et me laissaient, à mon réveil, un goût de miel dans la bouche. . . . Qui de ma génération n'avait pas visité la France *par la bouche,* comme on dit au pays? Un seul mot, *Paris,* suffisait pour que nous nous retrouvions comme par enchantement devant la tour Eiffel, l'Arc de triomphe ou l'avenue des Champs-Elysées" (36).
8. Didier Gondola's article focuses on the relationship between *la sape* and "dreamlike representation" (41).
9. See in particular Moudileno, *Parades* 107–14; Gandoulou, *Dandies* 58–63; and Thomas, *Black France* 179–80, 184.
10. "Nous nous réveillions le lendemain les uns sur les autres, tels des cadavres liés par le sort d'une fosse commune" (136).
11. "La lettre était claire et résumait notre volonté de perpétuer le rêve" (133).
12. Bazenguissa-Ganga and MacGaffey argue that the practice of *la sape* comes out of an opposition to social and economic exclusion in both the African city and the European one (107). In contrast, Elie Goldschmidt emphasizes the middle-class provenance of *sapeurs* from Kinshasa, arguing that the departure for Europe is motivated primarily by cultural, social, and personal concerns rather than economic hardship (220–23).
13. As Gondola notes, the term *mikiliste,* from the plural of *mokili* in Lingala (meaning "world" and connoting "Europe"), designates a young Congolese who has "made it" to and in Europe (28).
14. See Thomas, "Fashion Matters."
15. "Le vêtement est notre passeport. Notre religion. La France est le pays de la mode parce que c'est le seul endroit au monde où l'habit fait encore le moine" (78).

16. As Dominic Thomas puts it, "the migrant impulse [of the *sapeur*] is inextricably linked to the anticipated return to Africa" (*Black France* 157). See also Moudileno, "Fiction" 183 and Fall 49. Moudileno ("Fiction" 183) and Thomas (*Black France* 178) have both remarked on the narrative structure of Mabanckou's novel that highlights this movement between Africa and France.

17. See in particular MacGaffey and Bazenguissa-Ganga 56, 81, and Gondola 35.

18. On the deployment of a "reverse ethnology" in African novels on Paris, see Dramé and Mudimbe-Boyi.

19. The *OED* defines the tourist as "one who travels for pleasure or culture, visiting a number of places for their objects of interest, scenery, or the like."

20. On performance and authenticity in Congolese fiction, including Mabanckou's work, see Moudileno, *Parades*.

21. "Donc le Tout-Paris te connaît?" (73).

22. "Tout le monde me connaît à Paris et tout le monde m'appelle par mon nom lorsque je passe dans la rue: Charles Moki. . . . Paris est dans ma poche" (74–75).

23. "Le jugement dernier, c'est au pays" (136).

24. "On doit nous compter. Comme des marchandises. / On compte les têtes. On se trompe. On recommence. On se trompe encore. On recommence de nouveau. On nous répartit par petits groupes. Non, par pays finalement. C'est mieux. Il paraît que c'est plus pratique. C'est pour éviter que ceux qui ne savent pas parler et comprendre le français se retrouvent dans un pays qui n'est pas le leur" (219–20).

25. "au temps béni des colonies" (220).

26. "ôtant à cette langue toute son élégance" (220).

27. "Combien de fois, d'ailleurs, cher Jimmy, durant mon long séjour en France, ne m'a-t-on pas demandé si j'étais sénégalais? L'imaginaire a fini par façonner ce personnage générique que nous avons hérité de notre participation à la Première et à la seconde Guerre mondiale aux côtés de la France. Et répondant à mes interlocuteurs que j'étais congolais, il fallait encore préciser, avec patience et pédagogie, qu'il y avait deux Congo, alors même que les frontières entre l'ex-Zaïre (République démocratique du Congo aujourd'hui) et mon pays (République du Congo) ont été tracées par les Européens! Fallait-il aussi que j'ajoute que ma capitale, Brazzaville, avait été celle de la France libre pendant l'Occupation?" (94–95).

28. Pointe-Noire was the capital of the Moyen-Congo region of French Equatorial Africa between 1950 and 1958.

29. "dans cette dernière ville, qui est celle de mon pays, je serai aban-

donné à mon propre sort, dit-on, mais avec quelques billets de francs français dans les poches. Je ne connais pas Brazzaville. De là je prendrai le train, puis un véhicule tout-terrain m'emmènera jusqu'à mon quartier, à plusieurs kilomètres de la ville côtière du Congo, Pointe-Noire" (214).

30. "La France, c'était ni Marseille, ni Lyon, encore moins des villes inconnues de nous comme Pau, Aix ou Chambéry. La France, c'était Paris . . . " (88).

31. For an interview with Mabanckou about his blog, see Thomas, "New Technologies."

Works Cited

Casanova, Pascale. *The World Republic of Letters.* Trans. M. B. DeBevoise. Cambridge: Harvard UP, 2004.
Davis, Mike. *Planet of Slums.* London: Verso, 2006.
Dramé, Kandioura. "Bwanapolis or Africa-on-the-Seine." *Research in African Literatures* 26.1 (1995): 97–110.
Fall, Mar. *Les Africains noirs en France: des tirailleurs sénégalais aux . . . blacks.* Paris: L'Harmattan, 1986.
Gandoulou, Justin-Daniel. *Au Cœur de la sape.* Paris: L'Harmattan, 1989.
———. *Dandies à Bacongo: le culte de l'élégance dans la société congolaise contemporaine.* Paris: L'Harmattan, 1989.
Goldschmidt, Élie. "Migrants congolais en route vers l'Europe." *Les Temps Modernes* 620–21 (2002): 208–39.
Gondola, Ch. Didier. "Dream and Drama: The Search for Elegance among Congolese Youth." *African Studies Review* 42.1 (1999): 23–48.
Hanneken, Jaime. "*Mikilistes* and *Modernistas:* Taking Paris to the 'Second Degree.'" *Comparative Literature* 60.4 (2008): 370–88.
Holston, James. *Cities and Citizenship.* Durham, NC: Duke UP, 1999.
Le Bris, Michel, and Jean Rouaud, eds. *Pour une littérature-monde.* Paris: Gallimard, 2007.
Mabanckou, Alain. *African Psycho.* Paris: Serpent à Plumes, 2003.
———. *African Psycho.* Trans. Christine Schwartz Hartley. Brooklyn: Soft Skull Press, 2007.
———. *Black Bazar.* Paris: Seuil, 2009.
———. *Bleu-blanc-rouge.* Paris: Présence africaine, 1998.
———. "Le chant de l'oiseau migrateur." *Pour une littérature-monde.* Ed. Michel Le Bris and Jean Rouaud. Paris: Gallimard, 2007. 55–65.
———. *Et Dieu seul sait comment je dors.* Paris: Présence africaine, 2001.
———. *Lettre à Jimmy.* Paris: Points, 2009.
———. *Mémoires de porc-épic.* Paris: Seuil, 2006.
———. *Les petits-fils nègres de Vercingétorix.* Paris: Serpent à plumes, 2002.

——. "'The Song of the Migrating Bird': For a *World Literature in French.*" Trans. Dominic Thomas. *Forum for Modern Language Studies* 45.2 (2009): 144–50.
——. *Verre cassé.* Paris: Seuil, 2005.
MacGaffey, Janet, and Rémy Bazenguissa-Ganga. *Congo-Paris: Transnational Traders on the Margins of the Law.* Bloomington: Indiana UP, 2000.
Moudileno, Lydie. "La fiction de la migration: manipulation des corps et des récits dans *Bleu blanc rouge* d'Alain Mabanckou." *Présence africaine* 163–64 (2001): 182–89.
——. *Parades postcoloniales: la fabrication des identités africaines dans le roman congolais.* Paris: Karthala, 2006.
Mudimbe-Boyi, Elisabeth. "Travel, Representation, and Difference, or How Can One Be a Parisian?" *Research in African Literatures* 23.3 (1992): 188–95.
Ouologuem, Yambo. *Lettre à la France negre.* Paris: Serpent à plumes, 2003.
Sassen, Saskia. *The Global City: New York, London, Tokyo.* Princeton: Princeton UP, 2001.
Standley, Fred L., and Louis H. Pratt, eds. *Conversations with James Baldwin.* Jackson: UP of Mississippi, 1989.
Thomas, Dominic. *Black France: Colonialism, Immigration, and Transnationalism.* Bloomington: Indiana UP, 2007.
——. "Fashion Matters: *La Sape* and Vestimentary Codes in Transnational Contexts and Urban Diasporas." *MLN* 118 (2003): 947–73.
——. "New Technologies and the Popular: Alain Mabanckou's Blog." *Research in African Literatures* 39.4 (2008): 58–71.
"Tourist." *The Oxford English Dictionary.* 2nd ed. 1989.

Afterword
Europhilia, Francophilia, Negrophilia in the Making of Modernism

T. Denean Sharpley-Whiting

And yet, being a problem is a strange experience,—peculiar even for one who has never been anything else, save perhaps for babyhood and in Europe.
—W. E. B. Du Bois, *The Souls of Black Folks*

The power of place will be remarkable.
—Aristotle, *Physics*

That the prickly "impresario of Pan-Africanism" W. E. B. Du Bois's oft-cited formulation of the Negro as a problem and race as the enduring quandary of the twentieth century, was so clearly expressed in geopolitical terms is the stuff that has been relegated for the most part to biographical tomes (Lewis 566). And further that such geopolitical parsing would serve as a jump-off for his internationalist maneuverings and even shortcomings leads us into perplexing Du Boisian territory. As he rhapsodized over "the purple façade of the Opera, the crowd on Boulevard des Italiens and the great swing of the Champs-Elysées" (qtd. in Lewis 566), Du Bois in Paris 1919 was at last free from "the Thing—the hateful, murderous dirty thing which in America we call 'Nigger-hatred'" (566). From this feeling of freedom issued forth his vision of the Negro World, of a black internationalism where the French colonial project could ostensibly coexist peacefully, according to Du Bois biographer David Levering Lewis, with his own radicalism from above and with his cultural chauvinism concerning Africa. The Paris Pan-African Congress as organized by Du Bois would embrace the French colonial undertaking as "one of a splendid beginning" ("Association"; my translation).

The "fate of place," as philosopher Edward Casey suggests (borrowing an Aristolean missive), is then quite "remarkable" (xii).

Place determines reality. Places are concrete settings loaded with cultural, political, and social significance. Therefore, the seemingly contrarian political positions taken up by race radicals à la Du Bois and the figures of Négritude; the salons hosted, and later the launching of *La Revue du monde noir,* by the soeurs Nardal at their Clamart apartment; and the over-the-top-ness of Chester Himes's contributions to *La Serie Noire* are justly owing to the "place" where those creative, political, and social contexts were produced. And France, with its democratic ideals and Jacobin history, was that place.

Paris, more specifically, seemingly and seamlessly provided an escape from the doldrums of race (and gender) and racism. It represented the capital of opportunity and acceptance to African Americans and colonial subjects of the French empire in much the same way that America's Ellis Island and the Statue of Liberty just beyond signaled new and prosperous beginnings to the hordes of weary immigrants mired in poverty and hemmed in by an intractable European class structure. Interestingly, these yarns of opportunity and new horizons are importantly tied to race—in Paris, blackness, especially of the American variety, was like a prized social currency, circulated at swank soirees, erudite salons, artist studios, and happening revues, while the assumption of whiteness for America's newly emigrated allowed access to jobs, trade unions, and public spaces.

But just as several of the essays in this book recognize the psychological and history-making agency afforded by Paris, they also tackle and explode the myths of a color-blind and non-xenophobic France, giving light to the very complex roles blacks and their blackness played in the midst of French colonial practices and exoticism. Indeed, France ensnared many who sought refuge in its harbors at Le Havre in the *olla podrida* of French negrophilia. Serving both political and cultural ends for the French, who were known to exalt at any given moment japonism, orientalism, primitivism, or melanomania, the emergent Black Atlantic community profited nonetheless from the negrophilic mood and its liberalism, despite its exoticist and infantilizing tendencies.

Negrophilia was never really about the Negro—it was about France, its needs, wants, and desires. France traded in nationalism's violence for bohemianism, retrieved its cosmopolitan flair as its culture commingled with blackness as a sign of modernity, and embraced its colonial subjects with renewed vigor. Paris, particularly in the interwar years, became curiously lamented and celebrated as "un age de nègre." And in speaking for all of Europe, writer Paul Morand cautions that "ours is a Negro age" with its "slackening of morals, jazz, public lovemaking" (148–49). The fall of the Third Republic became for many the exacting cost of France's descent into decadence, debauchery, and "nigger-loving," as *négrophilie* was oft-interpreted by those xenophobic and nationalistic impulses that continued to grip parts of France, including sectors of Parisian society.

Despite the fleeting and troubling nature of negrophilia, it combined with black europhilia and francophilia to bring about the idea of a viable black internationalism—the wonderfully complicated and rich transcultural, multiethnic, and multilingual tapestry that has become the hallmark of modernism and continues to stoke our postmodern scholarly imaginations—whether we seek to plumb its depths for contradictions or romanticize it and the place, Paris, where it flourished. And as for Paris the city, it has taken on its very own personage in these narratives and like our postmodern pirouettes that cynically challenge concepts of community, race consciousness, and universalism—elements critical to that emergent Black Atlantic world—we also recognize that that Paris, the *Marianne* for black critical consciousness and expression, is no more and will never be again.

Works Cited

"Association pan-africaine et congres." Typed notes. November 10, 1921. Aix-en-Provence: ADO (Archives d'outre mer), Slotfom (Service de liaison des originaires des territories françaises d'outre mer) III, 29.

Casey, Edward. *The Fate of Place: A Philosophical History.* Berkeley: U of California P, 1997.

Lewis, David Levering. *W. E. B. Du Bois: Biography of a Race, 1868–1919.* New York: Holt, 1993.

Morand, Paul. *Black Magic.* Trans. Hamish Miles. New York: Viking, 1929.

Contributors

PIUS ADESANMI teaches in the Department of Comparative Literature at Carleton University. He is a two-time Fellow of the French Institute of South Africa (IFAS) and has contributed essays on literature and culture to several learned journals, literary reviews, newspapers, and edited books. His poetry collection, *The Wayfarer and Other Poems*, won the Association of Nigerian Authors Poetry Prize in 2001.

JEFFREY ATTEBERRY, at the time his article was written, taught at the University of California, Irvine.

KEVIN BELL is an associate professor of English at the Pennsylvania State University and the author of *Ashes Taken for Fire: Aesthetic Modernism and the Critique of Identity*. He is now completing a book on black experimental writing and cinema entitled *Drift Velocities: Black Fragments in Explorative Literature, Film, and Theory*.

JEREMY BRADDOCK is an associate professor of English at Cornell University and the author *Collecting as Modernist Practice*, which was published by the Johns Hopkins University Press in 2012. He is now working on a study of libraries and archives in the twentieth century.

MARC CAPLAN is the Zelda and Myer Tandetnik Professor of Yiddish Literature, Language, and Culture in the Department of German and Romance Languages at the Johns Hopkins University. His first book, *How Strange the Change: Language, Temporality, and Narrative Form in Peripheral Modernisms*, was published by Stanford University Press in 2011.

RANDALL CHERRY is a translator and writer living in Paris. He has published articles in *Nobody Knows Where the Blues Come From: Lyrics and History* and in *Temples for Tomorrow*. He has translated numerous works into English from French, notably the novel *Le Nègre* by the French surrealist author Philippe Soupault.

JONATHAN P. EBURNE is an associate professor of Comparative Literature and English at the Pennsylvania State University. He is the author of *Surrealism and the Art of Crime* and is currently working on a book entitled *Outsider Theory*.

MICHEL FABRE was professor emeritus at the Université de la Sorbonne Nouvelle in Paris. He was the author or translator of more than twenty books dealing with transnational black culture, including *The Unfinished Quest of Richard Wright, From Harlem to Paris: Black American Writers in France, 1840–1980*, and, with Ed Margolies, *The Several Lives of Chester Himes*.

Contributors

DOUGLAS FIELD is a senior lecturer in English at Staffordshire University, United Kingdom. He is the editor of *American Cold War Culture* and *A Historical Guide to James Baldwin*, and he is the author of *James Baldwin* in the series Writers and Their Work.

REBECKA RUTLEDGE FISHER is an assistant professor of African American literature and literary theory at the University of North Carolina at Chapel Hill. Her forthcoming book is titled *Habitations of the Veil: The Poetics of Metaphor before and after Du Bois*.

TERRI FRANCIS is an associate professor of film studies and African American studies at Yale University. She is the author of *Melancholy Muse: The Spectacle of Josephine Baker and the Erotics of Cinema*.

DAWN FULTON, associate professor of French studies at Smith College, has published *Signs of Dissent: Maryse Condé and Postcolonial Criticism* and articles on works by Calixthe Beyala, Leïla Sebbar, and Mounsi. She is currently working on a project on urbanism in Francophone literature of migration.

CLAIRE OBERON GARCIA is a professor of English at Colorado College. Her recent publications include chapters in *Henry James's Europe: Heritage and Transfer*, *From Bourgeois to Boojie: Black Middle-Class Performances*, and *The Harlem Renaissance Revisited: Arts, Politics, and Letters*.

RICHARD GIBSON began his career as a journalist with the Philadelphia edition of *The Afro American Newspapers* and continued with the *Christian Science Monitor* in Rome, the Agent France-Presse in Paris, and CBS News in New York. For many years an international correspondent based in Rome, London, and Brussels, he is the author of a novel, *A Mirror for Magistrates* (1958); a survey, *African Liberation Movements* (1972); and a workers' educational manual, *The ILO in the Service of Social Progress* (1995).

T. DENEAN SHARPLEY-WHITING is Distinguished Professor of African American and Diaspora Studies and French at Vanderbilt University and author, editor, or coeditor of twelve books, the latest of which is the *Norton Anthology of Theory and Criticism*, 2nd edition.

CEDRIC TOLLIVER is an assistant professor of English at the University of Houston, where he teaches African American literature and literary theory. He is currently working on a book project, *Of Vagabonds and Fellow Travelers*, which studies African diasporic cultural work in the early Cold War period.

MARK WHALAN is an associate professor and the Eve E. and Robert D. Horn Chair of English at the University of Oregon. He has published *American Culture in the 1910s*, *The Great War and the Culture of the New Negro*, and *Race, Manhood, and Modernism in America: The Short Story Cycles of Sherwood Anderson and Jean Toomer*; he is currently working on a study of American culture in World War I.

Contributors   355

JENNIFER M. WILKS is an associate professor of English and African and African Diaspora Studies at the University of Texas at Austin, where she is also an affiliate of the Program in Comparative Literature. She is the author of *Race, Gender, and Comparative Black Modernism*.

Index

Page numbers in italics indicate illustrations.

Achille, Louis, 120n1, 278, 280–81
Addams, Jane, 49n17
affaire N'Gustro, L' (Manchette), 237
AFP, 224, 236, 238–40, 242–43
Africa (journal), 282
Afro-Latinism, 277
Agence France-Presse (AFP), 224, 236, 238–40, 242–43
Agenda (Vergès), 242
Akademia Duncan, 237
Algerians in Paris, Baldwin on, 195, 196
Algerian War of Independence, 220, 223, 238; "Harrington" letter on, 234, 239; Wright on, 227
Alpha, Jenny, 79
Als, Hilton, 149–52, 154–55
ambiguity, structural, 296–97, 299–300, 306
Ambiguous Adventure (Kane), 10, 290–310 (ch. 12), 316–18
American Expeditionary Force (AEF), 54, 340
"Amid the Alien Corn" (*Time*), 226
animist tradition, 300, 302, 309n12, 315, 317–18
Anthologie de la poésie nègre et malgache de langue française, 286, 287
artifact, cultural, 17–49 (ch. 1); as Du Bois's guiding tenet, 33
Art négro-africaine, L' (Senghor), 294
"American Negro at Paris, The" (Du Bois), 23, 26, 32–33, 46n5, 48n12
anticolonialism, 60, 204–5, 218, 255, 276
Artaud, Antonin, 269n11

assimilation, as French policy, 1, 4, 8, 210, 278, 317
"Atlanta Exposition Address" (Washington), 105
Attitude de la France à l'égard d'esclavage pendant la Révolution, L' (Cooper), 78–79
Autobiography of W. E. B. Du Bois, The (Du Bois), 21, 27, 30–31, 47–48n10
Aventure ambiguë, L'. See *Ambiguous Adventure* (Kane)

Baartman, Saartjee, 98n3, 131
Baker, Houston A., Jr., on modernity, 104–5, 106, 110, 115
Baker, Josephine, 7–8, 124–44 (ch.5), 313; dance practice of, 135–37; films of, 128–29, 131–32, 135; Parisian success of, 129–30, 313
Baldwin, James, 8–9, 175–97 (ch. 7); as book reviewer, 179; as homosexual, 179; incarceration of, 184; leaving America (1948), 178–79; at Les Deux Magots, 149–52, 167; Mabanckou on, 341; in the South, 196
banana skirt, Josephine Baker's, 134–38
"Bandung: Beyond Left and Right" (Wright), 250
Bandung Conference in Indonesia (1955), 213, 230, 250
Banjo (McKay), 190, 314
Batouala (Maran), 276, 314
Being and Time (Heidegger), 257, 259–60
being-toward-death, 259–60, 262, 264

Index

Bennett, Gwendolyn, 64–66
Benveniste, Albert, 180
Beti, Mongo, 304–5
Beyala, Calisthe, 322
Black American Writers in France, 1840–1980 (Fabre), 227
Black Atlantic, The: Modernity and Double Consciousness (Gilroy), 3, 105, 103, 177, 183–84, 191, 195, 258–59, 306–7n1
"Black Bastille of Prejudice" (Du Bois), 69
Black Boy (Wright), 186, 230
black modernism/modernity, 7, 54, 62, 78, 82, 101–21 (ch.4), 118, 172, 313, 350–52 (afterword); Josephine Baker and, 128; *Présence africaine* and, 211. See also diasporic modernism/modernity; Euromodernity
blackness, cinematic, 140
Black Panther Party, 194–95
Black Paris, 2–6, 9, 11–12, 176, 313, 314–15, 318–19, 320–21, 326n4
Black Power: A Record of Reactions in a Land of Pathos (Wright), 228
black transnationalism, 3–4, 9–10, 61, 79–80, 193; questioned by Baldwin, 177–78, 184–85
black Venus narrative (Sharpley-Whiting), 131
Bleu-blanc-rouge (Mabanckou), 11, 332–45
Bone, Robert, 153, 173n2
Boyle, Kay, 230
"Box Seat" (Toomer), 111–13, 118
Brazzaville, 11, 333, 340–41, 342–43
Breton, André: on Césaire, 115, 284; Martinique visit of, 121n16
Brierre, Jean, 312
"bruit et l'odeur, Le" (song), 318–20

Cahier d'un retour au pays natal (Césaire), 101, 103, 107, 114–19, 284
cakewalk, films of, 136, 139, 140
Calloway, Thomas Junius, 26, 27; letter to Washington, 29–30, 44, 46–47nn5–6

Cane (Toomer), 101–3, 107–14
Caribbean region, 6, 7, 103, 104–5, 118, 277; Césaire demystifying, 115–16; surrealism of, 121n17; writers from, 106–7
Carnegie, Andrew, 37, 38–39, 46n1, 49n17
Casanova, Pascale, 3, 201, 343–44
Case of Rape, A (Himes), 246n9
CBS News, 226, 241–42, 243
Césaire, Aimé, 2, 7, 101–3, 114–20, 201–4, 219, 255–57, 277, 279, 281–82, 287–88
Chamoiseau, Patrick, 2
Chanderli, Jean (Abdelkader), 238, 241, 242
"Chant de l'oiseau migrateur, Le" (Mabanckou), 343
Chirac, Jacques, 319, 322
civil rights movement, 72n2; Baldwin and, 175–76, 188; Du Bois and, 60, 69; Himes and, 156
"City of Refuge" (Fisher), 61–64, 196n3
civilization, black "primitivism" hidden by, 126
"Close Ranks" (Du Bois), 56, 73n8
Cold War: culture as politics in, 9, 180, 182, 244; cultural conferences as part of, 214–16, 250; exile during, 178
colonial ideology, 84, 294
Colonial Exposition at Vincennes (1931), 278
colonial imagery, Josephine Baker and, 134–37
colonial policy, French, 4; letters denouncing, 234, 238–29; migritude novels on, 325–26
Color Curtain, The (Wright), 250
Columbus, Christopher, 103, 104, 105
Comedy, American Style (Fauset), 95–97
Coming Insurrection, The (2007), 1
Committee for the Defense of the Negro Race, 277
Communism: disputes with, 9, 229, 251–52, 256, 265; fear of, 69, 215–16

Communist Party: Césaire on, 255–57; racial politics of, 253–54; Wright on, 229, 251–54
community: diasporic, 211, 277; Heidegger on, 264–65; Parisian black American, 142, 180, 183, 190, 223, 232, 244; photos representing blacks in, 44; sociology of, 49n16; transnational, 177
Comte, Auguste, 33, 34, 36, 48n13
Congress for Cultural Freedom, 215, 230
"Conservation of Races, The" (Du Bois), 59–60
Cooper, Anna Julia, 78–79, 80, 81, 98n1
Copenhagen, Larsen on, 125–27, 142
Counts, Dorothy, 175–76
culture: African American, 18, 23, 33, 44, 45, 52–74 (ch. 2), 79, 108, 114; African Islamic, 303, 308n11; concept of, 9, 204–5; Parisian black, 9; and politics, 70, 105, 216–18, 219–20, 313; print, 212; transnational black, 2–3, 61, 102, 177–78, 184, 185, 192
"Culture and Colonization" (Césaire), 219

Dada, 313
Dadié, Bernard, 11–12, 316
Damas, Léon, 282
dance: Baker's dance practice, 133, 134–37, 139; black communality in, 288; cakewalk, 136, 139, 140; Maran on, 287–88; Paris and, 91, 134
danse des bananes, 134–36, 137
danse du ventre, 139–40
Dash, J. Michael, on modernity, 104, 105, 117
Denning, Michael, 173n2
deracination: migritude hero and, 322; Paris as site of, 316
diasporic modernism/modernity, 2, 6, 102, 200–221 (ch. 8)
Diop, Alioune, 9, 200–221 (ch. 8), 291, 294; education of, 202–3; on World Congress of Black Writers and Artists, 213
Diop, Christiane, 208
diorama, African village, 132–33
"double consciousness" (Du Bois), 250, 317, 318
Douglass, Frederick, 23–24, *24*, 25–26, 27, 99n9
Du Bois, W. E. B., 7, 17–49 (ch. 1), *24*; ambivalence to sociology, 19–20; anticolonialism of, 60; on black soldiers, 55; on Douglass, 24–25; on French language, 59–60, 70; on lynching, 30–31; and NAACP, 31; and "New Negro," 40–41; on prejudice, 69, 350; on sociology, 44–45; on Spencer's sociological method, 35; on U.S. anti-Communism, 216
Duhamel, Marcel, and Chester Himes, 162–63, 172
Duncan, Raymond, 237, 239
Dusk of Dawn (Du Bois), 35–36, 40–41, 44, 47–48n10
Dussel, Enrique, 313–14

economy, *sapeur*, 335–40, 342
Edwards, Brent Hayes, 55, 61, 177–78, 184, 185, 189–90, 211
egalitarian France, myth of, 1, 55, 57, 59
Elwitt, Sanford, 36, 37
"Emmy" (Fauset), 84–88, 97
"Encounter on the Seine: Black Meets Brown" (Baldwin), 183, 184, 189
"*enfants de la postcolonie, les*" (Ali Waberi), 321
End of a Primitive, The (Himes), 168–72
"Enigma of the Sorbonne, The" (Fauset), 80–81
"Equal in Paris" (Baldwin), 183, 184, 233
"Ethics of Living Jim Crow, The" (Wright), 52
Ethiopiques (Senghor), 275, 308n7
ethnological entertainment, 131–34, 140–42, 143n3
Etudiant martiniquais, l' (newsletter), 281

Index

Etudiant Noir, l' (journal), 281–82, 314
Euromodernity, 10, 313, 314
"Everybody's Protest Novel" (Baldwin), 179, 180, 181–82, 234
Exhibit on American Negroes (1900), 18, 21–23, *22, 25,* 27, *28,* 31–33, *43;* as autonomous African American cultural expression, 32; fund-raising for, 29–30
existentialism, 178; Wright's critique of, 9, 248–69 (ch. 10), 251, 257–59
exoticism: and gender, 127; modernist, 117; reverse, 338
Exposition Universelle (1900), 7, 17–49 (ch. 1)

Fabre, Michel, 10, 73n10, 129, 230–31; on *Cane,* 102; on the Gibson Affair, 224–27, 243, 244–46n3; on Senghorian Négritude, 275–88 (ch. 11)
Fair Play for Cuba Committee, 231–32, 241, 246n7
Fanon, Frantz, 6, 10, 18, 74n18, 117
Fascism, 265
fashion, *sapeurs* and, 333, 336–37
Fatima's dance du ventre (film), 139–40
Fauset, Jessie Redmon, 78–99 (ch. 3), 81; black Parisian imaginary of, 90–95; "French Imaginary" of, 82–84; "Nostalgia," 70; Paris-themed writing of, 7; visits to France, 91
"Fern" (Toomer), 109, 110–11
"Fire and Cloud" (Wright), 258
Fire Next Time, The (Baldwin), 188
Fischer, Ruth, 230
Fisher, Rudolph, 61–64, 70, 196n3
Fitzhugh, George, 36
fluidity: in novels of Chester Himes, 151, 154, 159, 165; of self-invention, 337
Folie du Jour, La (1926), 134–35
Fourth Congress of the Communist International, 253, 254

Foyer des Etudiants Coloniaux, 203
France: colonial failings of, 68; colonial guilt of, 130; as truly democratic, 55–57, 70–71
Franco-American Fellowship Group, 183, 184
"Freaks and the American Ideal of Manhood" (Baldwin), 179
"French and Spanish" (Du Bois), 59
"French Imaginary," 78–99 (ch. 3); Fauset on, 82–83, 90–99
French language: black soldiers and, 53, 57, 61, 63–64; competency in, 7, 58, 64–68, 85–86; Négritude writer and, 294
French Revolution, slavery and, 78–79
Frobenius, Leo, 282, 283

gardiens du Temple, Les (Kane), 309–10n19
gender identity, black women's, 78–99 (ch. 3), 124–27
geography, literary, 331–32, 343, 346n2
Ghana: Smith in, 242, 243; Wright's visit to, 227
Gibson Affair, 9, 223–46 (ch. 9)
Gilroy, Paul, on modernity, 103. See also *Black Atlantic, The: Modernity and Double Consciousness* (Gilroy)
Giovanni's Room (Baldwin), 8, 178, 188–93
Glissant, Edouard, 2, 83; on modernity, 104, 107
Gold Coast, Wright's visit to, 227
Goshorn, Alfred, 38
Great War of 1914–18, 52–74 (ch. 2)
Grimké, Rev. F. J., 55, 56, 57
guilt, French colonial, 130

hair, straightening of, 136–37
Hampton Album (photos by Johnston), 27, *28,* 47nn7–8
Harlem Renaissance, 7, 278–79; black soldiers and, 54; French culture and, 53, 70–71, 72n3; Négritude and, 313; *Quicksand* (Larsen) and, 141

Harrington, Ollie, 224, 230–31, 239, 242–43, 244n2, 246n8; forged letter of, 234
Harvey, David, on modernity, 219–20
Haitian Revolution, 104, 105, 120n6
Heidegger, Martin, 257, 259–61, 264, 265, 269nn14–15
Himes, Chester, 8, 9, 149–73 (ch. 6), 246n9; Baldwin's review of, 179–80
"Histoire sans importance" (Horth), 80, 83–84
History of African Civilization (Frobenius), 282
Hodges, LeRoy S., Jr., 226–27
Hoetis, Themistocles. *See* Solomos, George
homelessness, national, 191–92
homosexuality, in *Giovanni's Room*, 192–93
Horth, Roberte, 80, 83–84
Hose, Sam, 30
Hotel Tournon, 236–37
Hottentot, image of, 85
"Hottentot Venus," 98n3
Howlett, Jacques, 187
Hunton, Addie, 57–59, 70, 71
hybridity, cultural, 10, 318

Iceberg Slim, 74n17
identity, American, 187, 188–90
If He Hollers, Let Him Go (Himes), 157–58
imperialism: Baldwin on, 194–95; Paris as capital of, 200
Indochina, French colonialism in, 206
Inside BOSS (Winter), 244
International Committee for Cultural Freedom, 214
International Congress of Black Writers and Artists. *See* World Congress of Black Writers and Artists
International Day of Resistance to Dictatorship and War, 214
internationalism, black, 313, 326n1, 352
Islam: in Francophone Africa, 297–98, 303; in Paris, 322–23

Island of Hallucination (Wright), 9, 227, 228–29, 232–33, 235, 244
"I Tried to Be a Communist" (Wright), 252

Jackson, Lawrence P., 173n1
James, C. L. R., 235
Jamestown Tercentennial Exposition (1907), 32, 48n11
Jim Crow legislation, 31
Joachim, Paulin, 205–6
Johnston, Frances Benjamin, 27, 28, 47n8
Joséphine Baker: Star of the Folies Bergère and Casino de Paris (film), 135

"Kabnis" (Toomer), 109–10
Kane, Cheikh Hamidou, 10, 290–310 (ch. 12)
Keita, Salif, 319
Kennedy, John F., on Algerian independence, 238
Koran, study of, 292–93, 300–301, 303
Kouyaté, Garan, 282

Larsen, Nella, 124–25
Lasebikan, M., 186
Last of the Conquerors (Smith), 235
League for the Defense of the Negro Race, 278, 279
"Letter to Maurice Thorez" (Césaire), 255
Lettre à Jimmy (Mabanckou), 341–43
libel case, Richard Gibson's, 244
liberation, language of, 52–74 (ch. 2)
Life magazine, 225, 234, 239
literacy: in Francophone Africa, 307n5; of migration, 343–45
littérature beur, 320
Locke, Alain, 54, 278
Long Dream, The (Wright), 228
Loukoum (Beyala), 322–24
L'Ouverture, Toussaint, 105
lynching: of Sam Hose, 30–31; poem on, 113; of returning soldiers, 71n1

Mabanckou, Alain, 11, 330–48 (ch. 14)
Mack, Charles E., 66–68
Madagascar, anti-French revolt in, 206
Manchette, Jean-Patrick, 237
"Many Thousands Gone" (Baldwin), 189, 234
Maran, René, 4, 10, 275–77, 314; on Césaire, 287, 288; on Négritude, 287; on Senghor, 284–88; Senghor's view of, 283–84
Martinique, Toomer's *Cahier* on, 115
Marxism, Wright's critique of, 248–69 (ch. 10)
masculinity, models of, 53, 66
McKaine, Osceolo E., 70
McKay, Claude, 254–55, 314
metaphor, 20, 21, 41
métissage, cultural, 275, 278, 279, 282, 284, 318
metonymy, 20–21, 41
migration, literacy of, 343–45
Migritude writers, 11, 321; and transmodernity, 312–27 (ch. 13)
Miller, Christopher, 295, 307n5
Mirror for Magistrates, A (Gibson), 240
"Modern Culture and Our Destiny" (Diop), 216
modernity: birth of, 219–20; blackness as sign of, 351; vs. tradition, 304
Mudimbe, V. Y., 308n8
Murphy, Madeline, 231, 246n8
My Life of Absurdity (Himes), 160, 162–63
mythology, of Paris as promised land, 334, 338–39, 344

Nardal, Andrée, 279
Nardal, Jane, 79–81, 120n1
Nardal, Paulette, 80, 83, 120n1
Narrative of the Life of Frederick Douglass (Douglass), 99n9
National Association for the Advancement of Colored People (NAACP), 31
Ndiaye, Pap, 204
Nègre à Paris, Un (Dadié), 11, 316

"Négreries" (Césaire), 282
Négritude, 275–88 (ch. 11); Sartre on, 305
Négritude, Islamic, 290–310 (ch. 12)
Négritude movement, 5–6, 10, 97–98; Harlem Renaissance and, 313; Sartre on poets of, 106
"Negroes and Art, The" (Achille), 280
negrophilia, French, 351–52
"New Negro" (Du Bois), 40, 45
New Negro, The (Locke), 279
"New York" (Senghor), 327n9
"Niam n'goura ou les raisons d'être de *Présence africaine*" (Diop), 209–11
Nkrumah, Kwame, 227
Nnaemeka, Obioma, 319
No Name in the Street (Baldwin), 8, 175–76, 193–96
"Nostalgia" (Fauset), 70
"No to Nothing, A" (Gibson), 234
"Nous pas bouger" (Keita), 319
"Nurse Emma Payelleville" (Senghor), 285

objectivity, Wright on, 266–67
Observer (British newspaper), 239
"Of Mr. Booker T. Washington and Others" (Du Bois), 24–25
Orphée Noir (Sartre), 106
outside, politics of, 248–69 (ch. 10)
Outsider, The (Wright), 9, 251–53, 257–60, 262–67

Palace of Social Economy, 21, 22, 23
Pan-African Congress in Paris (1919), 60, 350
pan-African movement, 69–70, 350
Pan-American Exposition (Buffalo, NY), 31
Paris: Baldwin's relationship to, 176–77, 183; Fauset on, 90–95; German occupation of, 203–4; as promised land, 334, 344, 351; romance with blackness in, 142. *See also* Black Paris

Index 363

Paris Créole Blues (Alpha), 79
Paris Exposition (1900). *See* Exposition Universelle (1900)
Parisianism, 313, 326n4, 336
Payne, Daniel, 18
Peau noire, masques blancs (Fanon), 18
Penguin Books, 244
Philadelphia Negro, The: A Social Study (Du Bois), 33, 34
photographs, African American children, 41–44, *43*
Place des fêtes (Tchak), 324–25
Plum Bun (Fauset), 95
Pointe-Noire, Congo, 11, 333, 334, 337, 339–40, 342, 345, 347n28
polygamy, in Paris, 322–23
"Pork Chop Paradise" (Himes), 161–62
"Portrait in Georgia" (Toomer), 113
Postman Always Rings Twice, The (Cain), 181
Pour une littérature-monde, 331
poverty, as resistance to colonialism, 304
Présence africaine (journal), 8–9, 185, 200–221 (ch. 8), 315; emphasis on culture by, 205–6
Présence Africaine (publisher), 212
"Preservation of Innocence" (Baldwin), 181
primitivism, Josephine Baker and, 128
"Princes and Powers" (Baldwin), 176, 183, 186–87, 215

Quality of Hurt, The (Himes), 150–51
"Que m'accompagnent kora et balafons" (Senghor), 285
Quicksand (Larsen), 124–27, 141–42

Rabemananjara, Jacques, 203–4, 206, 207, 208
racial identity, Jean Toomer and, 107–8
racism, French vs. Anglo-Saxon, 223–24

Rancière, Jacques, 249
representation, of black bodies in public spheres, 142
Revue du Monde Noir, La, 83, 278, 280
Revue Nègre, La, 131, 137
riots, Parisian suburb, 1–2
rive noir, La (Fabre), 227
Rivet, Paul, 284
roman nègre, 276
Rose, Irene, 235–36
Run, Man, Run (Himes), 163–64

Saint-Louis, Senegal, 202
sape, la, 11, 333
sapeur economy, 335–40, 342
Sapir, Edward, 60
Sarkozy, Nicolas, 1, 2, 6
Sartre, Jean-Paul, 106, 207, 258; on Négritude, 305
Senegal: Kane's life in, 292; as stand-in for Africa, 341–42
Senghor, Léopold Sédor, 10, 275–88 (ch. 11), 294–95, 314–15, 327n9; Baldwin on, 186; education of, 277–78; Maran on, 284–86
Sharpley-Whiting, T. Denean, 131
slavery, French Revolution related to, 78–79
Smith, William Gardner, 224, 225, 234, 235–36, 238, 239
Société des Ambianceurs et des Personnes Elégantes (sape), 333
sociology: of community, 49n16; Du Bois and, 19–20, 31, 33–35, 39, 44–45; positivist, 48n13
"Sociology Hesitant" (Du Bois), 32, 34, 35, 44, 46n4, 48n12
soldats noirs, 54
soldier, African American, 53, 61–64, 70–71
Solomos, George, 180
Sorbonne, Fauset on, 81
"South in Literature, The" (Toomer), 108
Spencer, Herbert, 34–35, 49n15
Stalinism, 256–57
Stone Face, The (Smith), 242
"Stranger in the Village" (Baldwin), 178

Sufi religion, 309n18
Surrealism, 313

Taber, Robert, 241
taboos for interracial conversation, 52–53
Tanner, Henry Ossawa, 224
Tchak, Sami, 324
Temps Modernes, Les (journal), 258
There Is Confusion (Fauset), 95
"There Was One Time: A Story of Spring" (Fauset), 84, 88–90
"Theses on the Negro Question," 253–54
"This Morning, This Evening, So Soon" (Baldwin), 188
Thomas, Dominic, 6
Thomas, Sadie, 240–41
Tidjani-Serpos, Nouréini, 300–301
Time magazine, 226
Tolman, William H., 37, 49n17
Toomer, Jean, 7, 101–3, 107–14; racial identity of, 107–8
"Totem" (Senghor), 315
Tournon. *See* Hotel Tournon
Tovalou-Houenou, Kojo, 4
"Tracing Shadows" (Fauset), 92–95
"Tradition and Industrialization" (Wright), 249, 250, 266
transmodernity, 312–27 (ch. 13)
Tuttleton, James, 268n10
Two Black Crows in the A.E.F. (Mack), 66–68
Two Colored Women with the American Expeditionary Forces (Hunton), 57–58
Types of American Negroes (Du Bois), 41–44, *43*

Uncle Tom's Cabin (Stowe), Baldwin on, 181
Uncle Tom's Cabin (film), 139
underground economy, 333–34. See also *sapeur* economy

United Nations, 251
universal vs. particular, 248–69 (ch. 10)

Vergès, Jacques, 242
Vietnam: Baldwin on, 194, 195; anti-French insurgency in, 206
visibility, black female, 127

Washington, Booker T., 24, 27, 29; "Atlanta Exposition Address," 105
Waters, Benny, 240
"Wedding Day" (Bennett), 64–66
Wells-Barnett, Ida B., 24
When the Walls Fall Down: An Outlaw National Identity? (Glissant and Chamoiseau), 2
White Man, Listen! (Wright), 248, 249
Winter, Gordon, 244
"wish image" of Black Paris, 4–5, 11
World Congress of Black Writers and Artists, 175–76, 186, 212–13, 215, 249
World's Columbian Exhibition of 1893, 37, 38–39, 46n3
Wretched of the Earth, The (Frantz Fanon), 6
Wright, Richard, 9, 52–53, 201, 215; and communism, 229–30; death of, 229, 230, 231; and the Gibson Affair, 224–44 (ch. 9); at Les Deux Magots, 149–52, 167; Marxism and existentialism critiqued by, 248–69 (ch. 10); and *Présence africaine*, 209

Yesterday Will Make You Cry (Himes), 165–66
YMCA, 57–58

Zebda, 319
Zero (magazine), 180, 181

www.ingramcontent.com/pod-product-compliance
Lightning Source LLC
Chambersburg PA
CBHW020109010526
44115CB00008B/749